MOMMY, PLEASE DON'T DIE!

Mommy, Please Don't Die!

How a Childhood in Africa Shaped a Future American Surgeon

Nche Zama, MD, PhD

Contents

CHAPTER 1
Needle Phobia

"WELCOME TO GUTHRIE CLINIC!" she said with a broad smile and with obvious sincerity. I appreciated the welcome, but that did not ease my trepidation, for this was the laboratory medicine department. I was there to be "exsanguinated" as part of my preemployment physical. I was excited about beginning a new chapter in my career as a cardiovascular and thoracic surgeon. Nevertheless, I was truly nervous about this entire process of bloodletting. Don't get me wrong; I had no concerns that any surprises, such as illicit drugs, would be discovered in my bloodstream. The problem was between me and needles—our mutually, piercingly uncomfortable relationship. My arm veins are my witnesses. They can attest to this, as they often disappear whenever there is an imminent invasion by a persistent hypodermic intruder that plunges deeper and farther and stops at nothing until it encounters an innocent, frightened, tremulous, tiny vein, which it leaves eventually in a limp, listless, leaking state and feeling embarrassed for dereliction of duty in failing to protect the body's most precious lifeline.

As I sat in the corner of that claustrophobic room with nervous anticipation, waiting to be impaled with what I perceived to be a medieval torture device (which the phlebotomist affectionately called "just a small butterfly needle"), my memory took me back to the roots of my aversion to needles, syringes, and other such contraptions. Zipping across the vast expanse of the Atlantic Ocean, my thoughts led me to a village sanctuary thousands of miles away at a place in Cameroon, Africa, where my placenta still resides. A place called home: "The drum yard."

The compound where I lived with my five siblings and parents had three grass-thatched huts. One of them doubled as a kitchen and a bedroom for a couple of children. The other one housed the rest of the children, and the larger one was considered our parents' abode. The property had a wide, deep yard littered with large, empty metal drums, giving it the appearance of a schizophrenic artisan's workshop.

My father, a soft-spoken, illiterate man with a creative mind and dexterous hands, collected these discarded large oil drums because he used them to construct metal suitcases and storage boxes, which he sold to the villagers for about a quarter each. I had always imagined how thrilling it would feel to sit in one of the drums and roll around in the yard. With a unique capacity to read malfeasant minds, my mother had warned me against playing with the drums because of the perpetual danger of injury from their sharp ends. Unfortunately, as always, the curiosity demons within me prevailed. Without forethought, I tipped one of them over on its side, crawled in, and proceeded to engage in the most thrilling, rolling adventure. Unexpectedly, I noticed a streak of blood on my left hand. Somehow, I had cut myself without feeling any pain whatsoever. I crawled out of the evil drum as fast as I could; I darted across the drum-laden yard and into the hut, where my mother was sitting and preparing okra soup. "My God!" she screamed. "What happened?"

My mother did not play! She was a predictable, consistent disciplinarian. She had a jab so quick that it would've left a young, ferocious Muhammad Ali dysarthric and grasping for words. I know this for a fact as I have multiple reminders on several anatomical sites in my possession, ranging from the facial and palmar to the gluteal regions. A long-winded explanation by me about causation usually failed to convince her. Therefore, this time I chose wisely and abridged my response: "I don't know!"

I discovered that there was no greater emergency with my mother than the sight of human blood. Instantly, she ignored whatever she had been doing and whisked me off—half walking, half running—to the only hospital in the region. When we got there, I received the care I needed. The nurses, as usual, were kind and attentive. They cleaned and bandaged the laceration and had a few kind words to say about the "great warrior" I was. Through it, my mother remained focused and unfazed. Everything seemed to be going well. Then, suddenly, as if prompted by an afterthought, one of the nurses suggested an antibiotic shot to prevent infection and speed up wound healing.

To my recollection, I had never received a shot before. Still, when I saw what appeared to me like a menacing, foot-long piece of glistening steel threatening to impale and penetrate the most intimate confines of my innocent gluteal department, things didn't sit well with me. I went into defense mode, despite the nurse's assurances that "it was not going to hurt one bit." And then, without soliciting my permission, my mother promptly pulled down my shorts and hoisted me in a swift, gravity-defying maneuver across her lap. Such indignity! If the procedure truly wouldn't hurt, I wondered, why, then, was my fragile, innocent, three-foot-plus frame being forcibly positioned, butt naked and in a prone position, facing her massive feet and lying across the two unyielding, muscular, steely, ebony tree trunks called "thighs" on her six-foot-three frame?

Before I could exercise the luxury of further thought, suddenly, I felt the full weight of my mother's monstrous arm on my back while her other arm leaned heavily on my hamstrings. I knew then that democracy had been choked to death in that room, and the decks were stacked against me. Surrounded by three unflinching Amazonian women, having lost all modesty and decency—including minor rights to my own body—I knew my options were asthenic and fleeting at best. Therefore, I resorted acquiescently to the lone privilege my respiratory system could still afford me: *I moaned loudly and courageously!*

Promptly, one of the nurses rubbed an alcohol-soaked cotton ball on my butt cheek, and immediately I felt the sharp, painful sensation of a rapidly penetrating needle that seemed to traverse my entire pelvis. At this point, I released what the perpetrators must have perceived as a bloodcurdling scream. I had never before experienced such excruciating pain. Never! I tried to wrestle free from my mother's vise grip, but my gyrations were no match for her Herculean strength. Then, instantly, she relaxed and commanded me to stand up and be strong like a warrior! Just like that! No hugs, kisses, niceties—nothing to mitigate my pain or rescue my pride. I guess calling me a warrior was one of her numerous psychological strategies designed to squelch my protestations and temper my expectations for consolation. To add insult to injury, one of the nurses quipped, "That wasn't so bad, was it?" *Really?* I pondered silently. I wondered if she was referring to the completion of her saga or my experience with her dagger.

I had a feeling the entire experience had been a conspiracy. Through it, Mother had maintained a pragmatic, stoic, and matter-of-fact disposition. When it was all over, she pulled up my shorts, patted the back of my head, thanked the nurses, and briskly ushered me ahead of her and out of the room. "Let's go! I have things to do!" she said as she unleashed those enormously broad strides that frequently left me scampering breathlessly behind her imposing, majestic presence.

When we got back to the village, my mother wasted no time dishing out assignments for the rest of the day. I had to go and fetch water for cooking and bathing. That was about a mile trek each way. After that, I would have to sweep the dusty yard and peel yams for dinner. What the hell! I had just suffered a traumatic injury to my hand and had been the victim of a butt attack under the guise of medical treatment after an undemocratic, unilateral decision by perpetrators to humiliate me with a foot-long hypodermic needle. The experience had left me limping and smarting, with a needle I was convinced had broken off and was likely lodged somewhere in the deep recesses of my sacred pelvis. Lord knows how much damage and torture it would continue to exact on my anatomy!

Besides, whatever happened to justice, fairness, and equity? I had an older sibling! Why couldn't she help out and allow me to recover from the experience I'd just had? I began to wonder why my parents always singled me out and often gave me the most difficult assignments and never seemed to allow me any breathing room. They appeared to watch my every move each day. I was starting to envy my younger brother, who relished every privilege I believed I was being deprived of. I knew objectively I had not been slacking off...at least not while anyone was watching!

As I stood there pondering these things, with predictable consistency, my mother, in her eternal clairvoyance, reminded me that my right hand had not been injured, my legs had not received needle treatments, and that the rest of me was OK. I knew what would come next if I opted to appeal to my elusive—yet democratic—rights. Yes, I knew my parents. They were different. I had learned many hard lessons from them. I realized that whenever I would perceive controversies in their decisions and actions, my stubborn heart would need my rational mind to keep it in line. Therefore, with conditioned acquiescence and measured ass-saving alacrity, I deliberately grabbed an empty calabash and hit the dusty, meandering trail to the distant, murky river, all the while wishing I could be living with my grandma instead of my dictator mom.

CHAPTER 2

My Dad

MY FATHER, NDEH, WAS hammering away on a sheet of metal. He wanted to make it completely flat. Eventually, he would fashion this piece of metal into a box that would bring value to someone in the village. He had been at it for what appeared to be a lifetime. He was an uncompromising perfectionist. A peaceful, meticulous man with admirable dexterity, he was one of the most focused individuals I knew. He was a man of few words and no formal education who worked at a palm-oil plantation for many years before meeting my mother. I was told that my paternal grandmother's husband, Zama, died at a very young age, leaving my grandmother with two children, both girls. At that time, following tradition, she married her deceased husband's brother Abegly and had three more children with him: my father, an older brother, and a sister. My father's biological father, Abegly, had another wife with whom he had about five children. Overall, things seemed to have gone well in that polygamous setting, a common practice at that time and up till today.

I have been told that my grandfather Abegly was a very hardworking trader who traveled a lot to various villages, regions, and neighboring countries, buying and selling goods to sustain his family. When I inquired why my grandfather enabled all my father's stepsiblings to earn an education at least to a postelementary school level while neither my father nor any of his siblings were educated, I received conflicting answers from several elders. However, I remember my father telling me that when he was a child, he pleaded incessantly for his father to send him to school but was rebuffed. In those days less than 2 percent of the Cameroonian population was educated.

It was not unusual to find entire villages and regions where no one was literate and where there were no schools. When an opportunity did arise to obtain an education, boys were given priority. Girls rarely went to school. They were groomed to perform farming and household chores and to prepare for marriage. It was not unusual for some children to trek up to twenty miles or more just to attend elementary school.

After my grandfather refused to educate my dad, in desperation he left home and walked a long distance to reach the only government elementary school in the region, where, unfortunately, he was turned away because he didn't have tuition money. Angry and frustrated at the lack of support or resources to enable him to achieve his dream of getting an education, he informed his siblings and his mother that he would be traveling far away in search of other opportunities for himself. He left his village and embarked on a long journey all by himself in an era when decent roads were nonexistent. Therefore, he walked and slept on treacherous trails, navigating his way through thick, foreboding jungles, evading hostile tribes and grumpy creatures, and after a weary month of travel, his tattered, frail, and starving body arrived in Calabar, a southern coastal city in Nigeria. He had neither family nor friends. He had neither money nor possessions. He was all alone and was lacking everything but faith and determination.

He spent a few days roaming the streets of Calabar, unsuccessfully searching for menial jobs. Occasionally, he ran into a kind stranger who offered him a meal and a bed for the night. He was in a new country with a different culture and language and was beginning to feel despondent after a few weeks of struggling and not finding meaningful employment. In a short time, he became fluent in the local language. Then one day a chance encounter at a large open market would place him on a path that eventually would lead him back to his homeland. He spent that day roaming the market, looking for something to do and hoping to meet a generous stranger who might offer him a meal.

It was late in the afternoon, and he was feeling profoundly discouraged. As he was leaving the market, an older, distinguished-looking gentleman who looked to be successful beckoned him to come closer. The man had a few heavy bags lying near him. My father did not know what they contained, but he was curious. The gentleman asked if my father would help him carry the items to his house. Without a second thought, my father hoisted a couple of the bags on his head and carried the rest in each hand. The items were very heavy, but he didn't complain. After some time, they arrived at the man's residence, where he thanked my father profusely and asked if he would stay for dinner. My father obliged because he had no other options—at least none that came with a meal. The man was a Muslim who lived in a very big house and had four wives. He was curious about my father's accent and asked to know where he was from and how he had gotten there. After a lengthy conversation lasting well into the night, the gentleman asked if my dad would be willing to live in his house and work for him. My dad did not ask to know what type of job the man had in mind, but he was so desperate for work that he accepted the offer at once. That night he slept well, and his new employer woke him up around noontime the next day.

He spent a few years working as a servant for this Calabar man, taking excellent care of the man's household and cooking meals for his entire family. He worked from dawn to dusk without requesting or receiving monetary compensation besides free room and board. His boss's wives and the children were very kind to him. One day while Dad was performing his household chores, his boss asked him, "Young man, you are such a hardworking boy, and everyone in this household likes you. What do you want to do in the future?"

Without any hesitation, he responded that since formal education was no longer a possibility for him, he would like to train to be a mechanic. Interestingly, where my father grew up, you could count on one hand the number of cars. Calabar was a booming city with many cars, and something about automobiles was intriguing to him. The next day his boss took him to a mechanic shop and paid the required enrollment fee, and my father remained there as an apprentice for about two years. When his apprenticeship ended, he became a certified auto mechanic. At this point, he decided to go back home. He knew he could not practice his new profession in his village because there were hardly any automobiles there. However, he was aware of the fact that there were more opportunities in the southern part of the country, in the coastal region. Therefore, he caught a ferry from Calabar, and after a day's journey, he arrived in a coastal city in Cameroon called Victoria. Although he was happy to be back in his home country, he was feeling sad and lonely because he was missing his mother and his siblings. However, he knew that after such a long time away from his family, he could not return home empty-handed and without symbols of success because that would bring shame and embarrassment to him and his family. Moreover, he was now at the age of marriage, and appearing successful would make him a more attractive suitor to many of the eligible women in his village.

Employment opportunities in the coastal region were better in those days because of the existence of a large number of cocoa, banana, and palm-oil plantations. Although the majority of workers were Indigenous natives from that region, a good number of them came from the northern part of the country, which included my father's region. A few days after he arrived, my father went to a palm-oil plantation, where he joined a long line of job seekers at one of the management offices.

The overseer who was interviewing job applicants on that day was a kind man; he was well-spoken, of average height, and had a pleasant demeanor. When my father's turn was up, the overseer asked him about the type of work he was looking for. My father responded by stating that he was a mechanic. The overseer chuckled. There were no natives who worked as mechanics at that plantation. All mechanical equipment, including tractors, generators, and bulldozers, was repaired at a special shop in the region by European engineers. In a cynical gesture, the overseer pointed to a tractor with a broken engine parked several yards away from them. The tractor had been effectively discarded because the engineers had concluded that it could no longer be repaired and would only be useful as a source for spare parts. The overseer asked my father if he could repair it. Before my father could respond, the overseer was called back to his office. After my father graduated from his mechanic training program, his boss bought him a small set of tools as a graduation gift. While standing there waiting for the overseer and not knowing what to do, he decided to give it a shot and proceeded to dismantle the tractor engine. Before long he had it working. Neither the overseer nor his European counterparts could believe what they were witnessing. My father had done what they considered impossible. He was hired on the spot.

It had been a long, circuitous journey to get to that point, and my father was happy. He worked hard and diligently. He was always the first in and the last to leave. As the months went by, his boss gave him more and greater responsibilities with autonomy at the shop. His European supervisors were impressed with his capacity for fast learning and his unique sense of responsibility. My father would often tell us that their biggest regret was that he was illiterate. He could recognize numbers and letters from habit. Deep down inside him, he felt a void that he knew he would have to live with for the rest of his life. At his age, it was too late to go to school. The few opportunities available for elementary education in the country were reserved for children.

One day word came from his village that his mother was on the verge of death. She had not seen her son in many years, and she was severely depressed for that reason and had decided to go on a hunger strike, from which she was prepared to die if she could not see him. When the overseer received the message, he immediately sent for my father and told him to take a vacation and travel home to see his mother. My father thanked him, and as he was about to leave, the overseer summoned him back to his office and asked him to sit down for a moment. He recognized something special about my father.

"Young man, listen to me. You have been an excellent worker. Everyone loves you. The European supervisors say you are one of the finest natives they have worked with. I would recommend that when you go home to see your mother, you should also find yourself a wife to marry. You may be living here in this part of the country for a long time. It would be nice for you to have a family of your own. I have three very beautiful nieces. They are good family girls and are well raised. They work hard and are well-liked in the village. I want you to marry the youngest one. She will give you wonderful children."

My father was stunned but appreciative. The following day as he was preparing to travel back to his village, the overseer showed up at his hostel and gave him some spending money and a small package to deliver to his older sister, the mother of his nieces.

In those days, most marriages were arranged. When a man reached marital age—which was a very nebulous number as most people were illiterate and few people had recorded birthdays—his parents began the meticulous process of searching for a potential spouse for him. Girls from respected families who loved to farm and cook and were known to be cheerful, helpful, warm, caring, nurturing, and of course, attractive were highly sought after. Often, the young man's parents would meet the parents of the potential bride and get to know them better and also identify any possibly objectionable issues, peculiarities, or personality characteristics that could deter a marital union. Concerning the groom, characteristics and attributes such as being hardworking, strong, educated, engaging, friendly, and socially responsible were important.

Other factors such as being gainfully employed, possessing property, or having symbols of wealth such as farms or cattle were attractive to a bride's family. Of course, the established reputation of either family within the community brought tremendous weight to these decisions. Many qualifying requirements also varied from family to family, clan to clan, and individual to individual.

Dad was excited about the prospect of meeting the overseer's niece. He bought her a pair of shoes, dresses, a headscarf, and a special bottle of lotion. Additionally, he purchased gifts for her mother and sisters. He also bought gifts for his family members. Since coastal people had more frequent contact with Europeans, Western goods were much more readily available to them than to those who lived up in the mountains and the grasslands. Consequently, possessing Western goods represented status and prestige. In those days, there were neither paved roads nor public transportation. Therefore, it took him almost two weeks on foot to complete the almost-two-hundred-mile journey to his village after traversing a tropical rain forest, endless mountain ranges, and savanna grasslands.

My mother's parents were highly disciplined people. She was a middle child. Her older sister Lydia was entrepreneurial and unusually adventurous for a young woman in those days. On her own, she had traveled far away to the coastal region, where she lived and worked on several different plantations and owned a catering business. She was married but had no children.

She provided much-needed material and financial support to her parents and sisters. It is my understanding that her younger sister was the most vivacious and attractive of the three girls. Years after my parents got married, this sister died immediately after childbirth, and the newborn succumbed as well soon afterward. My maternal grandmother, Mankah, and her girls were subsistence farmers. Their father, Muasah, was a hunter and a palm-wine producer. He tapped local palm trees to extract palm liquid, which could be consumed fresh or fermented. It was hard work, and each day he left early in the morning to tap the sweet sap from numerous palm trees. After collecting the liquid in large gourds, he would take it to a neighboring town, where he sold it to local merchants.

My mother and her siblings were tall girls. My mother was probably the tallest woman in the region at about six-foot-three and had a reputation for possessing stellar culinary talents. She and her sister lived under strict discipline because their father wanted them to marry good men. Therefore, he did not encourage any frivolity on their part. Unfortunately, education was not considered a priority for the girls at that time. Uncle George, who was my father's overseer at the plantation where he worked, was their favorite uncle. He was the only person in his family who had attained a significant level of education. As a young man, he attended the only government primary school in the region and did so well that he was offered a rare opportunity to travel a few hundred miles away to the coastal region, where he pursued secondary school studies for a few years. This educational experience qualified him for several job opportunities, and ultimately, he was hired to be an overseer at the palm-oil plantation. His work was intense as he was responsible for hundreds of laborers. His position and status brought tremendous pride to his family. Ironically, because of his economic and professional status, potential suitors for his nieces had to be vetted more stringently.

On the other hand, the patriarch of the Zama clan had several male children, who included Abegly, Zama, Ghasarah, and Fowajuh. They were not only feared, revered, and respected as warriors, but they also were often the first volunteers on the front lines during times of war. Most of them were respected farmers, merchants, and community leaders. My father, Ndeh, was short (five-foot-two), shy, reserved, humble, and sensitive—hardly someone anyone would consider a competitive candidate in a bachelor lineup.

CHAPTER 3
My Mom

WHEN MY FATHER FINALLY arrived at his village, he made a beeline to Uncle George's (his overseer) family home, where he hoped to meet his future wife. He knew that if he went to see his mother first, she might not let him leave. Upon arrival, he was met by Uncle George's niece Monica, an extremely tall young lady, who walked up to him and asked if he needed any help. When she received the package from her uncle, it made her happy. Without wasting any time, Dad informed her he was there to meet her mother, Mankah, and her younger sister Rose. Mother Mankah happened to be at a distant farm with Sister Rose. Dad promised to return the following day. At that point, he got back on the road to his village.

In his heart, he began to feel something magical about the encounter with Monica. He was smitten by her. Something deep within him told him that he had finally met his better half. She might not have been the one he was supposed to meet, but she had suddenly become the object of his fascination. It must have been a sight to behold: his diminutive, sturdy, and toughened frame against a six-foot-three-inch giraffe of a woman.

He rushed home to see his mother, who was delighted to welcome him after so many years. The long-lost son had finally returned home a mature and successful man. His older brother Daniel couldn't contain his excitement upon seeing how much more physically mature his younger brother had become. The mood in the village was highly festive, and his mother broke her hunger strike and participated in all the welcoming celebrations. That night Dad couldn't keep his mind off the woman he had just met. What concerned him the most was how Uncle George would react if he decided to marry Monica instead of her younger sister Rose. The very next day, he got up early in the morning and headed out to meet his future mother-in-law. When he arrived, Monica and her sister were preparing a meal for their parents. After a few customary greetings and pleasantries, he grabbed Monica's hand and told her in no uncertain terms, "You are the one I want to marry!"

Her parents declined to express any opinions about his decision. After spending a couple of hours with them and sharing a few details about himself and his family, he returned to his village.

Monica's father, Muasah, was dissatisfied with what he had just witnessed and did not think my father was good enough for his daughter. Therefore, he discouraged Monica from pursuing a relationship with him. Monica, on the other hand, decided to follow her heart and so began a series of surreptitious love escapades that lasted several months. Stubbornly, she began to escape from her village to visit my dad and his family in his village without obtaining permission from her parents. When her parents got wind of this, they sent her male cousins to fetch her, but she was not dissuaded. On one occasion, word arrived that the men from her village were coming to get her. A couple of my dad's female cousins decided to hide her in a narrow attic in one of their huts. When Monica's cousins arrived, no one claimed to have seen her. In time, Dad's family, his sisters, and his cousins began to develop a fondness for Monica.

She escaped so many times against her parents' wishes that eventually her father, in a gesture of acquiescence, showed up at Dad's village on a surprise visit and asked to meet his parents. Everyone gathered in my paternal grandfather's house for the meeting, where a traditional meal was served. As soon as he began to eat, he paused for a moment and expressed an observation that he had no doubt the food he had just begun to eat had been prepared by his daughter Monica. He recognized its unique and familiar flavor and quality. Unbeknownst to him that day, Monica was hiding somewhere in that hut, and she had indeed prepared the meal he was eating. She was a rebellious girl who was still respectful of her parents.

After finishing dinner, her father declared that if his daughter was determined to marry my dad, he would not get in their way and that he was tired of fighting her decision. That said, he bade everyone good night and left. A jubilant Monica emerged from her hideout into a raucous and joy-filled room. Thereafter, there were multiple encounters between the two families to address important traditional formalities, such as bride price and other related payments required of my dad's family. These discussions and arrangements were concluded without acrimonious wrangling, and a bride presentation date was set. It came on a warm, sunny weekend in the dry season.

CHAPTER 4
Marital Union

ON THAT DAY, THE beautiful bride arrived with a large, festive delegation from her village, singing and dancing with excitement. The beaming bride, resplendent in her traditional garb, was met by some of the young girls from Dad's village, who took her to a prearranged location where she was stripped naked and generously anointed with fragrant oils and ointments. Her face and upper body areas were decorated with special dyes to complement her colorfully knitted skirt. Then the women began to sing about her beauty and the wonderful man she was about to marry. The air was electric. Dad was suited up in traditional regalia. The time had finally come for the official encounter between groom and bride. The formal ceremony, including traditional rites and blessings, was officiated by village elders. At the family shrine, fertility rites were performed, and sacrifices were offered to ancestors. In Dad's parents' hut, immediate family members from both sides gathered, and the marital union was consummated. By then a few hundred people from the village had assembled in the courtyard. They came bearing food, drinks, and gifts, and the celebrations went on for days. Food and drinks were in abundance. As a special expression of his love for her, my father surprised Monica with a unique gift, an Usher sewing machine. She was overjoyed as this was a monumental gift in those days. She would be the first woman in the village to own a sewing machine. Working at the plantation on the Atlantic coast had afforded him greater access to European appliances, contrivances, and other niceties that were unavailable in the hinterland.

Dad was having the time of his life. He had a beautiful wife and a loving, supportive family. He was back in his native land, where he felt secure and was ready to begin a new chapter in his life. At that point, he decided to quit his job at the plantation and plant his roots in Bamenda, his village. Together he and Mom built a small house miles away from the village, where they intended to start a family. Frequently, village members would stop by and ask the customary question: "Any children yet?"

Before long, children arrived. Within a year of their marriage, they welcomed a lovely baby girl named Kien. Mom, a highly skilled and celebrated dressmaker, decided to use her Usher sewing machine and share her skills with some of the young girls in the village. She also opened a food stand nearby where she sold homemade snacks, and she started a catering business supplying food items to a local school. Realizing she was spending too much precious time trekking places and running errands, she learned to ride a bicycle. This was considered revolutionary at that time. A woman on a bicycle had to be a passenger sitting behind a man and couldn't straddle the passenger seat either. Straddling was frowned upon. It was considered unfeminine, and as such, it drew universal ire and a "bad woman" label. A woman on the passenger seat of the bicycle had to sit at a right angle to the male rider with both of her legs suspended on the same side. The men didn't know what to say when they saw my mom riding a bike by herself. She was physically imposing, intimidating to behold, and unconcerned with their responses. Nothing seemed to bother her. She was a pragmatist with a big, kind heart who was always on a mission.

Dad was a skilled mechanic, but few individuals had cars or owned machines that needed his expertise. Therefore, he decided to produce metal suitcases and smaller boxes for students. He hammered out old, discarded oil drums and used them to construct boxes complete with latches and locks. He had a pristinely creative mind and was admirably facile with his hands.

Childbirth was a treacherous challenge for my mom. She suffered excessive postpartum hemorrhaging during my sister's birth and almost died. There were no hospitals in the region at that time, and deliveries were all done in village huts and attended by one or more village female elders. When she did become pregnant again, she decided to travel far away to an American Baptist missionary hospital in a different region, where she gave birth to me a few days after Christmas, on December 29. She suffered a severe hemorrhage again at that time and remained hospitalized for ten days after the delivery.

It's been said that she was extremely happy to have a son and was overly protective of me. She kept me close to her at all times. The day I was born, an uncle of mine who was a perpetually happy, hardworking, and generous man with a gregarious personality died suddenly. A small group of family members assembled to pick a name for me, and a unanimous decision was made to name me after him as a symbolic gesture to celebrate his reincarnation. Gleaning from the narratives that abounded about him, I can never measure up to him, and I wish the name had been assigned to someone else. Nevertheless, I will forever feel humbled to bear it.

Fecundity was not an issue with my parents as they went on to have seven children, Kien, me, Fru (brother), Siri, Mambo, Bih, and Anye (brother), along with a term miscarriage along the way, despite my mother's recurrent brushes with potentially fatal bleeding complications. Sadly, tragedy did eventually strike like a bolt of lightning in an unfortunate rendezvous between her and destiny.

CHAPTER 5
Grandma's Hut

THERE WAS A SPECIAL bond between my grandmother and me. Whenever we visited her, she often complained about how skinny I looked. Predictably, she would ask, "Don't they feed you?" Then she would proceed to heap colossal portions of food on my leaf.

Grandma lived alone. I never met Grandpa. He died before I was born. Grandma was beautiful and tall, of a slender build with shimmering eyes and a quick, disarming smile. She spoke with deliberate focus and walked with assured optimism. Her couture emphasized simplicity: topless and shoeless with a simple, colorful skirt and a variegated double strand of beads strung loosely around her beautifully sculptured waist. Her habitat also epitomized simplicity. She lived in a one-room hut, the walls of which were built with large sticks held together by ropes made from special tropical vines. The walls were reinforced with a "drywall" of red mud on the interior and exterior surfaces, and the roof was thatched with elephant grass. There was a single wooden-framed entrance no more than six feet high and about three feet wide. A wide wooden panel about four-by-four feet in dimension was used as a partial door cover at night to keep out stray animals, rats, snakes, porcupines, and other curious rodents. Ventilation was provided by a small window in the middle of one of the walls. This was kept permanently open.

Grandma slept on a very comfortable bed. The mattress comprised soft dry grass stuffed into a huge hemp sack and placed on a rectangular frame, which was constructed with bamboo sticks. My bed was positioned at a right angle to hers. Our beds were constructed in a similar manner and with similar types of material. Our pillows were small logs cut out from local tree trunks. It may be hard to imagine a wooden pillow, but I was quite comfortable with it. My bed did not have a mattress, just several long bamboo sticks laid side by side and held in place with interwoven roping material made of vine. It was *my* bed, and I didn't have to share it with anyone, in contrast to many other kids in the village who often had to share bed space with two to five other children. One day Grandma brought home a mat for my bed. It was a double-layered mat made of woven dried palm leaves. This provided a new level of luxury I had not been accustomed to. Life was great!

Unfortunately, we had many cockroaches that enjoyed living and breeding between the layers of my bed mat. So began the weekly ritual, usually on Saturdays, when I was required to carry the mat to the yard and shake it vigorously to dislodge them. Hundreds of cockroaches would fall out, and it was an exciting experience to witness so many of them scurrying away in every direction in the yard. Generally, grass huts were comfortable and provided tremendous respite, especially on hot days when temperatures soared into the nineties. When freezing temperatures descended on us at night, we kept the hut warm by burning logs of wood positioned between a triangular formation of large rocks in the middle of the floor. This arrangement served a dual purpose: heating and cooking. To make fire, my grandmother would vigorously rub together two flints adjacent to a cotton ball. The resulting friction would create a spark to ignite the cotton ball. I always found this procedure to be intriguing. It would ultimately take a science lecture in the future for me to appreciate its effectiveness. There were times when she would run out of cotton balls, and she would send me to the neighbors to fetch fire. I would collect a bunch of sticks tied together and rush over to a neighbor's hut, light them up, and return rapidly to our hut so that we could ignite logs of firewood in the fireplace. Grandma had a look of pride each time her Olympian grandson would arrive bearing a life-sustaining torch. On windy or rainy days, maneuvering the torch became an artistic challenge. I would walk backward depending on the direction of the wind or use my upper torso in a contorted attempt to shield the flames from being extinguished in the rain.

The inside dimensions of our hut were approximately eight by eight feet. This space was satisfactory for our daily existence. In a corner of the room, my father had constructed a shelf for our clay pots and other utensils. Cooked food was kept on the shelf in order to discourage intrusions by rodents and other marauding creatures of the night. There was a small attic-like space for storing food for general daily nutrition as well as preserving seeds in a gourd for the next planting season. It was my duty to climb up a ladder to retrieve whatever foodstuffs we needed on any given day. On occasion, I would encounter and chase away adventurous and rather elusive and unwelcome intrusive rodents. Going after a large rat seemed like so much fun back then. When I did successfully kill one, its humble flesh provided partial fulfillment of our daily nutritional requirement for protein. There were instances where a stray black snake in the hut would succumb to the same fate. Oftentimes, after a delicious meal of oily vegetables and cornmeal, I would wipe my greasy hands on my feet before going to bed at night. Ironically, this maneuver made me an attractive bait to a few midnight marauders, such as our ubiquitous rodents. On many occasions I was awakened by multiple rats nibbling away tenaciously at my toes and feet. I would shake them off and create quite a ruckus to discourage them from the carnivorous instincts that I preferred to monopolize. Whenever the commotion became intense and inadvertently awakened Grandma, she would usually solve the problem by immediately inviting me to seek refuge in her bed. Keeping her bed resting on four stilts and at a higher elevation than mine was a deterrent to rats and others. While she hugged me and kept me comfortably nestled in her warm embrace and protective arms, I would furtively plot the ultimate revenge on my rodent adversaries.

At that time tin dishes were just being introduced in our region, while a majority of villagers ate their meals from leaves. My preferred dishes were banana leaves. Many of the metal dishes would rust out after a few months and spring frustrating leaks through their rusted holes. However, one day I decided to eat some food out of a tin bowl that had been sitting idle in the hut for a long time, and I discovered that it had a hole in the bottom of it. I found a piece of thin aluminum somewhere, cut out a wedge from it, and used it to repair the hole by hammering the aluminum piece securely in place with a piece of rock. Grandma was so thrilled by my actions that she told everyone about them. Subsequently, the villagers began to bring their treasured rusted tin dishes for me to repair and compensated me in kind—food, fruit, or an occasional penny. This made my grandma extremely proud of me. (When I told this story to my daughter many years ago, her innate capitalist thinking triggered a funny response: "Wow, Daddy! You should've charged them for fixing their dishes, and you would have been rich!" As much as I admired her entrepreneurial spirit, I had to explain to her in simple terms why that idea of getting rich repairing dishes could never have been anything other than fantasy because the village GDP wouldn't have allowed it.)

With the exception of Sundays, when Grandma insisted that we get up early for the long, laborious trip to the mission church, she generally went farming up in the mountains miles away from the village. Occasionally, I would accompany her to help bring home some of the harvest, such as beans, corn, vegetables, and multiple other seasonal tubers. Whenever she returned from the farm, she would take a bath and proceeded to cook dinner, which we both ate with our fingers from the same banana leaf. Sharing a meal with her was always a special moment as she often left the better parts and portions for me. Grandma could always tell when I was feeling hungry because I would resort to humming softly and alternatively sulking. Lectures and lessons about life and living came after dinner as a daily occurrence. She would regale me with stories and parables generally intended to instill in me the importance of love, hard work, humility, concern for others, sacrifice, and sharing. Her very existence embodied all the values she professed.

CHAPTER 6

Life Lessons at the Farm

IT WAS ON ONE of the village farming trips with Grandma that I experienced an event that ultimately would profoundly impact my understanding of certain human behaviors, shape and undergird my personal and professional life, and guide me in my service to humanity.

As was customary in our village, the women assisted each other in doing farmwork—tilling the soil, planting, and ultimately harvesting the crops. A rotating schedule was agreed upon to make all this possible so that everyone would benefit from a collective effort and engagement. This formula was especially effective and compelling given that many of the farms were large and so much more could be accomplished collectively than individually. Men were not involved directly in the farming process. Their role was relegated to clearing the land of trees and tall grass with machetes or setting bushes on fire to eliminate obstacles and other physical constraints that women might encounter in the tilling process.

Preparing the soil for planting was labor-intensive! To till the soil, the women used hoes mounted on sickle-shaped pieces of wood. On collective farming days, the women left very early in the morning, and each woman was obligated to bring enough food to feed at least a few other group members. Upon arrival, they would immediately proceed to till the soil manually with their hoes and create about two-foot-high mounds of soil in long parallel rows. Generally, about twenty to fifty of these mounds were constructed in a day's work. The farming event was admirably organized, and it was a beautiful experience to witness these women in their magnificent, colorful body wraps, some with their babies perched precariously on their backs, as they tilled away rhythmically and seemingly without effort, creating symmetrical and precisely sculptured architectural marvels of soft earth. The entire scene was supremely festive and was an emotionally inspiring display of tradition and culture. On occasion, to energize the group, one of the women would belt out a familiar melodious tune, and the rest would chime in with beautiful harmonious cadence with the lead singer as the pacesetter. The rest of them would join in at different points in the song, and the result would be a creative, riveting chorus. While the women worked, the children played. There was an abundance of creative talent among the children. We wrestled, played hopscotch, and used whatever nature provided to entertain ourselves: oranges, mangoes, nuts, ropes, tall grass, and so on.

This would go on for hours before someone would announce a lunch break. Then the women would carefully drop their hoes and proceed to a clearing, usually under a tree canopy, where everyone would retrieve food from their baskets and proceed to share with the rest. Following tradition, multiple participants ate from the same leaf using their natural and universal utensils: their hands and fingers. Sharing a meal from a leaf was an entrenched tradition that had the effect of establishing and solidifying social bonds between individuals. It represented a powerful subliminal contract between individuals by establishing a sense of mutuality, collectivism, interconnectivity, equity, equality, and social responsibility.

On that particular day, everyone converged on Grandma's farm. She was hosting the event in accordance with the rotation schedule. She had cooked a lot of food in anticipation of the event. The other women also brought many different food items. Grandma was the first person to sit down when the lunch break was announced. Strangely, when the women arrived under the tree canopy, they maintained an excessive social distance from Grandma and me and proceeded to eat their meals from the same leaf, separate from ours. None of the women joined us to eat from our leaf or expressed any interest in tasting some of the delicious meals my grandma had painstakingly prepared. I was confused and bemused because such behavior was unusual and out of tradition. Although this observation sparked my curiosity, I opted to hold my peace. Grandma maintained a calm, relaxed demeanor and was enjoying the vibrant bond we had between us. As if she had been reading my mind, she looked straight at me and asked a question that has remain stenciled in my heart all these years: "Do you know why the other women are not eating with us?" I gave no response. She continued despite my intentional reticence: "It is because I am a leper." She proceeded to show me the digital stumps on her feet and hands as if I had never noticed them. Seemingly unfazed, she continued to enjoy her meal.

To me, there could be no moment more emotionally poignant than that. I was familiar with her condition, but she was obviously unconcerned about it. What mattered more to me was that she embodied kindness and was loving and caring. She meant the world to me. She was not a freak. Then I thought this couldn't have been the first time she had been reminded of her infirmity subtly or indirectly by someone. She must have been a victim of discriminatory attitudes in the past, shunned, despised, humiliated, and treated like an outcast because of the deformities she had acquired from her feud with leprosy. Yet she remained calm and dignified. Her voice had a loving, forgiving tone, and even during such a challenging moment, she was comfortable with herself and showed no expression of animosity or vengefulness for the actions of her friends. She spoke with regal poise, demonstrating strength and tenacity. Grandma always held her head up high. If she felt any emotional pain as a result of the overt loathsomeness by her "friends," she certainly did not let on. On my part, I couldn't help but feel a twinge of sadness and compassion for her. For the first time, I began to appreciate her deformities in a different light as I became more keenly aware of them. I looked up at Grandma with sadness in my heart and told her that I loved her and I hated her friends. She rebuked me immediately and, in no uncertain terms, said, "Oh no, hate destroys everyone! These are good women, and each one of them has some good in her. You must learn to love the good in people. An isolated failure does not define the sum total of any of these women."

She went on to explain how all life in the village was interconnected and that there was no perfect community because everybody had imperfections. It would be years before I would be able to discover the true meaning behind her magnificent words.

After lunch, the women regrouped and began to work again under the searing tropical sun. There was something about what I had just experienced and how it affected my mind and body in strange ways. My interest in playing with the other kids effectively vanished. I just could not shake off the sadness that had suddenly engulfed me. Observing a drastic change in my demeanor, Grandma prodded me gently to reengage my friends in play. I agreed for a moment because I didn't want to distract her from her work. All I could think of was getting back to the village. I could not care less about anyone there except her. The women continued to labor until sundown. When it was all over, everyone grabbed their belongings and headed back to the village. The return trek abounded with laughter, chatter, and banter despite what had transpired earlier at the farm. I was beginning to imagine that Grandma's upbeat, vivacious, and congenial attitude reduced tension and fostered a delightful state of camaraderie among the women.

As I look back over the years, I now realize she had a brilliant strategy to subsume her pain, set priorities, and maintain her power. On the way home, I found palliation in knowing that we had so much leftover food and I would be feasting in the days ahead. This realization certainly assuaged my feelings, although I wished the other women could have experienced my grandma's culinary talents. Their loss was my gain.

CHAPTER 7

Traditional Medicine

WEEKS AFTERWARD I BEGAN to have recurrent thoughts about the experience at the farm. Understandably, the decision for me to live with my grandmother was made by my parents when I was four years old because they realized she needed assistance and companionship. After all, she was elderly and alone and had been dealing with the ravages of leprosy. But most of all, I believe it was Grandma's idea for me to live with her because I was her favorite. She was loving, compassionate, and giving. Not long after I moved in with her, I began to witness horrific changes in her body. Her fingers and toes would slough off in front of my own eyes and leave fragile, smelly, dead tissue and sores, which I helped to clean and treat. Additionally, she needed my assistance in giving her baths. The loss of most of her digits resulted in a decrease in her coordination and dexterity so that at times I had to help her with handling unwieldy objects. I did not mind swatting annoying flies away from her sores and using sharpened pieces of wood to remove bothersome fleas buried deep in her hands and feet. I often wondered why she appeared to suffer no pain from her sores and stumps. The answer came years later in a medical school lecture on leprosy when I discovered that nerve damage is common in lepers. Understandably, society's unfair attitudes toward her were steeped in the widespread ignorance about the disease.

She was a deeply spiritual and religious person. Unfortunately, when she became a leper, she was not allowed to worship in person at her church. About two times a year, a pastor came to the village to give her Communion. That was always a special occasion. The pastor was a kind man who didn't seem to be bothered by her condition. I suspect that she might have been shunned by other congregants in her church and that the pastor had nothing to do with her "excommunication." I believe so because every time he came to give her Communion, Grandma would prepare the best meal of the year, which he ate with vigorous enthusiasm. On my part, I didn't like him. I was jealous of him because of the attention Grandma gave him during those visits.

Despite being a leper and being shunned by many, she showed no signs of animosity or slowing down. She didn't perceive herself as handicapped as she remained remarkably energetic, resilient, and upbeat despite occasional stumbles and falls. She even had a way of injecting humor into such awkward situations. She would look fondly at me and blurt out one of her "Granny" aphorisms: "You know an old person's cane is their child." To say she was my hero would be an understatement. I just loved and admired her immeasurably.

Ironically, Grandma was a native doctor. Her mind was a phenomenal pharmacopeia of therapeutic African herbs and plants. She was known to achieve cures for diseases that orthodox physicians struggled with. I had a terrible skin condition when I was a child, which left me feeling self-conscious among the other kids. I remember showing it to her and wondering if I would have to suffer the indignity of showcasing a large patch of my inflamed skin forever. She examined it carefully and then took me on a brisk walk in the woods, where she identified a specific leaf and rubbed it on my skin. Within days, my skin problem was eliminated.

Patients used to come to see her from far-flung places and stay in our hut. Some of them arrived on makeshift stretchers. The hut would become congested with people sleeping on every inch of the dirt floor. I would have to give up my bed to a patient and find comfort somewhere on the floor with some of the patient's family members. I often wondered how Grandma could remember the therapeutic value in so many different plants, herbs, and a thousand different natural products. She would disappear in the woods and emerge hours later with a basketful of countless remedies, which she would prepare diligently and use for treatment purposes. Her approach to treatment was holistic. Her treatment philosophy, which addressed both the somatic and psychic determinants of illnesses, was in line with Indigenous

African beliefs of disease causation by both spiritual and physical imbalances. Besides her herbal remedies, she included generous portions of massage therapy, meditation, and spiritual invocations. She treated every patient gently, attentively, and with loving care.

It was always a celebratory moment when, about a week or so later, a patient who had appeared so close to death would leave our hut looking invigorated and journey back to his or her home. Grandma even treated fractures successfully. I must confess that I never saw her solicit or receive compensation for her work. On a few occasions, I witnessed appreciative patients and family members who, of their own volition, offered her chicken, goats, or food items in appreciation for her work. On her part, she always appeared to derive immeasurable personal gratification from taking care of sick people in particular and humanity in general.

CHAPTER 8

School Wish

Uncle George, my maternal grandmother's younger brother, a retired plantation overseer, lived in a huge house adjacent to my grandma's hut with his four wives. Around the corner was the residence of my dad's brother Uncle Daniel, who was missing a right hand from a fire accident. Another uncle, Marcus, lived across the road with his doting wife, Esther, and their two sons. The vast majority of people living in my neighborhood were close relatives of my family. The atmosphere in our compound was always lively. With so many children around, life for a young boy like me could not be boring. There was always someone to play with, and the doors of every house or hut were open to everyone. We did not have many of the modern contrivances or luxuries, but we were content with the natural resources that abounded in our environment.

Human relationships meant more to everyone because of a strong, traditional sense of community in the culture. Our way of life embodied the true essence of that powerful African adage about how it takes a village to raise a child. When I needed anything and my grandma was not around, somebody in the neighborhood or the compound addressed the situation immediately, efficiently, and effectively, as though I were their biological child. By the same token, when I misbehaved (as I often did), I was summarily punished or disciplined accordingly by anybody in the neighborhood. The communal philosophy embraced the idea that the survival of the village was predicated on the physical and emotional health of its children.

My very best friend at that time was my cousin Thomas. He was the oldest child of Uncle George. Thomas was a few years older than me and had a lovingly vested interest in my well-being. He played the role of protector, teacher, friend, and disciplinarian. He was enrolled in a Catholic mission elementary school in a neighboring town, and he left early on school days on a long walk to school. I knew exactly when he returned in the afternoon, so I used to sit patiently at the roadside, waiting to meet him and help carry his books as we walked home together. I was fascinated with his depth of knowledge, and I was riveted by the new songs he sang in English. I adored his school uniform—a navy-blue shirt and khaki shorts. Thomas was my true idol, and he delighted in telling me about all the great things he was learning in school. He talked incessantly about his delight in learning English, recognizing letters and numbers, studying arithmetic, learning new songs, and many other things.

All his experiences captivated my attention. Hearing him talk about school convinced me he was having the time of his life and that learning was fun. Consequently, I felt as though I was missing out on many unique and tremendous experiences in school. During that time there was nothing I enjoyed more than to sit and listen to Thomas. Thankfully, he was very strong-minded, garrulous, and engaging. Whenever I was with him, I often preferred to listen more and speak less. I used to lie in bed at night dreaming about the experiences he had shared with me earlier and wishing that I could partake in them as well. Predictably, I began to harass my grandma regularly about my interest in attending school. Her response was always that I was too young. Each time my parents stopped by to visit, I would plead with them to send me to school so that I could be like Thomas. They always blurted out the same response, that I was too young for school and would not be admitted. It seemed to me as though no one was listening or was interested. They may have thought that I was not mature enough, but I knew that I was ready for the opportunity.

As time went on, I became less interested in mundane activities around me and wasted no chance to throw a temper tantrum. I found multiple excuses to be rebellious. I complained about Grandma's food, the water, the air, and my bed. I complained about anything that came to mind. Even the kids around me decided I had become too obnoxious to play with. One time I waited until my grandmother was going to sit down at dinner, and I immediately pulled the seat from underneath her. She fell on the floor, and in a fit of legitimate targeted rage, she grabbed a large clay pot and lurched in my direction. I bolted like a threatened deer in the Serengeti, and although she gave chase, her attempt at snagging me was no match for my youthful, agile limbs. I hid out in the woods for a while until I could slither back into the hut under cover of darkness. My intentional behavioral transformation was driving everyone crazy.

One day my parents made an unannounced visit to Grandma. She was sitting in the yard husking corn. Skipping the usual salutations, she began to complain about the new and repulsive changes in my behavior. As I listened to her narratives, I began to feel bad about my attitude and behavior. Most of all, I was worried about the immediate repercussions from my parents. I knew that I could be experiencing my very last moments on the planet at that time because my mother had a take-no-prisoners attitude. By a stroke of luck, within seconds my uncle Daniel appeared and saved the moment—and most likely my life—when, with ecstatic detail, he conveyed welcome news about a new Baptist missionary elementary school to be opened in short order a few miles away from our compound. My mother's gaze abruptly shifted in my direction. With a piercing look, a taut stance, a flexed elbow, and an emphatically extended thumb, she declared in no uncertain terms, "*He goes!*" I did breathe a sigh of relief at the stay of execution; however, the primordial fear of what could happen to me if suddenly I broke out in a song-and-dance routine kept my emotions in check. I wasn't off the hook yet.

There were not enough schools in the region at that time. Given the discrepancy between the large number of applicants and the paucity of educational opportunities, many children were often left disappointed. My behavior leading up to my mother's decision had been, at best, stupid. I had a little wisdom inside me to appreciate the possibility that her precipitous decision to have me enrolled at the new school, at that moment in time, was buoyed neither by a strategic impulse to capitalize expeditiously on an immediate and fleeting opportunity nor an emotional or affectionate desire for me to jump on the education bandwagon because of its future rewards.

Not wanting to be left out, my dad stepped forward in my direction. Unfailingly he lived up to his reputation as a man of few words: "If I ever..." I prayed for him to leave the sentence uncompleted. In a calculated, strategic maneuver steeped in experience and intended to deter him from further clarification of his position and from the completion of his sentence, I abruptly bowed down my head in a gesture of contrition and respect. I knew better. His incomplete message was loud and clear. I knew from my previous experiences with him that an admonition could be a "package deal," and complete sentences often heralded supplemental physical contributions that often left me with short-term physical deficits.

Realizing there was a real possibility that I might finally get my wish and attend school, I spent the ensuing days behaving like a model grandson. I was quiet, courteous, reserved, and overly responsible as I tried to compensate for all the wrong I had been doing. Even my grandma began to worry about the extreme behavioral shift in me. By her actions, I sensed she had forgiven me and wanted things to return to normal between us.

CHAPTER 9

Rejection

A FEW DAYS LATER, on a dusty January morning, Uncle Daniel aroused me at the break of dawn to tell me that he would be taking me to the Presbyterian elementary school to seek admission to the first grade. He had not heard anything about the new Baptist school since the rumors about its official opening were dispersed. I jumped for joy, grabbed a gourd, and sprinted a mile downhill from our hut to fetch water in the stream, where we routinely obtained it for bathing and other household and lifestyle needs. After taking a quick, cold bath, I darted over to my uncle's hut, where he was standing at the door holding a nice little surprise for me: a new shirt and a pair of shorts.

He helped me to get dressed. I rarely wore clothes. Almost all kids, like me, either walked around naked in the village or wore loincloths. A majority of the men and women in the village wore simple garments, grass skirts or loincloths. Traditional full-body garb and other more complex outfits were reserved for special occasions like weddings, religious ceremonies, and regional or national celebrations. With balmy weather practically all year round, there was no need for excessive body coverage at all times. The concept of "less is better" was quite apropos at that time as it related to individual attitudes concerning clothing. Therefore, when people returned from school, church service, or any other formal event, they immediately shed their complex outfits and replaced them with simpler alternatives.

Despite tradition, on that day I was on cloud nine in my new uniform. My behavior that morning was somewhat impetuous, and Uncle Daniel understood how badly I wanted to go to school. At that time, there were only three elementary schools in the region representing three denominations: Catholic, Presbyterian, and Baptist. Although many of my relatives were Muslims, there were no Islamic schools then. Uncle Daniel was a member of the Presbyterian congregation. In general, children attended the schools of their family denominations. However, not all children of school age were sent to school. Some families did not appreciate the value of formal education. After all, village children had numerous traditional responsibilities that were congruent with their ages and developmental levels.

Few truly "successful" individuals in the village could attribute their success to education. The most educated people were our schoolteachers, who were few in number and were highly respected and revered. However, their lifestyles were no different than those of many other members of their communities. Even when families were convinced or persuaded by the missionaries to send their children to school, more often than not, they sent their sons before their daughters. Daughters continued to help their mothers with household chores and farming duties until they left home to be married.

When my uncle Daniel and I arrived at the Presbyterian school, the grounds were bustling with noisy parents and their timid, anxious offspring. It was a new and unnerving experience for me. I saw a White man dressed in a blue shirt and long gray pants. He smiled easily and stopped intermittently to shout out commands in English. I could not understand him, but I assumed he was trying to organize the children in a line and prepare them for the screening interview. Admission to elementary school was not guaranteed. There were many students vying for precious few positions at that school. Therefore, children of congregation members and those who were deemed old enough stood a better chance of being selected. The selection process had many flaws and was hardly objective. Since most parents were illiterate subsistence farmers from neighboring villages and most babies were delivered in village huts, birth records were rarely kept. Age was relative. You knew who was older or younger.

As I stood there on that fateful day in the scorching tropical sun, wondering what was going to happen, I had a feeling that things might not end favorably. Before I could think of anything else, Uncle Daniel abruptly interrupted my dreamlike state, grabbed my hand, and yanked me over to one of

Mommy, Please Don't Die!

the lines where other anxious children like me were waiting. Suddenly, he pulled my right hand up across my head to my left ear. It seemed as though he had just lost his marbles and was attempting to dislocate my right shoulder from its natural attachments. I screamed in pain, but he was unyielding. He reached over, and with his right forearm stump, he applied intense upward pressure to my right arm at the level of my elbow while simultaneously pulling hard on my hand above my head. My protests were falling on deaf ears, and there was nothing I could do in front of the crowd to dissuade him from hurting me. *How embarrassing*, I thought. My helplessness was exacerbated by the physical disparity between us. I was beginning to think he intended to kill me for whatever demonic reason until I realized he was not the only parent testing out torture techniques on innocent children. I noticed that some of the boys were able to touch their opposite ears nimbly and without extreme physical coercion. After multiple futile attempts, Uncle Daniel gave pause. He stood there silently, as though he were considering alternative maneuvers.

In the interlude, we began to inch slowly forward toward a closed wooden door, and I wondered what sinister mystery lurked within those walls. I could see at least two children with their parents being ushered in rapidly, followed by the door slamming shut behind them. I did not see anyone exiting the same door, which gave me concern about what could be happening in there. The White man would open the door, scan the crowd for a second, always with a smile on his face, and then wave in the next candidate. The closer we got to the door, the more anxious I felt. What could be going on in there to all those children and their parents? Who was this strange-looking man anyhow? Why did he smile so much? Folklore had it that White people were magicians; they were kind, and they could always miraculously retrieve candy from their pockets to offer village kids. They could fly like birds. They had a spare set of eyes, and even when they took off the external set, placed it on a table, and left the room, they could still "keep an eye on things" despite their physical absence. They liked raw meat. Oh no! Now, that last one was concerning to me! My uncle was big and strong and…well, I don't know! Since I hadn't heard any screams emanating from the building, I felt reassured.

I was still pondering the bizarre nature of the unfolding events when the door swung open again. The same White man appeared, and this time he was sporting a broader smile, and his gaze was directed unflinchingly at me. My turn was up! My eyes darted up toward Uncle Daniel's face, where I found neither concern nor reassurance. Before I could voice any personal grievances, we were immediately pulled into a room and the door slammed behind us. We were standing in a spacious chamber with a large wooden desk in the center, loaded with stacks of papers and a few rulers. Behind it sat two neatly dressed ladies, one White and the other Indigenous. I scanned the room with cautious suspicion. No knives, no spears, and no cauldrons. What a relief! Then I noticed a partially closed side door leading to another room with chairs where a lot of kids and their parents were waiting. Ahead of us was a smaller door that remained completely shut. Soon I would discover that the outcome of the interview would determine which exit door we would take.

The ladies immediately explained to us that they would be asking questions. Since neither my uncle nor I understood or spoke English, the Indigenous lady served as a translator. My uncle was asked how old I was. He responded that I was old enough for school. This response did not seem to sit well with them. When asked about my birthday, my uncle responded that I was born around Christmas. At that point, the White man grabbed a ruler to record my height. Without wasting any more time, the women asked a barrage of questions in rapid succession. Exactly how old is your son? Has he attended any other school? Has he solicited admission elsewhere? Does he have any health problems? Without any further ado, one of the ladies walked out from behind the desk and demanded that I touch my left ear with my right hand from above my head. Although I had had a frustratingly painful experience earlier with this maneuver, I felt as though I had no option but to sweat through it again. However, despite a desperate attempt at contorting my torso, squinting, and grunting, I failed again miserably. I gave up and stood there for a few moments feeling dejected and looking at the women with imploring eyes. I knew I was ready for school. I didn't know how to convince these strangers about my determination to enter elementary school. I felt so powerless in that room; I was concerned my ethereal hopes would be dashed. I could not imagine what evil person could have conceived such a miserable way of determining a child's eligibility for elementary school.

In retrospect, I believe the genesis of that technique was the absence of chronological age information in predominantly illiterate communities, where obstetrical practices took place in local villages without any official records. The implicit subjective aspects of this technique are glaringly obvious. Because of natural physical disparities among children of any given age or geography, some children could perform that maneuver easily and successfully despite their younger age and without a forceful dislocation of their shoulder joint by a desperate parent. Additionally, there were children with added advantages who were afforded a greater degree of flexibility due to certain genetic conditions.

In my situation, judgment came swift. "Can't start school yet! Too young! Next!"

They showed us the door. It was a back door that led us down a narrow alleyway to the main road. Tears were streaming down my cheeks. I had just been rejected, and I was feeling hapless, helpless, hopeless, horrified, and despondent. Suddenly, Uncle Daniel's pace hastened. He did not seem to be concerned with my emotional response to what had just happened. He blurted out, "Let's go to another school." Then he continued, "Remember, my son, not every chase yields a catch!"

I was in no mood for any of his aphorisms.

Off we went, practically running through the bushes. After about half an hour, we arrived at a Catholic elementary school. Once again, I failed the hand-to-ear test and was encouraged to reapply the following year. I kept thinking about my cousin Thomas and his books. I kept thinking about all the exciting things he was learning and how he even spoke and acted differently than the rest of the little boys in the village. I envied him. Uncle Daniel didn't say much on the way back home. I knew he loved me very much by his words and, most especially, by his actions. All day he had tried unsuccessfully to secure a place for me at both local elementary schools, and he was clearly sad and disappointed, just as I was. To assuage my feelings, he reassured me that the year would go by fast and that I should be ready the following year as I would be a year older and physically better qualified for admission. I was not buying it!

I was so emotionally exhausted that day that I went to bed at an earlier hour than usual. I resigned myself to the fact that I would be lingering around the village another year before anybody would be interested in offering me a chance to attend school.

I was sitting in my grandmother's hut thinking about the events of the day when my mom showed up. She asked me to accompany her to another village where she was going to celebrate the birth of a child. It was about a ten-mile trek. We started off the next morning, and everything seemed OK. About five miles into the journey, I began to throw a temper tantrum. I told her I was not able to walk anymore, and I asked her to carry me. She looked down at my droopy face for a brief second and kept walking. I held my ground and refused to budge, hoping that my actions would give her reason to comply with my wishes. As I stood there pouting with my arms folded on my chest, I watched her walk nonchalantly at her normal rapid pace as if I did not exist. She was over a mile away in the distance when my brain kicked in and flooded my legs with renewed strength, and I took off like a cheetah until I caught up with her. Even so, she continued as though nothing had happened. She was so principled, unbreakable, and unswerving that I was determined to craft new strategies to break her resolve.

When we arrived at our destination, I met one of the boys who was slightly older than me and had just been accepted into the first grade and could not contain his excitement about starting school. This made me feel bad about my situation and effectively ruined the trip for me.

CHAPTER 10

Acceptance

SEVERAL DAYS WENT BY. Then early one morning, Uncle George showed up at my grandmother's hut and announced that the new Baptist elementary school would actually be opening the very next day. When Uncle Daniel got wind of this, his excitement was immeasurable. Once again, he ordered me to get ready the next morning. The school didn't have a schoolhouse yet, and classes would have to be conducted in a one-room hut that had been donated by someone in the village. That morning we hit the road half walking, half running. I was pleased to see that Uncle Daniel had not lost his enthusiasm. He was more determined than ever to have me enrolled. His persistence was ferocious and infectious. We walked a dusty road, encountering friendly villagers either heading to or returning from a popular farmers' market in the region. My uncle was on a mission, and I could barely keep up with him.

When we finally arrived, there was a throng surrounding the new teacher, Mr. Wankie. He was seated at a table in the tiny schoolyard in front of a hut. He had no assistant. At first, the scene appeared chaotic, with desperate parents pleading loudly for him to admit their children. This was a different scenario than our previous experiences. Through it, Mr. Wankie kept a remarkable composure, maintained order, and reassured anxious parents while assessing the candidacies of their children. Uncle Daniel refused to take his position in the queue. He muscled his way through the boisterous crowd, walked up to the teacher, and immediately began to plead with him, telling him that I was a good boy and would be the best student. He kept emphasizing that Mr. Wankie would not be disappointed by me. I guess there comes a time when some unsolicited advocacy is warranted, but frankly speaking, much of what he was telling Mr. Wankie about my character and qualifications sounded so alien that I honestly didn't know whom he was talking about.

The teacher asked me to step forward. He was a tall, imposing figure with hunched shoulders and a paralyzing gaze. He was fluent in the local language, and once again, he asked me to perform the dreaded hand-to-ear maneuver—which, predictably, I flunked. It all seemed unfair because I had not been allowed enough time to grow since the previous test a few days earlier. I was convinced all the options had been exhausted and there would be no schooling for me for quite some time. When the teacher turned around to walk back to his seat, I could hear him mumbling something I could not make out, but I was prepared for the worst. It would be my third rejection of the week, and for some reason, I was ready for it this time. It would not be as painful. Mr. Wankie sat down, looked at my uncle for a moment, and then shifted his gaze in my direction. He kept looking at me for what seemed like an eternity, and then he leaned back, hands clasped behind his neck, his generous lips twisted in a sardonic smile, and momentarily, while staring at Uncle Daniel, he expelled a few memorable, magical words: *"I will take him!"*

My heart stopped! I found myself gleefully hugging the teacher's table and my uncle alternately. When I look back over the years, no words come close to expressing the joy I felt at that moment, and I often wonder if the compelling reason behind the teacher's decision was my uncle's overwhelming and movingly desperate exuberance, rather than my having fulfilled the criteria for admission. I forget what the teacher said next except that we left the schoolyard ecstatically and precipitously. I couldn't wait to share the news with my parents, Grandma, and Cousin Thomas. I would have my own books! I would have a new and handsome uniform! I had just earned the coveted title of *student*, finally! Nothing could be more uplifting. From that moment onward, everything I did or thought about was in anticipation of my first day of school.

CHAPTER 11

Elementary School

I CAN STILL REMEMBER that first day of school. It was in January. The
leaves on the trees bore a thick coating of light-brown dust. The morning
air was cool and crisp. In a few hours, temperatures would triple. Butterflies
were floating lazily from shrub to shrub. Dragonflies were everywhere. On
the bush path to school, the dust was a few inches thick and cushioned
every step I took. It was the dry season, and the rains had been absent for
a couple of months. It was also planting season. The weather was so dry
and hot that the earth cracked into deep furrows, as did the soles of my
leathery, shoeless feet.

An old, rickety truck appeared out of nowhere, kicking up a huge cloud
of dust that remained suspended for minutes before settling on our bodies, vegetation, and everything within sight. That morning I had gotten
up bright and early, and I had run to the stream about a mile from our
house to fetch water for bathing and cooking. After taking a quick bath,
I ate some roasted corn and peanuts that my grandmother had prepared
and immediately darted out of the hut to go to school. I was all smiles and
beaming with joy when I saw my cousin Thomas leaving in the opposite
direction and heading to school as well. We exchanged pleasantries and
parted. He wished me well, and I reciprocated. I was decked out in a new
uniform, which frankly was not as comfortable because I had not been used
to restrictive clothing. There were too many buttons on the shirt, which
was a complicated mess. However, I didn't allow this to bother me one bit,
especially on onc of the most special days of my life. It was certainly not easy

graduating from a tiny loincloth to strange-looking clothes. The loincloth was practical, simple, and logical.

When I arrived at the bush path leading to the school, I heard the sound of a drum emanating from the distance. I would discover later that it was intended to alert villagers that school was about to start. There were no clocks in the village. The drum was hollowed out of the trunk of a large tree. Two sticks alternately hitting the opening of the trunk created a musical sound that traveled far across the village. That morning I was the first student to arrive and was welcomed by my new teacher, Mr. Wankie. He lived several miles away and walked to school every day. On the first day of class, we learned letters of the alphabet and numbers. There was no frivolity on the part of our teacher, and he despised playfulness.

After the first day of school, I was smitten. My mind never quite returned to the village after that day. My curiosity was boundless. I enjoyed learning the alphabet, numbers, and arithmetic. There were only about fifteen of us in class, and we considered ourselves privileged to be there.

Whenever I returned from school, I proceeded to teach my grandmother everything I had learned that day. She was always patient, and with a look of pride in her shimmering eyes, she would heap enormous praises on me, calling me by a new name: "Our king!" After school, I often shed my uncomfortable uniform as soon as I entered the hut and dashed out naked or in my favorite loincloth to join my friends at play. At times Grandma would still be busy farming (she often told me in the morning where she would be farming on a particular day), and I would go there after school to assist her in bringing home the harvest. We didn't have any contraptions such as refrigerators; therefore, food was prepared daily and had to be consumed the same day. We never had leftovers, and I never experienced complete satiety after a meal. Periodically, I would climb a mango tree for supplemental nutrition. I loved mangoes, and sometimes I would gorge myself on so many of them that I would wind up having explosive diarrhea for days. Another favorite of mine was avocados. On the way to school, I would shake an avocado tree or one of its branches until a few of them would fall to the ground. Then I would bury them for two days until they ripened. This would be my lunch or dinner.

Our elementary school teachers did not give us homework during the earlier years. All work had to be completed before the end of the school day. However, in the later years, things became more difficult. I used to bring home a lot of math homework, and unfortunately, there was nobody in the village to help me with my assignments. There were times when I would be so desperate for help with an assignment that I would turn to look at Grandma, who would simply look back at me and offer her only option: a prayer. She was someone who prayed before and after everything. Sometimes before a meal, her prayers would be so lengthy that I could feel the saliva welling up in my anxious mouth. If she kept her eyes shut during prayer, I would usually begin to eat stealthily.

My main focus at that stage was school. The entire village seemed to be committed to making sure none of the school children strayed from this focus. I couldn't wait to get up in the morning to go to school. My parents were particularly delighted and proud of me.

My older sister and I shared a special bond. She was highly intuitive and very smart. She spent most of her time with our mother. One day I asked my grandma why my sister was not in school. "Because she is a girl!" she responded. Our discussion quickly degenerated into a debate about educating girls. I was so insistent that my sister be offered an opportunity to study that I took my case to my uncles and my parents. Nobody seemed to be moved or convinced by my argument. (Recently, my sister reminded me in detail about the persistent advocacy work I pursued unsuccessfully on her behalf at that time. She is currently a proud parent of successful, educated children.)

Even though my father had no formal education, his exposure to educated supervisors and European expatriates on the plantation where he worked gave him an appreciation for the value of education. He was fascinated with my exercise notebooks, and I would often find him sitting alone and flipping through their pages. In the third grade, I began to teach my dad some of the things I was learning. His enthusiasm was infectious. I taught him the English alphabet and basic addition and subtraction. While I was teaching him, the look of fascination, enthusiasm, and tremendous pride on his face as he watched me furiously scribbling away on a piece of paper with Mom standing somewhere in the background was so precious and loving that such moments have remained very dear to me to this day.

Every first-grade child was given chalk and a small board on which we practiced writing our letters and numbers. Our teacher also brought an abacus to teach us to count. I particularly enjoyed some new songs we were taught by certain missionaries, such as "Rain, rain, go away, come again another day," and so on. These and many others were exciting because we sang them in a foreign language that was new to us and vastly different from our native language. At times we did not know or understand the meaning of the words we were singing, but that did not matter because we enjoyed the melody and the uplifting feelings we experienced while singing together. Understandably, the songs varied with the country of origin of the missionary. English missionaries taught us many songs about the king and queen of England. The American Baptist and Presbyterian missionaries brought "Swing Low, Sweet Chariot" and a host of other foot-stomping, hand-clapping melodies that we loved. I can only imagine the thrill and fascination of our parents when we took these new and exotic songs back to our villages. My grandma learned some of them and would sing along with me. Sometimes some of my aunts and uncles would pipe in and voilà! We would have a melodious impromptu native choir. Music was and is indeed a universal language.

Unfortunately, years later I discovered that some of the songs we had been taught were disturbingly inappropriate. We learned them phonetically, sang them, and enjoyed them without a contextual understanding of their words and meanings. Up till today, I remember one of those songs:

> Oh I went down south for to see my gal sing polly wolly doodle all the way. My Sally Ann a dowdy gal sing polly wolly doodle all the way. When I came to a river and I couldn't get across sing polly wolly doodle all the way. Then I jumped upon a nigger for I thought he was a horse sing polly wolly doodle all the way...

A new school building was constructed during our first year in elementary school. It had three rooms, brick walls, a dirt floor, and an aluminum roof! This was pure luxury, given that we had just spent a year learning in a tiny hut with a thatched roof. In first grade, we had to bring our bamboo stools to school every day. Our new school had wooden benches and desks, but our classroom was lacking a blackboard. One day the teacher asked us to contribute three pennies each so that he could buy cement and black paint to construct a blackboard on one of the walls. My grandma was quite visibly distressed when I brought home this request. First, she prayed hard, as she often did; then she went all around the neighborhood soliciting financial assistance. She had no money, and she did not need money for herself. It wasn't long before she returned with the full amount, which enabled me to proudly make my contribution the following day. Eventually, we got a blackboard, which is still in use to this day.

We were fortunate in my village to have a school building where classes could be held indoors. In many other villages, students received their education beneath the canopy of a tree. During the rainy season, things would sometimes become chaotic in the classroom as we couldn't hear our teacher because of the loud and continuous noise generated by the sound of fierce, torrential tropical rains beating against the aluminum panels on the roof. There was no ceiling to buffer the noise from the pounding rain on the aluminum roof. Additionally, the rains often came pouring heavily through large openings in the walls, which served as windows but without coverings. Occasionally, it rained so much that we were ankle-deep in water. Then we had to huddle in a corner with our teacher while anticipating a hiatus in the deluge.

Our teachers were all highly respected in the community. They received priority seating and service during every occasion in the village. The average monthly salary of a teacher was two dollars. Despite the low wages, their dedication was incomparable. All the teachers were strict disciplinarians and were dedicated to their profession. Corporal punishment was meted out daily. Everyone stood up in unison and greeted the teacher at the beginning of the day. If you were late for school, did not dress properly, or received a bad score in the daily math and language quizzes, or if you were boisterous during class, spoke, or acted with disrespect for the teacher, you would become the recipient of a painful encounter with the whip.

Each day after every quiz, students were asked to remain standing. Then the teacher would read out the scores, starting with the highest and proceeding to the lowest one. The performance of a student whose score was below an arbitrary cutoff point was considered poor. As each score was read, students who had achieved acceptable scores were allowed to sit. Everyone below a specific cutoff score would be left standing and invariably received a few lashes on the hand, back, or bottom. On occasion, a student who had received poor marks on a quiz would be hoisted on the back of a taller student to facilitate the delivery of lashes on the back of the hoisted student. I had a real problem with corporal punishment, which I considered inhumane and abhorrent. Whenever I was offered the choice of receiving lashes or staying after school to clean, cut grass, or perform other menial tasks, I would invariably choose the latter option. Thereafter, I became familiar with the preferences of some of our teachers. Several teachers didn't give students any choices except lashes. Frequently, if a particular teacher preferred giving lashes over other types of punishment, I padded my shorts and shirts in the back with leaves or clothing material before leaving for school that day to diminish the painful impact of the dreadful whip. All that protective padding probably gave me the look of a character in a minstrel show. Despite the stressful learning conditions we faced, we had no dropouts.

I finished my second and third years among the top students in my grade. I can remember going home each time and proudly announcing my performance to my parents and the seniors. My mother was often the self-appointed spokesperson for the tribe, expressing the same sentiments: "We are proud of you." Then she would immediately remind me, "There are many greater challenges ahead and more knowledge to be acquired!" After such a declaration, she often walked away quietly. Just like that! No nice words. No celebration.

CHAPTER 12

Village Games

THERE WERE STRONG BONDS between the few boys in the village who were attending elementary school. We met up on weekends in my uncle's yard and played games. One day when I was sweeping my uncle's house, my cousin Thomas showed up with some of the boys in the village. They had a homemade football and asked if I could join them in a game of soccer. Since no one could afford a real football, we often used oranges or grapefruit as balls. Needless to say, these did not last long because they would invariably be crushed during intense dribbling activity. Sometimes the balls were made of rubber obtained directly from the dried sap of rubber trees rolled into the shape of a ball. I was a lousy footballer with no rhythm or coordination in my feet. Frankly, I was more of a hindrance than a positive contributor in the game. I could dribble neither to and fro nor side to side, and most of the boys experienced tremendous pleasure dribbling circles around me. It was probably a comical spectacle to watch me playing, but that did not worry me because I loved the game, and I loved the social camaraderie that came with it.

Oftentimes before a game, the two top players in the village would be allowed to pick and choose players for their team, and I was always the last one to be selected in what was often a painful decision for either top player. Cousin Thomas was one of the best players, and he was admirably coordinated; he had nimble feet and tremendous balance. He defied gravity, and to watch him was like watching a symphony in action. He was my hero, and I adored him. Repeatedly, he would try to teach me some of his moves, but those efforts generally were hopeless. I just didn't have it physically, even though I enjoyed the game.

I can remember one particular day when someone came with a new homemade rubber ball, and we decided to test it out. The two key players began to select members for their squad. It turned out everyone was picked except me. While standing there, scratching my butt and feeling a mixture of embarrassment, dejection, and excitement, I looked across at Thomas. When our eyes met, I read his mind. Without missing a beat, he called my name out softly with much affection and sympathy in his voice. He had a complete team on his side, and I was the extra player he did not need and his opponents did not want. During a previous tournament, when I had played on the other team, I had scored three goals for them. Those were the only goals scored in the tournament. Unfortunately, some of my team-mates—especially the goalkeepers—were ready to kill me because I scored those goals against my team! The opposing team didn't mind it at all.

During the rainy season, we had a favorite game called mud fight. We made balls of mud and hurled them at each other. Sometimes the rainy season brought lots of hail, which we used to pelt each other for the fun of it. Village children never played alone or indoors. We invented many of our games using raw materials from our environment: fruit items, trees, and vines. I enjoyed building things with my hands. I remember building a wooden bicycle after seeing my uncle Samuel's bike. I chopped down a tree and fashioned a couple of wheels from its trunk. Using its branches, I was able to construct the frame and handlebars. I rode my wooden bike for a while before my cousin accidentally broke it. Furthermore, I had an idea about building a contraption that could fly. At that time I had never seen or heard of an airplane. The impetus for this instinctive idea was the long walks on tortuous roads with wet, thorny shrubs that Grandma and I used to take to faraway farms on cold, soggy mornings. On one of those trips, I imagined her and myself in one of my contraptions, up high in the blue yonder instead of walking the entire way.

CHAPTER 13

Fun Edibles—Termites, Critters, Snakes, and All

TOWARD THE END OF the dry season and just before the beginning of the rains, a favorite meeting place for children after school in the evening was the termite mound. In a sense, the mound had a special seasonal position of importance in local culture and tradition and brought out unique social dynamics. There was always heightened expectation and anticipation in the village for the day when termites emerged from the mound. No one knew exactly which day it would happen. Nonetheless, you could feel the anticipation in the air. Usually, someone would witness the initial activity at the mound as the first termites would begin to exit and fly away. That individual would then alert others, and before long the entire village would be notified and people would begin to arrive at the mound in trickles. First, the children showed up, and then a trickle of adults, followed by a throng of villagers.

Whenever the crowd reached a critical mass, people would begin to jostle for position. Children often arrived with wet baskets and stood around the mounds waiting for millions of termites exiting from thousands of pores at the top and sides of the mound before unfolding their wings and flying away. Amid excited rants, everyone had a specific task to accomplish. When you identified a particularly prolific pore, you placed a large wet basket over it to trap the winged arthropods in the wet lining of the basket, where the moisture acted like glue to their wings. Oftentimes the basket would fill up pretty fast with agitated termites. Some of us used to catch them and eat them on the spot. We did this by grabbing a few of them at once before they could fly away and then dropping them in our mouths and chewing rapidly. This action abruptly separated the termite's torso from its wings, and then as you were swallowing the torso, you simultaneously ejected the wings. Termites are soft and delicious and are also extremely nutritious.

They always exited the mounds in concert with ferocious, fiery ants as escorts. If you were not so vigilant and you grabbed a handful of termites along with a few straggling ants and dropped them all in your mouth, you would be the recipient of a painful sting from an ant, which might force you to spit out all the contents of your mouth in a hurry or make you hop around like a frantic cat on hot bricks as you endured its fiery, vicious biting action the entire way down to your stomach. The buzzing atmosphere at a termite mound was a chance for boys and girls to meet and express flirtatious behavior. Fathers generally showed up to watch the children in action, to resolve conflicts among children, and to make sure everyone played fair and avoided fighting over the more productive mound pores. Periodically, the mound events gave parents a chance to meet up and discuss important village matters while children were engaged in their usual activities. Even Grandma, who rarely left her hut in the evening, would slowly make her way toward the commotion. Not to be outdone, hunting dogs and house cats would join in, leaping in the air in an attempt to catch elusive termites trying to escape the commotion. It was rare but not unusual to see an occasional snake joining the frenzy. There were always flocks of hungry birds shrieking, tweeting, and chirping overhead while intercepting termites in their flight to freedom.

At the mound, you were oblivious to the rest of the world. It was akin to being at an exciting rock concert where the excitement would build up to a climax. At sundown, when the number of escaping termites was reduced to a trickle, people began to sing and chant in celebration of the evening as they headed back to their respective huts and compounds, feeling stuffed, appeased, and gratified. Those who were lucky enough to catch a large number of termites generally shared some of their bounties with others. Termite-mound activity represented a microcosm of African village life. Few events in the village were as raucous and delightful in the life of a child as this excitement at nature's bountiful seasonal banquet. Our parents would empty the large baskets filled with termites into a hot clay pot over a fireplace and stir the contents until the termites were adequately fried. Afterward, their wings would be separated from their torsos by blasting the pot contents with puffs of air while rhythmically shaking the pot. This action was followed by a dash of salt, a sprinkle of palm oil, and a few delicate spices to enhance their flavor. The termites were served with yams, roasted corn, banana, plantains, and other popular nutritious edibles. They were a much-cherished source of protein in our diets.

Weeks after the termite mound events, in the middle of the rainy season, nature would beckon villagers back to the termite mounds for another bountiful product, only this time the product was wingless. The mounds would be covered with sprouting mushrooms, which were highly valued ingredients in our dishes. To this day I can still smell the mound, taste the termites, and relive the excitement of that entire momentous experience.

I also enjoyed cricket hunting at night. Using a torch and a machete, we would head out to the bushes around the house in the dry season when we could hear them chirping. They would crawl out of their burrows, and while staying close to the entrance, they would intermittently chirp loudly. When you saw one in the glare of your torch, you quickly shoved the machete in the ground behind it to prevent it from crawling back into its burrow. Then you had to rapidly reach down and grab the prickly thing and drop it in a basket. This was a gratifying maneuver, and if you were not swift enough, the cricket would disappear back into its hiding place. We soon realized that these creatures were not very smart. Whenever you moved on to the next chirper, the one that got away usually reemerged and resumed chirping louder, as if to give you another chance to capture it. Nothing tasted more delicious than roasted or cooked cricket. Giant grasshoppers were also a much-sought-after delicacy. Whereas a successful hunt could yield a hundred crickets, catching a grasshopper was more difficult. I never caught more than a handful of them. They were best eaten salted and roasted on a stick.

I loved animals, yet I hated snakes. They seemed to be everywhere when I was growing up in the village. Snakebites were common. My grandma was convinced that a good snake was a dead one, and she was quite adept at killing them. Often, she returned from the farm with a huge snake that she boiled or roasted for dinner and served with vegetables, potatoes, or yams. Snake meat was delicious and tasted like chicken. She taught me how to catch and kill them.

Although encounters with snakes were frequent and generally nonlethal, if they didn't bother me, I would leave them alone. However, one afternoon I was enjoying myself, swimming in a river with some of my friends and having a hell of a time diving off tree branches into the muddy water, when suddenly I had an urge to have a bowel movement, and I ran into the bush to squat. Out of nowhere, a huge snake raised in front of me. It had a characteristically angry look, and for whatever reason, it did not seem to appreciate my intrusion. I understood what would happen next, but I was hoping that it would understand my urgent need to answer nature's call. Unfortunately, it made a fast move and struck me on the chest. I felt no pain from its bite, and I jumped up at once. I sprinted away without remembering why I had come there in the first place. When I arrived at the river's edge, suddenly, I felt dizzy and weak; my ears were ringing, and I had a splitting headache. I collapsed and lay there by the river, still conscious but very weak.

Eventually, I got up and trudged home wearily. That night, Grandma was concerned that I had not taken the appropriate traditional remedy for snakebite: a slug of female urine. According to tradition, drinking a woman's urine immediately after suffering a potentially fatal snakebite could be a lifesaver. (There may be a scientific reason for this tradition because female urine has steroids and their byproducts, which could act as anti-inflammatory agents!)

After that horrific encounter with a venomous bite, I began to treat every snake as an enemy. Not long afterward, I was playing near a river with a friend when suddenly a large black snake about six to eight feet in length appeared. Instinctively, I gave chase. As it slithered away, I became more emboldened. It went into the water, swimming quickly downstream as I was chasing after it, running along the riverbank. It came out of the water and slithered rapidly on the road, and I sprinted after it. Only when it disappeared in a thorny thicket filled with razor-sharp leaves did I give up the chase. I presume word was out in the reptile community that a crazed, vengeful native boy was on the loose and had to be avoided at all costs.

I can recall another day when we were all out in the woods gathering fruit and having a good time when one of the boys decided to answer nature's intestinal call. We all followed suit, hopped into the savanna bush, and fanned out in every direction. We could hear but not see each other. As usual, we continued our animated conversations. On that day, in the middle of our activities, a prankster yelled, "Snake!" The spectacle of naked native boys leaping out of the tall grass like Maasai warriors must have been quite a sight to behold. As it turned out, there was no real snake at all.

Overall the life of a village child was never boring. Boys and girls played separately. We employed our creative skills to craft entertainment options to keep our minds and bodies busy. In that idyllic setting, we learned the essence of human interaction and collective living. When you offended anyone, you offended everyone.

CHAPTER 14
Bed-Wetting

EARLIER ON IN ELEMENTARY school, I had what others perceived to be a serious problem: bed-wetting. Actually, I was scared of the dark, yet somehow, I used to dream that I was outside urinating in the bushes. Whenever I woke up, I would realize that my dream had deceived me as usual. Consequently, the adult men decided that I needed a major intervention. My cousin Thomas also had similar issues with bed-wetting. He was older than I, and word had it he had been successfully treated and that tracts of urine were no longer cutting across the floor in his room. However, the details about this mysterious treatment or intervention were not shared openly with everyone. There were a few unsubstantiated village rumors about fiery red ants, but I couldn't make sense of them. Therefore, I waited patiently to learn about what it was they were going to do to me.

In the meantime, I went about my business as usual, with only an occasional puzzling thought about why my bodily functions were of so much concern to others. After all, in the village, everyone lived well and peacefully with nature. We farmed, played, ate, and interacted naturally with each other in our environment. Every child learned proper social behavior and etiquette. I eased myself naturally, deep in the woods, and I used appropriate soft leaves to clean myself afterward. Whenever these were not available, the alternatives for toilet paper were myriad: mango leaves, orange peel, the soft bark of a tree trunk, corn husks, or corn silk could do the trick. Therefore, I was someone who was on good terms with nature, and I didn't understand what all the fuss was about and why everyone appeared concerned about my bed-wetting. After all, the dirt floor in our hut was quite "thirsty" and rapidly absorbed any liquid that was spilled on it. Nevertheless, I had moderate trust in the adult males, so I pressed Thomas for more details about what had been done to him. He mentioned something about a hill but refused to elaborate on it. I was concerned because it sounded like something traumatic he would rather forget.

Finally, on a chilly Saturday morning, they sprang one on me. I was rudely awakened by Uncle Marcus, and while I was still naked, he asked me to come with him but would not divulge where he was taking me. I got up and followed him begrudgingly but respectfully. In our culture, children were not encouraged to ask many questions. In some ways, it was a benevolent dictatorship. Soon after we left, we were accompanied by another uncle, Samuel. They were both very mild mannered and spoke softly yet deliberately. They escorted me to the backyard, and from there we walked past a banana orchard, mango trees, a corn farm, and a few bushes. I could feel the frigid drops of dew smeared on my shivering brown skin.

The farther away from the hut we walked, the more nervous I became. Since I was prohibited from talking to them, I chose to complain about the thorns hurting my feet and the dew on my skin, hoping in some way to lure them into a conversation. They ignored me and kept on walking, one in front and the other behind me. I had an inkling there was more to the trip than good ole male bonding. At one point I noticed we were bypassing a lot of anthills. I had a morbid fear of ants, especially the fat, fiery red ones—the kinds that lived in those big mounds. They were very large and reddish and were reputed to devour entire animals. I had had a few previous encounters with their snappy jaws, usually while innocently sitting on a bed of grass and conversing with my friends at school. On a few occasions, I had been awakened by vicious bites from a midnight ant attack in our hut.

We had walked an impressive distance, and my fears and emotions were starting to overwhelm me. It was akin to being involuntarily escorted to an execution. Suddenly, Uncle Marcus stopped, looked to the left, and muttered something to Uncle Samuel, who immediately grabbed me by the hand, as though he didn't want me to run away. I was dragged into the bushes. I screamed, "Let go of me!" but my cries fell upon deaf ears. Instantly we were facing one of the biggest anthills in the world, with a billion famished, humongous red ants crawling randomly and menacingly in every direction. They appeared to be organized in fighting formation, as though they had been anticipating my arrival.

At that instant, I experienced a new problem: urinary incontinence. Despite my fate being sealed, I wasn't going down without a fight. Uncle Marcus was trying to get a word in edgewise through my loud moans, deafening screams, and desperate kicks. He was saying something about how it wouldn't be so bad, and I wanted to ask him to prove it on himself first. Unfortunately, in the end my heroic efforts were dwarfed by the sheer strength my adversaries possessed. In an instant, my legs buckled, my testicles retreated in fear into their abdominal sanctuary, and before I could register another verbal protest, I was rapidly hoisted by those two burly brutes and involuntarily deposited on searing lava of gigantic, voracious African red ants. I was held down for what seemed like an eternity while heartless creepy critters, seemingly undeterred by my strident protests and whiny promises, rapturously devoured every inch of my bottom, thighs, and other innocent, sensitive parts. When finally I was lifted "compassionately" from Hell Hill and placed on a patch of soft grass, I continued to scream in pain because a few unsatisfied stragglers were still clinging tenaciously to my raw scrotum. It would take multiple attempts by me—and oddly by my "sympathetic" brutes—to dislodge the rest of those prickly little bastards from my bottom. With a psychotic look of "mission accomplished" on their faces, and seemingly feeling no compassion, my brutish uncles watched me walk with the gait of an injured chimpanzee while moaning desperately the entire way home.

They had successfully executed a plan that was steeped in tradition. However, if this was the village's idea of effective therapy for my problem, they were woefully misguided. That night, I had terrible nightmares about being chased all over the village by monstrous alien ants, and I wet my bed. Henceforth, every time I encountered an anthill, I would have a terrible urge to urinate. I shared my experience with Cousin Thomas, and after comparing notes, we both agreed that the therapy was cruel and unwarranted. It did not cure bed-wetting, but it gave us new diseases: myrmecophobia (a strong fear of ants) and unclephobia (an aversion to uncles!).

CHAPTER 15

Village Life

MY VILLAGE HAD A few thousand inhabitants, and we all spoke a common language, Mankon. Almost every hut had a small orchard around it where its residents grew crops such as bananas, plantains, yams, corn, peanuts, and beans. The numerous fruit trees produced oranges, mangoes, and other citrus fruits in abundance. By and large, natives took very good care of their properties. Adjoining each hut or household was a bathing area, which in essence was a small stockade made of sticks and palm mats in a square confirmation. It was roughly four to six feet in height and provided enough privacy for its occupants. We had three options for latrines: the bushes, a built latrine (which was essentially a deep hole in the ground), and a pigpen.

Normally when people were out and about on hunting, fishing, or farming trips, or just traveling between villages, they used the bathroom in the bushes or woods. For urination, the roadside, the edge of the bush, or any other outside location was acceptable. Some compounds had latrines that were constructed by digging deep, wide holes in the ground. A wooden platform constructed with a series of large five-foot-long tree trunks placed side by side was then positioned above the hole. The layout was completed by fashioning a six-inch-diameter hole in the center of the platform where a user would squat to eliminate intestinal and bladder contents.

I hesitate to elaborate on the last option for hygienic and aesthetic reasons. Pigs were highly prized for the income they provided during hard times, as well as the demand for their meat on special occasions. Among non-Muslims, pork was popular at weddings, funerals, and Christmastime. Pigs did not roam free at all in the village. They were kept in wide rectangular or square pens where they were fed leftovers or residual foodstuffs like yam peels, banana peels, vegetables, and spoiled fruit. Suffice to say that some members of the village community believed in recycling human waste. Therefore, a small opening wide enough to allow for a pig's snout was cut out in the pen at ground level. Adjacent to this opening was a contraption where people squatted to have a bowel movement. The pigs could sense a person's arrival (classical conditioning) and would immediately dash across the pen to where the hole was located. There they would wait, grunting with anticipatory impatience. The biggest risk implicit in this "toilet" option was an occasional vicious bite that occurred when an impatient pig's snout ventured out too far beyond the opening where someone was squatting. Therefore on my part, whenever nature called, my cautious preference was either the bush or a hole in the ground.

Growing up in an African village had many psychological advantages. There are numerous concrete support systems for children. Behavior was sanctioned within the framework of traditional rules and norms. When a child was not in school, he was at the farm, hunting, or participating in traditional activities and rituals. Every parent was your parent, and there was no distinction between father and uncle, mother and aunt. Grandparents were revered. They had the final word in every dispute. Cousins were called brothers or sisters. In a mixed family gathering with other relatives, a child understood, based upon context or discussion, whether it was his or her biological mother or aunt when a reference was made to "mother." Whenever my grandmother was gone farming, I simply went to one of my aunts' houses to eat. Sometimes I was offered a bed for the night if Grandma was late coming back from her farm. Whenever I did something wrong, the men and women of the village had no compunction about punishing me.

Village children were generally well disciplined. They matured rapidly, and it was not unusual to see seven-year-olds cooking, cleaning, farming, and taking care of younger siblings. Adult interactions between opposite sexes were discreet, and excessive public displays of intimacy and affection were frowned upon. Instead of using overt sexual language around children, adults preferred euphemisms and coded expressions. There was a universal disdain for curse words. As I got older, I became aware of the subtle meanings and intentions surrounding adult interactions. For example, children usually congregated for dinner in their mother's hut. Dad ate alone in his hut. On occasion, he invited some of the older children to eat with him in what was considered a tremendous honor. Women hardly ever ate from the same dish as their husbands or other adult men. After dinner, while conversing with your mother and siblings, your father might appear and ask, "When are the children going to bed?" Alternatively, he might ask the mother, "How long do you intend to nurse the baby tonight?" Children were oblivious to the actual meanings behind these questions, which were often intended to remind mothers about a scheduled conjugal visit.

In the case of my uncle George, who was a polygamist, all his wives and children assembled each night in his living room to share potluck meals. Sometimes other uncles, aunts, and their children would drop by with their kerosene lamps or candles and join everyone in a spontaneous festive setting, where adults told riddles and jokes and regaled us with stories about our ancestors, tribal conquests, and current events.

At a very young age, we learned to socialize and appreciate our elders and also how to interact comfortably with others. Children spoke only when permitted and had to address adults respectfully before making any statements. Children were not allowed to call adults by their names. They were obligated to use titles such as Papa, Mama, or Nemo (grandmother) or Tata (grandfather) when talking to an elder.

It was considered a great honor for a young person to be addressed as Nemo or Tata by an adult. Among the youth, seniority counted as well. Accordingly, older siblings, relatives, or friends had to be addressed by the prefix *Ndia*, followed by their given names. Ndia is a respectful term of endearment.

Our ancestors held a very special place in village life. Each compound had a shrine where families could communicate with their ancestors, thank them for specific accomplishments, ask for intercession during trying times, or solicit blessings for weddings, funerals, and successes in new ventures.

Christianity, Islam, and Animism were the prevailing practices in village communities. There were no faith-based conflicts at that time. Village life was communal. When someone's hut was lost in a fire, all the men congregated and rebuilt it. A newlywed who decided to build a home received immediate support and assistance from other village members. However, decisions about matters affecting the lives of villagers, such as the construction of roads, the settling of land disputes, or the mediation of disagreements between major tribal factions were the responsibility of the chief or Fon of the village, who was the traditional paramount leader. Fon Angwafor, a strong, benevolent man highly revered for his leadership skills, was the supreme leader of my village. He knew almost every family in the village, had the final word in most discussions and conflict resolutions, and was the ultimate trustee and curator of our culture and traditions.

There were three major celebrations in the lives of village people: birth, marriage, and death. The birth of a child always seemed to galvanize and delight the entire village. A steady stream of people would stop in to hold and bless the baby. No gifts were presented, just food and drinks to share with family and friends. Weddings were raucous celebrations with endless feasting and dancing. When someone died, word of the loss usually spread rapidly throughout the village. People would begin to congregate in the compound where the bereaved lived to mourn their passing and celebrate their transition into the afterlife. Grieving was intense, followed by celebratory events in which women cooked food and men brought drinks. Death ceremonies lasted about a week, and on the final day of ceremonies, family members of the deceased had their heads shaved bald to symbolize a final cleansing and a farewell to the dead. When a married man died, the accepted tradition was for his brother to marry the widow and raise her children like his own. Raising a child was everyone's responsibility in the village.

Village life was certainly not conflict-free. Consequently, there were traditional, well-established channels for conflict resolution between community members. Problems within a family structure were resolved in family meetings. Bigger conflicts between families usually called for impartial mediators and facilitators from the community or a high-level intervention by the Fon.

CHAPTER 16

Nasty Parasites

FEW CHILDREN IN THE village escaped the ravages of malaria and a plethora of other parasitic infections during childhood. Malaria, worm, and flea infestations were the most commonly recognized health problems. I often suffered severe episodic attacks of malaria, for which I received such treatments as chloroquine, special herbs, and exorcisms. The treatment option of exorcism was designed to address all illnesses attributable to curses that were thought to have been placed by an angry community member, relative, or ancestor. In addressing some of the ill-defined illnesses I suffered, a few practitioners often resorted to making incisions on the skin overlying my breast tissue to release "evil humors," followed by the liberal application of a mud-based concoction all over my chest wall while having me inhale the vapor from a hot herbal mixture in a hot clay pot positioned between my feet. At times they threw a large cloak over my head and torso to contain the therapeutic herbal vapors. Besides these and other interventions, I had my share of leech treatments for a slew of ill-defined illnesses. Oftentimes I wonder how I survived many of the infections in our village.

Without modern medicine, sometimes a disease was simply allowed to run its course, hopefully without killing its victim. A good example of this was a contagious parasitic infection we called scabies, which is caused by a burrowing mite with an affinity for buttocks. Whenever one of the children contracted it, before long the others would get it too. I had scabies at least once a year during elementary school. Because of the severe itching it caused, to relieve the discomfort, I would scratch my buttocks so hard that they would ooze blood and pus from the associated deep skin infection. It was not uncommon for village children to run around completely or partially naked after school. That habit invariably increased the chances of someone getting scabies from close contact. Each time I had scabies, I would dread going to school because the pus draining from the infection in my buttocks would stick to my short-pant uniform like glue, and any movement on my part would cause intense searing pain and threaten to peel away raw flesh from my entire bottom. When I did successfully wobble my way to school, I had to remain standing the entire day in class because it was painfully impossible to sit on those crowded wooden classroom benches while a thousand raw, blistering sores on my hapless behind were raining bloody pus. On an unlucky day, I would be stuck with a heartless teacher who would insist that I sit on a bench like everyone else. Then I would have to intermittently rock my bottom alternately from cheek to cheek, sit on my tailbone, or practically hoist my torso above the student bench with both arms on my side to avoid any disruptive pain and pray for a quick end to the school day.

In the realm of public health, practically everyone in the village in those days grappled with one or more species of parasites, worms, and a myriad other infectious agents. Up till today, I still shudder when I think of a particular flea known as a jigger that had a predilection mostly for human feet. There were so many of these tiny fleas in our communities, especially during the long dry season, when you could see them leaping from the dust everywhere and searching for a vulnerable body part to penetrate and destroy. Usually, the foot would be the most convenient target for them. Once it burrowed through your skin, it would become comfortably embedded in the flesh beneath the skin and then it would grow to almost half an inch in size. Initially, you would begin to experience severe persistent itching until its abdomen had expanded from producing thousands of tiny eggs. At that point, its immense size would stretch and damage the overlying skin and surrounding tissues, thereby causing such severe continuous throbbing pain in your foot that you could hardly sleep, walk, or mentally concentrate on anything else.

At some point in the flea's life cycle, it would begin to shed its tiny eggs, which you could see oozing from your feet. Oftentimes normal flesh surrounding the flea's cocoon would begin to rot and produce an offensive odor. It was not unusual to encounter someone physically debilitated by a flea infestation whose feet were completely consumed by these minimonsters. By and large, the jigger scourge was more common among poor shoeless individuals living in dusty, unhygienic villages. Whenever Grandma would observe me scratching my feet constantly and walking with an abnormal gait from having dozens of mature fleas in my feet, she would have one of the adult males physically restrain me before using a sharp splinter of wood to extract the bloated, unwelcome invaders from their dermal sanctuaries. Sometimes, through my screams and tears, the painful extraction procedure would take over an hour. Afterward, the bottoms of my feet would look raw, bloody, and frightening for about a week.

Having jiggers was the most irritating, embarrassing, and repulsive experience in every child's life in the village. Invariably, when a parent announced their intention to extract jiggers from a child's feet, immediately that child would run away as fast as possible for fear of enduring the painful procedure and the embarrassment of having one's peers witnessing your tears, fragility, and embarrassment. Knowing this, Grandma always launched a surprise attack on me and would always have a strong adult standing by to hold me down for that dreadful anesthesia-free operation. Eventually, when I entered secondary school and started wearing shoes almost routinely, those creepy jiggers begrudgingly left me alone.

There was a time when I suffered severe recurrent abdominal pain and discomfort and didn't know what to do, so I complained to my uncle George, who took me to the hospital, where I was diagnosed with "worms." I was given a concoction to drink, and early the next morning, I ran into the bush and evacuated ninety-five live, foot-long, pale-looking worms. Although I felt dizzy afterward, I was relieved. I remember a nurse reminding me to count the worms, and I still cannot figure out the reason for that order.

Long worm infestations were common at that time, and often we would share anecdotes about our experiences with them. It was not unusual to encounter a child who had passed a lot of long worms walking around with a residual worm hanging between his buttocks. Usually, an adult would grab the wiggly creature and pull it carefully from the child's rectum. Other people had certain types of worms visibly crawling underneath their skin.

At times you could see them crawling across their forehead, chest, or abdomen. I had an uncle who delighted in sharing updates with everyone about the current location of a worm in his body. On her part, Grandmother had a fascinating technique to extract these subcutaneous parasites. She would make a quick razor cut on the skin in the anticipated path of the worm and then wait patiently for it to arrive. Then she would grab the worm with a pair of homemade wooden tweezers that looked like chopsticks and with a twisting motion, gently and methodically, she would pull it out from beneath the skin. This was always a sensational *eureka* moment. It was not uncommon to encounter a villager with massive enlargement of his or her legs, scrotum, or labia due to severe infestations from this particular worm. How they suffered! There was no cure for this complication, which many attributed to a curse because of something bad the victim might have done. This disease is known in modern medicine as elephantiasis.

CHAPTER 17
Hunting

ON SOME WEEKENDS I delighted in going on hunting trips with the boys and men in the village. We would arm ourselves with sticks and spears and enter the woods in search of wildlife: big rats, snakes, porcupines, and other nameless members of the rodent community. Often, we had a hunting dog, which invariably would be a skinny, enthusiastic, cantankerous creature adorned with a collar bell. Our most fearsome game to hunt was porcupine. Its meat was prized, and I believe every dog had a healthy respect for its quills.

Uncle George had a hunting dog called Lucky. Lucky was intelligent but unlucky. I loved to see him wiggling excitedly, running ahead of the hunting team and leading the charge on a big hunt. One particular day we were on a hunt, and the adults had brought their guns. There was excitement in the air as we approached a grassy terrain several miles from the village that was known to be teeming with animals. One of the boys was sent to the middle of the bush to start a fire. Meanwhile, the rest of us were deployed in the perimeter, armed with sticks, spears, and machetes. The flames began to billow, and the burning elephant grass could be heard crackling from a distance. The air was filled with a plume of aromatic smoke from different species of burning vegetation. As the fire began to spread toward the periphery, the animals scurried away from the flames, only to encounter several hunters in waiting. That day I brought a spear for the hunt, and while standing there waiting for game to emerge from the raging inferno, I was caught up in a wave of excitement building among other participants.

Lucky began to bark incessantly, wagging his tail furiously and running back and forth, indicating that he was sensing something in the bushes.

Everyone stood still in a hunched, wide-eyed, hypervigilant posture with jaws apart and spears, machetes, and sticks at the ready! Then I heard some rustling in the bush. Out darted the biggest rodent I had ever seen. Its trajectory appeared to be on a collision course with me. Lucky got scared and sprinted away. One of the adults yelled, "Spear it!"

My torso froze, and so did my arms. Suddenly, whoosh! It ran right between my legs and disappeared into the woods. I froze for a while. Thank goodness cursing was not encouraged in the culture at that time because the adult members of our party had to have been exercising tremendous restraint from liberating a few generous and calming expletives. The boys didn't hold back their feelings, though. Frustrated with my inaction, they called me a wimp, among other expletives. On my part, I felt a deep personal sense of disappointment for failing to do the job as planned. I accepted the epithets and catcalls and decided that maybe I was not cut out for that hunting stuff after all.

At that moment Uncle George walked over, put his arm around my shoulder, and said, "When the heart is ready, the body follows." I didn't understand the meaning of this, but he went on to reassure me that, in essence, the hunt was sometimes more exciting than the catch.

CHAPTER 18

Uncle Daniel

UNCLE DANIEL WAS A bachelor. He had no children and considered me his son. He often took me to his church on Sundays. He was clean, compulsive, meticulous, and had few possessions. He also gave long lectures. Sometimes my bottom would begin to rebel against the hard, dry earth in the middle of his prolonged lecture or sermon. He was a great cook, a talented singer, and a dancer. Unfortunately, during his younger years, he had suffered a seizure, fallen into a firepit, and sustained serious extremity burns, which prompted an amputation of his right hand. He often joked about his stump and referred to me as his "right hand."

It was delightful for me to assist him with some of his daily needs and chores. Uncle Daniel used to tell everyone that I would become an important healer and leader someday, adding that I had been appointed by our ancestors to undertake an important mission. He was quite the philosopher. He would often remind everyone that for success to be meaningful, it had to be celebrated and shared in the context of the community. He believed strongly in self-motivation and the need to use whatever resources an individual had at their disposal to accomplish any goal without succumbing to a sense of despondency.

There was a huge mango tree adjacent to his house. On many occasions, I competed with my cousins to see who could climb farthest up the tallest tree. Sometimes we were reprimanded vehemently because there were potential risks for sustaining serious injuries. One day when none of the parents or elders was around, and despite a previous admonition by Uncle Daniel, I decided to challenge myself and see how high I could climb that mango tree. I climbed so high that I could almost see the entire village from a vantage point where I felt a surge of hubris in my accomplishment and relished the competitive advantage over my peers. My cousins were waiting below and marveling at my simian feat. I was visibly celebrating my achievement when, out of nowhere, Uncle Daniel appeared.

Ever so calmly, he motioned for me to descend. There was no way for me to run. I only had one option. I couldn't stay up there forever. Therefore, slowly and deliberately, I descended, knowing full well that I would be severely punished, probably with several lashes on my back. I crawled down a few feet and paused for a moment to assess his demeanor and then continued to slide down slowly while stopping every once in a while to assess the mood at ground level. Finally, I slid down to the bottom of the tree, anticipating some sort of punishment at any moment. He reached out and held my hand gently and reassured me that rather than punishing me, he would allow me to punish myself effectively and sustainably. His words sounded confusing to me. He did not appear to be in a hurry.

When we sat down in his house, he looked sternly at me and declared, "I want you to remember forever that I would rather have a live son than a dead hero." With that he dismissed me. In the meantime, my cousins had been keeping vigil beneath the tree, waiting to hear my screams from a whipping they were convinced I would get. The look of perplexity on their faces when I emerged unscathed was priceless. In a weird sense, they had been hoping that my punishment would somehow pacify their egos and diminish their collective sense of failure because they had not been able to accomplish the tree-climbing feat I had just completed. Ironically, at that moment I did not consider my achievement heroic. My uncle's words left me feeling more like a fool than a tree-climbing champion. It was the last tall tree I ever climbed.

CHAPTER 19
Animal Slaughtering

AT LEAST ONCE A month during the school year, we had chicken for dinner. I remember my grandma showing me how to sacrifice a chicken. She instructed me to grab its head, flip the poor creature over on its back, pin it to the ground with my right foot, and then slash its throat with a hunting knife. Just like that! She went on to emphasize that it was necessary to keep holding the chicken down until it stopped writhing, the blood ceased flowing, and its body became limp.

A day came when it was my turn to slaughter a big bird. First, I had to chase down the poor creature and catch it. That was not easy because I am certain it was aware of my dishonorable intentions. After a performance that brings to mind a Super Bowl tackle, I succeeded in capturing my avian nemesis. While holding it by the neck, I felt bad for what I was about to do to the innocent, unassuming, unoffending, and beautiful creature. In an attempt to assuage my guilt, I initiated a lengthy conversation with the chicken. Actually, it was more like a soliloquy intended to implicate Grandma and absolve me of any possible guilt before performing the ugly deed. Then all of a sudden, she yelled out from the hut, "Are you done yet?"

I grabbed the poor creature by the head, pinned it down with all my strength, and with glazed eyes, clenched teeth, and a racing heart, I brought down the machete rapidly, and the mission was accomplished. Dazed by this sudden performance, I had to remind myself immediately afterward to inhale. Subsequent performances were smoother as I developed a sense of detachment right before each sacrificial event.

Although I never quite moved beyond the level of "chicken butcher," other village boys became experts at slaughtering goats, sheep, pigs, and cows. It was considered an honor to be handed a knife by an adult to perform the initial cut. Sacrificing big animals was too great an emotional burden for me to accomplish. I usually preferred to avoid watching the initial cut in the throat, but then my eyes would light up when an animal's chest or abdomen was opened, and I would be fascinated with its internal organs, which I delighted in touching and feeling. I got up voluntarily at five o'clock on some mornings to accompany Uncle Sam the butcher and observe him slaughtering a cow. He would always allow me to cut out the heart, lungs, and other internal organs. I delighted in lecturing my friends and other willing adults in the village on animal anatomy as I knew it. To me, this experience with animals was more enjoyable than soccer. My hands were more predictable than my feet and legs.

My hesitation to sacrifice large animals did not deter me from becoming one of the most feared predators in the small-animal kingdom of the village. Rats, snakes, birds, stray cats were in abundance, and they took turns satisfying my curiosity for their internal organs. My unsanctioned surgical escapades left a few villagers feeling nervous and concerned. Given my interest, curiosity, and activities with small animals, I often wonder where I would've wound up had I been living in the United States at that time. Reformatory school, maybe? Taking multiple remedies for questionable diagnoses? Perhaps multiple visits to psychologists and counselors...who knows?

Frequently, I would catch jumbo Cameroon frogs and cut them open to study their insides. I was profoundly curious and fascinated with the workings of various internal organs, especially the heart. I can remember removing a frog's heart and running to my father with the heart still beating in my hand. It was so amazing! I asked him why the heart had not stopped beating, and Dad's response was "That's the way God made it."

CHAPTER 20
New School

EARLY ON, MY FAVORITE subjects in school were nature study and hygiene. In the later years of elementary school, I developed a passion for arithmetic. At the beginning of a new school year, we arrived to begin the fourth grade, but we were told that unfortunately there had been no money assigned to put up another school building. There had been no contingency plans for the continuation of our education. As we stood there confused, without knowing what to do or where to go, our teacher blurted out an apology, recommended we seek admission in other schools, and then promptly dismissed us and left. The Baptist school system had effectively failed and abandoned us. In their hopelessness, a few of the students began to weep. We all dispersed immediately and headed off in every direction. It was so sad. Six-to-eight-year-old children who had been brimming with joy and enthusiasm over the great education they were receiving and their proud parents who had accompanied them to school on the first day of classes were devastated with the news.

Since there weren't enough schools to accommodate the children in the region, class enrollment at every school was often at or beyond capacity. Even more moving and unfortunate was the fact that several of my classmates simply returned to their respective villages and never again attended school. I remember one of them, who had been my most fierce competitor and the smartest kid in our class. He was quiet and reserved, and his academic performance consistently earned him the top position and forced me to begrudgingly accept the second position every time! He was a quiet genius who never had less than a complete score in any subject or quiz. Of all the children in the class, he traveled the farthest to get to school. I knew nothing about him, his family, or his village. However, several years later, I ran into him, and I barely recognized him. He was doing menial work at a local market and looked miserable and wretched.

Some of the students who could not continue their schooling returned to their villages to herd goats and sheep and never again engaged in any formal education or training. I can only imagine how frustrating the impact of that travesty was in their lives. For me, going back to the village was not an option. Nothing could stop me from continuing my education. I was too deeply and emotionally involved with it to even consider other options. I was learning new things that captivated my heart and mind, and while my body resided in the village, my mind was exploring the universe. Education was transforming my perspective on myself and my tiny world. My curiosity was sharpened, and my appetite for more knowledge was heightened. I had heard about a bigger Baptist school about six miles from ours. Although I had never been there, I had a general idea of how to get there. Hence, without a second thought, I grabbed my books and hit the long, windy road over the hills to my destination. At that age, I was used to walking long distances by myself.

Upon arrival, I went directly to the headmaster's office to inform him about what had happened to my school. I recall him asking me what village I was from, and when I told him, he was quite surprised to learn that I had walked the entire distance alone, although I would discover on a later date that other students from villages even farther away than mine were attending that elementary school. He wasted no time in escorting me to my new classroom, which was clean and had a concrete floor, real windows, and a degree of vitality and sophistication that I was unaccustomed to. It had a ceiling too! The students were smartly dressed and looked confident. However, I felt intimidated, embarrassed, and inferior to my classmates. The teacher welcomed me and showed me my seat. My very own seat! No more benches for me! Life was great. So I began a new chapter in my educational mission.

My new classmates were friendly and cordial. During recess, a few of them invited me to play. I was particularly fond of two brothers, Martin and Andreas, who lived in the city. Their father was a successful trader, so they had money and always brought delicious home-cooked meals to school. Often, I would invite myself to lunch, and surprisingly, neither one seemed to mind my imposition. I reciprocated by assisting them with their homework. They were both smart students; therefore, realistically, I benefited the most from our friendship. To arrive at school on time, I had to leave very early in the morning, practically in the dark. Accordingly, I developed a terrible habit of not eating breakfast. Usually, by noon, I was feeling extremely fatigued, but I didn't know why. As time went on, I became accustomed to eating once a day in the evening or at night. I don't remember ever feeling hungry in the morning. One day as I was leaving for school, my grandma, out of concern for my "fasting" habit, gave me a piece of meat and a piece of yam to eat at school. When I turned the corner, I paused for a second to be sure nobody was watching, then I immediately tossed everything in the bushes and kept on going.

Every morning we lined up in front of our teacher to present our homework. Despite the physical challenges of traveling a long distance to school and not having anyone in my village to assist me with difficult assignments, I always made it a point to complete my homework. However, I dreaded presenting my work to my teacher because she tended to make loud comments, much to my chagrin, that I stunk terribly. She would ask loudly why I smelled like urine. Such open pronouncements left me so embarrassed and dumbfounded that I could not respond. I could always feel a dozen eyes scrutinizing me as all the students would pause and stare at me. After checking my work, she would practically fling the book at me disgustedly and proceed with the next student.

Interestingly, neither Martin nor Andreas ever commented on her actions. In some ways, I could appreciate the reason for her vile pronouncements. I had to get up extremely early each morning to get to school on time after traveling a long and difficult distance. I would often take a cold bath, and even though we had no soap, I still considered myself clean. Like many poor students, I only had one set of uniforms that I wore every day and took them off after school to keep them relatively clean for the next day. I can imagine that walking long distances in hot, muggy weather caused me to perspire more. When this experience was combined with wearing the same clothes every day, my inability to simulate the fragrance of a bouquet of red roses at that time seemed obvious. I decided that whatever the reason for her disparaging remarks, I was going to remain steadfast and do my schoolwork as usual. I had a goal, and I was not going to be deterred.

At the end of my first semester, to my greatest surprise, I was the top student in the class. When I showed up the following semester, the headmaster informed me that I would be promoted to the fifth grade. Accordingly, I had to skip the rest of the fourth grade. This was bittersweet because I missed my friends in the fourth grade. However, when I thought about my fourth-grade teacher, I was happy I did not have to confront her embarrassing remarks any longer.

CHAPTER 21

Transfer to New School

IT WAS AFTER MY first year in this new school that my parents decided to have me live with them because the distance I was traveling was excessive and also because there was a Presbyterian school nearby where I could seek enrollment as a transfer student. When my grandmother received the news, she was saddened by their decision but understood the reasons for it. My new school was much less challenging than the previous one. At least the distance I had to travel each day was significantly shorter than before. I was the youngest student in my class, and often I was bullied by the older boys. A particular boy threatened to hurt me if I did not bring him a mango each day. He was much bigger than I and was physically much stronger. Each day I ran to the woods after school in search of mangoes for him. One day he grabbed one of my favorite books on English grammar and vocabulary and summarily took possession of it. I cried and pleaded with him, to no avail. The sadness I experienced from losing that book was immeasurable, and even today, I am still bothered by that distant memory.

The bully kept me in a perpetual state of fear and anxiety. I was afraid to report him to my teacher because I didn't know what the repercussions would be. I was profoundly fearful of him. Unfortunately for me, my parents could not afford to replace the book he had taken illegal possession of. Happily, I was again promoted to the next grade that year, and I no longer had to share a classroom with him. As fate would have it, many years later, when I was on a humanitarian surgical mission in Africa, our paths intersected under unique and trying circumstances for him. It was refreshing to see that he had matured into a humble and thoughtful man. Although my thoughts streaked back to our elementary school days, when we met at that time, I chose not to remind him about the pain I experienced in elementary school from the loss of my cherished book, my frantic forages for mangoes to feed his savage cravings, and the maliciously prolonged state of corrosive anxiety he had kept me under.

It was glaringly apparent to me that my book and a thousand mangoes had done little over the years to enhance his social standing. However, at that moment I was committed to addressing a more serious problem he had on his hands. Yes, decades earlier I had given him my book and mangoes involuntarily, but our subsequent encounter necessitated a much greater gift than the two earlier ones. Most importantly, it would be voluntary and redemptive! I performed successful open-heart surgery on his delightful, effervescent ten-year-old daughter during that medical mission.

CHAPTER 22

Discipline and Molding

MOVING BACK IN WITH my parents was a challenge in many ways. My father was a disciplinarian. It seemed as though he expected perfection in everything I did. He would pause in the middle of something and give me a brief lecture on why perfection should always be my goal. He insisted that I study every night. Soon after I moved in, he bought a box of candles. After dinner, he would sit me in a room, where I studied by candlelight under his watchful eye. At times he would ask me to read to him. I found this to be comical because he was illiterate and didn't understand a word I was reading; however, the look of pleasure and satisfaction on his face in the glow of candlelight will forever remain dear to my heart. Sometimes I would wake up in my bed not remembering how I got there. Dad would explain that whenever I fell asleep studying, he would carry me to my bed.

He was a soft-spoken, focused, and very meticulous man. A master crafts-man with enormous patience, stamina, and resilience, Dad was so good at fixing things that his last name became Mechanic. I grew up believing this to be his true last name. Consequently, in elementary school, when at first I was asked to write my family name, I wrote down "Mechanic." In a sense, in those days it was common practice to call someone by their profession, such as Bricklayer, Tailor, Carpenter, Teacher, Nurse, Police, Lawyer, Engineer. If you were rich, you were simply called Money!

If you were devious in your dealings with others, you earned the per-manent moniker "Cunningman." Sometimes an activity, a performance, or an event in your life would earn you a permanent label, which became your name henceforth. So, for example, a woman who gave birth to twins would be called "Twin Mother" for the rest of her life. If you got caught stealing, your great-grandchildren would know you by no other name than Mr. Thief. Another aspect of this naming tradition had an interesting and comical twist to it. If you were an only child or were famous or celebrated for whatever reason, other family members would subsume their identities and share your nomenclature permanently: Mother-of-Jane, Father-of-Peter, Sister-of-Paul. Your family members could also earn your name by proxy—hence Mother-of-Thief, Father-of-Crook, Sister-of-Money, Son-of-Mason, et cetera. In a way, unethical behavior on an individual's part could earn them a dishonorable moniker, resulting in collateral damage to their loved ones, who became unwilling recipients of an ignominious indelible label. Fortuitously, the old African adage "I am because you are" is reflective of this tradition. You could go through life with everyone calling you something other than your birth name! Therefore, it was considered prudent to avoid any behaviors that could bring an embarrassing permanent label to the family.

Mom was more sociable than Dad. She hugged everyone and often invited total strangers to our home and cooked for them. She was actively involved in teaching and mentoring young women. I used to spend hours watching her work on her sewing machine. To watch her knitting sweaters was just as exalting. She was quick, precise, and highly coordinated. Her hands appeared to function autonomously of the rest of her body. She could discipline a child, carry on a conversation with someone, and knit at the same time without missing a beat. Whenever I spoke, she looked me straight in the eye without interrupting my words. On special occasions, she prepared rice and vegetables (usually with peanut soup). Rice was my favorite meal, and I would often feign illness to win her sympathy because invariably, she would ask, "My poor son, what can you eat? What must I prepare for you?"

My eyes would light up. "Rice!" I would exclaim before retreating to sick mode.

She would make me a delicious meal of rice and condensed milk. Mom truly had a keen interest in whatever I said or did. She had some chinaware that she didn't want anyone to touch. One day she caught me eating out of one of these items, and she was upset and reminded me that we were not "senior service" people. It was a reference to the educated and economically privileged who lived up in the mountains away from the rest of us. I guess she wanted to keep me humble and to be sure that I knew my place. I found her position quite puzzling because if those were her expectations of the family and me, I wondered why she would own dishes that were symbolic of wealth. Realistically, we were never going to be "senior service." I knew better than to share such thoughts with her. I suspected she had received the dishes as gifts from someone. At times she would say that she was saving them for a special occasion. It always seemed to me that this special occasion would never happen.

Mom seemed to focus more on me than the rest of my siblings. She always talked about doing something for others in the community, and on one occasion, she took me fishing along with a few of her friends. When we got to the river, they began to dump certain leaves in the water that must have contained a toxic substance because before long, I witnessed an amazing sight unfolding in front of me. Dozens of fish and snakes surfaced abruptly and died after gasping for air. We collected a lot of fish in baskets, and the women took them home. That day my mom prepared a large basket of fish and asked me to take it to one of our neighbors whose wife was sick. I loved to eat fish, and I would have preferred to keep most of it for our family, so I obliged begrudgingly. My parents were an endless source of timeless pieces of wisdom, many of which I understood only in the later years.

Soccer was the most popular sport among students at every level of education in the country. It was certainly the most engaging sport in my elementary school. The most popular students were soccer players. One day, I was invited to participate in a soccer meet between my class and an upper class at my new school. This gesture surprised me because most of the students knew that I lacked the minimum degree of coordination needed to play it.

Surprisingly, I scored a legitimate winning goal, and suddenly I became a sports hero! When I came home that day, beaming with exultation, I saw my mother toiling away in the kitchen, and I promptly relayed the news of my soccer achievement: "I scored the winning goal, Mommy!"

Unperturbed, she kept working at whatever concoction she was whipping up. Thinking she had not heard me, I loudly repeated a couple of times, "I scored the winning goal at the soccer game today!"

I will never forget how she shifted her gaze calmly, and with deliberate poise, she asked, "How did the team do?"

Perplexed by her response and thinking she might not have understood my announcement, I reiterated my accomplishment with emphatic prevalence. To my amazement, her response remained unchanged. Disgusted at her lack of appreciation for my athleticism, I decamped with the somber frustration of an unfulfilled ego.

Not long after that, I came home after school and complained to my father about how one of the older boys had grabbed me unexpectedly at recess and purposely knocked me to the ground in front of the other students. Then I told him how the bully's actions had led to my uniform being soiled and had been greeted with laughter by everyone. Dad's response was incongruent with my expectations. In his perpetually calm manner, he stated, in effect, "Son, you are stronger than your nemesis. You possess the most powerfully effective weapon on the planet. From now on, use it."

I wondered what he was referring to. The bully was twice my size, and worse still, my self-esteem had been disrobed mercilessly in front of all the female spectators on a dusty school playground. I needed to hold on to whatever pride was left in me. Realistically, I preferred to leave that whole David-and-Goliath thing in Sunday school class. To clear up any obvious confusion on my father's side, I declared, "I don't have any weapons!"

He retorted, "Yes, you do! Your brain!" Then he walked away, leaving me in a quandary and more bewildered.

There was a man who lived across the road whose son attended my elementary school. I remember a time when one of the class bullies beat up this man's son, and when he heard about it, he immediately grabbed a whip and went looking for the perpetrator to exact retribution. How I wished my dad could have responded in that same vein. Truly, I felt unprotected and vulnerable. He had an interesting way of motivating and challenging me at the same time. For example, if I did well on an exam and I earned the second, third, or fourth position, he would simply say, "Great!" Then, he would immediately follow that with "I wonder who was in the first position."

One day in the village, Mom called my attention to a European family in a van going somewhere. "Do you see that White man over there?" I looked where she was pointing. "I want you to learn everything he knows. If you can do that, you will have a better life."

Then she walked away, leaving me puzzled. I imagined that she had observed many of the Europeans who came to work in our village and how they did not appear to have any of the problems and struggles that plagued our people. They always seemed cheerful and upbeat in the way they conducted themselves, interacted with the natives, and did their work. Therefore, my mother must have attributed their successful lives to education. She wanted her son to rise to the same level of success they had.

My parents began to take turns as sentries, watching me and supervising me every night while I studied. My mom would light a candle, hand me one of my books, position herself a few feet away from me, and ask me to start studying. She always meant business: no sweet talk, no cajoling, no coaxing, and no affection! She could sit unflinchingly for hours at a time. One time she handed me a book upside down. When I noticed this, I thought about correcting the orientation of the book, but I decided wisely against that decision for fear of giving the appearance of playing games with my work and not taking it seriously. Therefore I proceeded to study the chapters upside down. It was quite a feat! As I sat there struggling with the unusual orientation of the print, I kept hoping that she would take a break and leave me alone. I read for about half an hour and then slowly lifted my gaze to see if she had left. Unfortunately, our gazes collided, and she gave me a nod, as if to assure me that she had no intention of leaving before the completion of my study session.

Periodically, I wished my parents could be like those of some of my friends. They gave me no slack whatsoever. Even my younger brother Fru did not have to experience the same degree of stringent attention I was subjected to. He always seemed to be having more fun than I. In a warped way, I felt as though in addition to my education, I was required by my parents to complete the collective education neither one had received. I was studying for three people!

CHAPTER 23

Family Structures

ALTHOUGH MOST FAMILY UNITS like ours were nuclear, polygamous practices were accepted and commonplace in the country. A good number of the friends I grew up with came from polygamous compounds. They were just as socially adjusted as I was. Polygamy had several inherent advantages. In such a setting, you had not one but multiple mothers. Therefore, if something happened to your mother, or if she were absent for whatever reason, there would always be another mother ready to step up to address your needs and take good care of you. Additionally, women in a polygamous situation supported each other with daily duties, such as farming, cooking, cleaning, and childcare, and in times of sickness. They were also available to each other for emotional support in times of death and countless other social crises.

Usually, in a polygamist compound, the wives lived in individual huts with their children, and the husband lived in a separate hut. Conjugal arrangements were established by mutual consensus. The most senior wife wielded tremendous power and influence over the husband and was accorded ample collective respect by everyone in the compound. In some cases, she played a pivotal role in the selection of successive wives. Frequently, junior wives received more attention from the husband. By and large, this did not result in any overt acrimony. Of course, this picture represents an ideal scenario. In some circumstances, social discord and conflicts abounded and usually were precipitated by jealousies and the perception by a member within the union that equity or fairness was lacking in certain situations, such as interactions between husband, wives, and children. Frequently, such conflicts were resolved peacefully and amicably in adult-only settings. However, malignant conflict situations often degenerated into acrimonious debates, public displays of pugilism, and rarely, divorce.

I witnessed the entire gamut of these events in my village. My dad often stated that he was happy with my mom and that "more women meant more trouble." The respect they had for each other was powerful and mutual. In a real sense, I cannot subdue my imagination as I visualize the tremendous physical disparities between them, and I imagine how comical it would have been for Dad to approach Mom to discuss his interest in having a second wife. In the interest of his physical well-being, I am glad it never happened.

CHAPTER 24
Family Time

WHEN I WAS IN fifth grade, we all lived together as a family. My older sister, who had been living with an elderly aunt, moved back home. It still concerned me that she had not been given a chance to attend school. My younger brother Fru was also in elementary school. Siri, who came after Fru, had a special place in my heart. She was playful and never wanted to leave my side whenever I returned from school. Her favorite playtime activity was hide-and-seek.

Our youngest sister, Mambo, had breathing problems, and on many occasions, she suffered asthmatic crises and would cry all day and night. I can vividly remember a time when she was so sick with high fevers, wheezing, and problems swallowing that Mom convened the entire family to a room and led us in prayer. First, we prayed to God, and then we prayed to our ancestors to intercede on the baby's behalf. By daybreak, she was doing much better. These episodes became less frequent as she got older. It was not until I was in medical school years later that I realized she had been suffering from recurrent tonsillitis. Unfortunately, the heart issues that likely resulted from this problem would precipitate her untimely death in her teenage years. Whenever there were any problems or challenges in the family, village, or town, Mom would convene everyone for a prayer session.

She was a perpetually spiritual optimist, a dreamer with strong entrepreneurial instincts. She used to prepare tons of fried *akra* (made of bean powder, palm oil, and spices) and sell it from a stand by the roadside. On weekends, she had me hawking a basin filled with this delicacy from my head all over town, on dusty roads in the hot tropical sun. She taught me how to attract customers by smiling often and announcing loudly, "Best akra! Best akra! Best akra!" as I crisscrossed the tiny hamlets bordering our village.

At times, the commodities would change. She would hoist a large basket filled with peeled oranges on my head and instruct me to target the residential localities of missionaries and expatriates. She knew from her experience that this was a demographic that possessed a strong passion for tropical fruits, which Indigenes took for granted because of their ubiquity. On lucky days, I would bring home a little less than a dollar. Mom would be overjoyed and would entertain me with a complicated celebratory dance move before crushing me with hugs and kisses. That always made me the proudest little boy on the planet.

I always wondered why she did not assign these commerce duties to my older sister Kien. I considered my sister Kien a brilliant saint with sparkling intelligence. She accepted more difficult responsibilities than the rest of us and never seemed to mind or complain. She assisted Mom with cooking, cleaning, and farming. She made sure my brother David and I had breakfast before setting out to school, and on days when Mom was late returning from the farm, she would prepare dinner for everyone. Sometimes she would get upset because I would refuse to eat breakfast. She loved everyone unconditionally.

Frequently, I got into trouble and had to be spanked or whipped. Whenever I would begin to cry rigorously, almost invariably, Sister Kien would start to cry in unison and would proceed to admonish whoever my punisher was. She showed vibrant curiosity in my schoolwork and an infectious interest in learning. Because she was soundly intelligent, I often wondered where life could have taken her had she received a formal education. Unfortunately, she, like many other young girls at that time, was a victim of cultural groupthink. My passionate denunciation of the prevailing tradition at that time of not educating girls always seemed to alight on deaf ears; hence my brother David and I took turns teaching her some of the things we were learning in school.

We had an interesting neighbor who had fought on the side of the British during the Second World War, after which he was honorably discharged, and like thousands of other African soldiers who had been exploited and dumped and abandoned without a pension and no financial base to under-gird themselves, after the war, he returned home a broken man. In hindsight, he represented a classic case of post-traumatic stress disorder (PTSD). He was loud, friendly, and gregarious and never seemed to have a care in the world. Unfortunately, sometimes he would break out in a panic in the middle of the day and begin to sing and bark out battlefield commands as though he were still at war.

One time he imbibed so much alcohol that he lost his way home and came lumbering into our house. He had a passion for the cheap local brew, and frequently, when he was in a state of inebriation, he would stumble harmlessly around the community, where humans, feline and canine creatures, trees, rocks, walls, and ghosts became recipients of his generous military salute. He was a wonderful man who, despite his bizarre behavior, abhorred violence, espoused love, cherished friendships, supported education, and always inquired as to know how my brother and I were doing in school, without failing to give us endless encouragement.

When I lived with Grandma in her village, I had no difficulty finding friends to play with. However, things were different after I began to live with my parents. Most of the boys in our neighborhood were older and had no interest in hanging out with me. I tried coercive strategies such as giving fruits and sharing some of my meager possessions with them, to no avail. At times, I felt lonely. One day I met a boy about my age with swaggering charisma who lived a short distance from me. He asked me to go fishing, and I jumped at the opportunity. He appeared to be genuinely nice and very polite, and he was protective of me. My mother liked him. Then one day he took me to a neighbor's house and asked me to climb through the window and steal some money for him. Without any forethought, I complied because I wanted to please him and strengthen our friendship. I found a few coins and gave them all to him. He was encouraged by my first successful home invasion, and then he wanted me to repeat the same thing in another house. Again I did it because it was a challenge, and I was seemingly good at it!

Several weeks went by. Eventually, he told me that he knew my mother earned money from her sewing business and her commercial endeavors. He asked me to steal some of it for him. Blinded by a utilitarian friendship and incognizant of my mother's omnipresence, I complied. This time "Fortuna and Tyche" deserted me. My luck ran out!

I was instantly caught red-handed by my mother. I knew better than to lie because Mom was extraordinarily brilliant. A pantomath! She was a true protagonist of a shock-and-awe philosophy; therefore, punishment always came swiftly and furiously. Generals Powell and Schwarzkopf would have applauded her tactics. I pleaded for mercy before spontaneously confessing to previous robberies. She was irate beyond measure. The last thing I saw was a gigantic limb akin to a baobab tree branch rapidly losing altitude. Then I woke up slurring, disoriented, and feeling the soothing comfort of a warm towel on my forehead with my older sister Kien at my side.

Days later, while recovering from the traumatic encounter with my mom's "weapon of bad boys' destruction," I limped out of bed to a stern lecture about robbery and was told in no uncertain terms that I must never again hang out with that boy or his friends. I thought about how unfair it was that he had reaped all the benefits of our escapades, while I got all the whupping. For a certain amount of time, I was made to live in mandatory isolation to avoid receiving negative influences from unsavory characters in the neighborhood.

Among a thousand lessons I learned from my parents was the importance of coming clean whenever I committed an infraction. I learned to avoid making excuses, giving long-winded explanations, or mounting any self-defense when I was in the wrong. Whenever I recognized, accepted, and took immediate responsibility for my actions and wrongdoings, my parents would spare me the rod. "It is better to learn a lesson than earn a licking," Dad would say.

Weeks after I got punished for stealing, I ran into that same boy after school and told him what my mom had said and done. He apologized and invited me to his house for a meal. Oblivious to past admonitions by my mom and the potential consequences of recidivism, I accepted his invitation and went over to his parents' home. I was sitting with him in his mother's kitchen, eating and having fun, when I was startled by the sudden appearance of a gigantic, menacing figure standing at the door. I prayed I was witnessing an apparition, but my organs knew better!

Within microseconds my brain froze, my jaw dropped, and my lungs paused. Not to be outdone, my anal sphincter tightened, and my heart took an unannounced break. Funny how your trusted body parts can declare, "You're on your own!" and abandon you in your hour of greatest need. To this day all I remember is the exquisite pain that came from being hoisted by the ears and assaulted at lightning speed with invisible limbs and the agonizing feeling of forced regurgitation before blacking out. It would be an eternity before I was allowed to play with another boy.

CHAPTER 25
Sociopolitical Challenges

WHEN A NEW GENERAL hospital was built in our region, my dad was hospitalized many times for treatment of his abdominal ailments. On one occasion he was at home recovering from a minor surgical procedure when, late at night, we were uncharacteristically jolted from our beds by a loud bang at the door. While still feeling pain and clutching his abdomen, he got up and walked slowly to the door. When he opened it, he was met by a few hostile-looking gendarmes. Without giving him a reason for their visit, they immediately whisked him off to a waiting van. Understandably, we were all confused, and our mother began to sob uncontrollably. We were at a loss as to what to do. We did not know why he had been arrested. Within minutes, they returned and whisked away Mom, even as she was fighting them off.

Our parents had just been abducted by vicious gendarmes, and we didn't know why. We were left nervous, scared, and crying. At daybreak, my sister Kien sent me to inform Grandma and our uncles about what had happened. When word of their arrest got out, one of our aunts immediately moved in to help us. My younger brother refused to eat and withdrew from everyone and everything. I continued to attend school but was not as motivated as before. Those were very difficult times. My older sister at once assumed Mom's role in the household during this time.

Weeks and months passed, and no word came from or about our parents. I was under the impression that none of the authorities cared about the disruptive impact of their absence on us children. Then one day our mother reappeared. It was an emotional and poignant reunion. We crowded around her and asked her what had happened. She told us that our dad was being held in a different prison building than the one she was released from and that he was being treated badly and was being tortured, but she refused to give us any details. Something in her eyes told me that her own experience at the hands of her jailers had been very traumatic. She went on to tell us that the reason for their arrest was political.

My uncle Aaron was a powerful member of a political party promoting democratic ideals. The government did not want this party to flourish and accused its members of agitation and sedition. They were repeatedly harassed, imprisoned, and tortured by the ruling party. Therefore, some of the party members had to flee the country to avoid persecution. This was a time when all political parties in Cameroon that were promoting democratic thought, concepts, or principles or embracing social freedoms were invariably crushed by the government's iron feet of suppression. Uncle Aaron was a lieutenant of the chairman of this party, who was known as Ndeh Ntumazah, a brilliant, powerful, inspiring, committed, respected, and engaging leader with incomparable oratorical skills.

They and others had received word that the government was coming after them and they would be arrested and would likely be killed. Therefore, under cover of darkness, they escaped and ran for days, coursing through jungles until they arrived in a neighboring country. From there, they continued on foot to Ghana, where they took refuge and stayed a while before obtaining asylum in Algeria, Guinea, and a few other welcoming nations.

When government operatives arrived and could not find the rebels, they became furious. Consequently, they went after their family members, hoping that through arrests and torture, the whereabouts of these "bad agitators" would be revealed. Mom also told me that she was interrogated for days about the whereabouts of certain important documents relating to the "illegal" party, which she knew nothing about. She was repeatedly and severely whipped and starved during this time, despite her innocence. Ironically, she had been unaware of my uncle's sudden escape from the country.

Mom appeared more irritable than I had ever seen her. She stopped using her sewing machine and abandoned her commercial endeavors. She wasn't as cheerful. Several days after her release from jail, one of her jailers, a policeman, visited us. I was home alone with her when he arrived. Mom appeared terrified and insisted that I stay close to her. He was a man of a different tribe and did not understand our language. She welcomed him politely and offered him a cup of water. On my part, I was afraid that he would haul Mom back to jail. He was a nefarious-looking character, tall and husky, in a tan uniform emblazoned with a zillion stripes on his lapels, shoulders, and shirt pockets. He appeared to be of considerable rank. He smiled at me and reached out for a handshake.

I watched my entire right upper extremity disappear inside his enormous hand, and then I quickly withdrew it. I did not like that man. I wondered if he had earned his stripes from human torture. Something about the way he looked at my mom made me nervous about his intentions. He offered me what amounted to a quarter, which was a ton of money at that time, and recommended that I run out to buy myself some candy. Upon seeing this, my mom gave me a brilliant tactical response. She nodded a universal sign of approval, but she immediately followed that with the word *no* in our tribal language, which he didn't understand. I stayed put. Even before the monetary incentive, I had decided that I would not leave her alone with him.

He tried a few more times to encourage me to leave, but to no avail. Then he became somewhat irritated. There was light chatter between them before he blurted out something about wanting to provide financial support for my education in the future since he understood that I was a smart student. Unfortunately, no amount of bribery, cajoling, or stroking could make me change either my opinion or my physical position. Frustrated, he stood up, shrugged, and told my mother he had to get going. At that moment, she inquired about my dad's condition and when he would be coming home. "It depends" was all he would say. He waited a minute, as though anticipating an action or response from her. Her reticence was deafening. On that note, he disappeared, likely frustrated about not getting what his evil mind had hoped for. Mom hugged me. Somehow, despite my youthful mind and impetuous spirit, we both understood what had just transpired. By the look in her eyes, she appreciated my role as a deterrent in the episode we had just experienced.

A few days later, my mom suddenly stormed out of the house, clutching her abdomen while writhing in pain, and bolted out to the hospital, leaving a trail of blood and clots in her wake. The diagnosis would be a miscarriage. We were all experiencing depression from the fear of losing her. Luckily, she overcame that unfortunate event and was discharged in a short time. Her strength and resilience were remarkable and inspiring. Every night we gathered by her bed, where she prayed for God's protection and the safe return of our father. I think she was actively trying to get things back to normalcy, realizing that our father's imprisonment might be protracted. Mom told us about the beatings she endured and the sufferings she weathered during her incarceration.

One day after her release, I remember sitting alone with her on her bed and asking her a million questions about her ordeal in prison. She looked at me in a solemn moment of indecision, cleared her throat softly, and told me one of the jailers had done something bad to her, which she didn't think I was old enough to understand. That conversation between mother and child stayed with me with amazing clarity until many years later, when my aunt revealed to me that Mom had been a victim of sexual violence perpetrated by a jailer. She had been raped—hence the miscarriage she suffered.

In those days, there was no communication or engagement by the authorities with families about the welfare of their loved ones who had been arrested and jailed for any reason. Every government decision was arbitrary, repressive, and totalitarian. Paranoia ruled and undergirded decisions, actions, and reactions of those in power and with power. Since concepts of truth, facts, justice, and fairness were relative, these were applied inconsistently and nebulously.

As the months rolled by, Dad's absence was beginning to take a serious toll on everyone. I missed him terribly. He was being held at a prison located high up in the mountains, many miles away from my elementary school. I could not focus on school because I was preoccupied with thoughts of my dad and wondering what he could be going through. My mother's ordeal was still gnawing away at my mind and rendering me powerless. Suddenly, I decided that I would forgo the rest of my school day, and I set out at once to see my father by any means necessary. The prison complex was nestled on a mountain, miles away from my school. Scaling the mountain on a treacherous trail was no easy feat for any child at that time. Spurred onward by desperation and love, I did it anyhow.

When I arrived, I found myself lost in an endless maze of massive buildings. Most of the buildings where the prison was located had been constructed by German colonizers in the early 1900s. The building designs were unique and interesting. Some of them were oval, others circular, and the community appeared to have been carefully planned.

I stopped a perplexed gentleman and asked him to assist me in identifying the prison house. I explained to him that I wanted to visit my father. He hesitated for a moment before pointing at one of the gated buildings in the distance. As I got closer, I encountered a colossal gate blocking the entrance to the prison complex. There was no guard in sight, so I peeked through its massive iron bars and saw a few men at a distance marching in military formation. I had no idea what to do next, so I sat on a rock by the gate and waited several hours, hoping to catch a glimpse of my father. While waiting, I could not help but cry because of painful, obsessive thoughts I was having that he was being tortured as my mom had been. Somehow, I had the feeling that I might never see him again.

It was getting late when I decided I had better go home. After arriving home that day, I didn't tell anyone what I had done. I lost all interest in school. Not long afterward, I stopped going to school altogether. Every morning, I left as usual as if I were going to school. Instead, I trekked up the mountain to keep vigil at the prison gate. In the late afternoon, I returned home. I never saw Dad. The frustration and anguish I felt during those trying times at the tender age of about eight were indescribable.

During his incarceration, Dad became ill. On several occasions, he had to be taken to the general hospital located about a mile from us. There were no prison ambulances; therefore, he was forced to walk while shackled and under guard to the hospital, despite his frail and vulnerable condition. On occasion, a kind and considerate guard would allow him to make a brief stop at our house so that he could see his family. These were embarrassing and painful moments because all the neighbors would come out and stare at him as though he were an alien monster.

Dad was a very proud and gentle person. It was disturbing to our mother and the rest of us to see him suffer. He looked older and emaciated and had scars on his face, arms, and lower extremities that had not been there before his arrest. My mother would fight back tears as she pleaded with the guard to allow her to feed him briefly before they departed. Some of the guards were considerate and accommodating. My mother always fed the guards as well. Dad spoke little. His words were always carefully selected, as though he did not want to incriminate himself, divulge any secrets, or expose his physical and emotional pain to us. He always asked how I was doing in school. "Fine!" I would lie. No details. The guards would undo the cuffs long enough for him to eat and then would reapply them as soon as the meal was over. This, too, was painful to watch.

Normally, after they left, Mom would convene the children so we could pray. Then she would reassure us that Dad would be coming home someday. For about three months, unbeknownst to my mom or anyone, I did not attend school. I spent every school day during that time at or near the prison grounds, where I remained determined and hopeful but never got a chance to see him. Sometimes I was soaked by the rain, and on a few occasions, a prison guard emerged from the building and chased me away. I often returned after he left.

One day on a weekend, I had just finished helping my mom with household chores and went outside to split firewood when I heard a familiar voice. I paused, spun around, looked up, dropped the ax, and ran toward my dad. I hugged him so hard he staggered. It seemed like the strength was gone from his legs. Many months of incarceration had exacted a toll on him. Mom and the rest of the family were bustling with joy and excitement as they rushed him. Then I witnessed something I had never seen. He cried!

Finally, the nightmarish experience was over for everyone. On my part, I was glad to see him free again—free from his guard, free from the repulsive prison garb, free from the hostile metallic cuffs. I was glad to see him free and home. He slumped into his favorite chair and immediately began to ask how each of us had been doing. He asked about our grandparents, aunts, and uncles. He did not discuss any of the events that transpired during his imprisonment.

That same night Uncle George came by. It was during one of their conversations that I heard the details of Dad's misfortune. He was arrested because the government assumed he knew the whereabouts of my uncle Aaron and was privy to information about the political party the government detested. He continued to share in stark detail the torture treatment he received almost daily. He talked about being subjected to various forms of torture, including genital electric-shock sessions. He talked about going for days with minimal nutrition and about sleeping on cold cement floors with no access to basic personal needs. My uncle George was so profoundly moved by Dad's narrative that he began to cry. In the middle of his suffering, Dad stated emphatically that his main concern during that time was the welfare of his family. It was thoughts of us that inspired and motivated him to maintain his composure and resilience. As I listened to him, I began to feel a surge of anger and hate for the reckless, repulsive actions of the authorities. I couldn't understand how anyone could perpetrate such evil on another human being. My mom and dad were good people and never hurt anyone.

Predictably, I failed all the exams that semester since I had made a willful decision to skip school. I had been a top student all along, and I truly felt a deep disappointment with myself. I remember sitting in the kitchen with my mother and watching her prepare dinner when Dad appeared at the door asking me a few questions about my grade report. Without a long, drawn-out speech, I revealed that I had failed. For a moment, he appeared to understand my response, but then he commented on money and tuition. In essence, he was bemoaning the loss of one dollar he had spent on tuition money that semester with nothing to show for it. As I sat there feeling bad about myself, he made a statement that, when I look back to that moment, reflects the greatness he represented. He expressed his responsibility for my failure. "Am sorry. It's all because of me," he said before slowly walking away. He was taking responsibility for something that wasn't his fault. How noble!

On the next school day, he accompanied me to school, where he met the headmaster and explained why I had failed. On his part, the headmaster seemed moved upon hearing about my dad's experiences, and he encouraged me to work harder.

Before long, things began to return to normal at school and home. A year after the terrible experience with the prison system, my mother gave birth to an adorable new family member, a sister named Bih. She became the favorite of everyone, including one of my uncles called Sam, the butcher. Therefore everyone called her Bih Sam. Our parents then had six mouths to feed.

CHAPTER 26
School Mentors

DURING MY LATER YEARS in elementary school, one of the best teachers I had was a lanky redheaded Peace Corps volunteer from Arizona who took a particular interest in my cognitive development. He fed me books from America, and I devoured them. I read incessantly, and every time I finished a book, he offered me another. It was he who told me that I must read extensively because, in the future, the ability to communicate eloquently and to excel in my understanding of written material would be of tremendous value to me. It was he who encouraged me to consider pursuing university studies in America after secondary school. He said this at a time when I had no concept of a university.

His pearls of wisdom were infinite. I am convinced that the reason for the intersection of our life trajectories was beyond serendipity. I have always considered his interest in my development, his optimism about my abilities, and his encouragement as pivotal in the successes of my academic pursuits. Because of him, I developed such a passion for books that at one time, I even tricked my father into buying me Jules Verne's *Around the World in 80 Days* when I was about nine years old. Since I knew Dad was illiterate, I often included a few novels of my liking on the list of required books for school. When we got to the bookstore in the city, Dad would simply hand the list to the manager and wait for the books. He would pay for them, and we would leave without his knowing that the list had been padded. I got a kick out of this! I knew he would complain about his meager financial resources if I asked him to buy me an extra book that was not on the official recommended book list.

During my last year of elementary school, I was assigned to a classroom with a more engaging and assertive teacher whose name was Mr. Fondeh and whose daughter was my classmate. He was a very engaging teacher and gave us a lot of homework. When he asked questions during lectures, he often looked in my direction for the answers. During this time, I had a crush on his daughter Rose. She was quiet, studious, and reserved. I often tried talking to her during recess, but she never paid any attention to me. I would bring her oranges and mangoes, hoping to spark her interest in me. Unfortunately, she would take them and walk away without offering me any encouraging feedback but would instead leave me twitching, aghast, and confused.

A million mangoes and oranges later, I got the message and discontinued any further romantic overtures on my part and reconnected with something less arduous, less complicated, that I had developed a tremendous appetite for: Shakespeare, Jules Verne, Mark Twain, Ernest Hemingway, and anything in print that I could lay my hands on, thanks to my trusted American friend and teacher. I decided there had to be a good reason for my mother telling me often to stay away from little girls because they could "mess up my head." I was a little too confused at that stage to understand the reason behind or importance of her stern advice. Each time she observed a neighborhood girl looking at me a certain way or trying to talk to me, she would immediately extract me forcibly from the scene.

CHAPTER 27

Uncle Manny

WHEN I THINK OF the environment where I was born, I think of big blue skies, endless vistas, and open spaces. Furthermore, I think of simplicity, easy smiles, facile social interactions, and a collective sense of community. I am not talking about a utopian world. There were abundant negative parts of our social tapestry. All in all, I continue to appreciate the importance of all those experiences, both positive and negative, that shaped my growth and development. Whenever I look back, I often appreciate how experiential learning shaped my future perspectives and actions in countless ways.

I had an uncle called Marcus who often stated that within each of us, there were two creatures, one bad and the other good. He often went on to say that the creature a person chooses to feed within them determines that person's trajectory in life. Each adult in my formative years seemed to have been given a divine assignment to teach me various lessons.

We had an uncle who lived nearby, Uncle Manny, who had an admirably close relationship with my dad. He worked in the city, and after work, he would stop by for a chat with Dad before going to his house. He was a tall, handsome, gregarious, charming, kind man who was a strong advocate for education. He had a son about my age and three smart and beautiful daughters. Their mom was somewhat reserved yet attentive to my siblings and me. She loved to cook and enjoyed visiting with us. One day, I was told that she had decided to move from the city to live far away in the village, where things were less hectic and where she could be closer to her farms. My uncle couldn't move because of his job. He had about a seventh-grade education, which made him one of the most educated people in the area.

Therefore, he was admired for this as well as his good character. He would occasionally offer some liquor to his dog to slurp so that it could become more aggressive.

After his wife and children moved away, he asked if I would move in with him, and I agreed without hesitation. Uncle Manny taught me how to be organized and the best way to keep a clean house. He was compulsively neat and clean and kept his surroundings in mint condition. During my stay with him, I learned to use a pressing iron, which was an interesting contraption shaped like a miniature metallic boot with a wooden handle attached to a lid, connected to the main body by a couple of hinges. To use the iron, one placed charcoal in its well and ignited it after sprinkling a little kerosene on the coals. I learned to accelerate the burning process by grabbing the pressing iron by its handle and swinging it around in an oscillating manner. Occasionally, while I was swinging the iron, the latch would disengage accidentally, and hot coals would become lethal projectiles.

Living with my uncle Manny made me feel socially sophisticated. He had a huge shortwave radio sitting in a cabinet in the living room. I had seen quite a few of these prized possessions in various homes. Owning a shortwave radio immediately elevated a person's social status to a much higher level. Young women swooned at the sight of a bachelor with a radio because he was considered more attractive, wealthy, and sophisticated. Consequently, owning one markedly improved a man's eligibility for marriage. When I moved to the village to live with my grandma, I remember the first time I saw a radio in my uncle George's hut. After he retired from his position as overseer at the plantation, he returned home with dozens of modern contrivances that were unavailable and unheard of in the village at that time. One of them was a shortwave radio.

I remember being riveted by beautiful music emanating from that bizarre-looking contraption positioned on a cabinet. Periodically, I sat for long stretches staring at it and soaking in all the news announcements and commentaries that it would spit out. Most radio transmissions were in English, with an occasional spattering of French and Spanish, none of which I understood at that time. Radio music was my favorite program, and although I did not understand the lyrics, I connected with the melodies. Out of innocence or ignorance, I thought that the mysterious boom box housed miniature creatures who generated all that talk and music. I marveled at their tenacity and resilience as they appeared to go on for hours at a time, until my uncle would decide to shut them up by a magic flick of his right hand against a part of the box. Every once in a while, the sound would cease from the box, and my uncle George, with deft and supercilious poise, would remove a cover in the unit and replace six cylindrical objects (which eventually I would discover to be batteries) in a specific manner, and the radio would be reanimated miraculously! It was my impression at that time that the six contraptions were nutrient sources for its diminutive occupants.

My imagination convinced me that the radio housed various groups of participants speaking an assortment of languages, having assigned responsibilities and duties. Some were strictly band members, others choir participants, and the rest were newsreaders. Therefore, when Uncle George got tired of listening to the choir, he would simply walk up to the unit without saying a word, and with a flick of his hand, he would direct the choir members to stop, and he would then usher in the newscasters. It wasn't until I traveled somewhere and happened by a radio repair shop that I made the unfortunate discovery that the true occupants of my favorite magic box were inanimate, unappealing vacuum tubes and tufts of intricately constructed variegated mazes of wires. How disappointing!

Uncle Manny loved to listen to the news on the radio. He was very passionate and demonstrative, and when he heard something he didn't agree with, he would scream at the radio, letting out an explosive "No!" Sometimes he would wave his arms menacingly as though he were an embattled participant at a political debate. Then he would suddenly calm down after the news was over and regain his normal demeanor and composure. Uncle Manny espoused and demanded perfection so much that he insisted I perform a task over and over until it was, in his opinion, perfect. He would demonstrate why the acceptable outcome was worth all those multiple attempts. Interestingly, he would occasionally interject that although only God could be perfect, the pursuit of perfection could elevate an individual to a higher level of excellence. It took many years for me to appreciate his philosophical thinking.

In general, living with him was a good experience. Unfortunately, sometimes he forgot to buy food, and at times after school, I had nothing to eat. It came to a point where I became so hungry that I would visit a few friends in the neighborhood in the hope of getting a free meal. I even resorted to foraging the woods for anything edible I could discover. One day, while sauntering aimlessly and looking for a solution to my nutritional insecurity, I observed a hen lovingly incubating her eggs adjacent to our house. I stood there for a moment in deep thought. A few ideas crisscrossed my mind, some of which Charles Darwin would have advocated and applauded. My malfeasance must have appeared intuitively obvious to the hen, as it readjusted its protective posture and began to eye me in the most sardonic, distrustful, suspicious, and scornful manner. To break the impasse, I waved my arms randomly while barking out inarticulate words. Still, she did not budge.

With Mr. Darwin's approval, I decided to take the bull by the horns because my patience was running thin. As I reached down to grab and dislodge her from a position that was deterring my access to a major protein repository, I was greeted with the most piercingly sharp and painful puncture in the back of my right hand. Upset at the hostility, intransigence, and disrespect she had shown me, I grabbed a broom nearby and smacked it across her head. While still angrily flapping her wings, extending her neck, and vociferously protesting my unwelcome intrusion, she backed up a few feet away from her eggs in a dare. In one fell swoop of perverted justice for impaling my innocent hand with her nasty beak, I took possession of all six pearly ovals. That night, after forgiving her for the terrible trauma I had suffered from her mean beak, and with my stomach wrinkles eliminated, I slept like a baby. Interestingly, I never saw her again. I wonder why.

On occasion, Uncle Manny visited a city bar to eat and drink with his friends after work. He would then come home staggering and too inebriated to appreciate my presence. At some point, I started a small garden in the yard and grew tomatoes, lettuce, and a few other vegetables to have some sort of reliable nutrition for myself. Often by the time he got home, I was already in bed. Occasionally, I was awakened to laughter and giggles and the sound of a female voice in playful banter. I had no idea what was going on.

One day he came home right after work, and a few hours later, there was a light knock on the door. I opened it to reveal a tall, voluptuous lady balancing a huge wicker basket on her head. She smiled as I turned to announce her arrival. Uncle Manny promptly guided her in with a gracious welcome, and she carefully placed the basket on the table. It was filled with delicious-smelling food. I remember that during this time, food had become my best friend. I never saw leftovers on my plate. I would eat everything and proceed to lick my plate and fingers with focused, artistic precision so that no drop or food particle was left behind. The very sight or smell of food elicited powerful systemic responses and a rush in me that drove me to consume any meal with abandon. Of all the people who had ever stopped by to visit my uncle, this lady was my favorite. She had come with food! We sat in the living room, and while they were engaged in small talk, my brain kept asking, "When do we eat?" I was poised to mount an aggressive attack on the fufu, vegetables, and corn that she had brought.

Then, suddenly, there was another knock on the door. I opened it and discovered a female interloper who had arrived at an inopportune moment. As I was letting her in, the look on my uncle's face spoke of disaster. To put it more practically, it was the look that you would have if you came home and found a couple of Martians sipping tea in your living room. I stood there by the door, waiting for guidance from Uncle Manny, but he appeared dumbfounded, as if he were in a deep trance, his lips parted, his eyeballs leaping from their sockets as their lids gave way.

Lady number two was a big woman in every anatomical sense. She had legs double my size and a gluteal department that appeared several minutes after she walked through the door. She looked at my uncle with a scowl and immediately lumbered across the room without saying a word. Then she took a seat across the table from lady number one. I don't think she even acknowledged my presence. The situation appeared ominous. There was tension in the air, and my uncle asked me to go to my room. Suddenly, I was torn between the choices of entertainment the unfolding events were presenting me: an "estrogenic" wrestling tournament versus a delicious dinner—or both! The floodgates of my salivary glands had been pried open by my famished vision.

Understandably, before heading to my room begrudgingly, I threw a droopy glance at the basket on the table filled with delicious food. No sooner had I closed my door than I heard a loud boom like the terrestrial collision of a meteorite. The commotion became louder, and I couldn't contain my curiosity. Because the language of communication in the living room had changed drastically, I was convinced that all hell had broken loose. Every other sentence was generously flavored with the word "mother" and a few other salacious expletives. I became concerned when I couldn't discern a male voice. However, I could hear both women loudly hurling epithets at each other. I was starving and, at the same time, dying of curiosity about the ultimate outcome of the events in the adjacent room.

Realizing that the other house occupants were preoccupied, I decided to sneak up to the basket of goodies and help myself to a few of its contents. Therefore, I pried open the door to the living room and stepped into a tornado with flying furniture, wigs, clothes, cups, dishes, and the scary sight of a big woman choking her adversary with a massive right hand and ripping clothes off the victim with her left hand, all the while pinning her down beneath her massive frame.

Uncle Manny was screaming, "*Stop!*" while trying to pull the big lady away from the smaller one, who was being choked, disrobed, and scalped. He looked desperate, and there was nothing I could do. I had never seen anything like that, and it was all too confusing. Suddenly, the big lady left her victim, stormed across the room half-naked, grabbed the basket of food, and headed for the door. Oh no! I sprinted after her, but it was too late. In one swift motion, she jettisoned the contents of the basket in the dusty yard. I stood there and watched with contemplative desperation. As she stormed back into the house to complete her mission, I ran into the yard, which was now littered with chunks of great food. What a waste! In the glow of my kerosene lamp, I proceeded to rescue as much food as I could, eating some of it on the spot and putting the rest in the basket, along with all the dirt and dust that had been smeared on it.

While walking back to the house, I was feeling angry about what the big lady had just done to the food. Then I discovered that the duel had ended while I was doing my respectable duty in the yard. The women were standing several feet apart and regarding each other with contemptuous scowls while my uncle was standing between them and attempting to salvage the night and his life. Suddenly, the big lady grabbed a piece of her apparel lying on the floor next to her, straightened up her back, briefly exploded a barrage of expletives directed at him and her adversary, and then stormed out of the room. Soon after, the other woman left without saying a word and did not even bother to take her basket with her. I was appalled by what I had just witnessed among adults. I retired to my room and soon fell asleep. The next morning, my uncle helped me clean the living room and the yard to eliminate the evidence. He was quiet and somber all day. After that incident, I never saw another woman at the house.

A few weeks later, I happened to be visiting my aunt (his wife) and cousins in the village where they had moved. She asked me how it was living with her husband. With youthful exuberance, I regaled her with the story of the fighting women. In my innocence, I failed to appreciate the potential fallout from my narrative. I told my aunt I didn't know why the women were fighting, adding that in my opinion, the big woman just didn't like the smaller woman. Predictably, my aunt confronted him with the story afterward. Needless to say, I got the life choked and whipped out of me by Uncle Manny for ratting on him. Soon after that, we parted ways.

On a different occasion, I was visiting him, and my other aunts from the village happened to be there as well. Then my dad showed up, and everyone seemed to be having a lively time in conversation till late at night. I always had a book with me wherever I went, so I retreated to one of the adjacent rooms to read. I had barely closed the door when I heard my name being mentioned. Then I overheard my father complaining about his stomach problems and how he had spent all his money on doctors and medicines. While listening with focused concern and sympathy, I overheard my aunt and Uncle Manny suggesting that my dad should remove me from elementary school and send me to work as a servant to a storekeeper in the city as that would address my father's economic woes. While listening to their conversation, I became frightened, sad, and worried. It would be a terrible thing to interrupt my education because I enjoyed learning and I didn't want to stop. As I continued to listen to their discussions about my future,

I realized that none of them had explored other options for financing my education, which at that time was only about three dollars a year. Nobody volunteered to offer financial assistance to my dad. Looking back through the years, I would rate what I heard that night as one of the lowest and most disturbing experiences I had. I couldn't imagine myself working anywhere when I would rather be in school. I was sleepless that night, tossing, turning, and shedding silent tears.

The following day I went to see my grandmother and my uncle George in the village. Both of them always seemed to be able to make important decisions in my best interest and frequently gave me comfort and optimism whenever my spirits were down. I told Uncle George what I had overheard, and he could sense my desperation. I cried and pleaded for his intercession on my behalf because I didn't want to leave school. They were both visibly upset and swore to never allow anyone to remove me from school. Their reassurances were comforting, and nobody would be terminating my education after all.

Those events were unfolding at a time when my curiosity for science was overflowing. I hung out occasionally at a radio repair shop near my house, where I observed the proprietor at work. Everyone called him "the boss." I asked him many questions about what he did and about the workings of radios, turntables, and reel-to-reel recorders. He enjoyed teaching me about his work because he appreciated my curiosity and interest in learning new things. He was a disciplined, immaculately dressed man who had a younger apprentice living with him. I used to help him with minor chores like dishwashing, cleaning, and laundry so that he would be motivated to teach me more about electronics. Early in the morning, after taking a bath in a shed behind the building, the boss would often walk back to his room in just his fancy underwear, which was not unusual behavior at that time in the village. One day, he got rid of a pair of his underwear. I found it in a trash pile in the bushes and retrieved it, washed it, and took proud ownership of it. It was the first pair of underwear I ever owned. I was in seventh grade at that time, and it was oversized, but I was happy with it. Owning underwear in those days was prestigious. I would often pull down my khaki uniform pants to the hip on one side briefly to show them off to my friends at school. That underwear lasted me through elementary and secondary school in Africa and across the mighty ocean to the United States, until I was able to afford a new pair in my college sophomore year in Massachusetts.

CHAPTER 28

Survival and Hopes

DAD WAS HAVING MORE frequent stomach problems, and he appeared to be increasingly desperate. He was hospitalized several times and could no longer work. Mom spent more time taking care of him and less time doing the things that enabled her to generate income. Consequently, there was not enough food for us. On occasion, I went fishing, hoping to bring home something to add to our meals. It came to a point where she could not afford kerosene for our bush lamp, so we had to resort to candlelight for studying.

Once I feigned illness to avoid studying, but she immediately collected a few leaves, made a concoction of something, and had me drink it. As soon as she did that, she handed me a book to read. On another occasion, I complained that I needed to go to ease myself in the woods. She gave me a break, and I disappeared into the bushes and held out a while, hoping she would be in bed by the time I returned so I would not have to study that night. It came as no surprise that she stayed up waiting patiently for my return, book in hand! At that point, I truly wished I had normal parents like my friends.

One day, after Dad had been discharged from the hospital and was feeling a little better, he gave us some bad news. The government had made a unilateral decision to build a road where our house was located, and we were obligated to move as soon as possible. They promised to build a new house for us. However, in the interim, we had to live with relatives. Before long, we packed our belongings and moved. Weeks later, I returned to the town, only to discover that our home had disappeared and a new round-about had replaced it. I was saddened by that discovery, especially since the government had replaced our house with a much smaller one, which was a hastily built shack, and we had received no compensation for the farm, trees, and crops that were around our old house. That experience took a toll on my parents. Once again, they were consumed by a state of powerlessness against the authorities. They had no recourse and had been forced to accept an iniquitous arrangement.

At the end of my final year in elementary school, I took a secondary-school entrance examination. Realizing that my parents could not afford the secondary-school education, I was hoping to earn high marks in the examination so that I could gain entrance into a prestigious government secondary school on a full scholarship. One of my brilliant older cousins, Fidelis Chi, had suddenly become a celebrity in the community because his stellar performance on that examination had earned him one of the coveted positions at a government bilingual secondary school in the nation's capital. Even my dad broke out in a rare dance routine when he heard the news. "Chi has done it," he sang with collective pride. The following year was my turn. I had done very well throughout elementary school, except for a few hiccups during my father's imprisonment. I registered and took the exam, and after a long wait, the results were announced on the national radio. I had flunked.

I didn't know what to do. Unfortunately, my performance from first to seventh grade was not factored into the final decision. According to the national education policy, the sole criterion for admission to secondary school after elementary school was an entrance examination. A student's performance throughout elementary school did not feature in the selection criteria. Top performers in this examination were offered full scholarships to attend exclusive government schools. Other top performers gained admission to missionary secondary schools. The rest of the students who performed poorly or had average scores were left with the option of less-selective private technical or commercial schools, which in those days were not as reputable as parochial or government secondary schools. Alternatively, one could opt to stay out a year and repeat the test.

My parents recommended that I seek enrollment at one of the commercial schools, which I did. I found their curriculum to be boring: ledgers, banking, typing, shorthand, and so forth. My self-esteem was devastated, especially since so many of my friends from elementary school whom I had outperformed were attending prestigious, challenging schools, and I was left to languish in suffocating boredom, learning things I had no interest in. My cousin Thomas, Uncle George's son, was attending one of the most prestigious secondary schools in the country, Sacred Heart College. During the holidays, I spent many hours poring over his chemistry, physics, and biology textbooks with rapturous admiration, even though I did not understand their contents. How I loved the uniforms of Sacred Heart College students!

During that time, I began to notice that my mom's abdomen was getting bigger. Then I discovered that another sibling might be on the way. A day came when she left for the hospital to give birth, and we waited patiently for the good news. Sadly, we were informed that she had lost the baby. The ensuing weeks were emotionally challenging for everyone, but eventually, life returned to normal. She was a true champion!

Not long after I started at the commercial school, my mother and I were sitting in front of our home when we saw a bunch of students from Sacred Heart College walking by on their way to the city. They were allowed time off each Wednesday afternoon and were permitted to leave the campus and visit the neighboring town for leisure or errands. My mother was impressed with their appearance, and she commented on how sharp and smart they looked in their short-sleeved white shirts and charcoal-gray pants accentuated with a red cotton vest adorned with delicate white stripes around both shoulder and waistline hems. She turned to me, and with an endearing look of wishful aspiration, she said, "My son, if I could see you in that uniform someday, I would die a happy mother."

From that moment on, I was determined to gain admission to Sacred Heart College. I knew this could only happen if I retook the secondary-school entrance exam the following year and scored significantly better than I had.

CHAPTER 29
There Is No Doctor

SEVERAL MONTHS LATER, HER abdomen appeared to be getting bigger again, and she seemed to be more disconnected from everything than I had ever seen her. She kept her emotions in check and was less expressive of her feelings. Unfortunately, one of her cousins died, and she took me to the funeral. On the way back, I remember her looking at me and telling me that someday she, too, would die. I didn't give it much thought because parental mortality was not something that I was overly concerned about at that age. However, soon after that, I began to have recurrent nightmares about getting lost and finding myself alone, and one day I dreamed my mother was offering me her most prized material possession, a wristwatch. This was a bizarre dream, especially since I had been punished a few times for playing with that watch.

My siblings and I were enrolled in school at that time, except for our older sister Kien and Bih, who was only three years old. Kien was living with Grandma, and two of my younger sisters, Siri and Mambo, were living with aunts. Only my brother and I, along with our youngest sibling, Bih, were living with our parents. Mom appeared to have lost the vivacity she used to have. She appeared to be even more pragmatic in her words and actions. For some strange reason, I began to experience recurrent episodes of anxiety and feelings of impending doom. On her part, she was obsessively concerned with my nutrition and well-being, and she had an uncharacteristic desire to feed me more food than I needed.

One morning, I left for school as usual. I had only walked a few yards when I heard a soft voice calling my name. When I turned around in response, I saw Mom standing in front of the door with a forlorn look adorning her usually cheerful morning face. Normally, she would smile and utter one of her carefully phrased admonishments: "Be a good boy today!"

This time she placed a gentle hand on my shoulder, and with articulate diction, she said: *"Forevermore, learn with your heart, and think with your mind!"*

I hugged her massive belly and took off. After all, there was nothing unusual about her words. In a bid to impart children with wisdom, it was not uncommon for African parents to weaponize advice with thought-provoking adages. Unbeknownst to me on that faithful morning, I had just received the final tool from her to add to an already overflowing toolbox, a useful toolbox replete with handy items that she and my father had given me over the years.

That afternoon, while returning from school, I ran into my uncle Sam the butcher, who looked unusually agitated. He informed me that my mom had just delivered a baby boy and was in a critical condition because she had lost a large amount of blood. She was in dire need of blood, and the hospital was soliciting blood donations. I feared the worst. I turned around immediately, made a beeline to the hospital, and went directly to the maternity ward. Hers was the first bed to the right after the ward entrance. Bright-red blood was dripping rapidly from the side of her bed and expanding the puddle beneath it. The sight of my bleeding mom with severely chapped lips, caked saliva around her mouth and chin, writhing and moaning in pain, upset me immeasurably.

With tears in my eyes, I reached out, touched her right leg, and announced my presence. In an instant, she grabbed my other hand and squeezed hard. Immediately, she began to proclaim loudly and repeatedly, "My son, I am dying! Please go home!"

I was shaking uncontrollably. Confused, frantic, and feeling helpless, I cried my eyes out. It was too much for a child to handle. With a desperate plea, I screamed, "I need you, Mommy! Please don't die!"

Then I kept on repeating, "Mommy, please don't die!"

At this point, a tearful nurse, who was very upset with the futility of not having any lifesaving options, walked up and gave me a hug, which I needed desperately. I remember her throwing her arms up in the air and repeating several times with an air of frustration, "There is no doctor!"

The hospital's lone doctor was tied up somewhere. Mom kept on moaning and pleading,

"Help me. Somebody help me!"

After what seemed like an eternity, her moans became weaker and weaker. And then delirium set in, and she started uttering confusing sentences. I held on tightly to her hand and assured her continuously, "Mom, I am still here with you. I am not going to leave you alone."

Then she insisted, "My son, please go home."

I continued to hold on to her right hand, squeezing it even harder and hoping to invigorate her. Tears were streaming freely down my cheeks and onto my shirt, and I could not stop my body from shaking. Suddenly, my father showed up and gently pried my hand away from hers before attempting to convince me that she was not going to die. He pleaded with me to go home and sleep so that I would be well rested for school the next day. I was unconvinced by his optimism; however, when I stepped away hesitatingly from her bed, I realized my legs had been generously smeared with her blood.

Furthermore, by my observation, the velocity of dripping blood had slowed down to a point at which I could count the drops as they collided without splattering in a large puddle on the uneven concrete floor. Comforted by the optimism of youthful innocence, I was convinced that a marked reduction in the amount of dripping blood was indicative of a significant improvement in her condition. With tremendous hesitation, I walked out of the hospital ward that night with my head slumped on my chest and feeling enormous sadness in my heart. The desperate words of that poor nurse kept haunting me and ringing loudly and incessantly in my ears: *There is no doctor!*

Despite my optimism, something inside me kept telling me I would never again see my mother alive. She was barely thirty years old.

(Whenever I am motivating students to consider a career in medicine, giving a lecture, or just talking to patients and community members or about health-related matters, people often ask me why I decided to become a doctor. Invariably, my response takes me back to those sad events that unfolded before me that terrible night in the maternity ward with my loving mom in profound agony and on the brink of death.)

When I left the ward to embark on a difficult trudge back to the village, I decided that night I would become a doctor so another mother would never have to suffer like mine, and no child would ever again, with tear-drenched eyes, have to experience what I had just witnessed. That night, I arrived at a crucial turning point in my life, during which I underwent a radical psychological transformation. It was as though a caption of those fateful events was incorporated in my DNA structure and subsequently transformed my life to become purpose driven. Gone were the childhood frivolities she had often condemned in me. That new DNA would be expressed in my studies and struggles, my longings and yearnings, and ultimately it would undergird my dedication to medical practice and human service. In essence, henceforth I would have to embrace a conscious psychological and physical withdrawal from the tumultuous, distracting world around me so that I might be able to focus on whatever preparation I needed to achieve my ultimate goal.

The journey home that night was arduous and dreary. My sad and confused mental state was sapping all the energy from my blood-soaked extremities. I couldn't go on any further. The burden on my shoulders was too much to bear, and I was feeling emotionally depleted. My heart was hurting from the fear of losing my mom, my love, my coach, my cheerleader, and my protector. Therefore, I decided to stop for the night at an uncle's home. I remember looking at my legs and deciding not to wash away Mom's blood from them. I crawled into a bed, and that night I dreamed my mother had died.

Early the next day, I was gently awakened by a sobbing uncle, who gave me the confirmatory bad news. Our loving, lovable, tall, beautiful, smiling giant was no more.

"Last night, your mother died peacefully. Her body was taken to your uncle George's home. You must go there now," he said.

I was overwhelmed with a sense of finality, emptiness, loneliness, and fear. Mom was smart, strong, and vibrant. She loved people, and she loved life. She cared about humanity. Could all this be a dream? In a profoundly demure state, I got out of bed without saying a word to my uncle, washed my legs, and set out to see my mother for the last earthly time.

By the time I arrived at Uncle George's house, a huge crowd of family, friends, and relatives was gathered in mourning. I went to the room where my mom's body was reposed. Uncle George was busy removing bandages from certain parts of her body while the women were preparing to bathe her. My siblings were sitting on the floor next to her body and mourning uncontrollably. My older sister Kien ran up to me, sobbing. Then it dawned on me that our youngest sister, Bih, who was only three years old at that time, was missing. One of my mother's friends had offered to keep her after my mother checked into the hospital. In an instant, I left to fetch her several miles away. On our way back, I tried to explain to her that our mother had just died. She was too young to understand. She straddled my neck while holding onto my head as we trekked back to the funeral.

Mom was wrapped in white sheets and placed in a wooden coffin that had been hastily constructed. She was then placed in the middle of the yard so everyone could view her body. While standing there crying and staring at her, I could have sworn that I saw a quiver in her eye. Maybe flames of hope were still leaping in my heart. Eventually, the elders took her body to a room to perform traditional rites, rituals, and prayers. After that, she was interred near Grandma's hut. The look of pain and the anguish of loss on the faces of my father and grandma at the moment her coffin was being lowered to its final resting place has remained seared on my mind and will remain there as long as my memory chords last.

Dad was inconsolable. He had to be restrained from jumping into the grave with her. In his immense sorrow, he cried out, "Monica, why did you do this to me? I want to join you."

My siblings and I were directed to a spot near the grave and asked to dump a little dirt on the coffin as a symbolic gesture to help us accept the finality of her earthly existence. We were feeling lost without our mother. Finally, with their shovels, the men filled the hole rapidly with more dirt.

The funeral lasted a week. It was a moving experience for everyone. For weeks afterward, I cried every night and could hardly sleep. She was my best friend in the universe. On one occasion, I found myself alone in her bedroom with memories of her inundating my thoughts. I reached out and grabbed one of her dresses, closed my eyes, pressed it against my face, and drew in a deep breath. In an instant, her scent flooded my senses. I couldn't contain my emotions. I was feeling so lost without her, and I didn't know what to do. Dejected, I sat on the edge of her bed and stared hopelessly at the ceiling. When my gaze shifted back down to the floor, it fell on a box in a corner of the room. Curiosity drove me to pry it open. Inside was a shiny set of chinaware that had never been used.

It was still waiting for that "special occasion" that Mom always talked about.

CHAPTER 30
Mom's Wish

SEVERAL DAYS AFTER THE funeral, a decision was made to split us up so that we could live with family members because of our father's frail health and his chronic abdominal problems. My sister Kien, my brother Fru, and I shuttled between the homes of Dad, Grandma, and Uncle George. This was not a problem because everyone lived close by. After Mom died, the baby boy she gave birth to was adopted by Cistercian monks in a neighboring village. Unfortunately, he died a couple of weeks later and was buried next to her.

As we were all still trying to adjust to the terrible tragedies that had befallen our family, Dad decided to do something remarkably heartwarming. Since Mom's grave was adjacent to Grandma's hut, he moved Grandma to a different abode nearby and extended the walls of her hut to encompass Mom's grave. Then he constructed a bedroom over her grave so that he could be near her until his death.

I kept experiencing bouts of depression, and books provided a welcome escape for me. Therefore, I read voraciously. I read everything I could lay my hands on. Unfortunately, we had no public libraries where I could go to satisfy my thirst for books. My redheaded American Peace Corps friend who had been an endless source for books had moved back to the United States. Not having any money to feed my addiction to books, I resorted to stealing. I became a book thief. However, I always made it a point to return every book I stole after reading it.

Grandma was getting older and weaker and couldn't farm as much. I often experienced severe hunger, and on occasion, I resorted to stealing food. Sometimes, in my desperation, I would steal cubes of sugar from someone's house and run away deep into the woods nearby where I could consume it in peace. My dad went through a prolonged period of what I now recognize as depression. He would often stand alone in a pensive mood and stare at a distance for long periods. On one of these occasions, my aunt Cecilia happened to be passing by on her way back from the hospital and decided to see how we were doing. When she recognized the state my father was in, she asked him how he was handling the loss of his wife. He responded that he was doing the best he could. And then she looked at me and asked him how I was doing. He informed her that I was doing well under the circumstances and that, most importantly, my schoolwork was coming along well.

At that moment, she told me to take my things and come with her so I could live with her and my cousins. She lived in the city and had about seven children at that time, a couple of them about my age. My cousins and I all got along, and it was a very loving family atmosphere. Aunt Cecilia was a highly spiritual person and had a powerful relationship with God, and she used to lead us in daily prayer. She exuded fairness and love in all her actions and activities. Living with her was a welcome respite, especially since I had just lost my mother and had a tremendous void within me. Aunt Cecelia in essence contributed enormously to filling that void.

A month after my mom's death, I began to plead with Uncle George to assist me in gaining admission to the secondary school of my mother's dreams, Sacred Heart College. One morning he asked me to join him on a short trip to see the principal of that school and solicit admission. He and I understood the odds were against me, but we were determined to give it a shot. He instructed me to dress appropriately. On his part, he wore a handsome traditional outfit. Then I hopped on the back of his bicycle, and away we went.

Sacred Heart College was a boarding school on a curvaceous mountain run by the Mills Brothers, a religious order of European missionaries with a primary focus on educational empowerment. After we got there, we waited patiently at the entrance to the principal's office for several hours. When he arrived, he greeted us cordially. His name was Brother Vincent. He was a handsome, wiry-looking Englishman with a brisk walk, a contemplative look, and an infectious smile. He stated that he was too busy to see us and asked if we could return on another day.

The next day, Uncle George insisted we go back, and when the principal discovered why we were there, he went into a tirade about school policies that discouraged the consideration of transfer students from technical or commercial schools because their education was inferior and those students would face enormous challenges and insurmountable difficulties with the curriculum in Sacred Heart College. With that, he wished us good luck and showed us the door.

That night, Uncle George insisted that we return the next day. This time he advised me to bring along all my grade reports from elementary school. We were battling a torrential downpour that morning on our way to "harass" the principal. He was not expecting us, but we waited patiently outside his office in a soaking downpour practically all morning. He was unpleasantly surprised to see us when he arrived, and without wasting time, he reminded us that his previous decision had been final. While appearing to be oblivious to the principal's statement, Uncle George began to plead passionately on my behalf with importunity, "Please, Brother Vincent, give him a chance. He is a smart boy. His mother just died."

I was shaking visibly. Looking frustrated and confused, the principal invited us into his office. Then, with stern composure, he explained that there were no vacancies in Form One, the first-year class I was interested in. He went on to explain that vacancies at his school were rare because it was a coveted and prestigious school. After an awkward moment of silence, and what may have been an afterthought, he revealed that the only class with a recent vacancy was Form Two. He had barely finished the sentence when Uncle George interjected with unbridled enthusiasm, "He will take it!"

The principal was caught off guard at that moment. He leaned back in his chair, scratched his forehead, and hurled a few dissenting words at my uncle. Undeterred, Uncle George continued to repeat, "He can do it! He can do it!"

On my part, I had resigned myself to the hopelessness of the situation, and I was ready to part ways with the principal at any moment and return to my preexisting reality. Suddenly, with a look of frustration, the principal asked to see my grade reports, and I obliged at once. He evaluated them carefully and remarked that I had earned excellent grades in French and English. And then he went on to explain the school curriculum at Sacred Heart College: "First-year students take a year of chemistry, mathematics, physics, biology, literature, history, geography, English, and French. Each of these courses is continued at a more advanced level in the second year (Form Two)."

Then, with emphatic prominence, he stated, "It is impossible for a student to skip the entire first-year coursework and begin second-year advanced courses without any knowledge of a year's worth of fundamentals."

As I stood there listening critically, the principal's explanation sounded logical to me. I didn't know anything about chemistry, physics, biology, or any of those other courses besides the two (English and French) that I had been exposed to. As if he intended to eliminate any further discussions, the principal reminded Uncle George that I had flunked the national secondary-school entrance examination. My uncle remained unflinching in his rebuttal. "His mother died! He is smart! He can do it!"

Exhausted by Uncle George's passionate exhortations, Brother Vincent capitulated. "All right!" he exclaimed.

Then he declared, "He is admitted to Form Two."

And then, as if he intended to save face in a duel he had just lost, he declared, "If he fails to rank among the top fifteen students in his class at the end of the first semester, he's *out!*"

A few years later, I discovered that I was the first student to have been admitted as a transfer from a commercial or technical school and the first student to have skipped an entire first year to join the second year in a five-year curriculum.

The principal wrote down my name and gave my uncle a list of my prospectus. Hat in hand and with graceful humility, Uncle George expressed his appreciation to the principal, looked at me briefly, and flashed a reassuring grin. In no time, we were cycling back furiously to the village like a couple of besieged Keystone cops. I knew the road ahead would be rough. I would have to figure out a way to learn a year's worth of physics, mathematics, chemistry, biology, and a slew of other courses while concurrently taking the same courses at a more advanced level with new classmates who would be further along than me.

When my father heard the news, his elation was subdued and somewhat tempered. He inquired about tuition and boarding costs. Sacred Heart College was a boarding school for boys. The cost for tuition, room, and board for the year was a hefty seventy dollars. He wondered where he would get all that money. I was afraid that the opportunity would elude me for financial reasons. Luckily, my uncle Daniel came through and offered to pay a portion of my fees. Uncle George took care of the items in my prospectus: shoes, uniforms, soap, and towels, among other requirements. The biggest challenge we encountered was finding shoes that would fit comfortably. There were only a few choices at the market; therefore, in desperation, I settled for a pair of sneakers a size too small for me. Not long afterward, I began to regret that decision. I would remove the shoes intermittently to give my feet needed relief from their constrictive effect.

As I prepared to enter my new school, once again I found an opportunity to be a "bad boy." My older sister Kien, who lived with Grandma, needed a utensil for her bathwater. I had seen her struggle to contain enough bath water for herself in a small, fragile gourd. Sensing an opportunity, I snuck in an item, "large plastic bucket," on the list of requirements in the prospectus given by the principal. To this day she still uses that bucket and enjoys telling everyone the story behind it.

CHAPTER 31

Sacred Heart College Student

FINALLY, A FEW MONTHS after my mom's death, with profound apprehension in my heart, I lumbered across the expansive threshold leading into the Saint James dormitory at Sacred Heart College, lugging a heavy metal suitcase (fabricated by Dad) on my head. After traversing its massive entrance glass doors, I stepped into a new chapter in my life's saga. I had just arrived almost two weeks after the beginning of the semester because I needed extra time to obtain tuition contributions from a few family members. There were about fifteen beds in that dormitory room, whose occupants were actively engaged in playful activities. My sudden arrival triggered a sudden uneasy silence. From the way they stared at me, one might have thought I had just dropped by from Pluto.

Confused about what to do, I just stood there, trying to make sense of the scene and deciding which bed would be mine. At that moment, one of them, tall and thin with an air of seniority, rocking an intimidating stare, walked up and helped me to a corner bed. He introduced himself as Fru, the dorm captain. My twin bed, a metal contraption with a spring mesh and an overlying straw mattress, was the most comfortable bed I had ever slept in at that time. That night, I was overcome with a sense of melancholy and could not help but imagine how delighted my mom would have been to see me matriculate at the school of her hopes, wishes, and dreams. In a twist of irony, I could not help but wonder if she had not sacrificed her life so that I could achieve that dream opportunity.

Early the next day, I was awakened by the sound of a trumpet to begin my first day at Sacred Heart College. I was feeling anxious because classes had begun almost two weeks before my arrival. Boarding-school life at Sacred Heart was highly structured and organized. There were several dormitory buildings, each one having an adjoining shower and toilet booths. The rooms were in spacious halls with adequately spaced, seemingly endless rows of twin beds. Each dormitory had a large closet with generous storage capacity for students' possessions.

The dormitory captain was a fifth-year senior student, and his bed was always located in a corner. His job was to supervise the students and make sure their surroundings were clean and they were well behaved. Furthermore, he had the authority to discipline students for minor infractions. He kept a duty sheet to assign various responsibilities relating to the upkeep of the dormitory and toilet facilities by the students. In general, the captains were benevolent, although there were a few tyrants among their lot who delighted in enforcing their power on powerless junior students by using abusive force. The school campus "alarm clock" was a third-year student in Saint John's dormitory, which was located at a higher elevation than the rest of the dormitories. His trumpet would sound at 6:00 a.m. to rouse students out of bed. After taking cold showers, we would don our uniforms and scurry over to the dining hall for breakfast, which generally consisted of hot tea (which we called "colored water") and bread with a little butter. Eggs and beans were served on special occasions like Easter and national holidays.

Classes began at 7:45 a.m. and continued until noon, when we broke for lunch, and then resumed until 3:00 p.m. Between 3:00 and 5:00 p.m., students were allowed to engage in sports and social activities. Mostly, we played soccer, Ping-Pong, or tennis. I had already developed a passion for Ping-Pong before coming to Sacred Heart.

My first day of classes was predictably nerve-racking. Because I had never heard of algebra, it came as no surprise that I flunked the first math quiz. To be more precise, I got none of the answers right. The teacher, obviously bemused, looked up after grading the quiz and asked, "Who's Nche?"

Embarrassed, I raised a weary extremity to acknowledge myself. I was admonished for my abysmal performance and warned to do better the next time. At that point, some of my classmates began to giggle. I sat nervously in a corner, hoping that the ground would open up and swallow me whole.

And then it was time for my next class, chemistry. The teacher walked in and announced that he was going to give us a quiz on some of the previous year's work to set the stage for a more advanced lecture he intended to give. My heart was pounding so hard that I could feel my head rocking. He began by reading out loud the names of certain chemical elements and compounds such as water, calcium, potassium, sulfuric acid, nitric acid, sodium chloride, and magnesium sulfate, and asking the students to write their corresponding chemical formulas.

Oh boy, not again, I thought. I was completely lost. The only word I recognized was "water." I had never heard of chemical formulas. In my desperation, I scribbled a bunch of meaningless words phonetically. Not knowing the formula for water, I wrote down *water*. The word *chemistry* did not exist in my native vocabulary. The teacher graded the quiz afterward, and once again, my perplexing performance prompted him to call me out, share my answers loudly with the class, and admonish me for earning a zero score. The class roared in laughter. I had become the unsolicited, unwilling headliner at the Sacred Heart "improv." I had no friends in the class, and I was feeling terribly lonely. On that day, I was highlighted during every lecture. Appalled with my performance on one of the quizzes, a teacher actually paused, commanded me to stand up, and unceremoniously asked me, "Who let you in here?"

I felt dejected and worthless as I sauntered back to my dormitory that afternoon. My enthusiasm for learning had been dowsed. The enemy of self-doubt was beginning to gnaw away at me while enormous dark clouds of extreme anxiety and hopelessness floated menacingly in my mental skies, overwhelming my fragile mind and disabling any preexisting ambitions within me. I felt so alone.

When I got back to the dormitory, a few students were sitting on their beds and discussing various esoteric subjects like clothes, shoes, cinema, trains, and the national soccer teams. They appeared to be oblivious to my presence. These students were from big cities, and a few had even lived overseas. Their world was entirely foreign to me. Most of them dressed in expensive clothes and wore fancy shoes. Others possessed gadgets and other items I had only read about in some of the books I used to steal. They spoke and behaved with confidence and intimidating swagger. The topics of their conversations affirmed the social crevasse between us and left me feeling inferior and increasingly self-conscious. Without uttering a word, I stood up and went over to the library.

I did not know where to begin since there was so much catching up I had to do. I found myself in a deep hole from which I had to craft a workable and sustainable strategy to free myself. I knew that to catch up with my coursework, I had to complete the previous year's entire curriculum while working simultaneously on current material. This seemed like a tall order, but I had no other choice!

In a deserted corner of the library, I opened a first-year chemistry textbook and began to study the periodic table. None of the figures and letters on that page made any sense to me, but I persisted for hours. After dinner, I joined the rest of the students in the classroom for a mandatory two-hour evening study session. That night, lying in bed thinking about my mom, I kind of wished she had not planted the seed of education in me. Then I began to engage myself with a little self-talk. I had been motivated to attend Sacred Heart College because of her death and a desire to address the conditions that resulted in her death. I began to question whether an exclusive boarding school was for me. That night, I had recurring dreams about my mother. In one of the dreams, she appeared visibly upset while holding a lighted candle, and then, as she would often do, she asked me to sit down, grab a book, and study.

I was jolted out of bed by the morning bugle. It was time to shower, eat, and begin another school day. Understandably, I experienced a sense of dread surging within me because I did not want to face another scalping by a teacher because of my poor performance on a quiz. I did not want to be used as an instrument for class entertainment, and I considered it a cruel gesture for any teacher to express his exasperation with my performance deficits in front of my classmates.

That morning, during literature class, my teacher began by asking how long I intended to stay at the school. He was teaching a course on Shakespeare's *Twelfth Night*, and I found myself loathing English literature. French was one of the few classes where my anxiety level was manageable.

My French teacher was a young lady from Paris who was encouraging and supportive of my efforts. I earned excellent scores on her quizzes and the best overall grade in that class. I always looked forward to her lectures as a welcome reprieve on my somber days.

On a particular day, everything seemed to be going wrong. Hardly any teacher left without saying something demeaning about me. To add insult to injury, after class, a few classmates teased me about my lackluster performance. I became paranoid and self-conscious on campus, and I was gradually disintegrating into minute pieces, feeling weak, and sensing the last drops of courage and enthusiasm leaving my body. I seriously considered quitting to avoid the possibility of dismissal. That afternoon during siesta, I was lying in my bed and feeling listless when I remembered Grandma's words during challenging moments: "God gives strength."

I jumped up and headed to the chapel. On my knees, I prayed to God, my mom, and my ancestors for guidance, strength, hope, and everything I could think of. Afterward, I felt energized and determined to work harder. I had known things would not be easy at Sacred Heart College. I realized it would be better for me to adjust my sails than to fight and eventually capitulate to the whims of academic winds. Now was the time for action.

Sacred Heart College was located on a hill and surrounded by many bushes and trees. I decided to build a hideout in the bushes where I could go and study in private. I needed tranquility. Using sticks and bundles of grass, I constructed a shed between eucalyptus trees. From that time onward, I would go there each day in the afternoon to study during the three-hour recreation break. I designed a schedule for myself and followed it religiously and with calculated discipline. I spent a minimum of six hours each day studying. In the afternoon, I studied in the bushes; in the evening and at night, I would study either in the classroom, library, or dormitory. I studied the course material for the first and second years simultaneously. Half of my session was spent concentrating on fundamental concepts from the previous year that I had missed. Then I would devote the rest of my time to second-year coursework.

Frankly, I had neither time nor interest in extracurricular activities. During this time, I developed varying degrees of insomnia. Unfortunately, the library was closed every night at 9:00 p.m. It was a small, poorly stocked library with books donated by American and British philanthropists. If a student was interested in reading a particular book, he had to wait in line for weeks before he could borrow it. This did not sit well with me. I lacked patience, and time was of the essence. Therefore, I found a way to jimmy the windows surreptitiously at closing time and returned later under cover of darkness. Then, I would scale the wall, stealthily enter the library through the window, and help myself to any book of my liking. Afterward, I would read it rapidly for a couple of days before returning it at night. This desperate activity may have seemed daring, but it was also risky because had I been caught, the result would have been instant dismissal.

The Marist brothers who ran the school were strict disciplinarians. They were dedicated, passionate, driven teachers and missionaries whose primary objective was to enable us to have the best educational experience in a culturally sound and ethically grounded environment. All students were obligated to abide by a set of structured, formatted rules and regulations. Punishment for minor infractions was decisive and swift. Major infractions, such as causing bodily harm to a fellow student or inappropriate verbal or physical behavior, could lead to suspension—or worse, dismissal. To be a Sacred Heart student was such a coveted opportunity in the entire country of Cameroon that only rarely did students deviate significantly from the rules. Only the "best minds" were allowed to matriculate.

Sacred Heart students consistently outperformed all other secondary schools in the internationally recognized United Kingdom–based standardized examination General Certificate of Education (GCE). The examination encompassed every course in the secondary-school curriculum and was taken at the end of the fifth year, immediately after graduation. The quality of education at Sacred Heart College attracted sons of diplomats, ministers, expatriates, wealthy individuals, and the rest of us.

CHAPTER 32

Renaissance Man

SOON, I WAS BECOMING better adjusted in my study regimen. With this principled and disciplined strategy, my performance started to improve within a couple of months. A few teachers began to stand up and take notice of this transformation. Nevertheless, I was still obsessively concerned about the possibility of being dismissed at the end of the semester. I had difficulty falling asleep at night because of issues with anxiety and self-doubt. I engaged some of the brightest students in the class in a bid to learn more about their strategies for success. A couple of students, named David and Joachim, welcomed me openly and embraced me warmly and spontaneously during those initial months.

The most notable of the top students was George Akwa, an intriguing, enigmatic character whom I worshipped with gleeful envy. He demonstrated consistent excellence in every class. He was a serious, astute, focused, and articulate boy who was cognitively gifted, spoke with mature confidence, and exuded an aura of sophisticated elegance and contemptuous dismissal in a way that intimidated me and often left me grappling for words. He commanded the respect of every student on campus with his intellectual prowess and his pacific demeanor. Oh, how I admired him!

One day I approached him to solicit his assistance with my math and physics homework, and I was truly taken aback by the simplicity and genuine interest he demonstrated in helping me, along with his intrinsic ability to demystify complex mathematical and scientific concepts that had previously eluded my bcfuddled mind. George knew his stuff and was a veritable genius!

After our study session, he asked me if I would be interested in learning judo, and I consented. At once, he proceeded to show me his moves.

He was my hero, and it was humbling to be in his presence. I followed him everywhere like a faithful puppy and emulated his every move. The more time I spent with him, the quicker my self-confidence and self-esteem evolved. He did not appear to be from a rich family, although he had an uncle whom he talked about who was a big shot in the police department. He did not possess a variety of clothes like some of the other boys, but he looked prosperous and regal for reasons beyond materialism. He earned everyone's respect primarily because of his stellar academic performance and his comportment. The teachers were all in awe of him and treated him with deference. Rich students interacted with him like ignoble sycophants. He was a true Renaissance man who could hold his own in any discussion on a variety of topics, ranging from Newtonian physics to the complicated sociopolitical practices in apartheid South Africa.

George was an enviable charismatic vocalist who sang like James Brown and drove young girls to the extremes of audiovisual ecstasy. He could talk about the American prairie as though he had lived in Wisconsin. He could move nimbly and seamlessly from Voltaire to Socrates, Aristophanes to Plato, and Euripides to Bacon. A brief interaction with him often left me feeling so pulverized and inadequate that I would rush on to the library with a desperate need for encyclopedic resuscitation. George was an insatiable and voracious reader. He frequently lent me some of his books. (I had sense enough to resist the urge to steal any of them.) I would often find myself caught up in a reverie about him, wondering if I could ever know as much as he did, perform as well as he did, possess the degrees of ethical composure and celestial confidence he embodied, earn the level of respectability he enjoyed, and sleep as calmly as I imagined he did.

CHAPTER 33

Survival Strategy

ONE OF MY CLASSMATES, G. B., became curious about my usual whereabouts in the afternoons. I told him about my lair and even took him to see it, thinking that he might be motivated to construct one for himself. He was not a particularly serious student as he drank alcohol and smoked cigarettes surreptitiously and excessively. Fundamentally, I thought he was very smart but was undisciplined and unhinged, and he had difficulty applying himself to his schoolwork because of his many distractions. When he saw my hideout, he thought it was a great idea and stated that he intended to build one for himself.

I gave him some pointers on how to do it while suggesting that he should keep it confidential because I didn't want anyone else to know about my secret academic survival strategies. Unfortunately, one day I discovered that someone had defecated right in the middle of my hideout. Disgusted, I left once and for all. One night, I overheard one of the boys in the dormitory revealing how G. B. had proudly confessed to the malicious deed.

My first semester ended better than I had expected. As usual, George Akwa was the top student in a class of fifty students, and I was number fifteen. This made me feel safe because I knew I had avoided dismissal by the skin of my teeth, but still, I was not completely satisfied. My confidence was still somewhat lacking. My uncle George and my father celebrated my performance while encouraging me to work harder. That Christmas break, I had the feeling that everyone in the family was treating me as extraspecial. I guess it had more to do with my being a student at a prestigious school than the grades I had earned.

In African tradition, success is communal; therefore, the mere fact that I was enrolled at a good school was an ego boost to everyone connected to me. I was pleasantly surprised when total strangers would walk up to me and offer encouraging words for my studies. During that holiday, I enjoyed sashaying around the neighborhood in my distinctive school uniform. My only wish was that my mother could have be there to see me in it.

The next semester I began to feel more confident in my classes. Our chemistry teacher, Brother Norbert, a Scotsman, was quite vocal about his observations concerning my improved performance. He started to invite me to his office, which doubled as a bookstore, to assist me with any challenges I was experiencing with my coursework. One day, he predicted, I would excel in chemistry.

CHAPTER 34
No Tuition Money

ONE DAY, THE NEW school principal, Brother Justin, came to our classroom and requested to see me in his office. When I got there, he informed me that my tuition had not been paid and that he had no choice but to suspend me from school. Unfortunately, I had to leave the campus just when things were beginning to turn around with my studies. My family had only been able to pay the first-semester tuition and fees.

When I arrived at the village, my father did not appear to be surprised to see me, and he promptly gave me bad news. I could feel his pain. The only source of revenue he had was a small coffee farm. In those days, villagers grew coffee and sold their beans to a cooperative. It was more like slave labor because they were paid less than two dollars per drum-sized bag of coffee beans. They were being fleeced, and their compensation was incongruent with their labor. I watched my dad looking sad and wondering what he could do to obtain the money I needed for my tuition. I realized he was having difficulty maintaining eye contact with me. Then suddenly, he turned his back to me and remained silent for quite some time. When he did turn back around, I noticed his eyes looked bloodshot. They were flooded with tears. It was a very sad situation.

It is a sad and difficult situation for any parent who cannot provide for his or her children. I felt bad for him deep down in my heart. Having financial insecurities placed him in a terrible emotional quandary, especially after losing our mother and having to take care of the children alone. I told him that I would sell firewood, mangoes, pineapples, or anything to earn a little money. I also suggested that my uncles might be able to help. For two long weeks, I picked coffee, processed it with him, sold mangoes and pineapples, and solicited financial assistance from relatives. In the end, I was able to collect some money, and I reenrolled. I was then under tremendous pressure to catch up with my classmates. Two weeks was a long time to be away from classes, especially since I was still on probation and was studying under the dark cloud of potential dismissal.

A month later, I was again summoned to the principal's office. To my surprise, he informed me that the rest of my fees, including boarding fees, had not been paid. Once again, I was asked to leave the campus. Two weeks later, I was back with the money. The cost of my education was causing much grief and anxiety to my father and a few relatives. My younger brother Fru had just graduated from elementary school, and Dad could not afford to send him to secondary school. Therefore, he went on to a monastery far away to work on one of their farms. I felt bad for him because he was much too intelligent to discontinue his education. I became paranoid every time I saw my principal. I avoided him at all costs.

One day, I was surprised to hear that my hero, the genius George Akwa, had been suspended for failing to pay his tuition. He was out for quite some time. On one of our days off, I paid a visit to him at his uncle's house near a fishpond and empathized with his situation. I was surprised how well he was able to maintain his spirits despite the stress he was likely experiencing. Our lives were similar in many ways. Being poor was rough, and my experiences were teaching me lessons about life's challenges. I had to work harder so I could hopefully overcome financial insecurities in the future. Eventually, George did return with his tuition money.

During the last semester of my second year and after my third suspension for money reasons, I did something that even today defies my comprehension. I sat down, and I wrote a letter to the minister of education in Cameroon. In that letter, I told him that I was a student in good standing at Sacred Heart College and that my father was poor and had tremendous difficulty in paying my tuition. I added that my mother had died and left my father the sole burden of caring for my siblings and me and that he was burdened with health problems. I pleaded with the minister to offer me a scholarship. After mailing the letter, I knew the odds of hearing from him ever were slim to none.

The fears of suspension and dismissal became overbearing. I became more and more withdrawn and sad. I would experience bouts of depression in the middle of a lecture, and I would start to cry inconsolably. Some of the teachers would simply ask me to leave. Others would ignore me completely. One time, after I left the classroom in a distressed state, one of the boys named Bartholomew followed me of his own volition to console me. He kept asking me why I was crying, but I couldn't bring myself to tell him the reason.

Not long ago, one of my classmates from years past surprisingly asked me about what used to precipitate my crying episodes. I guess I was just missing my mother so much, especially because I was going through difficult times and feeling lonesome and insecure. On top of that, I couldn't help but think about my siblings and how difficult things were for them and wondering how their caregivers were treating them. My father's poor health and his financial desperation were significant overriding concerns as well. In short, I was beset with all these emotions plus the other stresses and burdens of school. Whenever my problems and concerns became unbearable, I would simply break down and cry. Crying was cathartic to me. I knew I could not go back to the village without an education. There were no better alternatives in my life, and I just kept praying that I would ride out the perpetual storms and be able to finally earn an education that might guarantee a better life for my family and me.

In the years when I was a student at Sacred Heart, I loved Wednesdays. Students were free to leave campus the entire afternoon on that day. I took advantage of this opportunity to spend the rest of the day, including a few hours at night, catching up with my schoolwork or learning new material. One of the methods I employed to enable me to stay awake and study for long hours was to keep my feet soaking in a bucket of cold water while studying. With this method, I discovered that I could go on studying continuously for up to six hours.

On a certain morning, I was summoned to the principal's office. *Not again!* I thought. What now? I hesitated to go, but I had no choice. When

I entered his office, he seemed to have been anxiously awaiting my arrival. Immediately, he informed me that I had been offered a full-tuition scholarship by the minister of education. I jumped for joy. There was no way for me to rapidly relay the news to my father and the rest of my clan. I had to wait until the following Wednesday to travel to the village.

That same week, I received another blessing from God. My aunt Lydia, who lived hundreds of miles away on a tea plantation where she worked, sent me a little money. This was a particularly touching surprise because she earned meager wages and was barely surviving on a plantation worker's salary of about two dollars a month. Immediately, I sent a letter thanking her for her kind gesture, and I reassured her that I would work hard to succeed. She was my late mother's older sister, and she considered me her son.

After going through a particularly rough year, I passed all the required examinations and was promoted to Form Three. I had disappeared successfully from the principal's radar screen. At the end of the first semester in Form Three, I had an even greater surprise. I was ranked number four in my class. Naturally, the top position was held by George. I was beginning to feel a visceral surge of confidence propelling me to even greater heights of determination. Suddenly, I was being invited by some of the previously snobbish boys to participate in their campus activities. Others who never would talk to me were beginning to engage me in conversation. All these changes, although encouraging and stimulating, did not in any way distract me from my principles. Although I was buoyed by my grades, strangely, I could not shake the deep sense of insecurity and inferiority stemming from having an economically challenged, rural, and provincial background.

As my grades were improving, I had to recognize the fact that all my classmates were intelligent boys who were also highly competitive. It would have been easy to slip up if I had lost my focus. Some of the boys performed wonderfully in specific courses. When I think of math, physics, and chemistry geniuses at that time, formidable characters like Charles Sine and Augustin Ayuk and many others come to mind. Certain students possessed specific talents in history, geography, literature, and language.

We had a couple of students with phenomenal musical talent. One of the most gregarious of the classmates I would occasionally socialize with was named Ali. His personality was most amiable and uplifting. I never saw him unhappy. He enjoyed music, had an encyclopedic knowledge of all the top music stars, and was a huge, unapologetic Jimi Hendrix fan!

CHAPTER 35

University Preparation

IT WAS DURING MY third year in secondary school that the idea of studying abroad began to consume me. That summer, with my father's encouragement, I started a pineapple orchard where I grew about 250 plants.
When they were ready to be harvested, I collected them and sold them in
the neighborhood and the city. Then I used the proceeds from this and
other commercial endeavors to purchase aerograms to communicate with
universities around the globe, requesting information about undergraduate
education. I wrote to schools in Japan, China, South Africa, Europe, and
especially North America.

After a while, I began to receive responses with frequency. The most
positive responses were from North America. Among most of my peers,
America was the most appealing destination for education. We had several
members of the Peace Corps engaged in community projects as well as
education in our region. During secondary school, they were our favorite
teachers. Their casual and personable attributes resonated with many of
the students. They often set aside time to teach us about American life and
culture. Additionally, I learned about America in history and geography
classes, as well as some of the movies we were shown on Saturday nights in
the campus cafeteria. We considered it a land of dreams and possibilities.

I was studying in the library one day when I found a book titled *US
Almanac*. Within it, in alphabetical order, were names and addresses of all
the colleges in the United States. I could not contain my excitement, so I
copied down about thirty college addresses, and during the Christmas break,
I sold pineapples from my farm to buy dozens of stamps and envelopes and

wrote letters to all the schools requesting application forms and scholarship information.

Although I still had a little over two years before graduation, my desire to go overseas for further studies was overwhelming. Cameroon did not offer enough opportunities for advanced education. There was only one university in the country at that time. Unfortunately, it barred students from matriculating directly from secondary school. They were required to attend two more years of higher school before they could be considered for admission. Many bright students also were turned down because of a limit in the number of available positions and for other subjective reasons.

On one occasion, I spoke with my dad about my desire to study in America, and I never will forget his reaction. His response was that it would serve me better to look for a nice job in the city after graduation. He went on to say that places like America were for the rich and not for poor people like us. So, I approached my uncle George for a second opinion. He was more optimistic, and he said that if America was where I wanted to go, I would. I used to sit for hours poring over names and addresses of American colleges, and it got to a point at which I knew what town, city, or state each college was located in. Sometimes I wrote to authors whose textbooks I had read, requesting information about educational opportunities at their institutions. My mind was so consumed with thoughts of studying somewhere on the planet that most of my conversations with friends were centered around global educational opportunities. Even my dreams were suffused with visions of living in a foreign country and attending university there.

From a financial standpoint, the chances of me leaving the country to study overseas were practically nil. At times, I would visit the campus chapel in the afternoon and pray to God for guidance and support to enable me to earn a good education overseas so that I could free myself and my family from the seemingly endless grip of poverty and destitution. The only mail that I began to receive was from various universities worldwide. Some college brochures arrived in Russian, Japanese, or Chinese, which I could neither read nor understand, so I would simply leaf through the pages and enjoy the pictures in them.

We had an Irish priest who taught English and who frequently invited some of the students to his residence. I had hoped to solicit his advice concerning educational opportunities in his native country, and on one occasion, he stopped me in the hallway and congratulated me on my performance on an essay quiz I had written. Then he hugged me and attempted to kiss me. Confused, I pulled away and took off running. Understandably, my grades in that English class suffered, and Ireland disappeared rapidly from my educational radar.

My physics teacher, Brother Douglass, was a young and bright role model. I believe he was from London. He was very pragmatic, did not inject any humor in his lectures, and taught his classes with incomparable passion. Because of him, I developed a liking for physics. At that time we had a new principal, Brother John Phillips, who taught French. Henceforth he became my greatest cheerleader.

In Form Four, I developed a habit of reading each topic in an assigned text and then reviewing much more advanced material on the same topic in the encyclopedia. Consequently, my responses on exams contained more detail than the teachers expected. This would almost invariably impress them and confuse some of my classmates. One time, I was amazed that even George Akwa the genius appeared to be puzzled with my responses to a teacher's questions in a particular class. Afterward, he approached me, seeking to know what extra books I had been reading. During that fourth year, I was more relaxed and enjoyed a much greater level of comfort in all my classes.

I must admit that my secondary-school experience was unbalanced. I never played any sports and did not participated in extracurricular activities. I lived from book to book. In a sense, the root cause of this attitude was the unique circumstance under which I had been admitted. I read everything I encountered in print. My midnight forages in the library continued almost to the end of my secondary-school experience. I read books on psychiatry, surgery, astrophysics, aeronautics, philosophy, and so forth. I was scarcely without a book. Books became my most trusted companions and often provided an escape from painful memories. During this time, I had a marvelous friend, Meg Kilo, who was a student at Our Lady of Lourdes, a regional prestigious secondary school for girls, who was an avid reader and a clear thinker with beautiful penmanship, and we would often write each other and share our mutual love for books.

Overall, Form Four was my best year. It was the year when I became more integrated with myself. At the end of that year, for the first time, I finished at the top of my class. Getting there had not been easy. It had taken a mixture of pain, deprivation, hard work, consistency, and discipline and the support of my peers, teachers, and well-wishers. The realization that I had actually displaced my hero George Akwa from the top position in the class was surreal. In actuality, from that moment onward until our graduation, he never again soared to the top position in our class. Nonetheless, to this day, the respect and admiration I had for him are undiminished, and I still believe he is a smarter man than *I*.

I was elected student body president (senior prefect) before the beginning of my final year in secondary school. During the intervening summer between Form Four and Form Five, I worked on my father's coffee farm. On the days when there was no farmwork to do, I locked myself up in a room and studied all day. Some of my cousins and siblings used to come knocking at the door, but I would refuse to open it. At times, a crowd would gather outside wondering loudly if I was OK. It was always heartwarming to hear my dad reassure everyone that I would be fine because I had good company—my books. He would always remind them that I was a "hardcore student" and "kind of different."

Finally, after the summer break, I returned to Sacred Heart College to begin my final year of studies. I was taking ten courses at that time, and I had precious little time for myself. Besides my schoolwork, I had leadership responsibilities as senior prefect, and I had to firm up my plans to study overseas. In deciding on the choice of university, I almost invariably gravitated toward the ones with lower tuition, as I anticipated having full financial responsibility for my education. I remember our Peace Corps volunteers telling us that America provided many opportunities for employment to anyone who was willing to work. There were several big-name American schools interested in my candidacy, but when I saw how much it would cost me to attend those schools, I shied away from them. Some of them had bizarre names like Duke, Yale, and Dartmouth. In those days, we were unaware of the reputational advantages these strange-sounding schools held.

However, schools with names that included "state college" or "state university" sounded more like real universities, especially to those of us in socialist systems, in which state institutions were often better than private ones. For this reason, and the lack of career guidance, I concentrated my efforts on state colleges and state universities. The vast majority of my teachers were Scottish, British, Irish, or French. They didn't speak favorably of American schools and preferred for me to seek educational opportunities in Europe, but I was unconvinced. I talked so much about the greatness of America that one of the junior students began to call me "the American."

CHAPTER 36

Graduation

EVENTUALLY, GRADUATION DAY ARRIVED! Ironically, that day I found myself not feeling much excitement about the conclusion of my tenure at Sacred Heart. I remember sobbing quietly at the end of that day and feeling deep sadness within my heart. My mother was not around to see what I had accomplished and to be proud of me. My grandmother was in the village and was too frail to attend the graduation ceremony. However, my father did come by himself, and it was a special moment for both of us.

Everyone assembled in the school auditorium, including local dignitaries, politicians, and tribal leaders. When it came to the awards ceremony, I received several prizes for outstanding academic performance, chemistry, biology, and leadership. Each time I made my way to the podium, my vision was blurry from silent tears. I guess I was subconsciously overwhelmed by all the struggles, the emotions—the challenging road my little heart had traveled during four years of an intense educational program.

I liked my graduation gifts, which were mostly science books. One of the prizes I received was a book written in French and donated by a Canadian French teacher from Quebec province. It was titled *Living Words of Abraham Lincoln*. I still don't understand why I was selected to receive that particular book. Afterward, a photographer had me pose for a few shots, after which I received hugs and congratulations from my dad. No big parties, balloons, music, and so on. It was just cut and dried, and before I knew it, it was over in about an hour.

As my dad and I were preparing to part ways so that he could head back to the village, one of my aunts made a surprise appearance. She had heard that I would be graduating, and she had left hastily to come and congratulate me. She hugged me, and we spoke for a minute or two. And then she said something to my dad about how terrible he looked and about how much weight he had lost since my mother's death. She remarked that everyone had been commenting about how dejected my father was still looking almost four years after my mom's death. Then she attempted to persuade my father to marry someone who could take care of him. After all, he was only about forty-five years old.

Without a second thought, he stated emphatically, "I had the best years of my life with Monica, and I'm prepared to live out the rest of my life with those wonderful and loving memories."

Wow! *How touching to hear such a testimonial of deep love*, I thought. Decades later, I reflected on that experience and appreciated the profundity and power of his words.

After my father left, I trudged back to my dormitory and dropped off my prizes before heading over to the library. I had less than two weeks left before the beginning of the GCE exams. Only fifth-year students were on campus because the semester had ended. In the days leading up to the examination, there was minimal camaraderie among the students. I had already set my sights on leaving the country, even though I did not know how I was going to do it. After the examination, I collected my belongings and returned to the village.

Eventually, I received admission letters from a few American colleges. Coppin State College in Baltimore, Maryland, was the least expensive school I could attend. They sent me important documents to enable me to apply for a US student-entry visa. The basic requirements for me to travel to the United States were a passport, an American student visa, a plane ticket, and money for tuition and living expenses. I had none of these items, and I lacked the funds to obtain any of them. No one in my family had the kind of money I needed.

Feeling overwhelmed and very much in need of a retreat, I decided to visit the Cistercian monastery where my younger brother was working at that time as a farmhand. There, I found endless inner tranquility. I stayed a couple of months, helping the monks in various ways and praying for spiritual guidance. At the beginning of August that year, I returned to my village, only to discover that the results of the GCE examination had already arrived from London and that I had passed all the ten courses I had taken. As exciting as this news was, my ebullience was soon dampened by the absence of tangible possibilities to enable me to reach my ultimate goal: America!

CHAPTER 37

Passport and Visa

AFTER GIVING MY SITUATION a lot of thought, I decided to draw up an action plan. First, I had to work on obtaining a passport. I approached a wealthy relative who was highly connected in the government, and I solicited his assistance with the matter. Initially, he gave me the runaround, but I harassed him incessantly, knocking at his door daily until he got tired of me. Through his connections, I was able to secure a passport, gratis. Armed with a passport and a college admission letter, I took off to the port city of Douala, where a US consular office was located, and submitted an application for an American student-entry visa. Unfortunately, when I got there, I was asked to produce a bank statement to show that I had the necessary financial resources to travel, live, and study in the United States. I had never even heard of a bank statement. Furthermore, nobody in my family had a bank account.

Frustrated, I returned to the village and approached individuals in my region who were considered rich and solicited their support in giving me a bank statement to enable me to satisfy the visa requirement, but I was turned down by all of them. What was particularly frustrating in my situation was that I had just graduated with one of the top scores in the GCE examination that year, yet many sons and daughters of prominent political bigwigs who had not performed as well had been awarded scholarships to study in Europe and America. Such unfair and corrupt activities were not uncommon. Many top-performing students who lacked major political or social connections simply languished in their villages and communities after graduating secondary school. On my part, I was unwilling to give up. Therefore, despite the lack of the financial document I was missing, I decided to give the visa matter one more try.

The main US Embassy was located in the capital city of Yaoundé. I asked my father for a little money to enable me to travel there and give it another try. A few days later, I boarded a crowded bus destined for the capital city. It was a long journey that took two days on treacherous, serpentine roads. At nightfall on the first day, we arrived on the banks of a river where the road ended, and we had to traverse an enormous river on a ferry to continue the journey. Unfortunately, we arrived after the ferry service had been stopped for the day. Therefore, we spilled out onto dense jungle vegetation on a steamy tropical night, and under a moonlit sky, we kept company with a million restless insomniac and inquisitive mosquitoes all night. I was anxious and could not relax or sleep, not just because of all the marauding mosquitoes, nameless arthropods, and curious creatures of the night—but mostly because I was afraid that I would be turned down again for a student visa.

The following day, when I arrived at the consular office in Yaoundé, I organized my documents so that my GCE exam report card was at the top, and immediately beneath it, my secondary-school transcripts, a college admission letter with the associated I-20 US immigration document, and finally my passport. When I returned to retrieve my documents at the end of the day, edgy and apprehensive, I was greeted by the consular secretary, a freckle-faced lady who at once congratulated me on my secondary-school performance. Then she wished me success in my educational pursuits before adding that the consular office had also stated that based on my secondary-school performance, I would do well in an American college. She made no mention of a visa. At that moment, I did not know if my visa application had been approved or rejected. However, I deduced rapidly from her demeanor and her words that good news awaited my itchy fingers beyond the passport cover. I thanked her profusely and took flight!

After making my exit and feeling secure that I was beyond earshot, I pried open the passport to reveal a document that has enabled me, decades later, to share my story with you: an F-1 US entry visa!

I released a bloodcurdling scream: "God is great! America, I am coming!"

I was on cloud nine. This had to be among the most delightful days in my life. I wasted no time flagging down a taxi to the bus station. Every few steps, I would crack open my passport to reassure myself the stamped visa was still there and was real. I had not eaten all day, but that did not matter. On that day, I was convinced that my life would forever be changed and the story of my future would have no chapter for poverty and destitution. I was on my way to America.

I would work hard to succeed, and I would lift the rest of my family out of poverty. All these thoughts were crisscrossing my mind, but I must say that I was not unmindful of the rough road ahead. (To this day, the prospects of that impetuous teenager embarking on a long journey alone, to a new and drastically different culture, with practically no money and no family, invariably make me shudder.) Even though I was no stranger to adversity and challenges, I knew that the road ahead would be a struggle.

Often my father would say, "Because the road to success and freedom is thorny, many stay put." He knew a thing or two about struggles. As a teenager, he had left his village all by himself in search of opportunities in another country, trekking for weeks through the jungle.

My circumstances growing up had made me quite a contemplative child, and all these consuming thoughts and scenarios were ironically important in helping me to strengthen my resolve and buttress my optimism, while still accepting whatever inevitable path lay ahead of me.

A day later, I arrived home early in the morning and roused my dad to share the good news with him. For the first time, I heard him inject a sense of humor into his words. He said that Monica's little boy had graduated from the secondary school of her dreams and would be traveling to the land of milk and honey.

In practically no time, the news had permeated the entire neighborhood. And then Dad called me to his room, and in a demure moment, he asked how I intended to make the distant journey to "the end of the seas." He had no clue where America was located in the universe. I had not given any thought to the airfare, although I had heard that the average cost of a one-way ticket to America was at least 150,000 francs, the equivalent of three hundred US dollars in today's currency. We looked around and could not think of anyone with that kind of money to help me.

Therefore, my father decided to do the unthinkable: he sold all his land and his house for about the cost of the ticket. I felt really bad for him. I always admired his decisiveness when faced with a challenge. Hence, in a similar vein and without missing a beat, I promised him that someday I would build him a new house. I must say I was taken aback by his spontaneous response. He simply said, "Build roads for others. Build houses for your siblings."

Our house was sold for the exact cost of a one-way ticket to New York City. I traveled to a coastal city, bought a ticket at a travel agency, and returned to the village armed with a college admission letter, a passport with a visa, and a plane ticket. One of my uncles, a retired police officer, advised me to limit my contacts and pretty much stay at home during the few days preceding my departure. He wanted to be sure that nothing happened to me.

CHAPTER 38

Goodbye

A FEW DAYS BEFORE I left the village, the entire family, including my uncles and grandparents, assembled to celebrate the great news and pray for my safety, security, and success. I was taken to a special family shrine where the elders communicated with our ancestors and implored them to grant me clear vision and strength. Then, when everyone reconvened in a large sitting area, the women began clapping their hands, dancing, and singing about "the people's king" who would be traveling to "the ends of the earth" on a great mission. As they sang, a basket was passed around for donations to support me on my journey.

And then, as if on cue, everyone stood still, and a deafening silence descended on the crowd. They laid hands on me, at which point my father revealed a prophecy I had been oblivious to. He thanked God and the ancestors for allowing everyone the opportunity to witness the unfolding of a prediction dating back to my birth at the Baptist Mission hospital, a day's journey from my village. He told a story about my mother suffering a near-fatal hemorrhage after I was born. Ten days later, she was discharged from the maternity ward. As she was leaving the hospital grounds, a stranger stopped her and asked if he could hold the baby. Such a gesture was a common tradition in our culture at that time. Mom obliged. The man held me for a brief period, looked at my mother, and told her that her child would someday travel far away to the ends of the earth and would return and do great things. Then he handed the newborn back to its mother and vanished.

When Dad was done talking, there was not a dry eye in the room. On my part, I recognized that what was transpiring in that room on that day was transcendental and beyond symbolism, for it represented a unique blend of metaphysics and spirituality. I was uplifted by a force that can be described best by the concept of the *mysterium tremendum*, as defined by the celebrated religious thinker Rudolf Otto. That day I felt as if I were shedding old garments and donning new ones that were appropriate for the new phase in the life I was entering. A new level of responsibility was being thrust upon my shoulders. As the only one in the family who had attained significant heights in education and the first person who would be embarking on an even higher educational mission, I knew that the expectations for my future, as a leader and a pillar for the family, were enormous. As I looked across the room, I realized that everyone present had played a role in helping me to achieve my goals.

In keeping with our tradition, parents and elders took turns making speeches and giving advice and encouragement. Uncle George's brief comments were powerful: "Son-of-the-land, we send you to the future. Never shall you walk alone. When you scale the hills and mountains, when you cross the rivers and oceans, fret not. We walk with you."

As I look back over so many years, what I find particularly poignant is that everyone present that day talked about the importance of helping others and recognizing that the baton had been passed. My father often said that one must *never travel to heaven alone.* Therefore, if I became successful, I had a moral responsibility to help others to be successful.

Despite being poor people, no one among those assembled that day made any personal requests from America. Ultimately, about ten thousand francs (approximately twenty dollars) were collected. After everyone left, my father gave me the money, clasped his hands around mine, and once again prayed for God's guidance and a successful journey. Furthermore, he reminded me that the financial support I had just received was "seed money," and he expected it to yield a bountiful harvest for everyone. Then he hugged me, and we stood there for some time weeping. My siblings surrounded us in a circle, and we shared a collective hug and a few loving moments. On that day, I promised to take care of them and their offspring in the future.

On August 25, 1974, the yard in front of our house was teeming with men, women, and children from the village. They had all come to wish me a safe journey. Once again, rivers of tears flowed copiously. I began to experience lonesomeness and a high level of separation anxiety as I struggled to reconcile my aspirations for personal growth with my acute fears of social dissociation from the harmonious sanctuary where I had been nurtured. The village that knew me before I knew myself and protected me, embraced me, showered me with love and affection for over fourteen years was sending me to a foreign land for a purpose greater than my individual needs. My sisters, with tear-flooded eyes, were staring at a brother they barely knew. My brother was avoiding eye contact with me, but I knew the pain of separation in the very depths of his heart was just as intense as it was in mine. It would be inevitably exacerbated by distance, time, and circumstances. I had never really been "one" with my siblings. Life had placed me on a separate trajectory, away from them. At that moment, I found myself yearning for the elusive sibling bond between us that chemistry, math, physics, and a dozen other academic coconspirators had disrupted. Furthermore, the cord that connected me to the village placenta was being severed.

"It is time to say goodbye. I must leave you," I said with sadness in my heart.

Grandma reached out and held my hand. Her gait was unsteady, and her grip had lost its vigor to age and the perpetual ravages of leprosy. "My child, may you engage every situation on your journey with love," she said while weeping. Then, reluctantly, she released my hand. Again I sobbed as my dad was escorting me to the taxi.

With both arms jutting out of the taxi's rear window, I waved slowly and continuously at everyone, wondering if we would ever see each other again. Gradually, in the distant horizon, the gigantic eucalyptus and mango trees that defined the borders of my home began to fade away. They were replaced with a winding, weather-beaten reddish road riddled with a million puddled potholes struggling to accommodate the idiosyncratic whims of a dozen temperamental taxi drivers all hurtling toward the Atlantic coast, a couple of hundred miles away from our beloved mountainous grasslands. My mind was still lingering among my family members and others in that yard when a drizzle ensued, and I became acutely aware of parts of my anatomy that had been forgotten outside the taxi interior. Slowly, I retrieved my arms, and I stopped waving at space. After rolling up the car window, I settled in for a bumpy ride, literally and figuratively, to the international airport in Douala.

On the way, I stopped in Victoria for the night, and the next day I visited my friend Meg Kilo, who was on vacation in a small town near Victoria where her aunt lived. Meg was a marvelous individual and a trusted friend. We used to spend hours discussing literature, history, science, and social issues. I was particularly drawn to her compassion and simplicity. Although she was from a prominent family in the country, neither she nor her family members ever made an issue of our socioeconomic disparities. Her mom was always loving, doting, and kind to me. I was her son indeed. Therefore, on the day of my departure, August 28, 1974, I took a taxi to see her. After we shared a hasty breakfast, she offered to accompany me to the airport. I had never seen a plane, and I didn't know what to expect. I felt awkward with all the daunting formalities: luggage check-in, immigration control, and customs. Consequently, I was profoundly appreciative of her assistance in guiding me through these and alleviating my stress.

CHAPTER 39
Welcome to Paris

ULTIMATELY, IT WAS TIME to depart Cameroon. Once again there were more hugs and tears. I stayed close to the other passengers as we traversed the tarmac and scaled an almost vertical staircase into the Boeing 737 Cameroon airliner en route to Paris with a connection via Air France to New York City.

A lovely flight attendant helped me to my seat and asked if I was OK. I must have looked confused, intimidated, and just plain scared. To me, it was a new experience and a different world. When we were asked to attach our seat belts, I did not know what to do. I fiddled with the belt for several minutes while trying not to look ignorant or provincial. Everyone around me appeared to have a higher level of comfort with everything. Noticing my predicament, a pleasant lady across the aisle from me undid her seat belt and came to my rescue. "Young man," she said, "I can help you." Then, she attached the seatbelt for me. Sheepishly, I thanked her.

To make matters worse, the flight attendant started to make some kind of announcement about "in the event of a drop in cabin pressure" and "in case of an emergency water landing," and I was beginning to have second thoughts about the trip. However, it was too late, and the plane was already taxiing. I had read about plane crashes, and the thought of it made me even more nervous. After we were airborne, the same flight attendant returned with a cart filled with drinks and offered me some, but I refused. Then she returned with another cart filled with food, and I refused that offer as well. She pleaded with me to have something to eat, but I told her I was not hungry. Truthfully, I did not want to spend any part of the twenty dollars I had on me. I knew I would need it in America. Of course, I would discover sometime later that food and beverages were included in the airfare.

Several hours into the flight, my bladder was pleading to be emptied. Not wanting to disobey the seat belt law, I stayed put and continued to suppress the urge to urinate. Besides, I knew I could not open the airplane door or the window to urinate. I had no idea they had toilets on a plane. Back home, on long trips in taxis and buses, drivers stopped intermittently so the passengers could go into the bushes to relieve themselves. There were no public facilities in those vehicles and no rest stops with bathroom facilities on the roads.

When the plane arrived in Paris, I felt like my bladder was on the verge of rupture. I asked and was directed to a restroom, where I urinated until I felt dizzy. I was informed by an attendant at the Air France counter that I would be receiving a hotel voucher and that I would be taking a noon flight the next day, August 29, for New York City. After I received the voucher, I was directed to a bus stop nearby. As I was walking to the designated location, the kind lady who had helped me with my seat belt walked up and asked where I was headed. When I told her, she offered to give me a ride to her home to have dinner with her family and then drop me off at my hotel afterward. I accepted. As soon as we got on the road, I began to experience sensory overload. I had never seen so many cars, people, houses, and lights! It was just a confusing mess.

After dinner, I was sitting in her living room when she walked up to a large box in the corner and flipped the switch, and all of a sudden, images of a choir appeared. Finally, I was witnessing the miracle of television I had read so much about in secondary school. After we watched a few shows, she gave me a ride to Hotel Astoria. I had never been to a hotel, let alone slept in one. She dropped me off at the hotel entrance and gave me her address before disappearing into the street jungle. I grabbed my luggage, walked up to the receptionist hesitantly, and after presenting the hotel voucher in my passport, I signed a couple of papers and received my room key and a recommendation to take the elevator to my room.

Elevator? I had never seen one of those. I read the sign *Ascenseur* (French for "elevator") above what looked like a door and walked up to it while trying not to appear ignorant, and I stood there for a while, waiting for something to happen. I had checked in late, and no other guests were arriving at that hour. Then a bespectacled, wiry-looking Frenchman walked up, reached out, and touched a button. Voilà! The magic door opened. After stepping in, he held the door and asked if I wanted to join him. I hopped in promptly after him, smiling nervously before thanking him. I felt some movement, and up we went! When it stopped, my companion stepped out with a "*Bonne nuit*" ("Good night") and continued whistling a tune as he disappeared down a hallway leading from the elevator.

Then the door closed spontaneously, leaving me in deafening silence. I waited a while, hoping that it would now take me to my floor as it had the Frenchman. I coughed nervously and sat down on my suitcase. Still no action. After some time, it began to move in a downward direction. This gave me some relief because I assumed it was now going to take me to my floor. To my surprise, the door slid open at the entrance level, and an older lady stepped in. "*Ça va?*" she inquired.

"*Ça va bien*," I responded.

The elevator took off again and stopped on a remarkably similar floor as the one where it had deposited the gentleman. She disappeared, and the door closed. I began to wonder what the previous passengers had done to trigger a response from the elevator. A few moments passed before it started to move again downward. Then it stopped, and after a brief moment, it began to climb. The door opened, and the same lady who had just exited reentered. This time she was wearing a jacket and looked at me intensely before asking if I needed any help. I told her I was just trying to go to my room, but the elevator was not being cooperative. Then I showed her my room key. She turned around and hit a button on the numbers panel, and the elevator hiccupped a second before moving. Once it stopped, she announced my floor and instructed me to look for my room number down the hallway on a door. And then she said, "Welcome to Paris!"

I located my room, walked in, and dropped my suitcase on the floor. I was tired and frustrated with myself. The room was immaculate. I had never seen anything like it. There was a world map on the wall, and when I looked at it and realized the great distance between Paris and my hometown,

I began to feel a nostalgic yearning for my family. And then, when I looked across the vast expanse of the Atlantic Ocean, I was reminded that I still had a long way to go. I had never felt so alone and isolated. I sat down on the bed and began to weep. I knew I could not turn back, but I wondered if I could ever become accustomed to all the new and confusing things and situations I was experiencing. My senses were becoming overloaded. The mere depth of technology I had just confronted within twelve hours of leaving my homeland was intimidating and disabling. I stood up, still sobbing, and walked up to a door that led to a small bathroom.

My stomach was growling, and I felt an urge to relieve myself. So I hopped onto the toilet seat like I normally did in the latrines back home, squatted, and did my business. Then I waited for several frustratingly unnerving minutes for some kind of automatic flush event. While sitting there scratching my head, I reminded myself of the recent elevator experience. There had to be a trigger spot for the flushing mechanism somewhere on the unit. After stepping down, I searched all around it, even getting on my knees to peer at the underside of the seat assembly, but I found nothing! In desperation, I looked upward at the ceiling and found no rope or chain to pull and activate a flush. My self-esteem had already suffered a beating in the elevator, and I did not want a repeat of that in the bathroom, especially if someone were to come in the morning and see what I had left in the toilet bowl.

After several nerve-racking moments, I stood back and carefully examined the toilet setup. Then I saw a button that was flush with the top surface of the rectangular, boxy upper part of the bowl. Out of curiosity, I reached out and touched it and—*bam!* I was startled by a sudden cascade of water from somewhere into the bowl, flushing away its contents. I had just discovered how to flush a toilet after squatting on it as I had always done in the village, without leaving footprints. In a strange way, I felt proud of myself. Weeks later in America, I would discover that a seated position was the proper way to use that type of toilet.

It was the softest bed I had ever slept on. The pillows were heavenly. I woke up the next morning with just enough time to take a quick shower. This experience turned out to be less tasking and traumatic than the toilet one. I was famished, so I got dressed and took the elevator to the first-floor dining room, and I raided a basket of pastries, flushing them down with several glasses of milk and juice before catching a bus to the airport. That morning, the airport bus took us through parts of the city that I recognized from history and geography classes in secondary school. I saw Place de la Concorde, Arc de Triomphe, and les Champs-Élysées. How exciting!

In the afternoon on August 29, I boarded an Air France flight to New York. Seating next to me was an American student returning home after a year in Europe. When lunch was being served, he insisted that I eat something. I told him I was not hungry, but I was too embarrassed to tell him that all I had in the world was twenty dollars that I was afraid to spend. I was enjoying a conversation with the student when the pilot announced that we would be landing at JFK in a few minutes. At that point, my anxiety level soared again. I was realistic about the challenges ahead of me as I knew all along that life in America would not be a cakewalk because I did not have enough money. I just didn't know how much pain I would have to endure, but it didn't matter anyhow. I found solace in two words: "hope" and "determination."

CHAPTER 40

America!

"I AM IN AMERICA!" I whispered loudly to myself as if to reassure myself of a dream that had suddenly become real. After we disembarked, I retrieved my luggage, cleared customs and immigration, and exchanged my money for US dollars. I had been given a phone number to reach Sylvester, a relative in Brooklyn, so I asked the lady at the information desk for assistance in making a phone call. She directed me to a pay phone, but her speech was too fast for me to understand. I kept asking her to repeat what she had just said, but her responses were not helpful. So, I grabbed my suitcase and trudged a short distance to a row of public phones on the wall.

Although I had never used such a contraption, I read the instructions on it, lifted the handset, and dialed. I was interrupted by a voice telling me to drop a coin in the slot. Even though I had just changed my money to dollars, I was not familiar with American currency. Therefore, I stood still for a minute, trying to decide if I should return to the information counter for a more perplexing dialogue or seek help elsewhere. In an instant, and out of nowhere, a pleasant gentleman appeared and asked me if I needed help. I told him I had just arrived from Africa and was trying to reach someone for assistance. I added that not only did I not know the currency, but I was also unfamiliar with the pay phone. He appeared to be genuinely concerned. I showed him my money, and he said he had change for me. Reaching in his pocket, he came up with a few silver coins and gave them to me in exchange for my bills. Then he dropped another coin into the phone and dialed the number I gave him. *How kind!* I thought. I thanked him generously, and he disappeared.

Sylvester answered the call and instructed me to walk out of the terminal and take a taxi to 590 Flatbush Avenue in Brooklyn, where he would be waiting for me. I stepped out of the TWA terminal at JFK into a congested, perplexing melee, with a sea of cars and humans justling for position in the road abutting the terminal. Everything was moving at lightning speed, faster than I had just experienced in Paris. Cars were honking everywhere, and people seemed to be constantly yelling at nothing. Overwhelmed, with a pounding heart, I ran back into the terminal, where I took a few moments to compose myself before stepping outside again. Despite having learned English in school for many years, I had no idea what anybody was saying. I was about to turn around again and seek refuge in the terminal before someone yelled out, "Hey, bro. Need a taxi?"

He was holding the door open for me, and he looked like Jimi Hendrix. I paused and turned slowly around to face him. Feeling reassured by the look of familiarity he represented, I hopped into his cab. Instantly, he grabbed my suitcase, popped open the car trunk, and stowed it. Something about his demeanor and disposition gave me comfort.

As we drove off, soul music blasting from his car radio, I settled down and tried to relax but couldn't. He wanted to know where I was heading, and I gave him a piece of paper with the address of my destination, and he asked me where I was from. "Africa!" I said enthusiastically, adding that it was my first time in America and that I had come to attend college in Baltimore.

To this, he responded, "You look too young to be going to college." When we arrived at my destination, he told me the fare would be five dollars. I handed him whatever coins I had remaining after the phone call. He looked at me with a puzzled grin.

"Man, this ain't no five dollars. This is one dollar!"

I was just as puzzled as he was. I explained to him that I had arrived with money in a different currency, which I had exchanged and received twenty dollars, and that a kind gentleman at the airport had offered me change for that amount of money so that I could make a phone call. I had no more money left.

"Man, welcome to New York, bro. You just got ripped off! Never mind. It's on me. Bye."

On that note he took off and left me standing there, feeling like an idiot. The gentleman at the airport had seemed so nice. I had trusted him, and I was understandably disappointed with his actions. Back in my village, people went out of their way to provide honest assistance to strangers.

Sylvester came outside and welcomed me to New York. I told him I had not eaten anything on the flight, and I was hungry. For this reason, he took me to a restaurant around the corner, where he bought me my first hamburger in America and sat back to watch me consume it. I proceeded to eat the sandwich in a piecemeal fashion: first the bread and then the tomatoes, lettuce, and finally the beef. I was starving, but for some reason, the sandwich did not taste like real food and smelled like murky, muddy swamp water. I had never tasted anything like it. He laughed hard and proceeded to demonstrate how to eat a sandwich. This was my initiation into the American culinary culture. To wash it down, I slurped down a medium cup of vanilla milkshake, which was way too sweet for my liking.

Early the next day, I left to catch a bus to Baltimore, my final destination. He gave me instructions on how to take the subway to the Port Authority bus station. This was baptism by fire! After walking me to the entrance of the subway, he wished me good luck and hugged me, and I descended into the mysterious bowels of a restless city.

My suitcase was huge and heavy. It contained my books and a few clothes. I was having difficulty lugging it across tunnel walkways and up staircases. At one point, I was struggling with it, sweating profusely, and having difficulty keeping pace with everyone around me, when it looked like my train was about to leave. Out of nowhere, a kind young Black man walked up to me: "Come on. I'll help you." He lifted my luggage effortlessly and hauled it onto the passenger car as I scampered along after him. When I told him where I was from and where I was heading, he offered to accompany me to the Port Authority bus station. After wishing me a safe trip, he offered me twenty dollars and wished me well.

With some of this money, I was able to purchase a one-way Greyhound bus ticket from New York City to Baltimore, Maryland. The memory of that man still leaves me with renewed faith in the future of humanity. His warmth and kindness left me feeling so much better about America, especially after having been ripped off on my arrival at JFK. He appeared from nowhere, did a great deed, and then disappeared. He left neither name nor number—just his heart and compassion.

The journey to Baltimore seemed to take forever. While sitting on the bus, I began to wonder where I would stay upon my arrival in Baltimore since Coppin State College was a commuter school. The only thing I had was the name and phone number of the foreign-student adviser at Coppin, Ms. Robinson.

CHAPTER 41

YMCA

AFTER THE BUS ARRIVED at the terminal, I went to a phone booth and called Ms. Robinson. It was Friday, August 30, and when she answered the phone, she reminded me that the summer break had not ended, the school had no dormitories, and that the best advice she could give me was to stay at the YMCA until the start of school. I had a few dollars left. I used them for a taxi ride to the YMCA around the corner from the bus station. At check-in, confused and desperate, I informed the attendant that I did not have any money but that I was expecting some. I didn't know what else to tell him. Despite the puzzled look on his face, he grabbed a room key and escorted me upstairs to a tiny room with a sink. There was a common bathroom around the corner.

I shut the door and walked across to a large glass window. I was on the eighth floor, and I had never been that high up in a building. The street below was bustling with activity. I had finally made it to Baltimore, my destination, but I couldn't shake off an anticlimactic feeling consuming me. The world surrounding me was oblivious to my predicament and desperation. I had no money and no idea where I would be going after overstaying my welcome at the YMCA. I was just a kid, barely a teenager, alone in a confusing megapolis—and scared! I drank gulps of water from the room sink and collapsed on the twin bed, wondering how and where I would be able to get my next meal. Then I took a mental flight starting from my childhood and family, through so many trials, tribulations, struggles, wishes, and hopes in Africa, and across the ocean to the YMCA. I wondered if it had been worth the suffering. I began to wonder if my destination was a paradoxical paradise.

For two days, I kept to myself in that room, drinking only water from the sink and leaving only when I needed to use the bathroom around the corner. I had nothing to eat, and I was too scared to leave the floor or to go downstairs—or anywhere for that matter! After two days of self-imposed isolation, I heard a knock on my door, and when I opened it, I was greeted by a young man who introduced himself as a college student at Morgan State who was working part-time at the YMCA. He had just punched in to begin his shift when he saw my name on the guest list and discovered that I was from Cameroon and spoke French, and he was interested in practicing his French with me.

At that point, he reached out to shake my hand, and he welcomed me to Baltimore. I held on to his hand and wouldn't let go of it. I had not seen or touched a human being in a couple of days. He asked me if I would like to eat lunch, and I obliged, adding that I had not eaten in a few days. When he heard that, he took me to a McDonald's restaurant a few blocks away and asked me what I wanted to eat. I remember looking up at a panel above the register and not recognizing any of the menu items. Recognizing my confusion, he interjected and bought me a pie, a cheeseburger, and a drink.

We had a wonderful conversation over lunch. He was curious, inquisitive, remarkably fluent in the French language, and possessed an amazing wealth of knowledge about world history and geography. After lunch, we went for a walk in downtown Baltimore, and I remember feeling delighted and secure with him. I held onto his hand firmly as we walked all over the city. The overwhelming feeling of isolation that I had been experiencing a few days earlier was completely gone. While strolling in the street, he asked me if I had enough clothes. I told him that I had brought a few but that I had filled my suitcase mostly with my trusted companions—books! (Today I chuckle at the thought of this because, with so many books in America, my action was tantamount to "carrying coal to Newcastle"!). On that note, he took me to a department store, where he bought me a few shirts. Finally, we walked back to my room, and he left for the day. He had been so unbelievably kind to me that I was sad to see him go. He promised to return the next day and to bring me something to eat. When he did return, he brought me a peanut butter and jelly sandwich, which I adored. Henceforth, at the end of each shift, he would take me for a walk, and we would enjoy exciting conversations in French. A few days after I met him, he sat down with me to educate me about American culture and currency. One day, after thanking him profusely for all the kindness he had shown me, I asked to know his name. "Billy," he said.

Billy the angel!

Not long after that, one of the managers of the facility came to my room and requested payment for my lodging. I told him I had no money, but I promised him that I would, even though I didn't know where I would be getting it. I pleaded with him to allow me to stay a little longer, and he agreed. Unfortunately, he came back every day to remind me about my debts, and I became convinced he would have me deported. I expressed my concerns to my new friend Billy because he knew I did not have any money. I asked him where I could find a job to support myself, but he had no idea about that.

I was becoming increasingly desperate. I thought I could maybe do dishes in a restaurant and hopefully earn a little money to sustain myself. A couple of days went by without any word from him. I had no way to contact him, and I was concerned. As a consequence of my predicament, I began to experience insomnia. Since I depended completely on Bill for nutritional sustenance, I had nothing to eat during his absence and did not know what to do.

Soon, college would be opening, and I needed to register, but I had no money. I didn't even know where the campus was located and had no means of getting there! I had reached the nadir of my sufferings, and I was mired in hopelessness. So, I went down to the manager and told him I was prepared to leave the YMCA. Confused, he asked to know where I was planning to go, and I said I did not know. He must have sensed my desperation. I just wanted to leave the building and walk the streets. I had neither plans nor objectives for myself. He encouraged me to stay put, and I returned to my room and curled up in bed, thinking about my mom, dad, and family. I cried my eyes out to relieve my depression and loneliness.

In the middle of this conundrum, I gave pause to my troubled mind and got up to use the bathroom. In the hallway, I encountered an older gentleman who stopped and abruptly proceeded to strike up a conversation with me. He wanted to know where I was from. I appreciated his interest in my background, and I told him I had just arrived from Africa to attend college. Then he complimented me, saying that I was a handsome boy and that I was built like an athlete. He said I had beautiful eyes, beautiful teeth, and an attractive smile. He was heaping so many compliments on me in rapid succession that I began to feel ill at ease with him. However, I was just beginning to adapt to a new culture and new experiences, and I found many of them to be perplexing.

Suddenly, he invited me to his room, which was across the hall from mine, and I agreed without forethought. He appeared to be unoffending and genuinely interested in learning about me, my country, and my culture. As we talked, he became increasingly animated and asked to touch my hair. He wanted to know if I would allow him to comb it out in a big Afro style, and I consented reluctantly. Initially, he massaged my scalp. Then he got a hairbrush, and while standing behind me, he proceeded to brush and comb my hair while commenting on its silky texture. I was feeling relaxed, so I closed my eyes to relish the moment and enjoy the unsolicited scalp massage I was receiving while being intrigued by his animated style of conversation. Then when he walked around to face me while still combing my hair, I opened my eyes and was aghast at what I was witnessing. His pants were missing, and he was sporting an erection. I froze.

Suddenly, I became panic-stricken and consumed by fear and confusion. Reacting spontaneously, I jumped up and bolted out of his room. I could hear him saying something in an accent I was yet unfamiliar with, but I didn't pause to listen. I dashed back into my room, slammed the door shut, and locked it as rapidly as my tremulous fingers could manage. My heart was thumping faster than my brain could process the bizarre event that had just unfolded. I stood by the door for a minute in an acute confused state. And then slowly, I took a few steps forward and paused for a second, not exactly knowing what to do. After slumping into my bed, I heard a knock at my door. Still frightened, I refused to answer. Strangely, he asked if I would accompany him for a walk. Later on, he returned and slipped a note beneath my door on which he had written his home address and phone number. Feeling terribly scared, isolated, lonely, and vulnerable, I stayed in my room the rest of that day and the entire night. I never saw him again after that incident.

Early the next morning, I began to feel lost and down in the dumps, with no one to turn to and nowhere to go. I had an urge to use the bathroom, but I was afraid to walk out into the hallway for fear of crossing paths with that gentleman or anyone else. When I couldn't hold back any longer, I pressed my ear against the door and listened for any activity or movement in the hallway. Not sensing any apparent danger, I dashed out quickly, relieved myself in a hurry, and returned to the safe sanctuary of my room. Another concern nagging me incessantly that morning was the fact that I might be tossed out in the street because I had not paid my room bill. I had stayed up the previous night, singing and praying. Happily, later that morning, Billy stopped by with a sandwich and informed me that he intended to share my plight on the college radio station to see if someone in Baltimore would be willing to take in a homeless college student from Africa.

CHAPTER 42

Sam to the Rescue

A WEEK WENT BY, and one evening, I heard a knock on the door. An employee informed me that someone was waiting for me downstairs. I couldn't imagine who would be looking for me. Maybe he had the wrong guest, I thought. Nevertheless, I was curious and hopeful. When I got there, I saw a fashionably dressed gentleman who introduced himself as Samuel Asongwed. He had heard about me and my misfortune and had come to rescue me. He asked me to go back to my room and collect my luggage. Then he took care of my bill and helped me with my luggage, and we left the building. *Another angel!* I thought.

He didn't say much. His car was parked outside. As we approached it, the passenger door swung open, and a tall gentleman stepped out and pushed his seat forward so that I could slide into the rear seat. He introduced himself as Wali, a physician at Johns Hopkins Hospital. I was struggling to contain my excitement. In an amazing stroke of serendipity, a few years back, I had heard of a gentleman called Wali who was on vacation in Africa and who had earned both PhD and MD degrees. At that time, I had never heard of or met anyone with two doctoral degrees. I remember telling a friend that someday, I intended to earn two doctorates. There I was, sitting right behind him in the same car! After that initial encounter, I did not see him again until exactly twenty years later, when we crossed paths again at a different level on a different continent.

After a short ride, Sam dropped him off at his apartment near Johns Hopkins hospital before heading to his apartment about ten miles from Baltimore. That night, at his one-bedroom apartment, he placed a few

sheets and a pillow on the couch to make a comfortable bed for me. I was touched by his kindness and concern for my well-being, and I felt secure with him. He didn't ask me any questions! The next day, he came home with a brand-new set of pajamas for me. It was the first pair I had ever owned, and I couldn't contain my excitement.

A few Sundays after I left the YMCA, I told Samuel that I wanted to go to church, any church. There was an entire street filled with churches about four miles from his apartment. After scanning the yellow pages, he was able to identify a prominent Catholic church on that strip. Unfortunately, he had call duty at the hospital that day and could not take me there. Therefore, he showed me where to take a bus to the church he had selected. When I arrived, only a few congregants were seated. So, I took a seat on an empty row and waited patiently for the service to begin. Shortly, the rows in front of me were filling up rapidly. I didn't understand why no one else was sitting in my row. I got up to receive Communion, and on the way back to my seat, I realized that the church was practically full, and I was puzzled to see that mine was the only empty row. Furthermore, I was somewhat surprised when I realized that I was the only Black person among the congregants, especially since I had seen many Black people in the streets of Baltimore.

Later that night, I shared this experience with Sam, who always displayed active listening skills. He paused for a while before he responded by giving me a historical perspective, starting from the days of American slavery and the complicated relationship between the races in America. Then he discussed the civil rights movement and its impact on race relations in American society. He spoke objectively, without injecting any feelings of hate or animosity toward anyone, and he amazed me with his optimism about the future of human relations in America. In conclusion, he attributed such actions (as I had experienced) to ignorance. In essence, he condemned hateful and ignorant behaviors but not the perpetrators. I was beginning to appreciate that the spectral range of my education in America would not be confined to the study of atoms and molecules. My global experience would have to be holistic to be meaningful and would have to include a vital band on humanism and related psychosocial idiosyncrasies.

Growing up in an African village, a homogeneous world, I never had any reason to think of myself as a Black person. However, for the first time in my life, I realized I had color. In Cameroon, color was an irrelevant factor in interactions among us and between us and our European, American, and other expatriate friends. We sat next to each other in religious worship and social gatherings. Foreigners from Europe, America, Russia, and Asia whom I met in Cameroon were generally kind, peaceful, loving, and generous. Understandably, I had just arrived in a more complex heterogeneous world that required a real paradigm shift in my thinking about human relations.

CHAPTER 43

Coppin

WHEN SCHOOL STARTED, SAM drove me to the college campus so that I could register for my classes. It was a small, friendly college campus where I felt entirely comfortable on my first day and was embraced by everyone at every station of the registration process. I did not have any money for tuition, and to my greatest surprise, I was offered the option of paying by installments. At Coppin, there was a strong emphasis on education and a true sense of community. On-campus support systems were readily available and left no doubt in my mind that the school was motivated to support every student to achieve success.

Each morning, Samuel left early and dropped me off on campus before proceeding to Provident Hospital in Baltimore, where he worked. He always gave me lunch money, and whenever he had on-call duties, he would give me bus fare. On several occasions, I took the wrong bus and wound up somewhere in Maryland and had to rely on the kindness of strangers to redirect me home. Eventually, Sam decided that my commute was too hard on me, and we moved to a different apartment in the Woodlawn area, which was closer to my college, with convenient access to city buses. He bought a checkered sleeper couch for me. His kindness knew no limits.

On one occasion, I decided to walk home from school and took over two hours to get there, walking on a convoluted road through a dense forest. When I proudly announced to Sam what I had accomplished, I was admonished instead and told about the many murders reported in those woods. One day, after I had lived with him for several months, he asked to know my background. His primary motivation all along had been to provide me safety and security in every way possible so that I could concentrate on my education without a lot of anxieties and worries.

At Coppin State College, I majored in chemistry. My courses were not challenging because I had taken most of them in secondary school. My instructors were all very supportive, and I earned tuition money by working in the tutorial center, where I assisted students with math, chemistry, physics, and French. One of my favorite classmates, Shiminesh, was from Ethiopia. She was extremely bright, and like me, she was from a poor family. We were laboratory partners, and we shared a common desire to study medicine after college. I had tremendous respect for her academic prowess, and I was convinced she was smarter than I. Therefore, we were in a state of perpetual competition with each other for the top grade in a chemistry class that was taught by a brilliant, engaging teacher, Dr. McDermott.

Unfortunately, one late night, she was murdered at a bus stop in Baltimore as she was returning home from a nighttime job. I was so devastated by her sudden death, and I often imagine the immense emotional anguish her family must have experienced from her senseless murder. The students contributed about four thousand dollars to ship her body back to Ethiopia. One of the things that baffled me the most at that time was the high incidence of violent crime in the city of Baltimore. Growing up in Cameroon, I never heard of a single case of murder.

One of my classmates, Hazel, a registered nurse from Guyana, worked at John Hopkins Hospital. On one occasion, she engaged me in conversation and took me to lunch at KFC, where she bought me a whole box of chicken. I had never had so much chicken, and I consumed it with reckless abandon. Back in Africa, village children were accustomed to eating just the chicken heads and feet, whereas the adults ate the meaty parts.

During my first semester at Coppin, I met James Thomas in the tutorial center, where I was helping him with his French class. He made a positive impression on me and introduced me to his mother and sister. James must have perceived my naivete, as he was constantly teaching me American social life. There was a group of male students on campus with whom I would often sit at lunch, and frequently, they would advise me to stay away from American girls. I had no cognitive or physical experiences with girls because my strict, stern mother had effectively steered me away from them. Those boys would tell me all girls were bad, hurtful, mean, and distasteful. I believed them and cherished their friendship. One of them often gave me a ride home, and on one occasion, he initially took me to his home, where we sat in his room and listened to music.

One day, James pulled me aside after a French tutorial session and alerted me that the boys I had been hanging out with in the cafeteria were vying to see who would be the first to do something to me sexually. Cognizant of my naivete, I asked him what he meant by that, and he proceeded to describe in detail an act that I had never heard or read about. I was conflicted, repulsed, and flabbergasted by his narrative. On the one hand, those boys had embraced me seemingly with genuine intentions and were in many ways helping me at a critical transitional phase for me in a new culture. On the other hand, I had no experience with sexual intimacy at that stage and was fearful of any circumstances that could derail my education. I trusted James more than anyone on campus. He appeared to have my best interests at heart.

Hence, I immediately began to distance myself from the other boys. When I shared my predicament with Sam, he responded initially with such paroxysms of laughter that I thought he was going to have a grand mal seizure. Then he composed himself and proceeded to educate me about sexual behavior in America and assured me that those boys were not bad people but that I had to maintain a high state of awareness, vigilance, and caution with everyone because I was young and vulnerable.

One day, I received a call from Billy, who had helped me out at the YMCA, and he wanted to take me to an international students' event in Washington, DC. Although I had not seen him since I left the Y, we had stayed in touch by phone. When we got to DC that night, we found the venue to be crowded and noisy and not conducive to social conversation. In the wee hours of the morning, somewhere on Baltimore Washington Parkway on our way back to Baltimore, he disclosed to me that he was gay. Then he asked me if I knew about homosexuality, and I didn't know what to say, especially since I was still learning much about American society and culture. He kept on driving and didn't say another word.

A short while later, I spoke to him from my heart: "Billy. The only thing that matters to me is the kindness you have shown me. I was a lonely boy, lost in a new land. Without your compassion and love, I might not be alive today. For that, I will always be grateful to you."

He kept on driving and talking about the many international students he had helped along the way before meeting me. After dropping me off, I couldn't stop thinking about what a great human being he was, and I thanked God for having positioned him at that critical juncture in my life. I never saw him again. However, decades later, I would learn about his great and magnificent accomplishments in academics and human service.

Toward the end of the second semester, my chemistry teacher, Dr. McDermott, asked if I would be interested in working with him on a research project at the Goddard Space Flight Center in Greenbelt, Maryland, during the summer break. I accepted the offer. We would be undertaking a research project on nickel-cadmium batteries. Another student, Surapong, from Thailand, who had just graduated, would be joining me on the project. It was a tremendous honor to be selected to participate in such a prestigious opportunity. Dr. McDermott helped guide my college career. He had just graduated with a PhD in biophysics from Boston College, and during one of our conversations, he informed me that Boston offered an endless variety of enviable educational opportunities in addition to many employment possibilities for students.

I decided to act immediately on this and applied to several universities as a transfer student to study engineering and chemistry. MIT in particular was interested in my candidacy; however, they could not offer me financial aid to defray the prohibitive tuition cost I would have had to shoulder. I applied to multiple other schools in Massachusetts and received admission offers from all of them. Finally, I selected the Lowell Technological Institute (now University of Massachusetts) because of its great reputation in science and engineering and its reasonable tuition.

I spent that entire summer at Goddard. Surapong would pick me up every morning for the forty-minute drive to the facility. That summer, I earned $1,500 as a research assistant. When I informed my friend Hazel that I would be moving to Massachusetts for college, she bought me a set of sheets, pillowcases, and a bedcover. She had been a very thoughtful, trusted friend, and her kindness was overwhelming. Armed with so much wealth and an admission letter, I embarked on a new journey to New England exactly a year after arriving in the United States.

CHAPTER 44

Massachusetts

AT THAT SAME GREYHOUND bus station in Baltimore, Sam and his lovely girlfriend, Elmira, gave me their best wishes before I undertook a long journey to face new uncertainties in a distant state and city where I knew nobody. I had enough money to sustain myself for the first semester, and I had already decided to look for a job after enrollment to save money for the second semester. The trip to Boston took all day, and eventually the bus pulled into a terminal in the evening, and I caught a connecting bus to Lowell.

When I arrived at the university campus, I discovered that school had not started yet and the dormitories were still closed. Therefore I took a taxi to the Holiday Inn on the outskirts of the city, and three days later, I caught a bus back to the university campus, completed all the registration formalities, and was assigned to room 904 in a new dormitory tower. My arrival on the floor was welcomed with an unsettling cacophony of deafening music emanating from every open door down the hallway. Then I met my new roommate, Brian Nelson, a friendly guy who was an electrical engineering major from Connecticut.

I wasted no time in procuring a job in the campus dining facility, washing dishes and collecting trash. My boss, Tom Mahoney, treated me with respect and fairness. Frequently, he would pause while walking by and congratulate me on my work ethic and performance. On my part, I did the best I could; I didn't want to lose that job since quite a few students were looking for part-time positions on campus. He paid me $1.90 per hour. I had a persistent, overriding concern about my inability to meet my financial responsibilities the following semester. Therefore, I opted successfully to test out of sophomore calculus so that I could free up my schedule and pursue additional part-time employment. I also was offered an opportunity to be a math and chemistry tutor for at least ten hours each week.

One of the most influential people in my college life at that time was Dr. William Bannister, my organic chemistry teacher. He taught a night class, and when he heard about my financial insecurities, he was willing to accommodate my daytime work schedule by allowing me to take organic chemistry at night. I had absolutely no free time, as I was taking classes mornings and nights while juggling about two or three odd jobs during the week and on weekends. I could not afford most of the required textbooks; therefore, I used to visit the bookstore, copy down assignments from new books, and complete them back in my dorm room.

A few days before my first Christmas holiday in Massachusetts, Anderson, one of my friends from Springfield, Massachusetts, asked where I would be spending the holidays. I told him I had nowhere to go. I had no family in Massachusetts. He pondered a moment, and with eloquent frustration, he told me, "I would love to take you home, but my dad hates Blacks. He would go ballistic."

On that day, I decided to sit in a lounge by the first-floor entrance, and I watched as my classmates and their families and friends were lugging luggage and other belongings out to waiting cars and vans as they prepared to travel home for Christmas. In my solitude, I found myself experiencing jealousy and sadness in witnessing so much love, joy, happiness, and laughter percolating among my fellow students and their loved ones as they streamed out of the dormitory. In no time, I became the lone occupant in an entire twenty-floor building. I stood up and took the elevator to my floor. Things were not the same without my colleagues. I was all alone, and I did not like it at all, but I had no options. I missed their laughter, their arguments, and the loud, blaring, pulsating sounds and beats of Fleetwood Mac; Jimi Hendrix; the Grateful Dead; the Stones; Earth, Wind & Fire; and a roster of other college favorites. Room 904 now seemed like an auditorium without Brian. I remember seeing his younger sister looking lovingly at him with enormous pride while leafing admiringly through his physics textbook when his family came to get him, and as I watched her, I wished my circumstances were different so that I could experience the same love and pride from my siblings.

I must confess that I had packed up my things as though I were going somewhere so that I would not feel embarrassed and isolated and to avoid any uncomfortable, disabling questions from my dorm mates about my plans for the holidays. I sat on the edge of my bed for a few minutes and unpacked my suitcase. That night, the skies opened up and released mountains of snow all around the dormitory building. Intermittently, I would take the elevator to the lobby and peek outside. I had neither extra money nor a place to go.

The security guards took turns bringing me sandwiches each day. One of them, called Pierre, of Canadian heritage, was especially attentive. He would sit and chat with me to lift my spirits for at least half an hour while on his beat. I avoided venturing beyond the immediate grounds of the dormitory because of the extremely cold weather and excessive snow. Generally, I spent my days praying, reading, watching television, pacing the floor, riding the elevator, talking to myself, and reminiscing about home, family, and life. My love for books and my interest in reading, which had started way back in Africa, had multiplied severalfold when I arrived in America. Living in America was akin to living in a book heaven. Unlike in Africa, here books were relatively ubiquitous and generally affordable. Thus, a book lover could never get bored. Whenever I had a few extra dimes or quarters, I would visit a Salvation Army store near the university campus and purchase a pile of used books to add to my collection.

While sequestered in that dormitory building, I thought about how much money I could have been making during the long Christmas break from odd jobs here and there. Unfortunately, with all that snow and no means of transportation, I was stuck! The thought of Anderson and his kind gesture kept coming back to me. Living utterly alone in that twenty-floor dormitory building for more than a month was extremely painful, but I couldn't help but imagine the heartbreaking psychological burden my friend Anderson was laboring under at home with a father whose heart was burdened with cancerous hate.

On the Sunday before the beginning of the second semester, students began to return in droves to the dormitory in the late morning. This was a very exciting day for me. The snow around the building had been cleared, and I found myself loafing around at the entrance to the building like a Walmart greeter. I was excited to see my friends and colleagues back on campus. I remember volunteering to help anybody with their luggage because I was happy to have company again! The arrival of my fellow students gave me a boost of energy and reanimated my spirits. That experience of living alone for weeks in a cold concrete edifice affirmed my belief in community, and I prayed to never again experience that depth and duration of isolation and loneliness.

CHAPTER 45
Ron Russo

IN THE FIRST FEW days of the second semester, I met a student whose friendship has endured to this day. Ron Russo was from East Boston, and we called him Pancho. We met in the elevator, where he asked to know my name, and a conversation ensued. His father was the director of American schools in Europe, and he was very familiar with European culture and spoke multiple languages. Ron was lively and charming and had a sharp wit. He exuded energy and passion, and college girls swooned at the sight of him.

One day, I happened to be in the Ping-Pong room in our dormitory building when I saw him annihilate his opponent at table tennis. His style of play was extremely aggressive. After he was done with his first victim, he looked over in my direction and asked if I was interested in a quick tournament. There were many college girls in the game room that day, and Ron was in rare form. He was smacking the ball very hard, and I could tell I wouldn't be getting any breaks from him. Our female spectators were mostly watching him intently. Ironically, I liked his style of playing, but most of all, I wanted his friendship. I took the game to a tie and lost. He was the ultimate gentleman in winning, and he shook my hand, telling me how great I was at Ping-Pong. We switched sides, and again I played hard and gave him the round. At that moment, our session could have ended, but I asked for another chance. Once again, he won, and like a quintessential sportsman, he congratulated me openly and loudly for my performance. The girls were all drooling over him at that point. I left the room unceremoniously, feeling good about the game and my newfound friend Ron.

A few days later, he came to my room, and to my surprise, he wanted to know why I had allowed him to win. One of the students had just reminded him that he had trounced the college table tennis champion. Ron was a highly intelligent guy, and he realized that I had purposefully allowed him to win in the presence of his adoring college fans and groupies. A new friendship was born!

That night, he came back to my room and informed me that his father had just bought him a car, and he wanted to know if I would accompany him to a discotheque in Lawrence, Massachusetts. Without any hesitation, I agreed.

I had never been to a discotheque. Moreover, we were underaged, and I was concerned that we would not be allowed entry. However, when we got there, Ron asked me to position myself behind him and to keep my mouth shut. Then he used his charm to convince the bouncer to let us in. I don't know what exactly he said, but the bouncer opened the door for us cheerfully and enthusiastically. Promptly, we stepped into a mesmerizing chamber suffused with loud, pulsating music; flashing neon signs; a large, rotating, glittering disco ball suspended from the ceiling in the middle of a dance floor teeming with sexy vixens; and beautiful couples grooving to the hypnotically addictive rhythms of "Disco! Where the happy people go!" by the Trammps.

I had just discovered nirvana! Every joint in my impetuous teenage body was lubricated and anxious to whirl, twirl, and gyrate. "Let's dance with all those girls now!" I said as I was about to dash across the dance floor to a group of beautiful girls dancing with each other in a corner of the dance floor. Sensing my extreme juvenile impatience in a "candy shop," Ron grabbed my hand and tugged at it. With an air of seasoned sophistication, he commanded me to calm down.

"Don't rush! I'll handle this. Let's just watch them a minute," he said. Then he continued, "See those two girls dancing over there? I'm gonna go over and dance with one of them. As soon as you see me dancing, come up immediately and dance with her friend."

And then, most likely in an afterthought, for obvious reasons, he added, "And be sure to act cool!"

Like a faithful, anxious canine on its first hunting expedition, I waited briefly before hopping on the dance floor. Then I dashed toward him, uncoolly tripping over my own feet, waving my hands in the air, and gyrating my hips in the most uncoordinated manner, and before long, we were tearing it up with two voluptuous disco queens.

What a great life! I thought.

I was not familiar with any of the latest dance moves, but that didn't matter. I was thinking, *Watch out, party people! There is a loose nerd on the dance floor!*

I was spinning all over the floor like a wild man, hopping, kicking, shaking, jumping on innocent feet, and punching the air without any compunction. At that moment, nothing mattered because I was having a grand ole time dancing my little heart out! The lyrics of the music were speaking directly to me. My dance partner had a quizzical look on her face, understandably because of my bizarre, unpredictable, spastic, arrhythmic dance moves. I was lost in a worry-free disco euphoria, unconcerned about how I was being perceived by all the distinguished disco sophisticates surrounding me, who were probably wondering which cave I had just crawled out of.

Unfortunately, the night came to a close too soon; the music stopped, and the happy people began to shuffle out of the club at two o'clock in the morning. My ears were complaining about decibels, but the rest of my senses were contented. On the way back to the campus, I couldn't thank Ron enough for having allowed me to experience something new and delightfully sensational.

CHAPTER 46

Tuition Problems

A COUPLE OF MONTHS later, in the middle of the semester, I went to check my mailbox, and I found a pink slip. It was from the registrar's office, telling me that I had to move out of the dormitory because I had not paid the full amount of my tuition, room, and board. It was devastating. As I prepared to leave the college campus, I had deep concerns about my education because any prolonged absence from school could potentially affect my grades adversely and reduce my chances of entering medical school eventually. A foreign student, Raj, from India, heard of my plight and offered me his couch. Immediately, I found a job at a local plastics factory where I toiled for about two weeks while maintaining a part-time position at another job and earned just enough money to defray part of my tuition, and then I was permitted to reenroll. When the semester ended, I found one full-time and two part-time jobs for the summer. I had no days off the entire summer because I worked weekends as well. When school resumed in the fall, I was fine for a while.

At that point in my career, I began to think seriously about medical school. I met with my premed adviser and shared with him my desire to study medicine. Surprisingly, he was entirely negative about my prospects of getting into medical school. He said, in effect, that grades did not matter as much as other factors such as ethnicity and national origin. In fact, he was telling me that as an African and a Black person, my chances of gaining admission to an American medical school would be practically zero. This was one of the most demoralizing conversations I had ever had with a professor. To my surprise, he openly discouraged me from considering a career in medicine because, in his opinion, medicine was a highly competitive profession; therefore, it might be better for me to consider other options like laboratory technology, nutrition, or tropical hygiene, which were less competitive.

I left his office feeling somewhat dejected yet undeterred. The career options he mentioned were essential and great, but they were not what I wanted to do. Afterward, I had a conversation with a few of my fellow premed students in one of their dorm rooms and shared my experience with the adviser earlier that day. When they heard what I had to say, they were both stunned. On their part, they recounted how the same adviser had encouraged them to consider taking the medical school entrance test as soon as possible while also assuring them he would write excellent reference letters in support of their applications. I found it particularly puzzling because I had been their chemistry and math tutor for about a year. In the end, they both concluded that our premed adviser just didn't like me for some nebulous reason. I left it at that. I knew better.

Later on that semester, I received another letter in my mailbox, again advising me to leave the dormitory because I still owed tuition. This time, it took me a few days before I could find a couple of odd jobs in the city that would pay me enough over two weeks so that I could pay back some of my college debts. Once again, I came back and rejoined my classmates and worked very hard to make up for lost time. I began to work at least three part-time jobs while pursuing full-time studies. I could not afford a meal plan, and I had to rely on the goodwill of other students for nutritional sustenance.

One day on campus, I ran into Ron, and he was concerned that he had not seen me in the cafeteria for quite some time. I revealed to him that I was no longer on a meal plan. Upon hearing this, he came up with a strategy to feed me. Each day at dinnertime, we would meet in his dorm room in Leitch Hall and then walk together across the street to the student dining room in the main college tower. I would wait for him by a staircase entrance while he carefully selected multiple items from the buffet line to fill up his tray. He would then wrap several food items in paper napkins and sneak back to the dimly lit emergency exit area to address my nutritional insecurity.

No words can ever express the thrilling and jubilant feeling that I had each time he arrived with a bundle of delicious food items for me.

During this time, I frequently wrote to my family in Africa, but I did not share my struggles with them. I never wanted to tell them anything about my situation because I knew it would be profoundly devastating to them, especially since there was nothing they could do to alleviate my pain. I bought my first camera for about twenty dollars and often took a lot of pictures, which I included with my letters. Frequently, I received photos from family members as well, and it was always uplifting to see how my siblings and cousins were maturing physically. Unfortunately, sometimes it would take about two months for me to receive replies to my letters.

Box 2526 in the campus mailroom was my favorite destination in the afternoons after lectures. Whenever I received a letter from home, I would make a beeline to my room, jump in my bed, and allow the words in the letter to transport me on a mental journey back to my homeland. When I did reply to their letters, I laced them intentionally with optimism. Every few months, I sent about twenty dollars to my father for the family. This was a lot of money in those days. I remember assuring him that someday I would be able to take very good care of the family, even though I didn't know how I would do it, given my tenuous financial, social, and educational situation at that time. On his part, he never made any demands on me and only gave me encouragement and advice to be careful, to pray often, show kindness, and to work hard. These were recurring themes in his letters. Sending and receiving letters was not a straightforward process for my dad. Without formal education, he had to identify someone in the village who could write letters for him. Whenever he received a letter from me, he had to look for someone to read and translate it in Mankon, our native language.

CHAPTER 47

Homeless

SOMETIME DURING THE LAST semester of my junior year, I found myself again having to confront a third suspension because of incomplete tuition payment. This time, I had nowhere to go. I did not want my grades to suffer and potentially end my dream of becoming a doctor. Also, I did not want to be deported. Whenever a foreign student was on a prolonged period of suspension, immigration authorities would be notified and deportation procedures initiated. Therefore, I was understandably concerned. Working about three odd jobs and shouldering heavy coursework was too much for me. I packed a few essential items in a bag and left the rest of my possessions at Raj's apartment. Then I walked across a bridge to the library, where I stayed that night.

Luckily, I did not have many possessions. At about 10:00 p.m., an announcement was made of the fact that the library would be closing in a few minutes. At that point, I hid in the restroom until everyone was gone and the lights were out. Then I washed my face, came out, and spent the night sitting in a chair somewhere in a quiet corner. After spending a couple of nights in the library, I was afraid of being discovered by security eventually. I was feeling down, and I didn't know what to do. The only thing I could think of was to talk to someone who could hopefully help me. I went over to the science building and sauntered into Dr. Bannister's office at the end of the hallway on the fifth floor. I told him what I had been going through.

In the middle of my narrative, I became emotional and broke down in tears. He expressed deep sympathy for my situation. At some point, he stood up and walked across the street to get me a sandwich. When he came back, he apologized for not having the financial means to help me. He had children in college, and his meager income as a college professor did not afford him the luxury of adding another responsibility to his life. He mentioned something about certain students on full scholarship who were performing poorly in school, and he bemoaned the fact that I had good grades but did not qualify for financial assistance by virtue of my foreign-student status. Suddenly, he grabbed the phone and called Merrimack Magnetics, a manufacturing plant in the city that produced transformers, and recommended me for a job. The next phone call he made was to a local priest, with whom he pleaded to assist me in finding a place to stay.

I was homeless and hungry. After thanking him profusely, I left to meet the priest. Unfortunately, when I arrived, he told me that he did not have any more apartments or houses available for homeless people. However, on second thought, he mentioned a rundown church-owned building on Salem Street in Lowell, which was in a dilapidated state and which was unsuited for human habitation. I insisted on taking it because I was in dire straits. He gave me the address and keys to a third-floor unit.

The building was an old, abandoned structure resembling the Leaning Tower of Pisa. It had three floors with two apartments on each floor. The priest charged me twenty dollars a month for rent. I walked up a few concrete steps to the building entrance. There was a staircase that led from the entrance to an apartment on the third floor. When I stepped on the stairs, I felt a rattle, as if the entire staircase assembly would collapse. The first floor reeked of a thousand carcasses. I proceeded gingerly up the staircase to the third-floor landing, inserted the key, and walked into a pungent nineteenth-century kitchen that looked like it had not been cleaned since its original furnishing.

I found a room with a twin bed, where I deposited my bag. There were two other bedrooms. The air was stagnant and stifling. It smelled so bad I had to open all the windows. The bathroom needed a major cleanup. Every appliance in there was coated with layers of brown scum. I opened my bag, took out the bedcover, sheets, and pillowcases that Hazel, my nurse friend in Baltimore, had given me as a going-away present, and made my bed. There were no pillows on the bed. I had just received a letter from Hazel inquiring how things were going, so I left the apartment briefly in search of a pay phone, where I called her to inform her about all the difficulties I was having. Shortly afterward, I received a money order for a hundred dollars from her. She was such an angel! When I came back to the apartment, I started to clean but then realized that I would have to buy specialized equipment and chemicals to make the place truly habitable. Therefore, I decided to wait until I had saved enough money to address the myriad of sanitation problems in my new abode.

That night, I had difficulty falling asleep. I was famished, and the heat and humidity were unbearable. A pungent aroma permeating the apartment did not help matters either. In the morning, I went to a minimart next door and bought a bag of rice and a large container of Crisco oil. After cooking a huge pot of rice, I poured a generous amount of Crisco oil on it and stirred it for a while. That became my daily staple for at least a week. Despite the deplorable state of my new pad, one thing for sure that gave me security was that I had a roof over my head.

I arose early in the morning and headed out to Merrimack Magnetics to begin my new job. The factory was located on the banks of the Merrimack River in Lowell, Massachusetts. I was assigned to a desolate room in a dimly lit area of the factory that was lacking ventilation. You could taste the air in that room. My job was to strip insulated transformer wires with nitric acid. It was a dangerous job, and I was provided a lab coat, ill-fitting goggles, rubber gloves, and vats of nitric acid. There was an emergency shower in the middle of the room, which I prayed I would never need. At that stage, I had enough knowledge of inorganic chemistry to appreciate and respect the potential dangers of working with nitric acid. At the end of an eight hour shift, I was exhausted and dehydrated from excessive perspiration in the hot, humid, stifling atmosphere. I was afraid to ask for a fan for fear of upsetting my supervisor. Besides, I was gainfully employed and making a reasonable income of $1.90 per hour. I had to be careful to avoid spilling any acid on myself, but at times, I suffered an accidental spillage that penetrated the lab coat. This often resulted in excruciating, burning pain in the injured part of my body.

On one occasion, I inadvertently splashed acid on my face. Some of it got into my eyes, and I screamed out loud, stripped almost naked, and pulled the emergency shower handle. I was flooded with ice-cold water, and my vision became blurred. I was rushed over to Saint Joseph's Hospital in the city, where I was attended to by a kind doctor in the emergency department who was extremely chatty. After he flushed out my eyes and examined the rest of my body, he gave me a prescription and told me to go home and rest. I responded by telling him that I wanted to go back to the factory because I didn't want to lose my job. He asked to know why I was not in school, and I mentioned tuition problems. Then his final question was about my college major and career plans. When I told him I was interested in a career in medicine, he stared at me for a minute, shrugged his shoulders, and walked out without saying another word. I got dressed and went back to work, despite having blurred vision.

CHAPTER 48

Kind Friends

DURING THIS TIME, SOMEHOW Ron discovered where I was living. One day, I heard a knock on the door. People rarely came to the building. When I opened it, there was Ron with a paper bag filled with multiple paper boxes of Chinese food. He asked me if I was hungry, and I thought he was joking. Then I proceeded to eat ferociously. To Ron, I might have looked entertaining based on how I was eating because he took out a camera and snapped a few pictures of me. To this day they have remained a humble reminder to me of my journey in life. He stopped by often and always brought cheerfulness and some food.

After a couple of weeks of working, I had a few spare dollars, which I took to the dean's office and was promptly reinstated. I had a surprise visit also from Robert, a former student and great friend who came looking for me after I left the dormitory. He showed up at my new apartment, and after a brief conversation, he asked if I would like to go out for a meal at a restaurant. We rode in his brand-new burgundy Camaro to the Mai Kai, a Chinese restaurant in the city. There, I ate so much I had no room left in my belly. There was still a large amount of food left over: chicken, beef, shrimp, and rice. We had ordered the pu pu platter, which I liked. After the meal, Robert took out his wallet and extracted a credit card to pay for it and suggested that I take the rest of the food home.

Robert had been working at Honeywell as a computer engineer since graduating college. He was a highly intelligent, erudite gentleman with distinguished skills and tastes. In my opinion, he represented success: a great job, a new car, a big apartment, and credit cards! When we were done eating, I asked him a question that to this day he still reminds me of: "Do you think that I will be able to eat as I want and pay for it as you do?" Robert's answer was also a statement of motivation that I've never forgotten. He said, "Keep doing what you're doing. Study hard, and you will be able to."

College life had its ups and downs. During those moments when pain and stress abounded, one of the people whom I always enjoyed meeting and talking to was a perpetually positive and gracefully dignified student called Sharon B., of Jamaican heritage. She never appeared to have a care in the world and always had a kind word for my ears and expressions of empathy for whatever challenges I was facing. She was greatly admired and respected on campus because of her friendliness, maturity, and poise. She maintained a sharp focus on her schoolwork and displayed no interest in distracting social activities. She was everyone's psychotherapist.

During my first summer in the Salem Street apartment, Ron would often drive up from East Boston to see me. One night, he persuaded me to go out clubbing with him. I had worked all day until about eight o'clock at night and was extremely tired. However, the memories of our previous jaunt to Discoland were still fresh in my mind. Therefore, I capitulated despite my state of fatigue, and we drove to the same discotheque in Lawrence, Massachusetts. Fortunately, Ron succeeded in convincing the same bouncer as before to let us in.

That night, he was extremely energetic on the dance floor. Conversely, I found myself dragging because I was physically exhausted from my job. I danced a little, but mostly I stood and watched others perform. Right before closing time, Ron came up to me and said he had met two friendly girls who were willing to hang out with us and grab a bite afterward. That night, Ron was charming, magnetic, and dashing. He must have sensed a degree of hesitation in my body language, so he assured me everything would be OK with the girls and us. Truly, I felt nervous and timid about the whole idea, but I trusted his judgment. We sashayed out of the disco acting very grown up with two beautiful ladies next to us.

With Captain Ron in the cockpit of his Chevy Nova, we jetted back to Lowell, bopping to the addictive beat of disco music emanating from a temperamental eight-track player. I was sitting in the rear seat next to one of the girls and struggling to come up with a cool topic of conversation. She asked me what my favorite beer was, and I told her emphatically that I had never tasted alcohol and had no interest in trying it. She said nothing else after that. When the car shuddered to an abrupt stop at my Salem Street address, Ron announced, "We are here!"

The girls appeared to have been jolted out of a trance. As if on cue, they strained their necks through the car window, stared at my building and its surroundings for a few seconds, and looked at each other briefly before settling back in their seats. The girl sitting next to Ron mumbled something in his ear and turned to look at her girlfriend in the rear seat. I couldn't quite decipher what was transpiring. I opened the car door and tried to act cool by exclaiming, "Let's boogie!" No one budged.

I dropped back in my seat, perplexed at the absence of any physical response among my fellow occupants. Then I asked the girl sitting next to me what was going on. She replied crisply, "Take us back to the club." She and Ron exchanged a few words, which I could not understand over the loud music and raucous engine. Suddenly, Ron slipped the gear lever into drive mode, and off to Lawrence we went. Nobody spoke the entire way back. We dropped the girls off in the parking lot at the club, and they left promptly without a goodbye and didn't even respond to my good night wishes. I got back in the front passenger seat, and we took off.

On the way back, I kept asking Ron what all that was about. "Why didn't they wanna go with us? Why didn't they like us?" Ron kept driving while remaining silent, unflinching, and unmoved. I added that the girls had just missed an opportunity for a good time. Feeling quite mature, though indeed very ignorant, I began to wonder loudly why any girl would turn down two great guys like us. "Maybe they were intimidated or something," I said.

Finally, Ron appeared to have had enough of my rants. With a dramatic look of intensity in his eyes, he said with an emphatic calm, "Pierre [what he always called me], it's *the house*!" He said it with poignant honesty with an underlying tone of sympathy and resignation. His assessment was clear to me. There was no need for additional explanations. We drove in silence until we reached my address.

CHAPTER 49

First Car

DESPITE MY NEVER-ENDING FINANCIAL and other extracurricular insecurities, I finished my junior year on a high note, having done extremely
well in all my courses. I was searching for summer jobs in the local newspaper and found one with American Can Company in Merrimack, New
Hampshire, which was about thirty miles from me. I decided to buy a car,
even though I had never driven one. When I mentioned my interest in
purchasing a vehicle, a Nigerian commuter student offered to sell me his
for two hundred dollars. It was a Volkswagen square back with a manual
transmission and a "strong engine," as he told me. We met somewhere on
campus and sealed the deal. I knew nothing about cars, so I emptied my
bank account and bought it.

Afterward, he drove me back to my apartment and parked the car
alongside the building. After obtaining a Massachusetts driver's license, I
would get in my car each day, turn on the ignition, and sit there for several
minutes looking at the instrument panel. Then I would turn the engine off
and play with the gearshift handle for a while. I kept thinking about one of
my classmates from Hong Kong, whose car was also a manual. On several
occasions, he had taken me on fun rides in the surrounding region. I decided
that if he could drive a stick shift comfortably, so could I.

I was determined to drive my car, and one afternoon, I concluded that I
had done enough dry runs and was ready for at least a first-gear trip around
the block. I said a prayer and got into the car, put it in reverse, and stepped
lightly on the accelerator while releasing the clutch pedal. The car leaped
violently and stalled. I tried it multiple times until I was able to advance

a few yards backward. Then I turned the wheels to face the street while pushing the shift into first gear. Gingerly and nervously, I pulled out into the street, trying to control the loud, jerky, galloping, and whining monster. At this point, I was sweating profusely, as I appeared to be attracting too much attention from curious neighbors.

The poor engine pleaded to be released from the strangulation of first gear, and I'm sure the clutch was not too pleased with my indecisiveness either. I was embarrassed by all the attention I was getting in the neighborhood but was determined to push on. I avoided any acknowledgment of stop signs or red lights, for that matter, because I didn't want to get stuck in the middle of the street. After making a wide loop around the neighborhood, I pulled into my parking space, turned off the ignition, and switched my lungs back on. My shirt was glued to my armpits, and I needed a hot shower to dislodge it. A nervous-looking Puerto Rican lady across the street said hello, and I waved back but did not stop to chat. The next day, I was determined to advance to second gear and hopefully the third. It took a few days for me to move up to the fourth gear. At that point, I could smell freedom in the air!

In no time I was driving back and forth to Merrimack, New Hampshire. Having a car enabled me to access more job opportunities farther from my apartment. Additionally, it enabled me to discover my surroundings. The heating system in the car did not work consistently, and there was a large hole in the floor panel on the driver's side, which provided excellent ventilation and cooling on hot summer days. However, on cold winter days, I placed cardboard on it to decrease the amount of cold air blowing into the car.

I had a friend who was a college student in New Hampshire, and I would drive up on occasion to visit her. She was intelligent, compassionate, and beautiful and lived with her father. She, too, had lost her mother at a very young age. On one occasion while I was visiting her, we were eating a delicious meal of rice and chicken she had prepared when a buzzer at the main entrance to the apartment complex announced her father's arrival. In a panic, she jumped up and pleaded for me to leave immediately, telling me that her father hated Black people and did not want her talking to me. I feared for my life.

Thankfully, the apartment was on the first floor. I did a rapid survey of my surroundings, grabbed my car keys, and made a quick exit through the window. On my way back to Massachusetts, I gave much thought to the idea of hate and prejudice. I felt bad for her because she was a genuinely caring person who loved and embraced everyone, and I could only imagine the pain and agony she endured from living with an ignorant parent. I had significant difficulty reconciling the prejudice, racism, and beliefs I grew up with. Consequently, despite the enormous love and admiration I had for her, I realized we could never develop a strong and meaningful relationship without the sanctioning of her father.

Interestingly, about two decades later, we reconnected and enjoyed a few chuckles when she recounted a story about a question her father had asked about me when he was curious to know what had happened to "that African kid." Sensing an opportunity that had eluded her in the distant past, she responded with gleeful scorn, "He became a heart surgeon, Dad!" His jaw dropped. As a coup de grâce, she added, "He is the one you didn't want me to see." That experience many years ago with her father made absolutely no sense to me at that time, especially since I had been raised in a world where love and community transcended all else.

CHAPTER 50

Despair and Rescue

THE FALL SEMESTER OF my senior year finally arrived. However, when I went to register for my coursework, I was told that the university would no longer accept partial tuition payments from me. I had to pay the full semester tuition at once. I pleaded incessantly, to no avail, so I left begrudgingly and went back to my apartment. I didn't know what else to do. I had come a long way and was close to graduating in less than a year. Because I was not enrolled in school, taking the medical school entrance examination would have been a worthless endeavor. Although my dream of becoming a doctor had been a prolonged nightmare, I had remained hopeful. But it seemed as though that dream was on the verge of being completely shattered.

I sat on the smelly old couch, the only piece of furniture in my dilapidated apartment, and bowed down my head in prayer. Darkness and gloom surrounded me. I was facing an impregnable barrier of financial challenges with no glimmer of hope left in me. My future spelled deep gloom. I spent that entire day and night mostly staring at the walls in despair. The next day, I paid a final visit to the library. The librarian was cheerful as usual. I was not. I requested help with finding books on suicide. Hours later, I left feeling gratified.

It was an unusually hot and humid day. I plugged in a fan and set it right in front of me. The whining noise it created was, in a strange way, soothing to my spirits. I could not sleep that night. I thought about my childhood and my family and about all that I had gone through in the preceding three years. I asked God why my road had been so bumpy. I had arrived at a point where I could not continue, and I was not willing to go back either. My status as a foreign student prevented me from dropping out for a significant length of time to earn money. That would put me at risk for deportation.

At the break of dawn, I took a pen and paper and scribbled the most heart-wrenching note I had ever written and addressed it to Mr. King, the dean of students. In essence, I told him, "All my life I have known mostly struggles. I have known tragedies. I have been working since age five. I worked hard to be able to come to America in pursuit of an education so that I could change my life and my world. Despite being a good student, I have had to constantly confront disabling financial difficulties to the point that I can no longer continue my education. I see no options ahead, and I refuse to go back. Therefore, I am prepared to accept my limitations and to end my life."

It was a very short letter. After writing it, I felt a strange sense of relief, as if a heavy burden had been lifted from my back. I placed it in an envelope, sealed it, addressed it to the dean's office at the university, and dropped it in a mailbox nearby. It was Thursday afternoon, and I saw no reason to work that day. I had already decided how I was going to end my life on Sunday. That night, I slept well. The next day, I did not leave my apartment. I began having recurrent thoughts about my family and home. When I finally went to sleep, I dreamed of my mother. In my dream, she had me waiting somewhere for her, but she failed to show up.

After waking up, I wrote my father, telling him how much I loved him and our family. Then I said my prayers, ate breakfast, and proceeded to read a Mickey Spillane detective novel I had bought at the Salvation Army store. Gone were the anxieties and worries that confronted my restless mind each day at daybreak. There was an unusual air of serenity surrounding my mental space. I was at peace with my decision.

Suddenly, I heard a knock at the door. It was unusual for anybody to be stopping by at that hour, especially on a Saturday. I wondered who it could be. Without asking questions, I turned the latch and pried the door open. Standing there in a leisure jacket with a look of deep concern on his face was the dean of students, Mr. Leo King, and Dr. Scruggs, one of our psychology professors. I was confused. I had no idea why they had come to see me. How did they discover where I was living? I showed them the couch, and they sat down hesitatingly. They took turns asking me few questions, mainly about my schoolwork, my health, and my general social situation. The dean glanced inquisitively around the apartment and appeared to be concerned about something. Still, I couldn't make sense of the impromptu visit.

Then Dean King disclosed that he had received my letter. He wasted no time delving into the reasons for their visit. He counseled me against doing any harm to myself. He expressed an understanding of the difficulties I had been facing. Then he congratulated me on my academic performance in the setting of my financial woes. The psychology professor spoke at length about life's challenges and coping mechanisms. I felt particularly touched when he told me that he was convinced I was destined for major leadership and that I would make an impact on the lives of many in the future. "The world is expecting great things from you," he said. The dean concluded by assuring me that the university would offer me free housing in the graduate-student rooming house on Plymouth Street adjacent to the main campus and that I would be allowed to defer my tuition debts until sometime after graduation. I would, however, be responsible for my books and living expenses.

I was completely flabbergasted. I could not find words to express my joy and relief. Before I knew it, I began to cry. Considering the dark, foreboding night I had just gone through, that was a veritable shining daybreak. I couldn't stop thanking them. At some point, the professor whispered something to the dean, who asked me to collect my belongings at once because he wanted to take me to my new abode. A few hours later, I was living in a warm, comfortable room in an old mansion with an exciting bunch of graduate students from various states, nationalities, and ethnicities. My room was no bigger than a large closet, but it was clean, cozy, and carpeted.

I was appreciative of the unspeakable assistance I had received. I felt remorseful and ashamed of the decision I had made to end my life. Truly, I had hit rock bottom. I had reached a point of exhaustion at which I saw nothing but darkness and hopelessness around me, and I was prepared to capitulate to despair as a final response to my insurmountable challenges. I could not face the embarrassment of returning to Africa with empty hands and shattered dreams. I knew just how disappointed my family would have been had I been deported. The additional embarrassment they would have suffered in the community would have been unimaginable.

The dean and the professor were timely in their response to save my life. I had mailed the letter to the dean on Thursday, knowing that the postal system generally took three working days to deliver mail. Therefore, I had been under the assumption that the letter would arrive the following week after my death. Weeks later, I learned the letter arrived the very next day on Friday and caused a flurry of activity in the dean's office, which triggered a massive search for my whereabouts in the city. Thankfully, since many people knew that Dr. Bannister and I had a good relationship, he was notified about the letter, and it was he who suggested contacting the local priest, who then revealed my address.

In my new residence, I was surrounded by very smart graduate students enrolled in PhD programs in the sciences and engineering. A few of them from China and Korea helped with and guided me in my senior-level courses. Armed with renewed strength, I was more determined than ever to pursue my career objectives. One of the graduate students was doing exciting research in molecular biology, and I spent many hours with him on weekends learning about the fascinating intricacies of his research project. It was this experience that stimulated my interest and determination to pursue a PhD in chemistry as well as a doctorate in medicine with an eye toward medical research and clinical medicine.

CHAPTER 51

Last College Year

ONE OF THE MOST enriching encounters I had was with a mother who was looking for a college student to tutor her two children. I was introduced to her by Fume, a graduate student in physics from Nigeria who was familiar with my incessant inquiries about part-time job opportunities. Her name was Marilyn Reid, and the children were Angela (sixteen) and Eric (thirteen). Before long, I became integrated within their family structure, an experience that helped fill a huge void in my life at that time. Mrs. Reid was an administrative assistant at the Harvard Business School and had a forty-five-minute commute each day to Cambridge. At the end of her workday, she would frequently stop by the graduate-student house to check on me before heading home.

Her daughter, Angela, was bright, insightful, and gregarious. She loved to dance and frequently delighted us with her complicated disco moves. Teaching me the "bus stop" was a colossal feat on her part because I had no meaningful rhythm in my lower extremities. She was tall and beautiful, and several of my college friends were infatuated with her.

Eric had an amazing encyclopedic memory and could stun the sharpest academics on our campus with his understanding of philosophy, the arts, and other diverse topics. I didn't think he was being challenged enough at school. Mrs. Reid was like a mother to me, and I could always count on her objective advice, support, and encouragement. She taught me the basics: how to dress, how to do laundry, how to use cutlery, and how to shop for groceries. She had a unique yet realistic take on life that was full of optimism, and she never hesitated to share her unique and valuable insights with everyone.

When college became unbearably stressful and the demons of nostalgia and loneliness became unmanageable, I could always turn to her for comfort, hope, endearment, and reinvigoration.

By the early spring of my senior year, I had received a few admissions offers for graduate studies. My top choices for PhD programs in synthetic chemistry were Lehigh and Harvard. I had communicated extensively with Professor Woodward, a synthetic chemist at Harvard University, and was interested in his work. For a while, I decided to pursue an opportunity to work with him. However, when I interviewed at Lehigh, I was more impressed with the kind of research they were engaged in, and I accepted their admission offer soon afterward.

Subsequently, another offer arrived from Cleveland for a combined chemistry PhD program at Cleveland State and the Cleveland Clinic, emphasizing clinical chemistry, which I thought would be more relevant to my medical education eventually. Moreover, the clinic was one of the most reputable medical facilities in the world and abounded with endless resources. In the end, I decided to solicit opinions from a couple of my professors about which program to select. Their unanimous decision favored Cleveland. With my tuition woes postponed and a decision made regarding my postgraduate destination, I reduced the number of hours I was working part-time and focused my attention on schoolwork and good grades.

Eventually, graduation day arrived, and it was bittersweet. I kept thinking about my family back in Africa, and I truly wished that they could have been there to support me so that we could celebrate as a family. Therefore, on that day, I avoided the commencement exercises, stayed in my room, wrote letters to my family, and made plans for my graduate and medical studies. After graduating, I made it a point to thank Dean King and other key professors for the support they had given me.

That summer, I worked full-time at a factory in New Hampshire. One day, while I was returning from work, my Volkswagen broke down in the middle of the highway. When the mechanic evaluated it, he told me that I would need a new engine. I could not afford one, so I abandoned it. In the evenings, I tutored students enrolled in summer classes in college math and chemistry.

CHAPTER 52
Cleveland

IT WAS DURING THE summer immediately after graduation that I met a gentleman from Cleveland, Ohio, whose name was Clarence Fitch. He was visiting one of the administrators at the college, and when I told him I would be moving to Ohio, he shared his contact information with me. Toward the end of August, I packed my belongings and hitched a ride with a Korean student who was returning to school in Athens, Ohio, and he dropped me off in Cleveland at a YMCA. From there, I called Mr. Fitch, and he came and took me to his house, where I stayed a few days until I could locate a place for myself.

I enrolled in a PhD program in chemistry working under Dr. Robert Towns, a brilliant, humble, unassuming, extraordinary teacher who was also my adviser. He was indeed the greatest mentor any student could ever ask for, and to this day, the bond between us has remained strong. After completing the preliminary coursework for a doctorate, I embarked on a research project focused on trace elements in cardiovascular disease. My research project was done primarily in Dr. Town's laboratory, where I shared space with several other graduate students under his leadership. The rest of my work was done at the Cleveland Clinic, which had the best resources in cardiovascular medicine, and also at Case Western University, working on anatomic pathology with Dr. Abel Robertson.

On weekends I hung out with Mr. Fitch. At that time, he was also pursuing a doctorate in education at Northeastern University, which required him to make frequent trips to Boston. Therefore, he would often ask me to house-sit whenever he had to leave town. One day, he surprised me with an old Volkswagen of his, which was also a square back, like the one I used to own in Massachusetts.

On my first Christmas holiday in Ohio, I drove back to Massachusetts to visit my friends. It was a very cold, snowy winter that year. Other than having a fickle heating system, my car seemed to be running well. On my return trip from Boston, I encountered a terrible snowstorm in upstate New York around Albany. Understandably, there were very few vehicles on Highway 90 that afternoon. Then I reached a stretch of the expressway between Syracuse and Rochester that had not yet been plowed, and the road was deserted. I had just passed a sign announcing Canandaigua when the engine began to sputter. Instantly, I veered to the shoulder, at which point it ceased to function. I was in the middle of a winter wonderland, and the silence was deafening. Hardly any car passed by.

Snow was falling heavily, and visibility was extremely poor. I was all bundled up in multiple layers of clothing, snow boots, a winter hat, and a scarf. It did not take long for the heat to be gone completely from the car interior, and the temperature plunged to a deep freeze. My belongings were in a plastic garment bag on the rear seat. I waited for a very long time, and no one came. I began to shiver, and after some time, my bladder began to scream for attention. I held on for a while, but the urge became unrelenting. Consequently, I opened the door, stepped out, and rapidly relieved myself in the snow. My nose, lips, fingers, and toes were starting to feel numb. I had a fleeting thought to leave the car and seek help, but I decided against it.

On that day, after a couple of hours in the frigid wilderness, I thought I was going to die, especially after I began to experience an intense continuous burning sensation on my forehead. I pulled my winter jacket over my face and leaned against the steering wheel in a desperate attempt to alleviate my discomfort. I did not know what to do next. I had run out of options, and I was shivering so hard the car was rocking. I didn't want to die, and I kept praying out loud for deliverance. Then my emergency blinkers stopped working. All around me was snow and deafening silence. I reached over and grabbed a few shirts in the back seat, wrapped my hands in them, and leaned back against the steering wheel. I might have fallen asleep.

After a couple of hours, in a state of hopelessness and despair, I pulled the jacket back down from my face and looked straight ahead. Faintly, at a distance, I saw what appeared to be a pair of shimmering headlights heading east. Was I hallucinating? As they got closer, I recognized a state trooper's vehicle, and my heart leaped with joy. He pulled over on the opposite side of the highway, rolled down his window, and said something I could not comprehend from that distance. Therefore, I jumped out of my car while still bundled up like an Arctic explorer, stumbled awkwardly across the divider, and struggled to describe my predicament to him. My poor lips were too frozen to produce meaningful speech. I think he recognized that.

"Come on in here, son. It's hell out there!" he exclaimed.

He opened the front passenger door, and I hopped in, shivering intensely. He had deep blue eyes, meticulously cropped blond hair, and a square chin. Then he asked me how long I had been waiting. After I responded, he warned me of the danger of driving in such horrible weather. I told him that I was a student in Ohio and that I was returning home from a visit to Boston and I needed to get back to school. Hearing that, he offered me a warm chocolate drink from a large flask positioned on the floor next to me and a piece of candy. Then he got on the radio to summon a tow truck. He told me that there was a town not too far away where I would be able to find a motel for the night. "Here. You might need this." With that, he handed me a twenty-dollar bill! The officer's kindness was immeasurable, not only in terms of what he offered me but especially the way he treated me, which was both reassuring and heartwarming. I still credit him for saving my life on that fateful winter day. Somewhere on the highway after Albany, I had stopped and filled my tank, and all I had left was a five-dollar bill.

After the tow truck arrived, the driver hitched my car to his truck and asked me to join him in the front seat. The police officer wished me well and promptly left. He was another angel from God.

The tow truck driver took my car to a shop in Canandaigua, New York, where a mechanic informed me that it would be a few days before he could work on it. Then he directed me to a motel within walking distance from his shop. I did not have the thirty-dollar room rate he requested. After listening to my narrative of the events that had led me to his motel, the owner, an

Indian gentleman, allowed me to spend the night with the understanding that I would be paying him at a later date. I was honestly amazed by his trust and kindness. Therefore, I gave him my driver's license voluntarily and promised to return with the payment I owed him. The next day, I bought a Trailways bus ticket to Cleveland. A week later, I returned and paid the motel owner what I owed him. The mechanic succeeded in restarting my car, and I drove nonstop to Cleveland, feeling nervous the entire way and dreading the possibility of another complicating event.

CHAPTER 53

Return to Africa

AFTER MY FIRST YEAR of graduate school, I decided to return home on an unannounced visit. I missed my family terribly, and I was often homesick. I had been gone five years, and I was desperate for some family love. I didn't have enough money for the trip, so a friend of mine loaned me the cost of the airfare. This time around, I was not a novice at traveling. I had become a "travel connoisseur," a more confident traveler. Yes, I ate everything the flight attendant offered on that trip. I used the lavatory facilities on the plane with ease and comfort. In Paris, where I had to make a connection, I navigated my way to the appropriate terminal without assistance. Undoubtedly, in many ways, I found myself compensating for any previous faux pas from my inexperience with travel. I was attempting to assure myself of the progress that I had made since my first journey.

The flight arrived in Cameroon late in the evening. When the airplane door opened, my nostrils were suffused at once with familiar, delightful fragrances I had not experienced in several years. I was bubbling with anticipation of seeing my family, and without hesitation, I hired a taxi for the long overnight journey to my village in the highlands. The road was dusty and bumpy, but I enjoyed every moment of it. I was just plain happy to be back home! As my jet-lagged body got closer to the village, the familiar smell of the mountain air brought back many wonderful memories. Ubiquitous sounds of laughter and the perpetual sights of total strangers waving jubilantly at me in salutation were reassuring to my soul and my spirits. I was home. At last!

The taxi screeched to a stop in our yard. I leaped out, grabbed my luggage and a box full of gifts, and ran toward our house. My dad was outside, clearing the bushes a few yards away. "Papa, Papa!" I yelled. Unhurriedly and deliberately, he turned around, his head cocked to the side, and repeatedly squinted as though he were trying to discern the strange figure galloping toward him. In slow motion, he dropped his machete, cracked the broadest smile I had ever seen, and collapsed in my embrace, his frail arms wrapped around my waist with the desperate tenacity of an orphan. Abruptly, his eyelids parted wide, and his pupils glided slowly upward to meet my tear-flooded cheeks.

As we stood there locked in an eternal embrace, a million fragrant thoughts began streaming harmoniously through innumerable corridors within our memory banks, and I discovered a new depth in the love we had always shared. Hastily, he took me by the hand, and we entered the room where he slept, a room he had built over my mother's final resting place. There, on our family's hallowed ground, he poured a libation on the floor and spoke to her with the passion and wisdom of the ages: "Your son has returned from a long journey. Your majestic hopes have guided him well. I offer you gratitude."

After he said a few prayers to God and our ancestors thanking them for the greatness that had been bestowed upon our family and the community, his gaze shifted in my direction, and with a gentle grin, he uttered a few heartwarming words. "Welcome home, my son."

Through my tear-drenched eyes, I could see a huge crowd milling outside. Virtually every family member was assembled. We were hugging and shedding tears of joy. I was uplifted by the buoyancy of a thousand balmy smiles surrounding me in the same yard from which America had plucked me away from the bosom of a village awash with love many years earlier.

A few people commented about how different I looked. Some wondered why I looked so thin. Others simply regarded me with puzzled smiles. As I glanced across the sea of smiling faces, I noticed the conspicuous absence of my beloved grandma. My older sister, in a telepathic gesture, informed me that she had not been feeling well. Instantly, I made a beeline to her hut. When she saw me, she jumped up in sheer, wanton ecstasy, as if she were responding to a miraculous event, and gave me a prolonged hug while resting her weary head on my chest. When she finally released my torso, she began hopping on the spot, clapping her hands and singing gently and melodiously. Given her age and her physical condition, I was worried she might fall, but I did not want to douse her joyful flames either. Her grandson was the panacea she had been waiting for. Therefore I reached out and held her hand, and together we danced gracefully to the melodious sounds of her joyful exaltations. Finally, she calmed down, and still with an indelible look of excitement, she repeatedly exclaimed, "My son, you're back!"

As I sat in her dark, dingy, smoke-filled hut and recognized my old mattress-free bamboo bed with its wooden pillow still positioned adjacent to her bed, my memory flashed back across the distant lands I had traveled and the countless beds whose comfort my weary body had experienced over the intervening years. Then I realized that there could never be a more alluring bed than the one that knew me before I knew myself. It had something others didn't: *love!*

The years had taken a toll on Grandma. Leprosy had robbed her of a few more digits. Interestingly enough, her concern for my nutrition had not diminished after all those years. Her immediate priority was to prepare a meal for me, and I had no choice in the matter. I tried to convince her that I was not hungry, but she ignored me. I hated to see her toiling away in her condition just to feed me. Ultimately, I realized that the American democracy I had grown accustomed to did not exist in her hut. Nonetheless, it was indeed heartwarming to see her again. I loved her with every atom in me.

Uncle George stopped by Grandma's hut to welcome me home. I stepped outside to converse with him, and he asked many questions about America. I reminded him that about ten years earlier, standing almost exactly where we were, he had predicted that I would travel far and become highly educated. He had also reassured me at that time that I would be able to go to America if that was indeed my wish and desire.

On that first visit, I spent a great amount of time enjoying lovely conversations with my siblings. I was proud to see how much everyone had matured, and I am sure that individually, they felt the same way about me. My oldest sister, Kien, and a younger one, Siri, were both married with children. My brother was pursuing commercial interests in the city, and two other younger sisters were finishing elementary school.

I felt somewhat uneasy with all the attention I was getting. I was being treated like a hero, even though I did not consider myself special. Early in the morning after my arrival, I overheard an interesting conversation outside my window. A neighbor was concerned about what kind of food I might want to eat. She stated that my system might not be used to anything but "American food." And then another woman suggested scrambled eggs and rice because that's what, in her opinion, Americans ate. A vivacious debate ensued about the differences between the nutritional preferences of Americans vis-à-vis Africans. I was rolling with laughter.

After I took a bath, my older sister informed me that breakfast was ready. On the table were enough scrambled eggs, fried potatoes, and fried plantains to feed a battalion. I was left to eat alone. Then it dawned on me that in their minds, I had risen to a different social level in our community and was no longer the boy who had left several years earlier. I was a man who had just returned from "the end of the earth" and deserved to be accorded the same deference as the elders. They regarded me as a leader, and I had to conduct myself accordingly.

I ate a small amount of the food before joining the gathering throng outside, where I addressed everyone in my native language. They were enormously thrilled since many of them had erroneously assumed that I had lost the ability to speak it as well as I used to. In my speech, I expressed my profound gratitude for the gracious welcome they had given me. I assured them that despite the distances between us, I had not forgotten about them and that the love I had for each of them had remained strong in my heart through the years in America. They cheered generously in response. Then I announced that I had come home to enjoy their company, share some love, and rediscover and indulge in all the nutritious delicacies that the pursuit of education had deprived me of. They roared!

On that vacation, I visited almost every family I knew from childhood and expressed my sympathies to the loved ones of those who had died during my absence. Being more mature and having been exposed to a different culture had given me a deeper appreciation for the richness and interconnectedness of village life and culture. In my travels, I had not encountered the depth of true warmth, openness, and unity of community that was so paramount in the village. In many ways, the philosophy in Western culture, in which the pursuit of social and professional goals can leave a person psychologically dissociated from their community and foster rugged individualism and a "Darwinian spirit," was in stark contradistinction to the pervasive interdependence in an African village. In America, the degree of human interaction was often carefully calibrated, with individuals winding up lonely and physically isolated despite being surrounded by copious symbols of materialism, whereas in a village community, everybody was concerned with the life and welfare of others within the community and beyond. People shared openly and gladly their joys and their sorrows. In African village communities, love and compassion flowed with ease, and rarely did a person feel lonely.

In a twist of irony, some villagers imagined America in a different light. Many would have preferred to be living in America. They imagined a world with strong community bonds and perpetual social harmony, awash with wealth, suffused with endless love, and devoid of problems and suffering. In a sense, they were imagining a utopia! I surmised that their fantasies about America were derived from doctoral snippets in print media, captivating lyrics in American music, encounters with a few individuals who had acquired knowledge and skills from there, and familiarity with the benevolence of American expatriates and missionaries in various sectors in Cameroon.

When I visited a local hospital, I encountered extreme destitution and a marked deficiency in basic resources. There were many desperately ill patients languishing on the outskirts of hope in pathetic, dilapidated hospital wards. These were challenges I imagined I might have to confront at a future date. Every chance I got, I motivated the boys and girls in the village to stay in school and earn a meaningful education. I gave out a few books I had brought along. I noticed that my father was paying greater attention to my words than in years past, and my opinion was often solicited concerning family matters. Although I tried hard to avoid it, the elders wanted to include me in their ranks. Grandma delighted in reminding me and everyone else of my childhood escapades.

While my overall homecoming experience was positive, in certain ways I noticed an unsettling cognitive gap between me and others within the community. On an emotional and nostalgic level, I connected well with everyone. However, on a cognitive level, I felt like an alien. Our thought processes were hopelessly divergent in countless ways. To have a meaningful discussion with someone who believed tenaciously in witchcraft as the root cause for all events and occurrences like the weather, illness, death, failures, successes, birth was an insurmountable challenge. My attempts to inject scientific facts and explanations into some of their beliefs often fell on deaf ears. At times such resistant thinking, even among my siblings and family, left me feeling frustrated and lonely and wondering if all the education I had attained had not become an antithetical curse, isolating me from some of the very people whose encouraging support and motivation had culminated in my transformation. In a sense, I recognized that the solutions for this conundrum would have to come ultimately from me.

Overall, I had a beautiful visit, and when it came time to depart, I thanked everyone for a wonderful visit. I promised them that I would be back again. On the flight back to the United States, I reviewed the events that had transpired during my visit. I realized that although I was not in a position at that time to assume full financial responsibility for the education of my siblings and their offspring, I had to be prepared to do it in the future. I was their only hope. Most importantly, I had to come to an understanding that the onus to address and bridge the cognitive and experiential gap I had just perceived during my brief visit was on me since the opportunities that life had offered me demanded a leadership role from me in addressing such conundrums.

CHAPTER 54

Lovebirds

IN GRADUATE SCHOOL, I was assigned to teach a chemistry laboratory course for health science majors. One of my colleagues from China was teaching a similar laboratory course adjacent to mine, and our classes were connected by two doors. My Chinese associate had some difficulty with English language communication. While lecturing and supervising experiments one day, I noticed a female student carrying her instruments into my classroom via the rear connecting door. After the end of class, she came up to me and explained that she had made the move because she was having difficulty understanding my associate's accent. When she looked across the connecting door and heard me, she realized she would have no problem understanding me. Accordingly, she took her belongings and instruments and left her assigned laboratory position.

She sounded bright, pleasant, and quite motivated to learn chemistry. In time, she requested to join my after-class tutorials and often requested additional lessons. When she discovered that I was born in Africa, she informed me that she had previously visited Ghana with her mother and her brother. Hearing this tweaked my attention since up till then, I had met only a handful of students who had ever been to Africa. Her mother was a schoolteacher, guidance counselor, and nurse. Her father worked at an automobile manufacturing plant. She was neat, well-groomed, meticulous, and appeared to be more sophisticated in the way she spoke and dressed than many of the other students. Although it was not unusual for some students to arrive late for the group tutorial sessions, she was always on time. Over time we found ourselves spending many hours in conversation.

Her name was Denise, and she was curious about where I lived. However, I was embarrassed to tell her about my living situation because it was a tiny room with a bunk bed that I shared with a law student. To eliminate any possibility of her visiting me, I told her in no uncertain terms that my culture forbade premarital contacts between boys and girls. During that time, I ate once or, rarely, twice a day because of my limited finances; therefore, when Denise asked me why she never saw me in the cafeteria at lunch, I told her the reason was I did not like the food. However, I believe she knew better, because one day I received a call from her telling me she was downstairs in my building and that she had prepared a plate of food for me. Instantly, I forgot my previously stated visitation policy and ran downstairs to meet her, and we both went up to my room, where I proceeded to consume every bit of the delicious meal, comprising huge servings of meat, macaroni, vegetables, and more. I could appreciate the timeless adage about "the way to a man's heart is his stomach" working on me. It had been a while since I had eaten a delicious and fulfilling meal.

That day, she offered to do my laundry at her house. With a full and delighted stomach, I could not say no. I was receiving graduate school financial aid, which included a stipend of about three hundred dollars a month, which I used to pay for my room, feed myself, buy books, and send a few dollars back to my father in Africa. I budgeted no more than fifteen to twenty dollars a week for food. My main staple was packets of Chinese noodles, which I cooked on a hot plate in my room. Occasionally, I spiced things up and added a couple of hot dogs or a can of sardines to the noodles.

Not long afterward, she invited me to meet her parents. Her mother was an engaging and knowledgeable lady, and her father was demure, observant, friendly but deliberate in conversation. I was nervous around him, so I gravitated toward her mother. Over the ensuing weeks and months, my love for her was growing stronger. We both enjoyed eating out, window-shopping, and driving places. I saved enough money for a camera, and much to her chagrin, I became the psychotic paparazzo she never solicited. I relished every opportunity to capture her beauty and photogenic attributes on film each time we met. From that time on, every letter to my family included a portrait of her. We were both young, active, and happy college students.

Ultimately, I decided to leave the claustrophobic room I was sharing with my friend the law student; therefore, I moved to a one-bedroom apartment in downtown Cleveland, which cost me about a hundred dollars a month in rent.

Within a year and a half, we were married in a beautiful church ceremony, which was followed by a lovely reception at her family home. Many of the traditions and customs relating to the wedding were foreign to me, although I found tremendous excitement in the novelty of the events. Unfortunately, my family members could not attend. After the wedding, we jetted off to a Caribbean honeymoon at Club Med, which was a thrilling week of food and fun. On the way home, I was held back at the airport in Nassau, Bahamas, and reminded that I needed a new student-entry visa to the United States. I was obligated to remain on that island for a few days without my wife until I had completed the necessary visa application process. It was particularly difficult for both of us to be separated so soon after our wedding.

CHAPTER 55

Medical School

WHEN I RETURN TO Cleveland, we settled down in our new apartment and resumed our studies. I was more determined than ever to complete my doctoral work and begin the medical segment of my education. That year, I completed all the medical school admission formalities, but my greatest concern at that time was the cost of medical education. Some of the state-supported schools did not encourage my application because I was a non-resident. (Ironically, years later, some of those same schools were courting me with faculty positions.) Although I received invitations for interviews at several private medical schools, the travel and related expenses to those interviews were prohibitive. One day, I received a letter from the University of Cincinnati expressing an interest in my candidacy, followed by an invitation for an interview. I was excited because it was one of the most respected medical schools in the country. I responded that I could not afford to travel, and I requested to be considered for the possibility of a local interview by an alumnus of the school. When I did not hear back from them, I thought they were no longer interested in my candidacy. By then I had already received a few other admissions offers.

Several weeks passed. Then I received a surprise letter from Dr. Benjamin Felson at the University of Cincinnati medical school. He introduced himself simply as a radiologist. I had never heard of him. He said he was involved in the interviewing process and was particularly interested in my profile. He understood that I did not have adequate funds to travel and informed me that he and other members of the admissions committee could not make any decisions about my candidacy without meeting me in person.

Consequently, he would be sending me an airplane ticket to enable me to come for an on-campus interview. I was dumbfounded and thanked him profusely. A few days later, I was on a flight to Cincinnati.

The interview went exceedingly well, and Dr. Felson was one of the most affable human beings I had ever met. During the interview, one of the professors remarked that my transcripts did not show any courses in anatomy, biology, or related areas except biochemistry. My college education had been entirely focused on engineering, mathematics, and the physical sciences. The last biology course I had taken had been in secondary school. I remember reassuring my interviewer that I would have no problem with medical school anatomy and physiology classes. At that point, Dr. Felson chimed in and made a statement to the effect that any student with a strong background in the physical sciences and engineering would be able to learn advanced concepts in biology and anatomy.

Before my departure, Dr. Felson took me aside and told me that he was very much impressed with my academic performance and my past experiences and that he had no doubt I would do well in medical school. Therefore, he was going to recommend me for admission, and he would be glad to be my mentor if I decided to come there. I was shocked and overjoyed. When I was ready to leave, he gave me a big hug. I can't quite remember what else transpired that day. I was beside myself with unbridled joy and exhilaration.

On the return trip to Cleveland, I became emotional when thinking about all the support and goodwill gestures I had received all along at various stations during my difficult life journey up to that moment. So many of my experiences had affirmed the true meaning behind the African adage "I am because we are!" Not long after the interview, I received an acceptance letter, and my wife and I celebrated the news with her family. Then I began to make plans to move to Cincinnati. Concerned that I might have difficulty with anatomy since my only experience with it had been in secondary school, I bought a textbook of anatomy authored by Professor Crafts at the University of Cincinnati, and within a few weeks, I had read the entire book. My doctoral research was going along well, and I needed to put the finishing touches on my dissertation before starting my medical education.

Then tragedy struck again in the family. News came from Africa that my eighteen-year-old sister, Mambo, had just died from a postpartum infection. I had no idea she had been pregnant. Two weeks after giving birth, she allegedly began to have severe abdominal discomfort and died soon afterward. In my sorrow, I slipped into a depression, and I mourned her passing for weeks. During my previous visit home, I had encouraged her to remain focused on her schoolwork because I wanted her to ultimately pursue university studies. The poignancy of her loss was exacerbated by my inability to be there and support the family.

During those challenging times, Denise and I were also experiencing much acrimony in our relationship. We had been married less than a year and were having arguments and disagreements with increasing frequency. Unfortunately, we had no one to help or guide us. Her mother's solution was simply to show up and take her home. I had struggled hard to get to that point in my education, and I was afraid that a persistently bad relationship could derail my plans. Unlike her, education was the only thing I had ever known and trusted through the many challenges I had been through up till then. Looking back at that time, I see that I had inflexible and unrealistic expectations of her to have as great a commitment to her education as she did to our relationship. I was graduating and moving on to the next phase of my education but was still socially immature. But I was enormously driven and was laser-focused in school, and nothing else mattered more to me than getting an education. This created severe stress between us.

She was very intelligent and was still trying to find her purpose in life. To make matters worse, we were very young, and marriage had probably been a hasty decision. Unfortunately, after ten months of marriage, we divorced, and I began my medical studies after she moved back to her family home.

I rented a rooming house across from the medical school, and when classes started, I combed the region for part-time jobs until I found one in northern Kentucky as a chemistry laboratory teacher. The first few months in medical school were nerve-racking. My insecurities and self-doubt kicked in on the very first lecture. About 180 of us sat riveted in a huge lecture hall each day while energetic professors zipped through book chapters at warp speed.

On the eve of my first day in the gross anatomy laboratory, I could not sleep. I had never before worked on a cadaver. Besides, coming from a culture in which there was extreme reverence for the dead and numerous superstitions associated with death and dying, I was apprehensive about this aspect of my training. However, I knew I could not turn back. I had to face the inevitable. Therefore, when I left that morning for anatomy class, I was determined to act normally until I stepped into a large room with dozens of shrouded bodies and a stench of formalin, where, surprisingly, some of the students were engaged in banter and laughter.

I was assigned to a station with two other students, one of them a female. We introduced ourselves, and when I looked across the aisle and saw a stiff-looking cadaver surrounded by a few enthusiastic medical students, I felt as though I had more rigor mortis in my limbs than it had. Then I began to concentrate so hard on the shrouded body in front of me that I failed to hear many of the instructions coming from our teacher, Professor Norma Wagner. I remember her telling us something about respecting the bodies and appreciating them for helping us to become doctors. And then she instructed us to remove the body covers, although quite a few students had already done that.

I just stood there and stared. For a brief moment, I wondered if medicine was the right profession for me. My partners were waiting on me to make the first move. Suddenly, Dr. Wagner approached and put her arm on my shoulder. "Are you OK?" she inquired.

I hesitated. "I'm fine," I replied.

She continued, "It's OK. You will get used to it. Go on and remove the cover. Go on!"

Slowly and with intense deliberation, I peeled away the cover slightly until a pair of frozen eyes appeared to jump up at me. I winced a bit before stepping back while continuing to peel the cover completely from the body and revealing a very old, pallid, cachectic woman of medium height. Then we were instructed to flip over our respective cadavers on their faces so that we could access the anatomical area of interest for the day. Instantly, I slipped on a pair of gloves and a protective apron. Without wasting any time, my female colleague grabbed a scalpel and proceeded to dissect the assigned area at the base of the cadaver's neck. She appeared to have excellent dexterity and emotional control. I was deficient in both.

I was prepared to allow her to perform the entire dissection, so I grabbed the instruction manual and began to read the directions aloud until Dr. Wagner came up and insisted that everyone had to participate in the dissection. As she spoke, she reached down and began to demonstrate the process, using a scalpel and her bare hands. She was touching dead human flesh! My God, I could never do that! When it was my turn, I could barely look at what I was doing. Growing up in Africa, I had butchered many creatures without compunction, but this one was different! Our cadaver had been preserved with her eyes open, and she had appeared to have been staring selectively at me when I removed the shroud. That was an eerie feeling that I couldn't shake. Luckily, our time was up, and we had to leave for the next lecture. Boy, was I relieved!

The gross anatomy course was scheduled to last the entire academic year. On my part, I was thinking I wouldn't last a week. That night, when I returned to my apartment, I reeked of "cadaver smell" in my clothes and my skin. It was awful! I took a long shower and proceeded to heat a pot of beef stew I had prepared the previous day. When I sat down to eat, I looked at my plate, and the meat reminded me of what I had just been working on in the cadaver lab. That did it! Instead, I ate plain white rice and a peanut butter and jelly sandwich. As time passed, my comfort level with the cadaver improved to a point where I was often the first in and the last out of the gross anatomy lab. Periodically, I would return late at night alone to review some aspects of the cadaver anatomy. Eventually, I was dissecting it with bare hands.

On some weekends, Dr. Felson would call me to the radiology reading room, where he taught me how to read and interpret radiographic studies. He was a marvelous teacher who enjoyed inviting a few other students and me to his house for delicious meals and endless stories about his medical career. At that time, I did not know that he was one of the most famous radiologists in the world. His humility truly exceeded his fame.

Denise and I had frequent telephone conversations during my first few weeks in medical school. She was busy with her schoolwork and a job. She expressed a lot of interest in my medical experience, and I thought she would have made a fantastic doctor herself. She loved biology but didn't care much for the physical sciences. Then nostalgia began to kick in as I was struggling to manage the challenges of a new academic experience, so I invited her for a visit, and we had a marvelous time.

Not long afterward, she discovered she was pregnant. The news pleased me enormously. I visited her as often as possible and enjoyed taking photos of her expanding belly. Finally, in the springtime, she went into prolonged labor and gave birth to a beautiful, adorable baby girl we named Mankah ("Torchbearer"), after my maternal grandmother. I was tied up with final examinations and was unable to be there with her during that marvelous event. I could not wait to see her on weekends.

After a while, they both moved in with me; however, the efficiency apartment was too confining for our little girl, who needed more space. Therefore, Denise took her back to Cleveland, and for a couple of years, we visited each other often. During this time, our relationship again was experiencing tremendous stress. Our communication was dying, and our emotional connection seemed to be disappearing fast. Nevertheless, I visited as often as my school schedule allowed me so that I could spend time with our daughter, who was a delightful child prodigy. At six months of age, she could walk and perform activities beyond her developmental level.

On one of my visits, we took a road trip to Washington, DC, where we arrived late at night, and we drove around looking for an affordable motel. Eventually, we found one for about twenty-five dollars a night and settled in. Unfortunately, it smelled like a fish market in July, had an awful bed, and was teeming with roaches. We placed the bedsheets on the floor, laid our daughter on them, and took turns chasing away roaches from her all night long and couldn't wait to break free from that dungeon at daybreak.

The later years in medical school were more difficult. I was tutoring and teaching chemistry part-time in Kentucky while working on my doctoral dissertation, which I completed at the end of my first year in medical school. Afterward, I was able to successfully publish a few journal articles on my research findings. Medical school coursework was rigorous. To reduce stress, I embarked on an aggressive regimen of jogging and weight training. On one occasion, I met a delightful lady in the weight room, whom I assisted with her exercise routine, and we became good friends, had great conversations, and visited once in a while. She was pleasant, and I liked her maturity and poise. Eventually, we became intimate. She got pregnant and delivered a handsome adorable boy named Robie. However, the relationship between his mother and me did not evolve, though we maintained our friendship. I was now the proud father of two.

During this time, I was beginning my clerkships. The surgical clerkship in particular was both mentally and physically exhausting. My chief resident was not easy to get along with. She hardly smiled, and no matter how hard I worked, she was never satisfied. She made every effort to sideline me on her service, and she actively ignored my contributions to the care of her patients. I remember being on call with one of the interns, and we kept on working until about 2:00 a.m. We finally went back to the on-call room, where I slept in the upper level of our bunk bed. I must have fallen asleep within minutes because I was tired from having worked nonstop for about twenty-one hours. About thirty minutes afterward, the trauma beeper went off, and in my confused and disoriented state, I sat up instantly, and while failing to appreciate the true distance between my bed and the floor, I took a wild dive from the top bunk, landing on all fours. My glasses went flying in an unknown direction as various items in my pocket spilled out angrily all over the dimly lit floor. The intern had already bolted out of the room and was long gone.

I ran in the direction of the emergency room with my eyes feeling as though they were filled with sand. My mouth tasted awful, with dried saliva that immobilized my tongue. My brain was wondering what all that commotion was about. When I arrived in the trauma room, there was a legion of doctors, nurses, and X-ray technicians in attendance. Lying on the gurney was a rambunctious, combative young man who had sustained a few stab wounds to the chest and abdomen. I found a spot between the intern and a technician and stood there fixated on the patient. Then the chief resident came in and walked straight up to the patient, who was spewing profanities at everyone. She stood over the patient without uttering a word and gave him a stare that could hypnotize a belligerent polar bear. Amazingly, he fell backward on the stretcher and remained silent.

She proceeded to prepare and anesthetize a part of his midabdomen so that she could perform a peritoneal lavash. In this procedure, about a liter of liquid is pumped into the patient's abdomen to find out whether they have sustained any internal injury that could be bleeding. The result of the test was positive, and the patient had to be transferred at once to the operating room for emergent abdominal surgery. I went along, excited but exhausted. My legs were wobbly, and my brain had not fully awakened, but as I later discovered, I would not be needing the latter. The operation took three hours. I was awake about two of those and never saw what was being done. My right hand did, though. I was essentially a human extension to a metal retractor, and every once in a while, I would feel a quick, violent jerk on the retractor, which would remind me to readjust the position of retraction. From time to time, someone would acknowledge my presence and yell, "Pull harder!" Usually, this happened when I was drifting off to sleep.

I was positioned between two surgeons with my right elbow snug between their hips. After the operation, I was told to take out the retractor, but my arm remained frozen in place. One of the surgeons had to manually remove my hand and the retractor from the patient's abdomen. After twenty-four hours of service, I was ready to collapse anywhere in a quiet spot. Before going home, I had to complete my patient rounds and all related assignments. That was my introduction to the world of surgery. It was a physically and emotionally draining experience.

I worked hard during that surgery rotation; however, to my great surprise, the chief resident gave me a terrible evaluation. I knew the implications of having a bad evaluation. At that time, I had my eyes set on a career in surgery. Therefore, I was concerned that a bad evaluation would prevent me from getting a residency position. For this reason, I registered a complaint with the dean of students but received no feedback. Consequently, I began to consider other career options in medicine.

In essence, the chief resident's evaluation of me stated that I lacked the necessary cognitive and analytical skills to survive a surgical residency, based on her assumption that my silence during the rotation on her service had been a betrayal of my ignorance. I had not been demonstrating the usual attention-seeking behavior (the word starts with an *a* and ends with "kissing"), unlike other members of my cohort (all of whom received good evaluations). Her conclusion was made without any knowledge of my grades or the fact that I had just completed a PhD in chemistry while studying medicine.

During my medical rotation, a thirty-year-old man who had previously undergone treatment for testicular cancer came in with acute shortness of breath, with his wife at his side. They had two children. He looked pale and was gasping for breath. He was immediately given oxygen, and just when he was being prepared to be transferred to the ICU, he stopped breathing and suffered a cardiac arrest. At once, we began to resuscitate him. We must have worked on him for more than an hour, to no avail. It was awful! I had never experienced anything like that, and all I could think of were his poor wife and their children. I felt helpless. I accompanied his body to the morgue, where the attending pathologist asked if I would be interested in observing the autopsy. I agreed, albeit with some trepidation, and he allowed me to participate in the procedure. The patient's body was still warm, and I discovered that he had died from extensive metastases of testicular cancer in his lungs. I was beginning to feel the intensity of medical practice from these kinds of experiences daily.

When I returned home one night after witnessing the death of another young patient, I became overwhelmed with paranoia about my health, and I must have examined my testicles a dozen times that night, as I was sure that each time, I could feel a new and different lump. Just to be cautious, I paid an impromptu visit to one of the urology professors and expressed my concerns to him. We had been taught that testicular cancer was more common in younger men. The professor was attentive, patient, and understanding, and after a meticulous examination, I was declared free of unusual masses. For a while, I felt some sense of relief—until I sat through a lecture on brain tumors.

After learning about the unusual and subtle ways these tumors can present, I became concerned about my brain. I guess you could say I was becoming a hypochondriac. Once again, back in my apartment, I rummaged through my medical bag, removed a reflex hammer, and went to work pounding my knee, elbow, and other innocent joints in search of elusive problems. Then I opened one of my textbooks to a chapter with illustrations on neurological examinations and tried many of the techniques on myself. This went on for a while until finally, I resigned myself to fate. When we studied the cardiovascular system, I had an opportunity to observe a specimen of the human aorta, which is one of the main arteries in the body. It was chock-full of junk called plaque. Having seen this, I decided on certain lifestyle changes, and I eliminated cheese and butter from my diet. Additionally, I began to avoid every social situation where I could be exposed to cigarette smoke.

Then a few of my colleagues—Carl Ogletree, Kyle McCleod, and Chris Leggett—and I started an informal runners' club. Eventually, I eliminated beef, beef products, and pork from my nutritional regimen.

I spent my last year of medical school at Case Western and the Cleveland Clinic. It was wonderful to reconnect with my daughter and Denise. Our relationship improved and matured exponentially. Soon we were expecting another child. Ahleea, a cute, quiet baby, was delivered by Cesarean section. This time I was there in the operating room, armed with a camera and unbridled excitement. There were now three young members in the Zama clan.

CHAPTER 56
Medical Clerkships

As a senior medical student, I did a surgical clerkship at a local hospital in Cleveland that was an affiliate of Case Western Reserve medical school. It was an intense and demanding rotation during which I was allowed to function in the capacity of an intern. The medical student didactic sessions with the chairman of surgery were so popular that the conference room was always at capacity. Unfortunately, the chairman consistently ignored my presence or participation in the usual clinical discussions. Whenever I would raise a hand to answer a question, he would point at someone else. Even some of my peers began to notice this. It did not bother me too much because I was learning a lot and having fun doing it.

However, the chief resident, Abel Robertson, who was a highly skilled surgeon, was attentive to my educational needs and played a great role as my mentor during that rotation, even though I was a nervous wreck when I first started the rotation under his supervision. As I remember, on my first day on the service, he ordered bloodwork on a patient who was being treated for an infection. After struggling to draw blood from his arms, almost half an hour and a hundred puncture holes later, I reluctantly gave up. The patient's name should have been Job because he was more patient than I could've been. His poor arms were black and blue when I was done with him. When Dr. Robertson found out what had happened, I was ready to accept death as a fair and reasonable punishment for my incompetence. Instead, he calmly apologized to the patient and thanked him for his patience with the "future doctor," and then he proceeded to teach me about veins and the best way to draw blood. After that initial fiasco, and with his admirable patience, my blood-drawing skills began to improve with each subsequent attempt.

During that clerkship, I began to submit applications to surgery residencies across the country. At the end of the clerkship, I received a copy of my evaluation, which stated, "By far the best medical student we have ever had on this service. Despite being a medical student, he functioned very well and comfortably as a resident."

Encouraged by this evaluation, I discussed with one of the other medical students from Case Western Reserve University our mutual interests in applying for residency positions at that hospital. On his part, he was concerned about his low scores on the standardized tests we had taken in medical school. He submitted his application to the chairman and program director before mine, and a week later, I delivered my application in person to the chairman, but I never received the usual letter acknowledging the receipt of my application, nor was I ever invited for an interview, despite numerous phone calls and letters expressing my interest in his program. My friend, on the other hand, was excited when they invited him for an interview, and he received tremendously positive feedback afterward from the chairman of the surgery program. That rotation gave me renewed hope about my ambition to become a surgeon, even though the chairman had not shown any interest in me or my candidacy.

I had wobbled and equivocated after my first rotation in surgery the previous year, which had left me feeling discouraged with a lousy evaluation. I had even considered a career in psychiatry based upon a professor's positive impressions about my clinical skills on his service during that rotation. I had also considered internal medicine, which I liked very much. Dr. Felson had suggested that I shouldn't make any hasty decisions and that I should experience rotations in various specialties before deciding on a career specialty.

In later years, my experience as a missionary doctor in Asia, Africa, and South America would remind me of the rotation I did at the VA hospital in Cleveland. Resident doctors were pretty much responsible for the care and management of patients in that VA hospital. As a medical student, I was assigned a few patients. Ancillary help was rarely available; therefore, I spent countless hours working as a phlebotomist, transportation assistant, psychotherapist, and physician. I will always appreciate the patience and understanding that I received from those patients and the powerful role each one of them played in my training. Late at night, I would often sit with a veteran, listening to stories about their bravery, their fears, and some of the challenges they had to confront in wartime.

As we went through our training, medicine appeared to be more about the disease and less about the individual. The person was often dissociated from his or her illness or disease. Sadly, students became accustomed to terms like "the gallbladder in room 406," "the hysterectomy in room 310," "the coronary in the ICU," or "the tibial fracture in the recovery room." Medical students realized early on that there were no grades or credits assigned for sitting with an anxious patient at 11:00 p.m. and engaging her in conversation to understand her fears about an impending major operation.

I can remember being reprimanded by one of my professors for spending too much time with a patient. When I tried to explain to him that the patient had been scheduled for a leg amputation and was upset and tearful, he interrupted me abruptly, and in a sarcastic tone, he admonished me with "You are not a social worker!" This professor was a smart specialist, and although I did not consider him a good role model, he was a wonderful clinical teacher. His actions and words often belied a profound discomfort with having me on his service. Whenever I was privileged to offer an opinion about the clinical management of a patient, he would summarily dismiss my opinion as "jungle medicine." At the end of that rotation, he hand-delivered invitations to each student and resident on his service to a party at his home. I did not receive one. On the day of the party, as we were seated in the hospital conference room discussing patients, he reminded everyone in attendance about it. I was sitting next to him, and he turned around as though in afterthought and said, "You can come too."

A few of the students knew that I had not received an invitation, and after the conference, they wondered loudly why he treated me poorly, especially since I worked very hard. I did attend his party, just to avoid any potential animosity between him and me that could have affected my grade adversely. Not surprisingly, he did not even introduce me to his wife and children, as he did the other students. Interestingly, years later while working as a cardiothoracic surgeon in Cleveland, I was consulted to see a relative of his who was desperately in need of major heart-valve surgery. When I walked into the room to see the patient, sitting in a corner was my old friend, the enigmatic professor from days gone by at the VA hospital. I greeted him and everyone in the room, sat down on the patient's bed, held her hand, and proceeded to explain her problem and the processes involved in achieving a surgical solution for it. She was tearful, asked a few questions, and was demonstrably appreciative of our dialogue. I hugged her, and when I left the room, I felt the most powerful redemptive force surging through my body. Ultimately, the patient did very well. Her brother did not recognize me from the past, but that didn't matter. I was thankful for his role in making me a better doctor.

In those days, there was a powerful hierarchy in medicine, and medical students were largely voiceless. Voicing a disagreement with certain professors could lead possibly to a failing grade. I had to constantly draw on lessons that I had learned as a child in Africa about living above hate and looking for goodness in others. That professor at the VA was a good clinical teacher who had poor bedside manners, and I was glad to have had the opportunity to learn principles of medicine from him. How I applied that knowledge was my responsibility.

I came to a point at which I had to examine my true feelings about what kind of doctor I wanted to be. To make such an important decision, I reflected on the information I had accrued during my formative years in the village while observing my grandma's interactions with her patients. She treated each patient as her family member. Not only did she apply her knowledge of natural products to cure diseases, but she also sat with each patient and applied both physical touch and compassionate listening in her treatment protocols. Such a holistic approach to medical care—which she espoused so honorably, in my opinion—represented a greater value proposition to the patients she served. I decided that it would be a practice philosophy I would embrace in my career as a doctor.

I went back to the Cleveland Clinic to do most of my final year rotations. I had previously spent a few years there as part of my training for a PhD in chemistry. Although a good part of my doctoral research had involved the clinic, most of that exposure had been at the research institute.

My initial assignment was a surgical rotation with Dr. Victor Fazio and his team. I had been encouraged to consider that particular rotation by Beth, Dr. Fazio's assistant, whom I had tutored in chemistry class in years past at Cleveland State University. Dr. Fazio was a notable colon and rectal surgeon, and I was impressed with his commitment to teaching and research. He ran a busy practice but never appeared to be in a rush. I was the only medical student, along with several residents and a couple of fellows on his service, and because we had a lot of patients to care for, on most days we began rounds at 5:00 a.m. Routinely, I would make prerounds and collect all the necessary patient data to assist the residents in making their clinical decisions.

One day I was called to assist Dr. Fazio with a difficult and complicated operation. While observing him in action, I was overwhelmed by his technical dexterity and his smooth demeanor. In the middle of the operation, he paused, and I could feel the warmth of his gaze on my forehead. Thinking that I had done something wrong, I immediately began to search for an apology, and I looked upward slowly until my frightened eyes collided with his paralyzing gaze. Then, with a deliberate motion, he handed me his instruments. "Go ahead and perform the anastomosis [reconnect the bowel ends]," he commanded. He had just removed a large tumor from a patient's small intestines. Now he wanted me to reconnect the intestines by stitching both ends together.

I had observed this procedure only a few times before but had never actually touched bowels in surgery. Usually, the senior resident would be the one doing it and not a green-faced medical student. On that day, I was the only "body" available to assist the surgeon. I felt a huge lump in my throat. My heart was beating at the base of my tongue, and I was sweating in places where sunlight couldn't reach. I took the forceps and the needle driver from him reluctantly. Then the nurse asked me what kind of suture I wanted for the procedure. I did not know much about sutures. There were a million different ones! The room went so silent that one could hear a pin drop.

I turned my head, and with somber, defeated eyes, I glanced at the nurse. She had probably seen that look before on many a beleaguered medical student. I did not have to say a word. Promptly, she offered, "Doctor, you need this one" and gave me the appropriate needle preloaded on a needle driver. With forceps in my left hand to stabilize the intestine, I began to suture the ends of the intestines together, as I had seen it done before. After a few stitches, I paused for his assessment. At that moment, I felt as though I were performing on some stage with a packed audience in attendance watching my every move. I looked up at the surgeon for reassurance but mostly because I was hoping he would take over the operation and end my misery. Unfortunately, the only response I received was a castrating chuckle.

Therefore, I resumed stitching nervously, with every sweat gland in my body functioning at maximum capacity. Suddenly, the surgeon quipped, "Don't rush; the patient should be ready for discharge when you are done." I ignored his "words of encouragement" and continued. When I finished the first layer of the anastomosis, the nurse immediately came to my rescue and handed me the specific suture to complete the last layer. Finally, I was done! I stepped back cautiously and braced for a major reprimand, at which point the surgeon grabbed the intestine and carefully examined what I had just accomplished. Then he took off his gown and gloves, spun around, and waltzed out of the room. "Go ahead and close!" he barked before disappearing.

Confused, I turned again to my savior, the nurse, and she handed me all the appropriate sutures and instruments I needed to complete the job. A minute later, she stepped up closer to the operating table, paused for a moment, and stated, "You are the surgeon now, Dr. Zama." Then she added, "You know, he likes you. He never lets medical students do anything!"

I responded, "Thanks, but I am scared."

I was suturing the skin incision when the nurse whispered, "He is back." I looked up, and I saw the surgeon standing at the door, and in an instant, he asked me to stop by his office afterward. *This could be my last day on Earth*, I thought. True to form, and sensing my concerns, the nurse allayed my fears, "You will be fine," she said. Afterward, I accompanied the patient to the recovery room to be sure nothing went wrong. Dr. Fazio was waiting for me in his office.

He was a busy man, and on some days, he performed as many as ten operations. He also had residents, fellows, and medical students to teach. Every morning and usually between operations, he would make rounds on his patients. Additionally, he was a prolific writer. I didn't know how he could juggle so many responsibilities yet maintain his sanity and composure. I walked into his office and took a seat by the door. He always addressed me as "Dr. Zama," even though I was still a student. Without wasting any time, he told me he was pleased with my work and he hoped that I would be back to train at the Cleveland Clinic. And then his face turned serious as he leaned over his desk facing me and stated emphatically, "You have excellent hands. You should seriously consider surgery. I would be delighted to help you."

Ironically, I was uncomfortable hearing this. I was interested in a career in surgery, but my self-esteem was low. I had been demoralized by my experience with the chief resident on my first rotation in surgery. Besides, I could not imagine myself ever becoming as good as Dr. Fazio or joining his ranks. To me, he was a godlike figure. He had heard about my interest in medical research, and he emphasized that he would be glad to assist me with any research project of my liking. The longer we chatted, the more relaxed and comfortable I became with him. I discussed my interest in studying trace metal transport in inflammatory bowel diseases such as Crohn's and ulcerative colitis, an idea that he considered intriguing. We had a prolonged conversation about different topics, including my background and origin. At the end of our meeting, I left his office feeling both invigorated and reassured in my choice of a career in surgery.

From that day on, Dr. Victor Fazio, chairman of the department of colon and rectal surgery at the Cleveland Clinic, became my mentor, teacher, and confidant. Ultimately, several other doctors would participate in a similar capacity at various stations in my rigorous journey to becoming a surgeon.

CHAPTER 57
General Surgery Residency

I APPLIED TO RELATIVELY few residency programs in general surgery. Almost invariably, wherever I would go for an interview, I would be advised to stay at the Cleveland Clinic. At times, a few program directors would tell me they did not think I would rank them high on my list because of my Cleveland Clinic connection. Eventually, when the ranking results came out, I was matched with the Cleveland Clinic after all. This turned out to be the best option because I was familiar with the clinic, and most importantly, I would not have to move my family.

We were renting the upper floor in a two-family home owned by Denise's grandmother. Although the house was in the heart of "the ghetto," we had no safety concerns. There was tremendous love and a strong sense of community around us. Our children were safe and relatively comfortable. The older girl tended to climb into her newborn sister's crib and snuggle, but Denise and I were afraid she might inadvertently smother her younger sister. Even more disconcerting during this time was a major home invasion by rodents that brought back nostalgic memories of my African village. We had rats with strange body clocks! Whenever the lights went out, they considered it a wake-up alarm and emerged in countless numbers. As we were deathly afraid of them attacking the children, I would often jump out of bed intending to commit murder, but somehow, they would always seem to be aware of my intentions and would disappear in an instant.

Denise's grandmother and five other relatives living downstairs seemed to have a cozy symbiotic relationship with those critters and didn't appear to be concerned with them as much as we were. To address this problem, I went out to purchase rat traps at a hardware store nearby, where the sheer number of rat traps at the store gave me obvious concerns about our neighborhood.

After setting the traps, we would turn off the lights and retire to our bed. Within seconds we would have a new problem on our hands: relentlessly snapping trap noises causing me to get up every half hour to remove dead rats from happy traps. Finally, we decided our nighttime lifestyle was not sustainable. It was time to move to a rodent-free home!

During this time, Denise was helping out at her mother's daycare center. Eventually, she landed a job as a social worker on a $15,000 a year salary, and with my contract promising me an annual salary of $17,000 at the Cleveland Clinic, we thought we would be rolling in the dough! At that point, we decided to purchase our first home. We found one (in a different neighborhood!) with an asking price of $48,000. Neither of us knew anything about real estate, and we agreed to buy it without negotiating. On my part, I found the prospect of homeownership to be appealing for all the traditional reasons, including the freedom from rat traps.

After a hurried closing, we moved in at once, and our family began to relish the essence of the American dream! The house had air-conditioning, a two-car garage, and a small study for me. The way Denise decorated it, you would have thought we were living an opulent life in a chic Beverly Hills mansion. It was immaculate! I decided to surprise her with a new set of wheels because our temperamental AMC Concorde was becoming a financial leech. So I went down to a Nissan dealership and bought a new Sentra with air-conditioning and an AM/FM radio! Our budget did not allow for cloth or leather seats; therefore, I settled for plastic ones. It was a joy to witness the excitement on Denise's face when she received the car, and for a while, we were feeling like the Jeffersons. When the car seats became unbearably hot in the summer, I installed protective seat covers. Eventually, I bought a reliable used car for about five hundred dollars for myself.

On July 1, I officially started my internship at the Cleveland Clinic and was assigned to a month service on the surgical division at St. Vincent Charity hospital, our affiliate teaching institution. My chief resident, Mark, was bright, confident, capable, and attentive. On my first night on the service, we were called to see a gentleman who had been brought in with a gunshot wound to his chest. The trauma room was chaotic, and the patient had no detectable pulse. The situation was grave, and Mark took charge, announcing that the patient's chest had to be cut open at once to save his life. Then he handed me a pair of sterile gloves and proceeded to rapidly clean the patient's chest with iodine solution and then ordered me to perform the procedure at once, although I had never done it.

I realized immediately that there was no time for vacillating because the patient was dying. Trauma situations do not offer a surgeon the luxury of academic discourse, so without any forethought, I took a scalpel and slashed open the patient's left chest between his ribs. Suddenly his lungs popped out in my face, and Mark yelled, "Clamp the aorta!" My memory from anatomy class in medical school reminded me that the aorta was situated way deep inside the chest. I plunged my right hand in there while pushing the lungs out of the way with my left hand. I couldn't find what I would call the "aorta," but I applied tremendous pressure anyway.

Instantly, someone yelled, "We have a pressure!" At that moment I felt something beating against my lucky shaking fist. I was compressing the aorta, which allowed the heart to fill with blood and initiate a pumping action to keep the body and its organs alive. The patient had suffered multiple chest and abdominal injuries and had lost a great deal of blood, so we were rapidly transfusing blood and essential fluids into his veins. The cardiothoracic surgeon on call was notified, and he instructed us to immediately take the patient to the operating room. With my hands still in the patient's chest and compressing his aorta, we rushed him to the operating room with his blood generously splattered on my chest, limbs, feet, and shoes.

When we arrived in the operating room, I was relieved by one of the trauma surgeons, who looked at me and remarked that I needed a shower immediately because I was dripping with the patient's blood. Within minutes, a cardiothoracic surgeon arrived and took over the care of the patient. Back in the locker room, I ran into Mark, and he complimented me for my response and reminded me that my actions had saved the patient's life. Then he asked, "How does it feel to do an emergent thoracotomy on your first day in residency?" My response didn't need words, because the adrenaline rush I was experiencing was reflected in my expansive smile. At that moment, I realized that I had just made a transition from medical student to doctor, and that's how everyone would view me henceforth. That new title had come with new and greater responsibilities and expectations. That night, I was too excited to rest or sleep. I was all over the hospital, making rounds over and over again, checking up on our patients, and checking laboratory values.

The trauma patient came through his operation and did well. Surprisingly, a few years later, when I was a senior resident on the same surgical service, I was called to see a trauma patient with an abdominal gunshot wound. It was that same patient! We took him to surgery, and after repairing his injuries, he recovered rapidly and requested to be discharged from the hospital. Afterward, I had a conversation with him about his social situation and his affinity for bullets. Unfortunately, it was difficult to get an honest response from him. He stated that on both occasions, he had been minding his own business when someone had decided to shoot him. I warned him to be careful because the next encounter with a penetrating missile could be his last. As if in defiance of my admonition, he presented a few months later with gunshot injuries to his lower extremities. Again, he survived his injuries after a prolonged hospitalization. At that point, we began to call him by an affectionate moniker: "Mr. Sylvester," the cat with nine lives.

CHAPTER 58

Medical Role Models

THE CLEVELAND CLINIC HAD some of the best doctors in the world, who were also fabulous teachers. Many of them became my role models for such reasons as clinical and technical expertise, bedside manners, and social consciousness. On the vascular service, the attending surgeons were all outstanding doctors who were also technically gifted. Dr. Hertzer, a supremely compulsive and meticulous man, represented a pristine combination of compassion, passion, and technical excellence. No margin of error was accepted by him as perfection reigned in his world! There was not a single resident who did not feel intimidated in his presence. He had a soft gaze that could turn steely and penetrating in a split second. He loved to teach and was so hard on himself that he would maintain a tense demeanor during an entire operation.

On one occasion, I scrubbed with him on a carotid artery operation in which his first assistant was a fellow, a more senior resident-in-training. Everything seemed to be going well—just the way Dr. Hertzer preferred it, of course. Then the unforgiving happened. He broke a tiny stitch while he was tying a knot. Under normal circumstances, when this happens, the surgeon simply places a new stitch and resumes the tying process. The operation had been going so well that Dr. Hertzer was engaged in a lively discussion about tennis while other team members were in a state of tense relaxation. You never quite wanted to be too relaxed or too comfortable when "Stormin' Norman" (as we affectionately called him) was in action. The weather could change any second. Therefore, when the stitch broke, a steely silence at once descended on the room.

Dr. Hertzer very slowly and deliberately laid down his instruments, removed his surgical gloves and gown, took two steps backward from the patient, spun around, sprinted to a corner where he stood facing the wall with his hands in the air, and for a few minutes, he belted out a steady stream of bloodcurdling curses at himself, including a sprinkling of "goddamns" and "Norms" intermingled with "Jesus" and "sons of something" in the most unconventional combinations.

Not a soul stirred. You could discern the rhythmic bellowing of the mechanical ventilator, which was supporting the anesthetized patient. You didn't even want to clear your throat or move your body an inch for fear of diverting his attention to you. Then, just as suddenly, he walked methodically out the door to scrub again. During that interval, his powerful presence was still palpable in the room; therefore, no one spoke a word. He returned, gowned and gloved, and without missing a beat, he resumed the operation precisely where he had left off and picked up the conversation exactly where he had paused in midsentence. As usual, the final result of the operation was a magnificent work of art. After the operation, we waited until Stormin' Norman had left the room before engaging in normal pleasantries. Of course, we did this only after taking a few deep breaths individually.

Sometimes during an operation, if you were not performing your role as a first or second assistant to the fullest of your abilities, you would realize it at once because of the change in Dr. Hertzer's body language. If the surgical field happened to be flooded with blood and your suction technique was suboptimal, he would go into stop-action mode and just stare ahead at a vacuum. The usual response by the intern or resident would be to overreact and suck so rapidly, furiously, and vigorously that they would run the risk of inadvertent tissue injury. Conversely, with one of the other excellent surgeons, Dr. O'Hara, there would be a pause, and he would make an emotional plea, "I am drowning!" This had a subtle psychological effect of urging you to make an intense effort to do a better job clearing the surgical field while feeling bad for having been standing there and not paying attention.

The other two outstanding vascular surgeons, Drs. Beven and Krajewski, were more laid-back, and as such they provided an excellent reprieve and balance from their more intense associates. Dr. Beven notably walked briskly and greeted everyone in the hallway, waving at total strangers while whistling a tune on his way to an operation. Nothing seemed to bother him. He was Mr. Cool. During an operation, whenever he encountered a serious problem, he had a classic response: "Hmm, this is a tough one," and he would keep on operating calmly. Dr. Krajewski was an outstanding teacher. He never lost his composure, and he allowed us greater supervised autonomy during surgery.

Whenever Dr. Hertzer was on call on a weekend, we would prepare for a few hours of intense patient rounds. You never wanted to be in a position in which you could not provide the information he needed to make a decision about a patient's condition. Things could turn ugly in a second. He would not yell at you, but there was always something in the air. On many occasions, I would be on call, and after a long day's work, I would finally crash in my on-call room at about 1:00 a.m., hoping to get some shut-eye between obligatory nurses' calls. And then a strangely familiar office number would appear on my beeper. At once, I would call back, and at the other end would be Stormin' Norman. "Can we make rounds?" he would ask, half commanding, half suggesting. You might say, "No, I'm tired and sleepy. It's one a.m.!" Or you could respond eagerly, as if you had been hoping excitedly that he would be making such a request at that ungodly hour.

I remember the first time Dr. Hertzer allowed me to operate while he assisted me. It would've been more humane for him to have alerted me a few years in advance so that I could've prepared myself better for such a memorable event. The patient, who had no kidney function, needed a vein in his forearm to be connected to an adjacent artery to provide vascular access for his dialysis treatments. After his forearm had been prepared and draped in the usual sterile manner, Dr. Hertzer and I sat across from each other with the patient's forearm on the table between us. I performed my usual maneuvers to prepare myself for assisting him: deep breathing, shoulder shrugging, coughing, clenching and relaxing my fist, flexing and extending my ankle joints. Then I was good and ready for "the boss," as we referred to him sometimes.

Soon after we settled in our seats, he looked across at me and said, "You are doing this." Oh no! I was not prepared for that. But I had no choice, and the nurse instantly handed me the instruments. I was so nervous that I almost made the incision on my wrist instead. Sweating profusely, I isolated the patient's vein and artery, and I was prepared to connect them, but my hands were trembling uncontrollably, and I was hoping he would take over the operation. Then, in a gentle voice, he said, "I am concerned about your surgical skills."

Boy, that just about tipped me over! I felt as though I was being immersed in a cauldron, and I couldn't stop shaking. To make matters worse, he asked, "Are you nervous?" I almost replied, "No! Just dying. No big deal." There's nothing more nerve-racking than someone asking you if you're nervous when you are visibly nervous. It only makes matters worse. Only God knew how I managed to complete the operation on that day. Afterward, I honestly did not think I had the right stuff to be a surgeon.

Ultimately, although he was hard on himself and others, Dr. Hertzer had a heart of gold, and like the other physicians and surgeons, his foremost goal was to train us to be excellent, compassionate surgeons. I saw him rip apart a certain senior fellow on many occasions, only to wind up giving that fellow a remarkable recommendation, which enabled him to gain an enviable position somewhere; eventually, he became a famous surgeon and enjoyed an illustrious career. On my part, eventually, a beautiful bond developed between Stormin' Norman and me as my understanding of what he truly represented and my respect for him became stronger.

On the general surgery service, I enjoyed my internship experience with Dr. Robert Hermann, who was the chairman of that department. He was a surgeon's surgeon and a great leader whom I struggled to emulate in almost every way. He was a sharp dresser who wasted neither motion nor energy, operated fast, and make quick decisions. His area of interest was complex liver, gallbladder, bile duct, and pancreatic surgery. Often, he would purposefully request that I begin the operation alone, and I would struggle with it for about an hour before he would show up instantly and talk me through the procedure. He was a patient teacher with a remarkable bedside manner, which I admired. For the longest time, he kept calling me Nick, but I was too afraid to correct him, and eventually he corrected himself. Because Dr. Hermann's feedback on my abilities and progress was often spontaneous and frequent, I was able to evaluate myself better and concentrate on those areas where I needed improvement. As a chief resident on his service, I functioned almost entirely independently.

Drs. Vogt and Brougham, skilled, dedicated clinicians, teachers, and liver transplant surgeons, were younger attendings, and naturally, they interacted more with most of the residents on a social level. I was always happy to go on liver procurements with either of them. In the early days of liver transplantation, it was not unusual to spend fifteen hours in an operation after having spent about five hours on a procurement run. Other attendings, like Drs. Fazio, Jagelman, Weakley, and Lavery, were such engaging teachers that for a while, I considered a career in colorectal surgery, especially after I published a lead article in a peer-reviewed journal with their support and assistance during the first few months of my residency.

Other surgical attendings contributed immensely to my education at the Cleveland Clinic, such as Dr. Grundfest, who was a highly intelligent, unassuming, patient, and skilled surgeon; she was consistently fair in her dealings with the residents and staff. Dr. Steiger was a congenial, affable, and talented teacher whose lectures in surgical nutrition have enabled me to provide a higher level of care to thousands of patients.

Sometimes I worked anywhere from 80 to 120 hours a week, which was physically demanding, and in those days, you had to look and appear strong and ready to rock 'n' roll at all times, even when you were dying from fatigue. The surgery residency was very competitive, and someone was always ready to replace you if your performance was deemed unsatisfactory.

By and large, during the many years I spent studying and training at the Cleveland Clinic, I was treated fairly by most doctors and scientists. One of the few exceptions was a certain attending surgeon who was in charge of the surgical residents and who would often either consciously or otherwise ignore my presence during his conversations and interactions with other residents. On several occasions, his communication with me would be laced with hostile language designed to intimidate and leave me with the impression that he wanted to affirm his authority over me.

During my first year of residency, I received word from Africa that my sister Siri was near death from complications following surgery for cervical cancer. The following day, I took a previously scheduled yearly in-service examination in surgery. I was an emotional wreck at that time, and once again I was facing the possibility of another tragedy in my family. Therefore, I arranged to go to Africa after the examination.

When I arrived, I examined her and discovered that she was suffering from a complication of her surgery and had an infection brewing in her abdomen. After I successfully convinced her doctor that she needed an operation, he agreed and took her to surgery, where he drained over a liter of pus from her abdomen. Subsequently, she woke up and was feeling much better. She was my younger sister, who had gotten married at an early age and had four lovely children and a wonderful husband. Unfortunately, after I returned to the United States, she developed more serious complications and died a few weeks later.

CHAPTER 59

Hostile Teacher

WHEN THE IN-SERVICE EXAMINATION results came back, I discovered that I had done poorly. Therefore, a meeting was arranged with the residency director to discuss my performance. On the day of the meeting, I went to his office and greeted him when I walked in, but he didn't acknowledge me. He was standing behind his desk and wasted no time with formalities or pleasantries. He began immediately by wagging his index finger at me and announcing, "Boy, you are a disgrace to this place!"

That certainly caught me off guard. But it was only a preamble to a hostile meeting scheduled to discuss my overall internship performance. He continued to wag his finger while yelling, and among many statements he was spitting out about how horrible I was, he said I was flunking out and that it would take minimal effort on his part to replace me. Then he mentioned that my examination scores were "the worst he had ever seen" and that all the attending doctors disliked me and were uniformly disappointed with my performance in every aspect of my training. I didn't believe him, but I couldn't say anything because I was still reeling from shock.

Finally, he wanted me to be careful in the way that I interacted with everyone at the clinic because nobody liked me and there had been many complaints about me. Except for my performance in the in-service examination, I did not agree with anything he was saying. His words sounded more like the final nail in the coffin than cautionary advice to me. I had observed him on several occasions purposefully stand with his back toward me while he was engaged in a lively conversation with the rest of my peers.

On one occasion, I had obtained permission from the department chairman to motivate students at a local inner-city high school to consider some of the careers in the health-care industry. When I returned to the clinic that day, I was confronted by this hostile residency director, who expressed intense anger over my brief absence because he had assumed that I had left to engage in an unethical or illicit activity involving drugs. On my part, I informed him that I had never taken any illicit drugs—never even smoked a cigarette or tasted alcohol. He responded with more threats. Therefore, as I was standing in his office and hearing how nobody at the Cleveland Clinic liked me or had any good things to say about me, I decided it was high time for me to defend my position respectfully.

First of all, I apologized for my poor showing on the in-service examination but reminded him that my academic record had been consistently good up to that point and explained that unfortunately, the news about my sister's condition, having arrived just before the test, had had a definite impact on my performance. Furthermore, I reminded him that like other interns, I was still green in many ways but that I intended to continue to work to become a better doctor because I had a true love and passion for medicine. At that juncture, for reasons I will never know, he lost it.

"Shut up, sit down, and listen to me. Don't you get uppity with me with all that fancy talk, boy!" He exploded.

He had not offered me a seat when I walked into his office, so I had remained standing. Before I could respond to his commands, he sat down and then stood up rapidly and yelled again, "Sit down and shut up, boy!"

I kept my anger in check. He appeared to have a romantic affinity for the appellation *boy* when barking orders at me. It made me cringe, but I chose to ignore it. Then his next question was really explosive: "Boy, you're doing drugs, ain't you? I know. Come clean with me!"

I refused to answer. It was the second time he had asked me that question.

That was more than the usual session with a program director to review an in-service performance and offer advice or encouragement. It was obvious to me that he harbored a burning desire to exert his authority, particularly over me. The venomous ranting did not stop there.

"You are the worst intern we have ever had!" he yelled.

At that point, his entire face turned a reddish hue and his facial veins became markedly distended. Ironically, I became concerned for his health. He went on to say again that he would not hesitate to fire my "dumb ass."

I cannot quite remember all the terrible things he said to me that day. I sat in front of him watching his index finger wagging relentlessly a few inches from my forehead. I was feeling emotionally exhausted from his tirade and physically exhausted from the 120 hour-a-week work schedule I was maintaining. I had been told by one of the doctors that I had been the number-one pick in my entering class. How had I suddenly become "the worst" by every measure and in every way?

I thought about my sister who had just died and the beautiful children she had left. I thought about my family, and I wondered if I should just pack it up and call it quits. I decided otherwise because at that moment it dawned on me that he was hurting more than I could ever be. His emotional blowout was out of proportion to my poor performance on the examination. I refused to be the exorcist for his demons. Therefore, with a calm voice, I apologized for any distress I might have caused him and promised to do better. I had to keep my self-esteem in check so as not to exacerbate the festering acrimony between him and me. I reminded myself of a recent occasion when he had invited all the residents to his house without me. I had not been bothered by his actions because that incident had not been the first time I had experienced such marginalization by someone who was my superior and teacher. One of the senior residents whom I liked and admired very much and who was a consummate friend had remarked that the attending did not like me because he was "a good ole boy."

Later that night, after making rounds, I headed home. Then, abruptly, I changed my mind and drove instead a few miles in the opposite direction to Lake Erie, where I parked my car and sat quietly on a huge boulder on the shore. I needed alone time for some deep thinking and a little self-talk.

It was a moonlit night, and I could appreciate shimmering and undulating reflections on the lake from the parking lot lamps. I sat there alone, thinking about many things. I reflected on all that I had gone through up to that moment, and I reminded myself about the great responsibilities on me at that time and many other challenges awaiting me in the future. I decided that I would neither protest my director's actions nor allow him to defeat me. I was convinced that if I reacted angrily, I would be playing right into his hands, which was precisely what he wanted so that he would have an excuse to dismiss me from the program. I was aware of a couple of students in the preliminary surgery category who were waiting for an opening in the full-fledged categorical residency I was in and would have been delighted to take my place. The residency programs at the Cleveland Clinic were among the most coveted and the most competitive in the country, and there would have been no shortage of residents to replace me.

I thought about how I had started in Africa with a blueprint for my life. That blueprint included a vision, goals, and a recognition of my purpose in life. Additionally, I had developed principles that would guide me and keep me focused. With a solid blueprint, I knew I could always rebuild my dream structure if prevailing forces should ever damage or destroy it. I realized that to become successful, I had to live and look beyond hate in any form. Hate was nothing but a distraction intended to derail my purpose. While still on my journey, and without power, I had to resist the temptation to engage in senseless fights that could prevent me from continuing on that journey. To capitulate to evil and hateful forces would imply abandonment of my purpose, my principles, and my blueprint. In essence, I would be ceding control of my life, my freedom, and my independence. Therefore, I had to keep my eyes on the prize without ever losing control or ownership of my blueprint.

So I made a firm decision to never capitulate to hate!

I got back in my car and drove home to my family with a determination to improve my performance in the next in-service examination. It would be my best weapon. Consequently, I spent several hours each week holed up in my basement studying. Occasionally, to avoid the inevitable drowsiness from fatigue while studying, I resorted to a time-tested technique from high school to maintain wakefulness by keeping my feet soaking in a bucket of cold water.

CHAPTER 60
Work, Study, and Family

DENISE OFTEN TOOK THE children to a movie, a park, or her parents' home so that I could study in peace. This was very difficult for me since I enjoyed playing with them, but my crazy schedule did not allow me any time to spend with them. However, whenever I arrived home at night, they would jump on me and refuse to allow me respite. Sometimes Mankah especially would stay up late waiting for me to get home, and then I would carry her to her bed, tuck her in, and kiss her good night. Whenever I had a long stretch without seeing them, with youthful glee and innocence, they would ask me to call my boss and obtain permission for me to spend more time at home with them.

On a particular night, Mankah stayed up until about midnight, and when I got home, she ran to the door, hugged me, took my hand, and walked me to her bedroom upstairs, where she stood still for a while, expecting me to say something. When I didn't make any comment, she asked me, "Daddy, what do you see?" I still couldn't figure out what I needed to see. Suddenly, it dawned on me: she had done a meticulous job making her bed. She had a beautiful canopy bed, and I was impressed with her performance, especially since she was barely five years old. I told her I was extremely proud of her; then I hugged her and tucked her into her bed.

Ahleea would often refuse to leave me alone, even when I was extremely tired. Sometimes, trying to read a textbook of surgery with her sitting on my lap leafing through the pages was a true exercise in patience. Sometimes, I would be so tired after a hectic day at the hospital, but I would be overwhelmed with guilt about not spending enough time with them, and I would take them and their cousins to the movies. Such occasions provided me a great opportunity to sleep during the movie and be rejuvenated. On the occasional free weekend, we participated in one of our favorite family pastimes: scenic driving. Cleveland's suburbs boasted some of the most prestigious neighborhoods and elegant mansions in the country. Therefore, Denise and I used to take the children on a fantasyland tour of the upscale mansions. Sometimes we visited new developments and attended open houses at some of them. The children loved these opportunities to pick and choose their favorite dream houses.

My communication with the rest of the family in Africa during the years at the clinic was severely limited. I had little free time, and I was chronically exhausted. My focus was almost entirely on surviving residency. As far as my residency director was concerned, I continued to try to win his understanding, friendship, and respect, and I worked even harder to earn his support and appreciation. Despite my efforts in getting him to appreciate my true nature, he remained resistant, but I knew there was a soft spot somewhere in him. After subsequent in-service examinations, I couldn't understand why he would not invite me to discuss my performance, and his silence kept me on pins and needles.

My daughter Mankah became very ill with pneumonia during my residency and was admitted to the pediatric ward. Having her in the same hospital where I was training was very emotionally difficult for me. She hated needles, and she cried incessantly at any attempt to insert intravenous access in her. I saw her several times during the day, and I practically lived in her room whenever I was on call. Her doctors and nurses were wonderful, and although it bothered me to see her hooked up to so many drips, thankfully, she recovered from her infection and was discharged in a stable condition.

On another occasion when I was on call, I received a frantic call from Denise that Ahleea had sustained an injury to her forearm. She was brought in to be evaluated and was found to have suffered a dislocation of her wrist. While her hand was being positioned for X-ray studies, the dislocation corrected itself, and she felt better and happier. In those days, I was observing so many children with horrible diseases that I was always concerned about the possibility of one of my children developing a dreadful medical condition. I would poke and prod them frequently in search of problems that did not exist.

For a while, things at the hospital were in a steady state of hard work, long hours, and intense learning. During that time, I was honored to receive an award for excellence in research, which was followed not long afterward by another research award from the Cleveland Surgical Society. Then a new general surgery attending arrived with new procedures and surgical techniques, and I was assigned to his service along with another senior resident. After a month he called me to his office and began by telling me in unequivocal terms that I was not a good resident and that I would likely fail the board examinations in surgery after graduation. He continued to lecture me about his impressions that I was not reading enough since I never seemed to volunteer answers to the questions he would often ask the residents during rounds.

He stated that my knowledge was not up to par with that of my colleagues and was not congruent with my level of training. He concluded by saying that I should carry a book with me at all times like some of the residents did. On my part, I noticed that his communication pattern with other residents was patronizing and subservient, whereas when he talked to me, he would sound more dictatorial than instructive. He told me that he had spoken with the previous program director, who confirmed that my performance was substandard. In my mind, I kept a constant reminder of the African saying "Lose what's big by chasing what's small."

At the end of the session, he wrote a highly negative evaluation of me. His assumptions about me were completely wrong. In his very twisted mind and words, he expected me to know everything about anything. He often admonished me openly if my responses to a question were not exactly what he had wanted. I was under tremendous stress working with him. Interestingly, one day, a resident observed that the attending probably enjoyed putting me down to prop himself up. It was my judgment then and still is that he was an insecure surgeon with below-average skills in a community of superstars. Therefore, I became a convenient scapegoat for him. Later on, when I did access my file, after reading his evaluation of me, I was so angry that I pulled it out and gave it to my chairman, who, in a feat of anger, shredded it. All these subjective biases, preconceived notions, and hasty generalizations about me were psychologically difficult to live with.

In general, despite the tremendous stress I was under during residency, I enjoyed good health. I did, however, experience one episode of severe abdominal cramping with diarrhea, for which I made an appointment to see an internal medicine specialist. When I arrived for my appointment with her, I felt rather strange sitting in the waiting room with other patients waiting for her, although the receptionist did not know that I was a resident doctor. After waiting about an hour without any word concerning the doctor, I figured she was busy taking care of other patients. Therefore, I walked up to the receptionist to find out how long it would be before the doctor could see me or, if possible, if I could make a new appointment for a later day. You would have thought by the receptionist's reaction that someone had awakened her at 2:00 a.m. to borrow salt or sugar.

She snapped back at me, telling me in an angry tone that the doctor was busy and that I could leave if I chose to. Defeated, I sat down and waited a while longer before I was called in to see the physician. When the doctor came in, she obtained a complete history of my condition and proceeded to perform a physical examination. She did not know that I was a resident doctor either, and I saw no reason to share that information with her. First and foremost, I was a patient. She then asked me to lie down on my side, and I suspected she was going to perform a rectal examination, but I wasn't sure. I could not see her, but I overheard her mumbling something to the nurse. At that moment, I felt a cold hand on my buttock, followed rapidly by the thrusting of a finger into my rectum. Reflexively, I jerked away from her, and she responded by yelling at me to stay still. It was a very unpleasant, painful experience, and she didn't even apologize for her crude actions. After the examination, I got up, dressed, and walked out. I could still feel a phantom finger in my anus for days afterward, and I decided that the whole experience could have been different. I wondered how many other healthcare providers treated innocent, unsuspecting patients in that same manner. It was certainly not the way I intended to practice medicine in the future.

CHAPTER 61

My Passion

IN THE MIDDLE OF my residency training, I had to decide whether I wanted to remain in general surgery after the five-year training or to continue to a subspecialty. I had the opportunity to spend some time on the thoracic surgery service at the Cleveland Clinic, which was an entirely different world of surgery. The thoracic operating rooms were physically removed from the rest of the surgical specialty suites. There, I worked primarily with Drs. Rice, Cosgrove, and Lytle. From the beginning, they embraced my involvement and interest, and I never questioned their resolve to teach, support, and guide me. I had already spent an enormous amount of time in various surgical subspecialties before coming to the thoracic service.

One day I asked Dr. Cosgrove if I could observe an open-heart operation, and with enthusiasm, he encouraged me to join him in a surgical suite, where I stood timidly in the corner of the room and watched as many complicated preparatory activities were taking place. There was an enormous heart-lung machine buzzing in the middle of the spacious room. The anesthetist was aspirating drugs from various bottles and carefully placing the syringes in order on a console. Three nurses were counting and arranging instruments and suture material on a large steel table. Everything appeared to be moving at a faster pace than in the other operating rooms. Meanwhile, the patient, a middle-aged gentleman, was lying faceup on the operating table and did not appear to be nervous. Eventually, the anesthetist put the patient to sleep with an injection, and then he inserted a breathing tube into the patient's windpipe.

After the patient had been cleaned and draped in what appeared to be a very complex routine, a rear door opened, and the surgeon appeared. After donning a gown and gloves, he asked for a scalpel, which he used to perform an incision in the center of the chest. Then the nurse handed him an electric saw, with which he split open the patient's breastbone. My eyeballs were still struggling to stay in their sockets when, suddenly, I saw the heart beating live and vigorously. It looked nothing like the one in gross anatomy lab. I was mesmerized! After thousands of complicated steps with clamps, needles, and many long pieces of tubing, the patient's heart stopped beating, but mine was still thumping hard. I could not see the rest of the operation, but I remember that when he completed the procedure, he grabbed a set of paddles, barked out a few instructions, and then zapped the heart with them. Instantly, it jumped back to life and began beating with renewed vigor. I was sold! That was what I wanted to become: a cardiothoracic surgeon.

I had already enjoyed a month with Dr. Rice learning about general problems with lungs and other organs within the chest. Therefore, the opportunity to observe heart surgery was the icing on the cake for me. Then my memory took me back to my village in Africa and my fascination with the frog's beating heart. I remembered how excited and puzzled I had been with its tiny heart beating in my hand. *Could it be destiny?* I wondered.

Soon after I joined the cardiothoracic service, the senior fellow left permanently for some unknown reason. I remember Dr. Rice giving me the former fellow's beeper and telling me, "You are now the fellow. Can you handle it?" After he said that, I think he realized I might start living in the hospital because the cardiothoracic service was extremely busy. I called my wife and informed her that she would not be seeing much of me for a while. Henceforth, I practically lived at the hospital. Occasionally, at night, I would be consulted to perform complicated procedures such as bronchoscopies to help a patient in the ICU breathe better. I was learning and practicing management protocols for patients after heart and lung surgeries and working as a critical care specialist, even though I was only a second-year resident. The harder I worked, the greater the support I received from the thoracic surgeons. On one occasion, Dr. Rice called Denise to tell her that I was OK as I had not been home in a long time. I missed my family, but I could not pass up that great opportunity to immerse myself in what I considered my true calling, my passion. I had started out dissecting innocent frogs in Africa, followed by several years of researching trace metals in heart disease, for which I earned a doctorate in chemistry. Therefore, there was no doubt in my mind that I wanted to be a cardiovascular and thoracic surgeon.

Approximately a year later, I began to apply to a few universities to study and train in cardiothoracic surgery upon completion of my general surgery residency. I can recall being interviewed by a famous professor at Yale who challenged me on a controversial chemistry issue concerning heavy water that was making national headlines at that time. He was visibly shocked and surprised at my detailed knowledge of the subject. Luckily, I had just read about it the previous night to relieve my boredom in the hotel room. At that interview, several other candidates from various programs in the country and I all congregated in a room at lunchtime, where we shared information about our backgrounds. For unknown reasons, after I heard what many of them had accomplished or were doing, I was left feeling so intimidated that I figured my chances of gaining admission to the Yale program were slim to none.

My next stop was Boston, a city I was familiar with from my college days. The interview at Harvard was grueling. I met with at least eight Harvard professors, and by the time it was over at four o'clock in the afternoon, I was mentally depleted. Several other candidates from strong, prestigious institutions were interviewed that same day. They were all brilliant and well-published in peer-reviewed journals. I had also published articles, and I had earned a PhD, but for some reason, I was consumed with feelings of inadequacy against the other candidates. After I returned home from that interview, without consulting or telling anyone about my decision, I wrote a letter to the Harvard program director and withdrew my application. Then I took an interview at a program in the South, which I liked very much.

About a week later, I was summoned to Dr. Hertzer's office because he had an important matter to discuss with me. He, along with Drs. Fazio and Rice, had written powerful recommendations on my behalf. When I sat down to listen to what he had to say, he immediately informed me that he had received a phone call from Dr. F. Henry Ellis, a famous Harvard professor, who was curious as to why I had withdrawn my application since, to his knowledge, I was the first candidate ever to have done that. Also of interest was the fact that everyone involved in the interviewing and selection process had picked me as their top candidate for admission to the Harvard program. Without wasting any time, Dr. Hertzer proceeded to give me some "fatherly" advice about the importance of getting an education at the best institutions. It was a short meeting, and when it ended, his advice to me was simple: "Get your ass back in there!"

I immediately contacted Dr. Ellis and arranged for another visit. A few months later, I received an admission letter from Harvard. I called Denise with the news, and that night we celebrated at a buffet restaurant.

CHAPTER 62

Empowerment

SOMETIME DURING MY FINAL year of training, I was working late one night preparing for a lecture I had been scheduled to deliver the next day. When I went to the surgery department to use the copying machine, I found a sheet of paper that someone had forgotten beneath the lid. Curious, I turned it over, and to my amazement, I was staring at a five-year summary of the performance of surgery residents on the national annual in-service examination. To my greatest surprise, I discovered that not only was I not the "worst resident," as my director had told me, but my performance also had been better than many of the more senior residents.

Hurriedly, I made a copy of it and ran home to share the news with my wife. Feeling empowered, I returned to the hospital the next day still demonstrating respect and humility in all my dealings, although my spirits and confidence were soaring, and I was determined to not allow myself to be humiliated or deterred any longer. Then I went to the department secretary and requested to see my file, and I was surprised by all the consistently good evaluations I had been receiving. Not long after that, I was in an outpatient clinic with our expert thyroid surgeon, Dr. Esselstyn, when he pulled me aside and made positive comments about my performance in general and particularly in one of the most recent in-service examinations. His comments gave me renewed confidence and spurred me to work even harder.

One day I was called urgently to the operating room. When I arrived, my nemesis, the program director, was having tremendous difficulty addressing troublesome bleeding in a patient's abdomen and appeared visibly shaken. He requested that I replace the junior assistant who was helping him. When I saw the problem confronting him, I provided the level of assistance he needed to control the bleeding. At that point, the nurse leaned over and whispered, "Thank goodness you came." Then he left me alone to complete the operation and walked out without offering any thanks or appreciation for my assistance. Before long, a different attending assumed the role of program director. He was engaging, fair, and objective, and I truly enjoyed working with him. Sometimes, he would take me on recruitment trips to various medical schools.

Then one day, I received a surprise call from the previous director because he wanted to discuss treatment options for one of his patients. At the end of that conversation, he went into an emotional tirade about the problems he was having with the CEO of the hospital. He had been told that he was not productive enough and had been asked to leave. While I was shocked to hear him speak in such detail about his predicament, I had the impression that he needed somebody he could trust to talk to. He could not stop talking as he decried how he had been treated and talked about how shameless and uncaring the hospital leadership had been to him. He talked about their lack of humanity and appreciation for his services. There was tremendous sadness in his voice. He mentioned how the decision to fire him had adversely affected his wife's health by exacerbating her preexisting health problems. I felt sorry for him, and I couldn't help but wonder why he had chosen to spill his guts with me after all the hell he had put me through over the years. Eventually, he found a position somewhere, where he finished his medical career.

Not long after that, I was admitted to Harvard to train in cardiothoracic surgery, where I wrote an article featuring one of his previous patients. I included his name as a coauthor of the article, which was published in a prestigious European surgical journal, and I mailed him a copy of it but never heard back from him. I still believe he was a good man.

CHAPTER 63

Chief Resident

MY FAVORITE YEAR AT the Cleveland Clinic was the last year of my training. As chief resident in surgery, I enjoyed a greater degree of freedom and responsibility, and I took a particular interest in teaching and helping to train junior residents. Almost all of my teachers allowed me significant latitude in the care of our patients.

It was also during the final year that I received a surprise phone call from an uncle who had been a highly successful businessman but had hesitated to assist me financially when I was leaving Africa. That call came from a New York hospital, where he had been diagnosed with a large liver tumor. He sounded desperate and stated that he was penniless. I was concerned about his condition. Immediately, I made arrangements to wire him some money from our meager savings and then took my family on a road trip to visit him because I was concerned about him. When we saw him at the hospital, he was extremely happy and visibly moved by the outpouring of love from all of us, especially the children. After speaking with his surgeon and reviewing all his studies, I was convinced that the tumor was too large and extensive to be removed, and I discouraged him from going through surgery because he would likely die from the operation. Even his surgeon agreed with my opinion.

In my attempts to further dissuade him from having surgery, I reminded him that he was a very important person in Africa and that it would be awful for him to die like a dog in a foreign land. Alternatively, if he returned home at once, he would have enough time to spend with his wife, children, and community members and put his affairs in order before his ultimate demise. With Denise and the children waiting in the hallway, I spoke to him privately and passionately about his medical situation. After I finished talking, he looked at me and expressed his sadness and the guilt he had been experiencing because he had helped so many sons and daughters of his friends at a time that I needed him the most, but for whatever reason, he had ignored my overtures for assistance. I responded by openly affirming my love for him, for indeed I believed that despite a history of misguided and improper judgments, he was a great human being. At that juncture, I walked out briefly and then returned with my family so that they could bid him farewell. I was convinced they would never see him again.

After we returned to Cleveland, I called him, and in the course of our brief conversation, he expressed a desire to have the operation against my better judgment, and I wished him well. A week later, I received a phone call from that hospital announcing his death. About a year later, when I returned to Africa and met his family, I felt a strong personal need to help them. One of his children in secondary school was very bright. Therefore, I went to his school principal and paid his tuition for the remaining school years. I believe he had an honest desire to study, but unfortunately, he must have been fighting a few psychological battles, not the least of which was the death of his father. Sadly, he requested disbursement of his tuition money from the principal and quit school permanently.

Finally, graduation day arrived at the Cleveland Clinic. I brought my family with me to share the joy of that special occasion, and to my greatest surprise, I received the prestigious George C. Crile Award. It was indeed a humbling surprise. Afterward, Denise arranged a reception for me at the Cleveland Clinic Inn, where several family members, including a few of my college professors, were in attendance. I was touched by all the warmth, love, and support from everyone, and I found it hard to fathom what I had gone through all those years. I could not have done it without the help and support of many people. At the same time, I was mindful of the continuing challenges I would be facing in the days ahead.

CHAPTER 64

Harvard

WITHIN DAYS, WE SOLD our cozy little home, rented a U-Haul truck, and moved to Cambridge, Massachusetts, to begin a new adventure. A few days later, I began a new phase in my educational journey at Harvard Medical School and Beth Israel Deaconess hospital under the leadership of Dr. Sydney Levitsky, a powerful academic with a passion for teaching and research. Dr. F. Henry Ellis, a phenomenal teacher and surgeon with unsurpassed knowledge and skills in thoracic surgery, took me under his wing. Other professors and attendings, such as Drs. Wilford Neptune, Robert Duncan, Stephen Leahy, Karl Karlson, Peter Maggs, and Joseph LoCicero, were phenomenal teachers and superstars in their own right.

During the Boston years, I was rarely home with my family. I put in about 120 hours or more each week with in-house on-call duties every other night. The physical, emotional, and cognitive demands in cardiovascular and thoracic surgery were stringent and required constant attention to detail because any slight mistake could lead to the death of a patient. Heart surgery patients presented unique challenges both during and after surgery; therefore, I spent many nights at the bedsides of patients who were unstable after heart surgery.

The Harvard training programs at that time lacked diversity. Once again, I "was highly visible" wherever I went, and I discovered that over the years, I had developed a greater capacity to remain focused on my work while ignoring negative distractions. Frequently, I would be interrogated by someone about how I had gotten there. Eventually, I came to realize that it was not a question concerning the mode of transportation. For some reason, none of my cohorts seemed to be confronted with similar inquiries.

My training included congenital heart surgery at Boston Children's Hospital under Dr. Aldo Castaneda, a great teacher, a gifted surgeon, and a superbly gregarious gentleman, who was at that time the most globally recognized name in his specialty. My experience at Children's Hospital was extensive, varied, and highly structured. Drs. Meyer, Jonas, and Henley, other prominent surgeons on the service, were excellent and consummate teachers. It was always a delightful experience to participate in the care of a child with severe congenital heart problems and to witness the joy in a parents' eyes and their gratitude after the successful surgical correction of a child's problem.

Conversely, some outcomes were heart-wrenching. I will never forget a newborn who was transferred to us late one night for the treatment of a severe heart problem. The child had been born with his heart sitting outside of his body, a condition referred to as ectopia cordis. He had a few other abnormalities as well. I recall the nurse and I stayed up all night with the baby, keeping watch over its delicate body and correcting any blood and circulatory problems that arose. His parents took turns staying up with us. The tiny baby was their only child. Unfortunately, despite our valiant efforts, he succumbed to his congenital heart condition. I was deeply saddened by his death, and I felt as though we had failed the patient and his parents.

Moving on to the next patient after losing a patient on that service was always difficult for me. Each experience with life or death on the service taught me about the real impact of illness on the fabric of a family. When a child or adult was sick, their loved one became sick. Each time a patient began to turn the corner and was feeling better, you could witness a "recovery" on the part of the patient's family and loved ones as well.

The long hours that I put in daily, including the prolonged intervals of absence from my family, took a toll on all of us. Mrs. Marilyn Reid, who had been a very supportive cheerleader of mine in college, was living next door to us. She nurtured a wonderful relationship with the children, especially Mankah, whom she enjoyed cooking with. Unfortunately, my children were understandably unhappy in Boston. They did not like their new school and missed their cousins back in Cleveland, where they had great support systems. Consequently, we all agreed on a difficult decision to move them back there after our first year in Boston.

It was also during this time that I received a sad letter informing me about the death of my beloved grandmother. All those difficult events combined to rock my foundation, but I had no other choice except to keep the focus on my training. I spent whatever few spare moments I had studying for my board examination in general surgery. I had to pass both the written and oral exams before I could eventually qualify to take the examination in cardiothoracic surgery. I was particularly concerned with the high failure rate among new graduates. The process of becoming a certified cardiothoracic surgeon was complicated and difficult. After medical school, you had to train for a minimum of five years to become a general surgeon before you could enter a training program in cardiothoracic surgery.

Additionally, in order to qualify to take the certification examination in cardiothoracic surgery, you had to have passed both the written and oral exams in general surgery. It was a rigorous process, and I was so concerned about the possibility of failing the general surgery board exam that as soon as I took it, I made plans immediately to retake it. I was also afraid that if Harvard discovered that I had failed the general surgery exam, they might ask me to leave.

A month after taking it, I received a letter from the American Board of Surgery, which I could not bring myself to open. On that day, I received other mail as well, mostly utility bills, which I opened immediately. I kept thinking obsessively about how my future career hinged on the contents of that envelope. Eventually, I sat down and mustered the courage to open it. To my surprise, it was a short letter that started with *Congratulations*. I screamed with joy. At least I had overcome the first major barrier on the final stretch of an endless educational journey. A few months later, I went to San Diego to take the oral exam in general surgery, which I passed. Everything seemed to be on the right track at that point.

At Boston Children's Hospital, I was sitting in the cafeteria one day and enjoying lunch with one of my friends, Dr. Didier Loulmet, who was there in training with me on the Harvard surgical service. It had been a particularly rough week on the service, and among the many topics we discussed that day was the lack of highly specialized surgical care in other parts of the world, especially in developing countries. In the end, we both decided that after graduation, we would travel the world and perform surgeries for free in poor countries. Afterward, I gave more thought to the prospects of realizing such a goal, but I did not have an implementable strategy in mind at that time.

Eventually, Didier left Boston before I did and moved back to Paris. Then I met a famous French surgeon, Dr. Carpentier, a luminary in cardiac surgery, who was a visiting professor at Harvard. After a brief conversation with him, he invited me to Paris, where I could receive further training in complex heart-valve surgery. Excited, I obtained permission from my chief, and a few months later, I flew to Paris, where I spent a long time training under him. It was during this time that I overheard him in a conversation with someone in the operating room talking about a letter he had just received from Cameroon, Africa, asking if he could send a team to perform pediatric heart surgery. It stated that many children were dying from congenital heart problems and there were no heart surgeons to help them. I listened intently and with interest.

Afterward, I approached him and informed him that I was originally from Cameroon and that I would be delighted to accompany him on a surgical mission after graduation. I was particularly drawn to his humanitarian instincts. He often traveled to poor countries to provide lifesaving surgical care. It was his influence that ultimately guided me in my pursuit of medical humanitarianism.

After I returned from Paris, I began to receive calls from prospective employers. I also was being hounded with threatening calls from collection agencies demanding immediate payments for the tens of thousands of dollars I owed in medical school loans, although I had begun paying some of them after medical school. One day, Dr. Levitsky called me and offered me a faculty position at Harvard Medical School after my graduation. I spoke to Denise about it, and she was not thrilled with the idea of living in Boston. Both Dr. Loop, cardiothoracic surgeon and CEO of the Cleveland Clinic at that time, and his wife, Dr. Bernadine Healy, had spoken to me on several occasions, expressing their mutual desire to have me on the staff of the clinic after my training in Boston, but I was not keen on returning to Cleveland either. However, when I did tell Denise about a job opportunity in York, Pennsylvania, she was more agreeable to that option.

Eventually, I completed my education and training at Harvard, and a private graduation party was held for me at Dr. Levitsky's home, where many of the faculty members came to celebrate with my family and me. Afterward, Dr. Peter Maggs gave another reception for me at his residence. I had accepted a job offer from York, Pennsylvania, and when Dr. Maggs heard about it, he offered me an unsolicited loan for $5,000 with no term limits to facilitate my transition to professional life. It was a timely, most appreciated, and spontaneous gesture that I will never forget.

At a brief reception, the critical care nurses at the Harvard Deaconess teaching hospital offered me numerous presents. Afterward, I went to the parking garage, where I sat in my car for a moment staring at my surroundings. Then a realization hit me, and I looked at myself in the rearview mirror and saw an incredible reflection reassuring me that I had finally made it. The long, tortuous academic journey had just ended. Finally, Monica and Michael's little boy had accomplished the mission he had embarked on decades earlier. It seemed surreal, even at that moment.

"I am a cardiothoracic surgeon!"

I professed it to myself thunderously, as though I needed to reassure myself that I was not in a hallucinatory state. With my Nissan Sentra in first gear, I crawled out of the garage to a traffic light, where I shifted into high gear after taking Brookline Avenue and allowed the Harvard Longwood community to slowly fade away in my rearview mirror.

I was tootling along the Charles River on my way to Cambridge and thinking about stopping for a quick bite near my apartment on Harvard Square when, suddenly, I was overcome with emotion as I began to think about the long journey I had traveled, which began in a tiny African hut and ended up at Harvard—a journey filled with ethereal hopes and seemingly endless challenges. I thought about all the unsung heroes whose sacrifices, generosity, love, and prayers had made that journey possible. I thought about how so many of them had died before my dream could be realized.

I thought about all the angels who had been stationed along that difficult road and about God's persistent guidance to me when all hope seemed lost.

I thought about Uncle Daniel's valiant efforts to position me at the starting line on that journey, Uncle George's persistence, and Grandma's eternal heavenly lessons. I thought about my parents keeping watching over me in the glow of candlelight or a kerosene lamp while I studied. I thought about my own family, which had been sidelined by my career. Finally, I thought of that great nurse crying out in desperation (*"There is no doctor!"*) while my heavily bleeding thirty-year-old mother was in the throes of death. There are many other thoughts that were too heavy for me to bear at that moment.

I pulled over to the side of the road. Alone, on a moonlit night along the banks of the rippling river, I paused my mind and allowed the tears to flow mightily from my weary heart. After I regained composure, my wrinkled stomach reminded me of my dinner plans. Like that of the ever-flowing river, my journey was not over.

CHAPTER 65

The Cardiovascular and Thoracic Surgeon

We moved to York, Pennsylvania, where my family was welcomed with open arms, and I joined two senior surgeons at a community teaching hospital. I remember my first operation as a principal surgeon. I barely slept on the eve of the procedure, and I had to keep on reminding myself that I was no longer a student. When I walked into the operating room, I was trembling. Thank goodness the poor patient was under anesthesia. Surprisingly, the moment my scalpel made contact with his skin, I became calm, and the operation proceeded without a hitch. I had finally arrived, and I was "the surgeon." No professor was waiting to bail me out in case I got into trouble. This was it, and I was it.

After the patient was transferred to the ICU, I refused to leave his bedside because I was worried about every possible complication. I'm sure his nurse was wishing that I could disappear for a brief moment because my nervousness was becoming an issue. Nevertheless, I was experiencing a rite of passage, and my confidence continued to grow with each operation. We bought a house in the city and enrolled the children at a local elementary school.

Despite our best efforts, we were having difficulty adjusting to life in York. Therefore, we agreed to move back to Cleveland and join a friend of mine in a practice at the teaching hospital where I had done some of my training. The children were particularly happy because they were reunited with their grandparents and their cousins.

Not long after we moved to Cleveland, my practice volume experienced explosive growth, and at one time, I was working at five different hospitals. Additionally, I was involved in many community programs with youth and the elderly. Every chance I had, I made visits to elementary and high schools to encourage students to consider careers in the medical field. I was honored to have a highly organized and compassionate office manager, Mary McGowan, who was truly indispensable and kept me focused. Within my first year out of training, I successfully passed both written and oral board exams in cardiothoracic surgery. I recall receiving a congratulatory letter from Dr. Levitsky at Harvard. It pleased me that he still took an interest in my career. I was working even harder than I had during my residency and was singularly responsible for the tuition needs of over two dozen nieces, nephews, and cousins, as well as my children. Additionally, I was responsible for health care as well as other living expenses for almost every family member in Africa. I still shopped for clothes at Value City, Woolworths, and Zayre, much to the chagrin of Denise, who rightfully thought I deserved better-quality clothes and comfortable shoes.

One day, a friend and fellow physician approached me with concerning thoughts. He wondered why I was driving an old, rusty Nissan Sentra. He proceeded to tell me about the importance of perception, adding that "people may be thinking that you are not cutting well," meaning that I might not be perceived as a good surgeon because I was driving a cheap old car. That did not bother me. I had principles, priorities, and family responsibilities to address. Besides, I wanted to pay off my medical school loans as soon as possible and then purchase a family home.

During that first year in Cleveland, my cousin Fidelis Zama, who was working at the United Nations, fell ill and needed urgent surgical intervention. Interestingly, the previous year, I had mentioned during a casual conversation with another cousin that I had a feeling almost like precognition that I would be operating on Fidelis in the future. When I received a frantic call from his wife about his condition, I knew that something terrible was happening. He had been diagnosed with a severe inflammation around his heart, which was dangerously compressing it. After I made a few phone calls to his primary care physician and addressing a few logistics, Fidelis flew in from New York to undergo a lifesaving operation for his condition. No sooner had he arrived than he was taken immediately to the operating room because his heart was under tremendous pressure and was at risk of stopping.

After I entered his chest and repaired the problem, he remained a few days in the hospital and then continued his recovery in our home. I remember trying unsuccessfully on the telephone to convince his wife, Delphine, to stay put and that he would be fine. Understandably, she was upset, worried, and unconvinced. Therefore, she took a flight at once to Cleveland to be with him during his recovery.

CHAPTER 66

Trauma Alert and the Difficult Patient

I HAD AN EXCEPTIONALLY busy practice and worked long hours. One night at about 2:00 a.m., I received an urgent call from the emergency room at one of the local city hospitals. A police officer had just been shot at the scene of a drug crime, and the perpetrator had also suffered a penetrating injury. The officer arrived at the hospital without a pulse. The admitting resident doctor did not know what to do, so when he called me, I asked him to open the patient's chest between the ribs and begin cardiac massage before taking him to the operating room. He thought I was crazy because the patient was pulseless. Then I jumped out of bed, still in my pajamas, and raced down to the hospital. The roads were clear, and I was driving as fast as I could. The surgical resident called my cell phone and told me the injured officer was on his way to the operating room. I had about ten minutes to get there, and I was feeling tense and concerned about him.

Then I saw flashing lights in my rearview mirror, and for a moment I debated whether I should ignore them or stop. Frustratedly, I pulled over, rolled down my window, and waited for the officer. After he walked up to my car, immediately, I began to explain my situation to him, but he was unconvinced. He commented on my pajamas and asked to see my license, which I did not have because I had left the house precipitously.

"Then I have to detain you," he said.

I pleaded incessantly with obvious desperation, and I was practically in tears. I asked him to call the hospital and confirm my identity. Still, he was unmoved. At that moment, my phone rang again, and the same resident informed me that he had been able to open the patient's chest and was actively performing direct cardiac massage while heading to the operating room. Then I told the police officer I was rushing to work on a police officer who had been shot. Reluctantly, he let me go, and I drove away as fast as I could. After I arrived, I quickly changed into scrubs and dashed over to a busy operating room, where everyone was trying to resuscitate the police officer. The first thing I noticed was a large pool of blood on the floor. His chest was filled with blood, some of which was spilling out onto the floor.

I immediately connected the patient to a heart-lung machine and stopped his heart from beating. He had sustained severe penetrating injuries to his left lung, heart, diaphragm, spleen, and liver. A bullet had penetrated across the muscular wall of his heart into a heart chamber, from whence it was propelled by the pumping action of the heart to his lungs. It remained lodged in a critical blood vessel. For a moment, I couldn't decide how to remove the bullet from the vessel, which was deep inside the lung substance. Then I had an idea to insert a thin fiberoptic scope generally used by urologists, and I was able to retrieve it through a large hole in one of the main blood vessels above the heart. After a couple of difficult hours, we successfully repaired all his injuries, and his heart resumed its beating action vigorously.

Promptly, I was called to the adjacent operating room, where the shooter himself, who had been shot by the police officer, was also in need of my services. The trauma surgeons were already working in his abdomen and suspected he might have other injuries in his chest. Therefore, I opened his chest with the trauma team and repaired all his injuries as well. At 6:00 a.m., exhausted and haggard-looking, I sauntered into the family lounge filled with police officers and delivered the good news.

"Surgery was successful!" I announced.

The police officer who had stopped me earlier and almost arrested me was crying inconsolably. I had just operated on his best friend. I was feeling completely washed out as I was driving home that morning and wondered if the officer had not suffered irreparable brain damage from his cardiac arrest and the loss of a significant amount of blood from his injuries. To my surprise and delight, he woke up without any deficits.

The second patient also had a smooth recovery, despite his extensive surgeries. About a week later, the officer was discharged home to his family, whereas the other patient was transferred to a jail cell. The entire experience had been gratifying. Several months passed, and then one day I was called by a resident doctor to meet someone in a rehab unit within the hospital. I shook the stranger's hand, wondering nervously who he was. The doctor laughed out loud and proceeded to remind me of a police officer who had been declared dead on arrival in the emergency room department. I was acutely overwhelmed with emotion at the realization of his identity.

And then the doctor took me down the hall to another treatment bay and introduced me to a different gentleman. This time his peculiar uniform gave away his identity. Additionally, he had a few armed individuals guarding him. I hugged him also. He didn't recognize me, but he couldn't stop thanking me for saving his life. Afterward, I thought, *This is why I became a surgeon.*

In my practice of surgery, I have had innumerable memorable experiences with many patients. Some of them have been entertaining and enriching, while others have been profoundly inspirational.

I vividly remember being called by a brilliant colleague, Dr. Koch, to see a patient in need of coronary bypass surgery. Before I could say anything, he warned me that the patient would be a challenging individual. However, he did not expound on this statement, and I did not inquire to know more about the patient either. When I walked into his hospital room, I found him propped up in his bed with the lower half of his body completely tucked away in the sheets. His hands were glued to the edge of the sheets, as though he intended to pull them over his head. I greeted him and introduced myself. No response. He appeared to be staring through me while at the same time strangulating his bedsheets.

I informed him that I had come to discuss the need for an operation for his condition. Then as I proceeded to sit on the edge of his bed near his feet. He shifted them away so swiftly that I was concerned he would fall off the opposite side of the bed. I felt compelled to reassure him that I had not come to drag him off to surgery, and I told him that I only wanted to discuss his situation and the treatment option of surgery, adding that he was under no obligation to consent to the operation. After spending about half an hour explaining heart disease and heart surgery, including making instructive illustrations to enhance his understanding of the problem, I assured him that if he did decide to have an operation, I would take excellent care of him like my family member. Still, he did not say a word.

I thanked him for his time, placed my business card on his nightstand, and extended my hand to shake his, but he showed no reaction or response to my gesture. Again I thanked him, wished him a nice day, and walked out. When I got to the nurses' station, I took a look at his chart and discovered to my amazement that he was a pastor. The entire experience had been, at best, perplexing. When I returned to my office, my secretary handed me a message from the patient I had just met. He was requesting to see me again to discuss surgery. Baffled and curious, I returned to his room. I had barely opened the door when he asked, "When can you operate?"

Wanting to capitalize on a window of opportunity he had just offered me, I responded, "Tomorrow!"

The next day, he underwent a quintuple bypass operation and enjoyed a smooth postoperative stay in the hospital before being discharged to his home. When he returned on a follow-up visit, he was still not talkative, but I noticed he appeared to be more relaxed with me. A few weeks later, many telephone calls began to come in. On the other end was a man crying and thanking me for all the wonderful and attentive care I had given him. At first, I found it somewhat weird. Sometimes, he would tell me how meeting me and being under my care had transformed him and other patients of mine he knew of. Still, I was confused, especially with the crying part. I discussed it with my office manager, who could not understand the reasons for his prolonged tearful and emotional response to my care.

Then one day he arrived at my office unannounced, and in what might have been a cathartic moment, he related his experiences growing up in a racist home and community. He talked about harboring strong feelings of hate toward those of a different race, even as he preached God's word from the pulpit every Sunday. Then he ended by telling me how the encounter with me had opened his eyes and had transformed him to a point where he had forced himself to reassess the position he often took on race matters.

He had also begun to talk openly against racism and ignorance. He told me how much he loved me and that he had been preaching about love and racial unity from his pulpit every Sunday since his operation.

As I listened to him, I was profoundly touched by his experiences, as well as the redemptive effect on him of heart disease and his surgical experience. Indeed, here was a new and different man sitting in front of me. He was a great man whom I admired and respected. As someone who abhors racism and discrimination in any shape or form and who was born and raised in a community where racism was neither taught nor learned, I certainly appreciated his honest exaltations and the transformation in his views about others as a result of our faithful encounter. For me, knowing him reinforced my belief that everyone has some good in them and has the capacity to change their beliefs from negative to positive. That experience also reinforced my belief in our common humanity and the importance of treating everyone kindly and respectfully without any expectations of reciprocity.

CHAPTER 67

Medical Missions

TOWARD THE END OF my first year in practice, I began to think often about conducting surgical missions in poor countries. Additionally, I developed an interest in bloodless techniques for heart surgery. We had two wonderful coordinators who happened to be Jehovah's Witnesses, with whom I worked to set up a program to perform heart surgery without transfusion blood or blood products. Many of the techniques in this area grew out of the religious teachings of the Jehovah's Witnesses. Interestingly, as the program grew, the vast majority of our patients requesting surgery without transfusion of blood or blood products were non-Witnesses.

I used to operate on patients from other states, and some of them would arrive in dire straits after having been admonished by their health-care providers for refusing to accept blood transfusions. Among them were patients who had been told they would meet certain death if they did not accept the transfusion of blood or blood products. Our program was successful, and I developed an appreciation for the human body's ability to tolerate significantly low blood levels. I believe my skills as a surgeon improved appreciably as a result of taking care of those patients.

Performing bloodless surgery forces you to be assiduous and meticulous in the conduct of any operation since there is no option for transfusion in the case of severe blood loss. The outcomes from bloodless heart surgery were so encouraging that I began to imagine the value in applying those techniques in resource-poor communities in developing countries where blood-banking technologies were rudimentary or absent.

Consequently, I contacted my friends in France, and we hatched a plan for a mission to Africa. Then, I submitted requests to a few pharmaceutical companies and major medical-product companies for donations and received so much equipment and so many medicines and supplies for heart surgery that I ran out of storage space in my office. After putting together everything I needed for a complex cardiac surgery mission, I flew to Paris and met with the rest of the team: Dr. Michelle Dellarat (a world-class anesthesiologist), Dr. Didier Loulmet (a cardiac surgeon), Lyon (a perfusionist), and Christine (a nurse intensivist). Dr. Carpentier had too much on his plate at that time and could not travel with us.

After a meeting in Paris in which we reviewed our mission strategies, we boarded a plane to Africa and arrived in Yaoundé, Cameroon. To me, this was truly an auspicious moment in my life. There I was, coming home to finally serve and give back to the community I had left two decades earlier. Dr. Wali Muna, a renowned cardiologist and hospital CEO, met us at the airport on arrival, and we were well received and were housed adjacent to the hospital. It occurred to me then that Dr. Muna did not recognize me on our initial encounter. Therefore, I jolted his memory by taking him back exactly twenty years earlier on a street in downtown Baltimore, Maryland. He was the Johns Hopkins doctor sitting in the front seat of Samuel's car when the latter came to rescue a skinny, frightened, anxious, homeless teenager at the YMCA. His jaw dropped, and his lips couldn't stop quivering. After a prolonged stare, he blurted out an incredulous "No!"

I assured him I was that same kid.

"But I was told an American cardiovascular and thoracic surgeon was coming with the French team," he stated.

"Well, I am the surgeon you have been expecting," I responded.

"You were looking so emaciated and miserable that day years ago at the YMCA. I didn't think you would survive!" he exclaimed in jest.

I could tell he was teary-eyed, and I hugged him. While speaking loudly and with guarded intrigue, he stated that in his wildest imagination, he could have never predicted that the wretched kid he had met at the YMCA would someday turn out to be a Harvard-trained heart surgeon who, in the future, would come to his aid on a different continent. I think at that moment, we both understood that life is unpredictable and that an individual's current situation does not always determine their future. We hugged some more, and again, he welcomed us to his hospital.

I learned afterward that he had left Johns Hopkins and accepted a position in the cardiology department at Yale, where he remained few years before moving to Africa to fill a desperate need for cardiologists. My French team members were aghast at what they had just witnessed. It was obvious that they were unfamiliar with my past. Predictably, that night they bombarded me with a thousand questions about my life journey.

On the following day, we assembled in a conference room and reviewed the medical records of all the patients who were being considered for surgery, and we agreed to operate on all of them. We had about ten days to accomplish our mission, and time was of the essence. The next morning, we started early. Dr. Loulmet was a gifted surgeon with a high level of emotional intelligence. We had previously worked together during our training in Boston and were at ease with each other. We decided that we would alternate the role of principal surgeon with successive cases and assist each other during every operation.

I was the principal surgeon, with Dr. Loulmet assisting me on the first operation, which involved a thirteen-year-old girl who was suffering from severe shortness of breath associated with mild exertion. She had been born with an abnormal connection between her aorta (the main artery in the chest, which is connected to the heart and carries oxygen-rich blood) and the pulmonary artery (the main artery connecting the heart to the lungs and carrying oxygen-poor blood). After Dr. Dellarat put the patient to sleep, I made an incision to enter her left chest, identified the problem, and proceeded to correct it. Unexpectedly, we ran into severe "audible" bleeding, and her chest filled up rapidly with blood. We had to identify the source of bleeding as soon as possible. There was an essential piece of equipment that was useful in controlling such troublesome bleeding. Unfortunately, they didn't have it there.

Meanwhile, the patient's blood pressure continued to drop, and Dr. Dellarat was struggling desperately to keep it reasonably high with powerful drugs and intravenous fluids. There were several medical observers in the room, including a television news crew. I asked for a few other instruments, but the look of panic on the nurse assistant's face spoke volumes. They did not have what I needed. The tension in the room was so high that you could smell it. We were frantically trying to save the patient's life, and despite my state of frustration, I had to remain calm.

In cardiac surgery, one has to always prepare for a surprise occurrence or a dramatic and potentially catastrophic event at any moment, along with the possibility of sudden death. A cardiac surgeon must think and respond fast. When confronted with massive bleeding during surgery, it only takes a few heartbeats before the heart goes into a lethal rhythm and possibly stops beating. The composure of the surgeon in an acute crisis is critical in determining the mood in the room and often the outcome of the operation.

Speaking loudly and firmly, I requested a piece of equipment I often used for a different purpose. I remember packing it for the trip as an afterthought. The circulating nurse dashed out and returned momentarily with it. Fortunately, after several heart-pounding, adrenaline-surging minutes, we succeeded in controlling the problematic bleeding. Despite having rescued the situation, my assistant and I kept up the pace and continued operating without pausing until the patient's problem had been addressed to our mutual satisfaction. Finally, the anesthesiologist assured us that the patient was stable. We finished up, closed her chest, and made a beeline to the locker room to regain our composure. That was only the first of three operations scheduled that day.

We saw several children born with holes in their tiny hearts that needed to be fixed. Almost all of them would have been facing certain death without surgery. When a television reporter approached me for a summary of the first operation, I declined and offered instead to present a summary at the end of our mission. I was feeling too much stress, and I needed to channel that stress exclusively to the surgical responsibilities ahead of us. Within an hour, we were back in the operating room for the second and subsequently the third operations.

Christine, our superb intensive-care team leader, stayed busy with post-surgery patients. We had a six-year-old girl with a severe congenital heart problem. After I opened her chest, I decided that she would likely require a heart transplant because of the severity of her heart problem. Therefore, I closed her up, and we contacted Paris immediately afterward and arranged to transfer her there for the advanced care she needed. Her family was distraught and overwhelmed with our decision, and we spent an appreciable amount of time explaining the situation to them while reassuring them that she would get the care she needed in France at no cost to them. All of our patients were children from poor families, and financial support for our mission had been provided entirely from charitable donations in France and the United States.

One of the children we operated on was only four years old and had been born with a huge hole in his heart, which we repaired successfully and without complications. I will never forget that within two hours of the operation, the kid was out of his bed and walking all over the ICU. His mother was beside herself. He had not been doing much walking before the operation because he had no energy. Operating on the human heart was something people did not think was possible in that environment; therefore, people considered us miracle workers. Moreover, the idea of working on the human heart didn't sit well with many of the Indigenous people because of certain cultural norms and spiritual beliefs that the heart was a repository for the soul, feelings, personality, and character. Therefore, the idea of someone touching, opening, or cutting a heart to fix it was not accepted easily.

I remember the parent of a child we had just treated who kept asking if we had touched his daughter's heart and cut it open with a knife. The more we tried to explain the procedure in as few simple words as possible, the more I realized we were doing more harm than good because the child's father began to look pale, sweaty, and possibly on the verge of fainting. Therefore I stopped the explanation in midsentence and assured the family that the child would be OK.

After each operation, we went to their family members to discuss our findings and explain what we had just done. Almost invariably, they would begin to cry even before we had said anything. Nothing could quite match the looks on the faces of those parents upon hearing that their child had gone through a successful operation. To me, nothing could've been more gratifying. Many of those children had been suffering immensely since birth.

Unfortunately, there were still a lot of children at the end of the mission who could not receive the surgical treatment they needed because we had run out of supplies and time. It disturbed us to leave behind any child who needed our services, and I truly wished we had had more supplies and equipment to continue operating for as long as it was physically possible. We could only help the most desperate patients, even as we knew that the rest of them would likely face death from their medical problems. I was told that the whole country was abuzz with the news of our mission and that updates on our surgeries were making daily headlines in print media and also on television. Christine and Dr. Dellarat took turns staying up all night with the patients to avoid any untoward outcomes with them.

One morning toward the end of our mission, I asked Dr. Muna if we could pay a brief visit to my family in the village. My team members were excited about the trip, not only because they were desperately in need of a short reprieve from our work schedule and wanted to enjoy the beauty of the countryside but also because they did not believe that I had been born there or any of the stories about growing up in a village. After a scenic ten-hour drive on a private bus, we arrived late in the afternoon, and when we pulled up to my father's compound, there was sheer pandemonium. Every family member, relative, and neighbor came out to greet us.

My father was the last one to emerge from his smoke-filled room, his illuminating smile preceding the rest of his body. To my greatest amazement, he greeted us in broken English, telling my colleagues that he had seen them on television. On their part, my colleagues were stunned at the site of the diminutive, fragile old man in a loincloth with a radiant smile.

"Is this really your father?" Dr. Loulmet asked with a tone of incredulity.

"Yes. This is the man who is responsible for all those surgeries I have done," I responded. Michelle Dellarat looked at the surroundings—the milling crowd of adults and several naked children—and couldn't believe her eyes.

"You are American! You are not from here!" she exclaimed in jest.

Still, Dr. Loulmet was unconvinced. He turned around to face me and expressed his amazement and difficulty at understanding how I could have come from that world to the United States. I reassured him and the rest of our team that my origins were precisely where we were standing and that my dad was indeed my biological father. They chuckled.

"My placenta is buried here," I declared.

As we were standing there and interacting with the curious throng of villagers, I apologized to my dad for failing to make contact with him since our arrival in the country and for failing to notify him in advance about the mission. I told him our team had been busy performing surgeries on sick babies and that the mission had been intense and absorbing. He interjected and addressed my team in our language. In essence, he said, "Welcome to our land. On behalf of everyone here, I thank you for the great work you are doing to save lives. In doing what you do, you are saving the lives of families and our nation."

One of my colleagues commented, "Wise man!"

While referring to my apologies, he made a profound statement that reflected his basic philosophical bent about life and human service and evoked many memories, both sweet and sad, from my past. He spoke in our native language and said, "Son, when I heard all the talk everywhere about all the great healing work your team has done, I felt good in my heart. You and your friends have done well. May God bless all of you. When I saw you on television, I had only one wish: that your mother and many others who have journeyed ahead of me could have been there to relish that moment with me."

With that said, he turned around to walk back to his room. I knew he would not want to spoil the moment and have my friends see him cry. Reflexively, I grabbed his hand and followed him. At the entrance, he paused and made this riveting statement: "Do not apologize for not having enough time for me. I understand. I am happy. Now you belong to the world."

Hearing such powerful words, I grabbed a stool and sat in front of him. At that moment, he reminded me of an event that occurred soon after my birth. He had told me that story before at the time when I was leaving the country for the first time. He talked about the prophetic words of the total stranger who held me after I was born and predicted that someday I would travel far away beyond the seas and would return to do great things. Then he added, "I am glad I have lived to see this revelation. Now I am on the road. I wish your mother had lived long enough to witness this with me. I will tell her everything when I meet her again."

We sat there for several minutes, discussing family matters. I imagined how exciting it had to have been for my dad to see my team and me on national television at someone's house in the neighboring town. Television had just been introduced in the country. So I offered to buy him one and install electric power in his room. He refused. I offered again to build him a new home with electricity and running water and to get him a car with a driver. Still, he refused. He said he was content with what he had. He did not want to live above anyone around him. He also was afraid that thieves would come and rob him if he had all those material things and "White-man" conveniences. As we talked, I had this awful feeling that he would not be around many more years.

My friends were waiting outside. We had to get back on the road to Yaoundé. I stood up and held his hand and told him that I loved him. Parting was very difficult for me. I thanked him for giving me strength, courage, and wisdom. "Papa, broken hearts beckon us. We must return to the hospital," I said.

We stepped outside, and he blessed us with a few powerful words.

"May we travel safely," he said.

I turned around in an instant and saw my father standing among the rest of the family, waving at us. In my silence, I could feel the poignancy and the wisdom of his words in my heart. My father never ceased to amaze me with his simplicity, wisdom, and ability to bring clarity, dignity, and humanity to any situation.

My colleagues were still struggling with the incongruences between the world I shared with them in the West and the one they had just witnessed. On my part, I was marveling at the greatness and humility of the little man with a large mind and a big heart, whose tenacity and wisdom I had admired ever since the flames of awareness were ignited within me.

Our visit was brief, and our weary bodies needed to be rested before returning to work.

As the bus chugged along, I couldn't help but think about my dad and wonder what path life might have taken him on if he had received the formal education he had so desperately yearned for as a child. Then I discovered the answer in his supreme words to us before we departed: May *we* travel safely—stated in the true spirit of collectivism.

Back at the hospital, we were greeted with the good news that all our children were doing well. We were told that ours had been the first successful pediatric cardiac surgical mission ever in that part of the world. In my opinion, the success of that mission was attributable to the laudable altruistic efforts of many people on three continents. The day before our departure, we enjoyed a reception given by the hospital administrators. Several social and political dignitaries were in attendance, in addition to some of our patients and their families.

On the flight back to Europe, we were all physically exhausted but spiritually energized. Sitting in a crowded cabin on that flight to Paris, I looked across at my colleagues and thanked them for a wonderful mission. They were the most compassionate, giving, and caring human beings I knew, and I truly felt honored to have joined them on the mission. We joked and cajoled the entire flight to Paris. We were all eager to participate in future medical missions; therefore, we began to make plans for the next one.

On the connecting flight to the United States, my mind drifted back to something I had read about a man of a different nationality, a doctor who had decided to make his home among the disenfranchised and marginalized lepers in Africa. I began thinking about the timeless words of Dr. Albert Schweitzer: "There is no greater good than human service. The purpose of human life is to serve, and to show compassion and the will to help others."

I believe there is truly nothing we cannot accomplish collectively to advance the cause of humanity.

CHAPTER 68
You Belong to the World

ABOUT SEVEN MONTHS AFTER our successful medical mission, our team was back in Africa again on another pediatric congenital heart surgery mission. The seeds for medical humanitarianism had been planted in our hearts, and I began to travel every year to donate equipment and supplies and to teach, operate, and assist caregivers in various African countries, Southeast Asia, and South America.

Unfortunately, my personal life was not so good. Denise and I bought a new home, but within a couple of months of moving into it, our relationship began to crumble. We had decided many years earlier that we would remarry in a formal ceremony after I was settled in a comfortable practice. However, that was not going to happen. Our situation deteriorated to the point that I moved out of the house and spent many days and nights in an apartment, wondering where my life was heading.

During that year, I traveled to northern Africa on medical missions, spending several weeks in the Republic of Chad. There I met with President Idris Deby, who was hospitable and was seriously interested in having me provide direct clinical and tactical medical assistance to his people. On one of those missions to Chad, I traveled with my friend Richard. Together we visited a few remote and resource-poor medical clinics in the country, providing assistance and guidance.

Working in the Sahara was physically draining. Sometimes temperatures would rise to about 140°F in the middle of the day. Additionally, I made a few humanitarian trips to South Africa, where I not only performed surgical interventions, but I also donated medical equipment and supplies. On one of those trips, I had the privilege of meeting a few notable South Africans, like Bishop Desmond Tutu and the renowned heart surgeon Dr. Christiaan Barnard, who had performed the first successful human heart transplantation in 1967. I also had a chance to meet a few civil rights icons who had endured immeasurable suffering under the evil system of apartheid.

On one occasion, I took a ferry from Cape Town to Robben Island, where one of my heroes, Nelson Mandela, and several other political prisoners had been incarcerated. This was an emotional visit, especially since I had read much about him and his fellow freedom fighters and about the indignities and human rights deprivations they had endured. I also traveled to other African countries, such as Tanzania, Kenya, Zambia, and Zimbabwe, where I visited numerous health-care facilities to learn about health-care challenges in those countries and to offer my assistance. Those and many other journeys to developing countries taught me unique lessons in geographic medicine and gave me a profound appreciation for the sacrifices that doctors, nurses, and other providers had to make regularly under terrible conditions of economic deprivation in quasi-democratic systems of government.

Southern and eastern African regions presented a plethora of geographic wonders for the enthusiastic traveler. I also found time during my missions to indulge in a few natural wonders like the Victoria Falls in Zimbabwe and the Serengeti in Kenya.

I had read about most of them in my geography classes in elementary school and had them on my must-see list of places. To get to Victoria Falls, I caught a flight from Harare to the town of Victoria Falls and stayed in a historic hotel a few miles from the falls. From there, I trekked across a bridge over the Zambezi River to the Zambian side of the falls. There, I went swimming in the Zambezi River itself, up to a few feet from the edge of the falls, while being mindful of a menacing, contemptuous bloat of hippos frolicking upstream.

While perched on a huge boulder by the river, I could see the roaring and restless Zambezi as it was plummeting down a cavernous gorge. Emerging from the gorge was a serene mist displaying a spectacular rainbow. I met an adventurous premed student from Chicago who was traveling alone across Africa, and she convinced me to scale down the gorge further downstream to experience the Zambezi River up close. After navigating slippery and treacherous trails, finally we arrived at the bottom of the canyon, where we encountered the mighty, ferocious river with its impressive cataracts, howling on its way downstream to Mozambique. Sitting on the banks of the river and looking up at the bridge I had crossed to get to the Zambian side, my mind drifted back to the 1800s, and I imagined David Livingstone marveling at the same wonders of nature surrounding us.

The continuation of my journey landed me in Nairobi, where I took a memorable safari and witnessed a riveting spectacle of a thousand wildebeests on their migratory journey across the Serengeti. The sheer numbers and variety of wildlife on that trip were impressive. Giraffes were the most dignified animals I saw up close. I have always considered them my favorite animals: tall, beautiful, gentle, and regal. Just like my mother.

Venturing deep into the Serengeti in the security of a Land Rover and encountering many packs of ferocious lions reminded me of a story I had read or heard somewhere about the Maasai culture. It said that as part of an initiation requirement, a young Maasai warrior transitioning to manhood had to prove himself by killing a lion. As our vehicle lumbered across the grassy terrain and I witnessed all those ferocious lions salivating at the sight and smell of human flesh, I concluded that there could be another story about a Maasai boy who vehemently refused to enter manhood. I would be that happy wimp who preferred to skip manhood and tend goats and sheep instead.

After the safari, I caught a flight from Nairobi to Douala. I wanted to visit my father and the rest of the family. As always, we were ecstatic to see each other. On the last night of that visit, we stayed up late talking about everything. It was one of those rare moments when all of my siblings and a few of my nieces and nephews were all together with Dad, enjoying general conversations punctuated with laughter and sprinkled with occasional cultural humor. Dad was in a great mood. Later that night, I asked everyone to stand up, and we took turns hugging him and telling him how much we loved him. It was indeed a beautiful, memorable sight to witness my siblings hugging him and the grandchildren expressing their love and respect for him.

When it was time for me to leave, Dad grabbed his kerosene lamp and walked quietly with me to the main road a few yards away and waited until a taxi showed up to take me to my hotel. He reminded me to convey special greetings to Mankah, Robert, Ahleea, and their mothers, and I promised him I would. Lying in bed that night and reviewing the events that had occurred earlier that day, I realized there had been something unsettling about Dad's demeanor, but I could not decipher it.

CHAPTER 69
Arthroscopy

IN DECEMBER 1995, I underwent arthroscopic surgery on my right knee. Mary, my office manager, was truly an angel for driving me to the hospital for the procedure, waiting until it was over, and then taking me back to my apartment. In my absence, she kept everything organized at the office and did a fine job of communicating with my patients. The operation itself was a traumatic experience. I had opted for epidural anesthesia; however, the analgesic effect was not optimal, and I experienced excruciating pain during the procedure.

A few days after the operation, I could barely move. I was sitting in my living room and staring at my right knee when I noticed that it had ballooned to about double its normal size, and the pain was unbearable. My right foot was becoming numb. Something was wrong. In my closet, I kept boxes of medical supplies for my future missions. While still in excruciating pain, I dragged myself across the room to the closet and rummaged feverishly through the boxes, but I couldn't find what I was looking for. With heightened desperation, I spilled the contents of all the boxes on the floor. Suddenly, I saw what I needed.

I was getting weaker by the minute. I could feel my heart thumping faster than usual. I placed a box of alcohol swabs on the coffee table and opened a package of 60 mL syringes and a box of sterile needles, which I spilled on the couch to look for the largest bore needle I could find. I was now armed with a large sterile syringe, a large bore needle, and tons of alcohol swabs. The phone was right next to me. I called a friends who was a kidney specialist and asked for his assistance in taking me to the emergency room. He agreed at once and informed me that he would be on his way to get me. My knee was throbbing. My lower extremity felt like a thousand-pound boulder attached to my hip.

With alcohol swabs, I carefully cleaned the inside part of my right knee and inserted the needle at that location where the skin was glistening under tension. When I drew back on the syringe, it filled with blood. I kept aspirating blood and emptying the syringe contents into a trash bin next to me. I don't remember how many full syringes I aspirated. When I couldn't aspirate any more blood, I pulled out the needle, applied pressure over the hole with a piece of gauze, and wrapped my knee with a bandage. In an instant, I began to feel tremendous relief in my right leg. A few minutes later, the numbness in my leg was gone.

As a doctor, I knew I had not addressed the cause of the bleeding and that my relief could be short-lived if I did not get to a hospital soon enough. My friend Dr. Mbanefo arrived and drove me to the hospital emergency department, where, within an hour of my arrival, I was back in the operating room having my knee joint explored.

I have no recollection of what happened immediately after the operation, but some of the nurses kept on telling me that I had been combative and incoherent in the recovery room. I was embarrassed to hear this. What I do remember clearly is having severe pain afterward and experiencing constipation and urinary retention from all the narcotic pills I was receiving. That entire saga gave me renewed respect for my patients and their sufferings after surgery. The highlight of my after-surgery care was having difficulty with urination. I remember standing in the bathroom and grunting forever but being unable to urinate. When I looked up, I was embarrassed to see a big, tall nurse staring at me with the look of commander in chief, and without waiting for any excuses from me, she barked, "Are you done yet?"

"No!" I responded.

Then she left the room without saying another word. I got back in bed and tried to relax. Minutes later, she returned with a urinary bladder catheter kit and dropped it on the bedside stand. Then, with a perfect country accent, she warned me, "If you ain't peed yet by the time I git back, I'm gonna have to git it outta you."

Boy, that did it! I knew what she would have to do to empty my bladder for me. I had written that order a zillion times for my patients. I didn't want to experience it myself. The thought of that particular nurse doing it was daunting and scary enough. Oblivious to my pain, propelled by my fright and the need for expedient action, I jumped out of the bed with desperate alacrity and hopped into the bathroom.

"Please, bladder, don't fail me now!" I pleaded.

It is never a pleasant experience when you have to plead with a body part to help you out. I sat down and grunted as loud as I could until I felt a warm sensation in my groin, followed by an audible trickle and then a waterfall.

"Hallelujah!" I exclaimed.

I had just been spared physical and psychological trauma by "Andrea the Giantess"! Unfortunately, I was also having nausea due to constipation, a side effect of the narcotics. I had tried several remedies to no avail. As soon as I got back in bed, my wonderful nurse walked in. "Did you go yet?" she barked.

"Yeah," I answered.

As though she didn't trust me, she asked to see the evidence, and I directed her to the bathroom. Then she asked if the laxatives had worked. In a flash, I decided I didn't want her manipulating my sacred backside. So I lied.

"Yup! I went," I answered with droopy confidence.

Then I got nervous. How could I explain leaving evidence of urine in the toilet without evidence of the other stuff? She stood there, giving me a look reminiscent of a mother acknowledging a transparent lie. Surprisingly, she turned around and left.

Oh boy! I never want to be a patient again. Never!

After I was discharged, many of my friends and colleagues came to visit and assist me. I wasted no time getting back to work and would frequently hobble to the operating room and stand for hours doing open-heart surgery because I was feeling bad for some of my patients whose elective surgeries had been postponed because of my physical ailment. I limped around on crutches for a while, and under the attentive expert care of my physical therapist, gradually, I regained strength in my extremity.

CHAPTER 70

Goodbye, Dad

IN MARCH 1996, I spoke with my daughter Mankah about bringing my father to the United States for a visit. She was excited and thought it was a great idea. Then I sent him a letter delineating my plans for him. I wanted him to experience a new culture and to receive a general medical checkup. I knew he would be excited to see his grandchildren and to experience firsthand this great land about which he had heard so much over the years.

I intended to show him where I had attended college and some of the not-so-glamorous places I had lived during those very difficult and challenging earlier years. These were places, events, and experiences whose narratives I had willfully kept away from him for fear of causing him unnecessary duress. On that particular week, I was having recurrent dreams about him, and I began to make arrangements to fly to Cameroon and bring him back with me.

Early one Saturday morning, I was awakened by a phone call from my brother. He was crying uncontrollably, and I couldn't decipher what he was saying. When he finally calmed down, he shocked me with the horrible news that our father had died in his sleep. When my children heard the news, they were devastated. Immediately, I started to make arrangements to go home and give him a dignified burial. I was still experiencing difficulty with my knee and required crutches occasionally.

After preparing myself for the journey, I took off early one morning and caught a flight to Africa. When I had seen him six months earlier, he had alerted me at that time that he was "on the road," meaning that he would be dead shortly. At that time, he told me he was handing over all family responsibilities to me. I thought about how we had taken turns hugging him and how on our last night together, I had a feeling that I would never see him again. He had lived a faithful and meaningful life and had refused to marry after my mother's death. At least they were finally together.

I thought about his difficult childhood and the many challenges he had confronted. I reminded myself of the great technical skills that had enabled him to make elegant boxes in a flash out of large, ugly oil drums. He was a man with incredible focus, patience, tenacity, and resilience. I thought about the sadness and tears in his eyes every time I got kicked out of school for nonpayment of tuition. I thought about how he had smiled so richly just a couple of years earlier when I had arrived with my friends to visit him during our surgical mission. His smile could always cast a cheerful ray on my heart. He was perpetually optimistic about my future. Whatever the case, I knew that I would never be the same without him.

Before I knew it, I was sobbing in the dark confines of the airline passenger cabin, and I could hear the whining engines propelling us south and across the vast and seemingly endless expanse of the Sahara Desert. Then I dozed off. When I awakened, the plane was preparing to land in Cameroon.

After completing the usual immigration formalities, I was met by Dr. Wali Muna, who helped arrange reliable transportation to take me to my village. The journey up to the highlands was both physically and emotionally arduous. I was feeling overwhelmed with concerning thoughts of the inescapable responsibilities ahead of me. After arriving in our village, I held a family meeting, during which we pledged to stay strong and close. Dad's body was still in the morgue. Luckily, my cousins were all there to help me in every way. The many years I had spent in the diaspora had left me rusty in my understanding of important traditional rites; therefore, I found comfort in knowing that others would guide and assist me. My uncle Wankie, a renowned architect, was particularly helpful in coordinating a funeral program.

I discovered that my dad had joined a local Christian congregation, where he had been an active participant and kept a record of his monthly tithes. As a child, I never actually saw him go to church, although he lived the life of a practical Christian. After collecting his body from the morgue, we brought him home to receive final traditional rites before taking him to his church for a funeral service. In eulogizing him, I expounded on his legacy and the impact his wisdom, love, and skills had made through his children on the lives of many. He was a simple, illiterate man with a colossal heart and enormous love for humanity. I stated how he had refused to remarry after the death of our mother. As he often stated, the love he had shared with her was so rich and bountiful that he was willing to exist on it for the rest of his life. My lovely niece Yvonne tearfully read a few special words she had written about the impact of his life on every family member and the community.

Afterward, we left the church building and headed for the burial in our compound. That afternoon, he was laid to rest next to our mother. I felt a deep sense of emptiness in my heart as I regretted not having spent as much time with him as I would've liked. I realized the demands of my career and the geographic distance between us had been a factor, but that awareness was not consoling to me. On the night he was buried, my brother informed me that Dad had left some items in a box for me, so I went alone in his bedroom, where I opened a suitcase to see its contents. That suitcase brought back many poignant memories because it was the same one I had taken on my maiden voyage to America decades earlier. On one of my visits to the family, I had brought it back and left it with my father.

It was a treasure trove of surprises. It contained a carefully executed will stating unequivocally his decisions about the distribution of his property as well as information about his savings account with a local credit union. I was not amazed to discover that Dad had remained frugal to the end. He used the money I sent him to help others and make donations to his church, and the rest of it he kept in that account. Despite his enviable financial status in the community from having a successful son, he had none of the trappings of wealth and preferred to live the simple life of a villager. He never wanted to look better off than the people around him. His brow would crease in an expression of discontent whenever I suggested anything to do with spending money.

The box contained traditional robes, which he left for me. Then I reached a pile of old envelopes, and when I opened the first one to read its contents, my heart stopped. I was staring at an almost twenty-two-year-old letter that had been mailed from America. In it, the writer was telling Dad how he was adjusting to a new life in a new world. He wrote about his studies, the odd jobs he was doing to take care of himself, and the nostalgia and the love he was feeling for his father, siblings, and everyone he had left behind. He wrote about his hopes of reuniting someday with everyone in his family. It ended by encouraging Dad to be sure his siblings stayed in school, adding that someday he would be able to assume the financial responsibilities of educating his nieces, nephews, and other family members. Then he concluded by stating that he had enclosed a twenty-dollar bill for Dad. I thought about how excited Dad must have been to receive a letter from America, and I imagined him scouring the village for a student, maybe an elementary school student, who could read the letter for him and translate it into his language. I could see the glow in his eyes and the pride in his heart from hearing the words of the writer.

I sat there and read all the letters in that suitcase. Each of them was filled with hope, optimism, and encouragement and addressed many issues and concerns about the family. They all ended with expressions of love for everyone and always mentioned every family member and close relative by name. I was familiar with the writer. I could visualize him in my conscious mind, and I imagined him going through all those experiences he wrote about. With deep compassion, I admired the workings of his mind at that stage in his life. Sadly, after so many years, I had forgotten the sufferings he had experienced during his earlier years in America. However, reading his letters evoked those memories with distinctive clarity. I was amazed at his optimistic communication, which contrasted with the real-life difficulties he was experiencing at that time. There was no mention of the challenges he was facing with hunger, homelessness, educational and financial insecurities, and loneliness. As I sat there thinking about that young man, I truly wished I could go back in time and meet him to know him better, to hug him, hold his hand, and assure him that there would be better days ahead. Ultimately, that troubled young man became transformed by his experiences, and eventually he evolved into me.

When I went back and read Dad's will, I was not surprised by the last statement on the paper. True to form, he advised everyone "to live in peace and love" and to "avoid arguments and contentions." Indeed, he was a great man.

After the funeral, I called a meeting of the family, and while speaking to my nieces and nephews, I extolled the virtues of education, hard work, and integrity. I promised to provide financial assistance to anyone who made it to college. Dad's passing meant that the torch had been passed to his offspring. I had the torch. His shoes I knew I could never fill, but I was willing to try. I headed back to America with a heavy torch and oversized shoes.

CHAPTER 71

South Africa and Street Children

A FEW MONTHS AFTER the death of my father, I met with Denise to discuss our relationship. We both agreed to get back together. I moved out of my apartment and rejoined her and the girls. Things were awkward between us for a while, and our communication was still not as smooth as we would have liked, but it was certainly better than it had been before our separation. We took a family vacation to Hawaii, and that same year, we traveled to Cameroon to visit my family. On that trip, we were hosted at a delightful reception by a prominent businessman, Mr. Victor Fotso, and his wife, Julienne. Many months later, this couple visited us in Cleveland when he came for a routine medical evaluation.

I continued to make missionary trips overseas to provide general medical and surgical care in developing countries. Some of those missions took me to South Africa again, where I helped out at a community clinic. On one of them, I was invited as a visiting professor to the University of Natal Medical School in Durban, where I delivered a grand rounds lecture to the cardiothoracic surgical service at Wentworth Hospital. Afterward, I received a phone call requesting my consultative services on none other than Nelson Mandela, who was stricken with chronic pulmonary problems. I was told that he had heard about my humanitarian medical missions, which he applauded. This came as a big surprise, and I was enormously humbled for being solicited to address his medical problem.

During one of several trips that I made to South Africa, I was also extremely honored by another memorable encounter with Bishop Desmond Tutu, spiritual leader, social activist, and Nobel laureate. He had heard of my volunteerism and wanted to meet me. He was giving a speech in Cape Town, and when he was notified of my presence, he came off the stage to greet me and thanked me personally for the help that I had been giving his people. There could be no greater honor than to bask in his humility.

On that trip to South Africa, I was invited to a family reunion in Bloemfontein by a friend I had met during her stint in Cleveland ten years earlier, when she was traveling with a group of visiting international social workers. After the event that night, at about 10:00 p.m., I was on my way back to my hotel when we passed a large group of about fifty children hanging out at an intersection in the center of Cape Town. Curious, I asked my friends what they were doing there at that late hour, and when I discovered that they were homeless street kids, many of whom were orphans, I was heartbroken. Furthermore, I learned that they survived principally on scraps from dumpsters and the generosity of an occasional motorist. Having just had a full and gratifying meal at the previous event and then heading to a comfortable hotel room, I couldn't help but imagine how it would be to live like those innocent children. Therefore, I asked my friends to stop so that I could chat with them, but they declined, citing security risks and the possibility of being robbed or assaulted by the children. I dismissed their concerns and insisted on talking to them. Reluctantly, my friends stopped, and I hopped out of the car in my lime-colored suit in the middle of the square, scuttled over to a perplexed and curious group of boys, and immediately introduced myself to them.

"My name is Dr. Zama. I am an American doctor visiting your country," I blurted out enthusiastically. A dreadful silence descended on the crowd as every eyeball was studying me from head to toe. I was beginning to feel momentarily awkward when one of the younger-looking boys stepped forward, and with a sheepish grin, he uttered a few universally heartwarming words: "Welcome to our country."

Reflexively, I asked, "Are you guys hungry?"

"Yus sur!" they responded in a thunderous chorus with their beautiful, melodic accents. I had asked the question from my heart but without a logistical strategy in mind of how to fulfill their nutritional needs. It dawned on me that the kids had to be quite familiar with the area and would know which restaurants were open at that time. Suddenly, as I was preparing to pose the question, one of my friends got out of the car, sprinted across the street toward us, and asked if I was OK. I responded by inquiring whether there were any fast-food joints nearby. Luckily, around the corner was a Kentucky Fried Chicken restaurant.

"Let's go eat!" I commanded excitedly, and like the Pied Piper of Hamelin with all my boys in tow, we strolled eagerly to the restaurant in random chatter the entire way. Unfortunately, when we got there, we discovered that the restaurant had just closed its doors about ten minutes earlier; through the enormous glass windows, I could see the workers busy cleaning up the place. At once, I began to knock at the door insistently to get someone's attention. Subsequently, a gentleman appeared from the back room and saw the crowd of anxious children leaning against the window glass panels, and with a look of understandable concern, he made a gesture with his hands informing us that his restaurant was closed for the night. Undeterred, I motioned for him to step up closer to the other side of the locked door. Then I pulled out my American passport and waved it at him. That did the trick! He cracked the door open, and immediately, I introduced myself and rendered a plea: "Greetings. I am an American surgeon on a medical mission. These children are hungry, and I want to feed them. I know you are closed for the night, but I appeal to your heart to help me feed these homeless children. Please help them. I will pay for their meals."

His mouth was still agape, as though he were fielding a surging contest between his mind and his heart. At that moment, he glanced at the restless crowd of kids occupying every inch of concrete between his door and the curb, and his eyes popped. "All these boys?" he asked with a look of concern.

"Yes. You can do it," I reassured him in a gentle voice. On that note, he turned around and ordered his crew to get ready for some action. Gladly, his heart had just won the contest. At that point, he swung open the main door to let us in. The look of anticipatory excitement on each of those boys was precious and eternally indescribable. I told them to order whatever they wanted and in the quantities they desired. After everyone had been served, I paid the bill, thanked the restaurant staff profusely, bid farewell to a bunch of happily satisfied boys, and expressed my profound gratitude to my friends for their patience and understanding.

That night, in the comfort of my bed at the Portswood Hotel Waterfront, I couldn't stop thinking of the struggles of those boys and their futures. Their plight is our plight. My gesture had been barely a drop in a massive bucket. The next day, I learned that the radio airways and print news were filled with narratives of my fun escapades with the boys. The restaurant manager had been so moved by the experience that he decided to share it with the media.

CHAPTER 72

Williamsport

AFTER RETURNING FROM SOUTH Africa, my next mission took me to Chad in the Sahara. I had stayed in touch with my former chief and mentor at Harvard, Dr. Sydney Levitsky. Before leaving on that mission, I discussed my career ambitions with him, and he expressed an interest in having me back in Boston on the Harvard faculty. I did promise to take him up on that offer after returning from Chad.

However, in the middle of the Sahara Desert, I received a surprise telephone call late one night from Richard, a cardiothoracic surgeon I had met in York, Pennsylvania, a few years earlier. He was calling from Williamsport, Pennsylvania, where he had moved to start a new surgical program. I wondered how he had been able to locate me, and he informed me that he had called Harvard looking for me and had been informed that I would be joining them in a few months. Then they told him where I was. I didn't have the energy to talk that night, but I was curious about what he had to tell me. He wanted me to work with him in Williamsport. He was convincing enough during the conversation that I conceded without giving much thought to offer.

"Sounds like a plan," I responded.

I had heard about his excellent surgical skills, and I assured him I would contact him as soon as I got back home so that we could finalize an agreement on the proposal. The first time I had heard of Richard was while I was training in Boston. Dr. Levitsky often referred to him as one of the finest students he had when he was in Illinois. After training in Missouri, Richard had moved to Texas to run a heart transplant program at the University of Texas in Galveston before taking up a new position in Pennsylvania. I imagined he and I working together and building an enviable surgical practice. I was also excited about the challenge of starting a new program in a rural community setting.

When I returned home, I discussed the opportunity with Denise, but she was not interested in moving. However, I remained hopeful that she would change her mind. Unfortunately, our relationship deteriorated to an irreconcilable point, and after we parted ways, I moved to Williamsport, where I rented a home owned by a local orthopedic surgeon.

I had barely emptied the moving truck of my possessions when I received a phone call from the hospital requesting my assistance with a patient in need of urgent coronary bypass surgery. He was a prominent local attorney with severe coronary artery disease. My partner was not available, and I was on call my first day on the job. Although I was a new surgeon, the patient and his family did not question my credentials or skill set. Not only was my surgical team new to me and unfamiliar with my protocols, but I also had never even met the anesthesiologist. Despite all these potential constraints, the operation went smoothly, and the patient was discharged after an uneventful recovery.

I was happy to be in Williamsport, where the entire community welcomed me with open arms, and I enjoyed a very busy and challenging practice. To address my spiritual needs, I joined one of the local churches and enjoyed participating in local events, giving community lectures on heart disease and healthy living.

I remember seeing an eighty-five-year-old man in my office who had a severely abnormal heart valve and severe coronary disease as well. He was also in congestive heart failure and had been turned down for surgery by every surgeon he had consulted. He pleaded for my help, stating that he wanted to live longer, and he had a very supportive family. He was also a retired pilot and wished to resume flying. Despite having some trepidation, I agreed and scheduled his operation. After performing extensive coronary bypass surgery, which included replacing one of his heart valves, I waited for his heart to resume its beating function, but it did not. I tried every trick I knew in the book to reanimate his heart, but it refused to cooperate.

Anxiety began to permeate the operating room, with every member of the surgical team standing motionless and feeling apprehensive of the obvious outcome. I knew the patient had several family members and friends waiting in the family lounge. I, too, became nervous, and at one point, I wondered whether I had made the right decision to perform his surgery. Then I realized I needed an option more powerful than scalpels and sutures to help the patient. I bowed down my head and started praying, and I was not embarrassed to do it. Everyone in the room was watching me. I said, "Dear God, please make this heart beat strong for this man."

I prayed a short and desperate prayer. Then, when I opened my eyes and peered at his heart through my surgical telescopes, I saw it beating vigorously and practically jumping out of his chest. We were overjoyed! Interestingly, when I walked into the family lounge to announce the completion of his surgery, I discovered that his family members had been praying at about the same time I had been soliciting God's intervention. Henceforth, I have continued to pray before every operation, as I am convinced that prayer can heal and renew and determine the outcome of surgery.

One of the special encounters I had in Williamsport was with a patient who presented with a large lung tumor and was desperately in need of an operation to remove the affected lung. He was a tall, unassuming gentleman who smiled easily. His wife was pragmatic and courteous. They were both highly intelligent people, and after the usual introductions and formalities, I reviewed the findings on his X-ray with them and proceeded to recommend a major lung operation, possibly involving the removal of an entire lung. Without wasting any time, she began to fire off many questions in rapid succession about my qualifications: Where did I train? How many of these operations had I performed? What was my track record? She had an unflinching, highly penetrating stare, and she meant business. I must admit she caught me off guard. Conversely, her husband simply sat there relaxed and peaceful. After ululating my responses, I cleared my brow and waited for her verdict.

"We want you to do the operation," she stated.

His consent for the surgery may have sounded conciliatory, but I was nervous about the possibility of a complication from the operation, and the thought of facing her wrath afterward was not a pleasant one. Mr. Davidson did undergo a successful pneumonectomy, which is an operation to remove an entire lung on one side. When he was under my care, I got to know his wonderful daughter, Joanne, a prominent local attorney; her husband, Mike; and their lovely children. The Davidsons also had two sons, one of whom was an actor on a TV show called *Pacific Blue*. When he came to visit his father in the hospital, it triggered an astronomical estrogenic upheaval event among the nursing staff. Ultimately, Mrs. Davidson adopted me as her son, and I have continued to enjoy a lovely relationship with her family.

I cannot forget the experience of meeting and treating certain patients who came to me as a last resort. I remember distinctly Kathleen Many, a magnificent fifty-eight-year-old lady suffering from diabetes. She had just recovered from a heart attack and was referred for surgery but was rejected by a surgeon. She had recurrent problems with heart failure and lived about one hundred miles away from the hospital. During one of her admissions, I was asked to see her in consultation. She was in terrible shape and could barely breathe. After performing a careful and thorough examination, I decided to operate on her the next day. Sitting next to her was her daughter Kim. When Mrs. Kathleen Many heard I had agreed to do her surgery, tears rolled down her cheeks. It was then that I learned about the ordeal she had been going through with her heart disease, and I was moved by her desperate plight. The next day, I performed a quadruple bypass operation on her, and she did extremely well, recovered, and resumed her normal life with her family. Then she began to shower me with presents. She was a remarkably talented craftswoman, crocheting and creating beautiful needlework, some of which still adorns the walls of my office about two decades after her surgery.

I was honored to work with a fabulous team of doctors and nurses, both on the floor and in the ICU in Williamsport. My operating room staff was skilled and dedicated. One of my best friends was Norma, a brilliant nurse who was exceptionally kind and compassionate. During my stint in Williamsport, my son, Robert, and I often exchanged visits. I enjoyed helping him with his school assignments. He had quite an aptitude for mathematics and the sciences and a very curious and inquisitive mind. On one of his visits, we spent the entire day on the Penn State campus, which he loved, especially because football was his favorite sport. I had wanted him to attend boarding school, and I remember writing to him about two hundred boarding schools across the country, hoping that one of them would tickle his fancy, but none of them did. Eventually, he transferred from a local public school to a Catholic elementary school, from whence he eventually graduated successfully.

One day, my partner, Richard, came to me and said he had something very important to tell me. We went to a quiet locker room, where he revealed a few major problems that he was confronting in his relationship, which was falling apart. I was immensely surprised. After all, they were considered a power couple in town, and they had appeared to be supportive of each other. Then he dropped a bomb. He was in a relationship with one of our operating room staff members, who was an attractive young lady married to a local banker. She was also a highly skilled perfusionist with a pleasant personality. Richard's wife was a marvelous lady with a tremendously welcoming heart who had been a perfusionist and had allegedly been instrumental in recruiting the lady he was having an affair with. After giving birth to their son, his wife had decided to stay home and raise him.

Upon hearing such shocking news, I reminded Richard that because we were cardiothoracic surgeons, we were always in the spotlight and that he had to be careful with his actions. Conversely, he was unconcerned about how the public would perceive the matter. He was an excellent surgeon, and he began showing up ruffled with anger every day and talking about how his wife was making his life miserable. His new girlfriend always seemed to be able to cheer him up whenever she was around. One day, he informed me that he and his wife had separated and that she had moved with their son to a different house in the city. Subsequently, his girlfriend left her husband and moved in with him. He showered her with expensive gifts, and they appeared to be a happy couple. She was a genuinely nice person but was oblivious to the disaffection of the nurses and doctors toward their relationship. Soon they were often traveling, and I was on call every day around the clock. He had powerful allies in the administration who chose to look the other way.

At a certain point, I was carrying an entire load of our surgical service alone, and I went to the vice president of the hospital to request a raise. Initially, when I joined the practice, I was told that after about six months, if I enjoyed working there and if my performance was satisfactory, Richard and I would each earn the same salary. That was a gentlemen's agreement. Foolishly, I trusted everyone and agreed to it. A year later, I found myself sitting in front of that administrator and asking him to revisit our previous agreement, but he appeared to be unfazed. He listened carefully and then told me in a few words that the hospital had no money. He was a man who often expressed his relationship with God during our conversations, and I must have met him on about three different occasions to discuss salary equity between Richard and me, but all my appeals were falling on deaf ears. He would just sit and patiently look at me as I ranted about how I was doing most of the work and getting paid less than my partner.

On my last visit to his office, I told him how disappointed I was with the institution for betraying my trust in it and for reneging on a verbal agreement with me. I told him that I had not become a doctor because I wanted to make a lot of money; my motivation was to help others, and all I wanted was fairness. I learned a few years later in the newspapers that my partner had been receiving a salary that was five times greater than mine! During my last meeting with that administrator, he said something bizarre: "If you want a salary increase, then you should go and talk to your partner."

Consequently, I became aware of the subtle psychodynamics that were operating at the leadership level. Richard and I were equally trained associates employed by the same system, but he held sway with the administration, whereas I was just a foot soldier. At one time, after he left for an extended period, I performed a new procedure on a local nurse who needed a heart-valve operation. It was the first time to my knowledge anyone had performed that technique or used that approach in the state of Pennsylvania. Upon his return, he heard about it and was not pleased. I think he was jealous.

Then he informed me that the hospital vice president had requested to meet with us. What transpired at the meeting was ridiculous, illogical, and shocking. The vice president was reticent throughout the meeting, while Richard played the part of his ventriloquist. He turned around facing me and said the vice president had recommended that the only person who should be doing new procedures in the hospital was the one who had been there the longest. This made absolutely no sense. All I wanted to do was to be part of a team and to work in a fair and understanding environment. Their decision did not even consider the most important thing: the patient's best interest! At that point, it became crystal clear to me that I had no future there.

Ironically, Richard continued to solicit my support and seek solace in my house whenever the friction between him and his wife would get to him. At the same time, he continued to connive with a willing and gullible administration to undermine my contributions. Nevertheless, I kept my focus on my patients. One day, my friend Norma stopped by, and while we were having a conversation and watching television, the doorbell rang, and the person at the door identified himself as Richard. Norma had always been uncomfortable around him at the hospital, so she decided to go upstairs and wait until after he had left. That day, he was in a fury about his wife. He said "the bitch" was making his life miserable and that he wished she would just go away.

At that time, they were going through a difficult, acrimonious divorce. I tried to share a dose of reality with him by asking him to give her whatever she wanted and contest nothing. I reminded him that his job was too stressful to have to take on additional stressors. Besides, whatever he would give her would be helping their son. He looked at me carefully and then blurted out that the problem with me was that I was too nice. I concentrated on getting him to calm down, and then he left, still brimming with frustration and anger.

Toward the end of 1998, I realized that the divorce proceedings were becoming increasingly intense because he was taking more time off. He had never looked more beleaguered. He told me the hospital had decided to reduce his salary by about 50 percent. This did not make any sense because our productivity had remained relatively unchanged. I knew I earned less than he, but I did not know his exact salary. Someone said he had made arrangements with his friends in the hospital to reduce his salary so that his spousal and child support burden would be lessened. All I knew was that because of his frequent trips to the courthouse and his lawyers, I was left to shoulder most of the responsibilities in our practice.

Then, at the beginning of the year in 1999, he decided to take a vacation. He informed me that he would be staying up in the mountains at his camp. The following week was a very busy one for me, and I got home at a late hour each night that week and went straight to bed. As usual, the phone calls kept coming in from the hospital with patient problems that needed to be addressed. Then I received a phone call from his wife. I had seen her only a couple of times in twelve months. She wanted to chat and was distressed about something. She asked if I had seen her husband, and I informed her that he was on vacation. She told me that I needed to watch my back at the hospital, adding that she knew her husband was up to something. She stated that he was jealous of me. Then she repeated a few times, "I know he's up to something."

Unfortunately, because of my physical exhaustion that night, I did not ask her the basis for her suspicions. Instead, I apologized for being tired and reminded her that I had been putting in long hours alone at the hospital and was very much in need of sleep. Additionally, I apologized for not having been communicative with her since the beginning of their divorce matter. Most importantly, I told her I didn't want to take sides. A few days later, she called again to say hello, and once more she stated that he had been acting strangely. Something was bothering her. It was late at night, and I was tired, but I felt bad for appearing to be nonchalant about her emotional plight. Therefore, I asked her if we could meet and chat over the weekend on Sunday afternoon at 3:00 p.m. at a local restaurant, and she agreed. She was a great human being, and I knew she would understand that I was too tired to chat.

Friday, the next day, was cold and snowy. Two days later on Sunday, as promised, I completed my rounds, and at 2:30 p.m., I was just finishing up a mountain of paperwork on my desk when my beeper went off. It was the medical staff director of the hospital, who was interested in the whereabouts of my partner. I told him he was on vacation and could be reached either at his camp or his sister's house a couple of hours away. When I asked him why he was looking for Richard, he told me that the state police were the ones looking for him.

"Why?" I asked.

"Miriam is dead."

I just about fell out of my seat. "Dead? That can't be! I have just been rushing to finish my work so that I could meet her for lunch," I told the medical director. Then I added that she had probably committed suicide because of the stress of losing him.

Soon, the news of her death was all over town. Further details began to emerge every hour. It turned out that on Sunday, she had been uncharacteristically absent from Sunday school, and her friends were concerned. So they went to check on her and found her sprawled on the kitchen floor in her house. She had been shot from her backyard.

On a snowy Friday, two days preceding the discovery of her body, Richard had allegedly picked up their son on a regular visitation schedule and had driven to visit his sister, who lived hours away from Williamsport. Interestingly, he often expressed animosity toward his sister. So I wondered why he would have decided to embark on a two-hour trip in snowy weather, driving his new BMW sedan with his son to visit her. An extensive murder investigation ensued. At that time, he was no longer productive at work, but the administration continued to support him. I convened a meeting with them and reminded them that public perception was hurting the hospital. Something had to be done, and maybe he should be asked to resign. Everyone agreed. A few days later, the hospital reneged and supported him to stay. Rumor had it the CEO of the hospital was his personal friend.

CHAPTER 73

The Guthrie Clinic

A FEW WEEKS LATER, I received a call with a job offer from the Guthrie Clinic. I spoke with Dr. Lynn Smaha, who was a cardiologist there and who was also the president of the American Heart Association. They were looking for a chief for the Division of Cardiothoracic Surgery. The chairman of surgery at the Guthrie Clinic, Dr. Sushil Gupta, was particularly aggressive in the recruitment effort. Eventually, I agreed to visit the Guthrie Clinic for an interview only because I wanted to get Dr. Gupta off my back. As it turned out, the interview was enjoyable, and I considered it a good, challenging, and worthwhile opportunity. Moreover, I did not want to remain forever mired in a soap opera scenario in Williamsport with no clear vision for the future; hence, I accepted the offer from the Guthrie Clinic

There were few available houses to my liking on the market near the hospital in Sayre, Pennsylvania, at that time. Therefore, I bought a lovely old house across the state border in Elmira, New York, which had been built in the midtwenties by the Kennedy family, who owned Kennedy Valve Company, a manufacturer of fire hydrants and drainage systems. Owning that home was a project in itself: tearing down walls and updating plumbing and wiring. One night, I came home after a prolonged educational trip to San Diego to discover a four-foot-deep swimming pool in my basement left from a few days of heavy rains. Thank goodness for Walmart and a reliable sump pump; I was able to prevent my home from floating away.

I didn't mind the thirty-minute commute to the hospital every day. In general, my colleagues were very easy to work with, and the nursing staff was phenomenal. I became immersed in my work on the very first day at the clinic. I had visions of a world-class cardiovascular center. Therefore, I convened a meeting of cardiologists, surgeons, and administrators to develop strategies designed to transform our hospital into a center of excellence within five years. Sadly, there were a few staff members who, for unknown reasons, could not see themselves as world-class and would have been content with the status quo. However, I remained unyielding, and ultimately, even the most difficult of them eventually acquiesced when they recognized that success could only be attained when we functioned as a team and as a unit.

Under the leadership of Dr. Scopelleti and Mr. Stensager, astute and visionary CEOs, and Jeff Tiesi, an energetic cardiovascular service line administrator, our division flourished. In the first few months, I discovered a cardiac surgery program at Arnot Ogden Medical Center in Elmira that had "died," and I volunteered to help them. After meeting with their leadership, I was given a chance to jump-start it for them. Operating at two hospitals about thirty miles apart was challenging. One day, I actually performed three open-heart operations at the Guthrie Clinic in Pennsylvania and drove across the border to the Arnot Ogden Medical Center in Elmira and did three additional heart operations. Such a feat could not have been possible without strong, competent, and supportive nursing and operating room staff members at both institutions.

However, over time, that hectic schedule began to exact a tremendous physical toll on me. One night, I crashed my car on a rocky edifice because I was so tired. I considered that accident a warning sign, but I had been too stubbornly foolish to slow down.

I was honored to work with a great team of doctors at the Guthrie and the Arnot. My managers, Michelle and Debbie, kept me organized and focused. Ultimately, I was overjoyed when we were recognized among the top one hundred cardiovascular centers in the country after less than three years of my joining the Guthrie. This was indeed a remarkable recognition of true teamwork. During my tenure there, I enjoyed teaching and motivating students and residents, and I often gave lectures at Cornell University to premed and bioengineering students and never hesitated to grant permission to any student who was interested in observing heart surgery. I believed that it was important for them to learn about heart disease by allowing them to see heart surgery and possibly become motivated enough to consider a career in medicine or surgery. Furthermore, I was convinced that exposure to an actual operation could convince people to practice and promote healthy lifestyles and potentially reduce the chances of developing heart disease, which is still the most common cause of death.

Although my professional life was consuming, I still found time to enjoy my family. My oldest daughter, Mankah, was attending Howard University at that time and performing very well in her studies. Her younger sister, Ahleea, and Robert were both finishing high school and doing very well. I was responsible for the educational expenses of my nieces and nephews in college and private secondary schools in Africa. At one point, I had about twenty students on my scholarship list. I had always preached the value of education and could think of no better investment than their minds. Sometimes during my travels on a medical mission to poor countries, I would offer financial assistance to a few young people who were motivated to acquire an education in their native land.

Of the many operations I performed at the Guthrie, there were a few that still stand out in my memory. I remember being at the surgery department Christmas dinner in 1999, feeling bored and praying for my beeper to go off for any reason so that I could leave. Suddenly, my prayers were answered. There was a gentleman in the emergency department who had just collapsed on stage while playing Scrooge in a Christmas play. He was transported by helicopter to the Guthrie Clinic and was suspected of having a serious surgical problem. I got up and took my entire surgical team with me to the hospital, a short distance away. The patient was a retired seventy-nine-year-old geology professor. Suspecting a potentially lethal tear of his main aorta called an aortic dissection, I asked for a confirmatory diagnostic test, but the cardiologist responsible for doing it could not be reached. Therefore, I asked for a different test that could be done by a radiologist. He was called in, and he arrived promptly.

However, while the patient was lying on the gurney in the radiology suite and waiting for the test to begin, I was informed by a concerned nurse that his blood pressure had dropped to a dangerously low level. Fearing the worst and realizing that our radiologist was working in slow motion, I made a quick decision to take the patient at once to the operating room without a definitive diagnosis. I realized that if I didn't respond immediately, he would likely die on the spot from a cardiac arrest. There were a few people who opposed my decision to operate at that moment without a diagnosis; however, I refused to debate the pros and cons of my actions. There comes a time when a surgeon must make an unpopular decision and act on his or her instincts and experience to save a person's life. Sometimes an inner voice tells you what others may not perceive. That night, I followed my instincts because there was no time for illusions or philosophical debates.

I grabbed the patient's gurney and ran down the hallway to the operating room, where he was positioned on a table and put to sleep. After I sawed open his chest, I was greeted by more than a liter of fresh, free-flowing blood. Just as I had suspected, the gentleman had suffered an acute type A aortic dissection, which was and still is one of the most lethal conditions known to medicine. I immediately arrested his heart and lungs and hooked him up to a heart-lung machine. Then we proceeded to work furiously on him, and after several hours of intense and extensive surgery, we were successful in addressing his problem. He did have a rough and challenging time in the ICU during his recovery, and eventually, he was discharged home to his loving wife and children. Every year around Christmas, I was reminded of his love and appreciation for our efforts in saving his life by the cards and letters he would send me. Nothing could have given me greater gratification than seeing his wife of so many years overflowing with joy because death had not separated them. His outcome affirmed the importance of teamwork and made the challenges of operating on him and caring for him all the more worthwhile.

It is hard to forget another memorable patient encounter during my second year at the Guthrie Clinic. She was a forty-year-old Hispanic lady with eight children who arrived in the emergency department, was barely responsive, and was diagnosed with a lethal heart condition. When I first met her, she was already paralyzed below her hips as a result of her problem. Initially, I decided against any kind of surgical intervention because I felt her condition was beyond remedy. Then one of the nurses informed me that she had just received a phone call from one of the patient's daughters in Florida who was requesting to talk to me. I took the call, and as soon as I introduced myself, she began to cry out loud. "Please do not let my mother die. Please help her. She is the only mother we have, and we love her. Please do not let her die. We are praying for her."

I could not get a word in edgewise. She kept crying harder and louder. It was sad and painful to hear her sobbing. Experience told me that there was no reason to operate on a patient who had already developed severe neurological deficits from her problem. Suddenly, I was overcome both with emotion and a flashback to my distant past. I was confronted with the image of my own mother as she lay dying from profound hemorrhage. I could hear the passionate plea of that caring nurse desperately bemoaning the absence of a doctor who could save her life. Therefore, I declared, "OK. I am taking her to surgery now. I will call you as soon as I am done."

I called my team and asked them to get ready because I was on my way with the patient. As always, they were prepared and ready. The operation took six hours. She bled profusely after she was transferred to the ICU, and I had to reopen her chest on the spot in her bed. There was no time to transfer her back to the operating room to address the problem. After controlling the bleeding, I decided to leave her chest wide open for twenty-four hours to give her sore heart a chance to recover before taking her back to the operating room for definitive closure.

Unfortunately, her paralysis persisted, and despite numerous evaluations by neurologists, there was no hope for the return of function in her legs. Subsequently, physical therapists began to work with her daily, and arrangements were made to address the obvious physical challenges she would have to contend with after discharge. I was drawn closer to her and her family, and on one occasion, I asked one of her children how they were managing without their mother. The question opened up an emotional floodgate. She was sobbing while telling me how they were barely making it and were all working odd jobs to put food on the table. Even their fourteen-year-old sibling was out hustling to support the family. Their mother had been balancing two full-time jobs before becoming stricken with her heart issue.

I just couldn't walk away from their plight. Therefore, I requested a hospital social worker to meet with the children and help them with getting some kind of federal or state assistance. Then I offered a large sum of money to the oldest daughter to help feed her family and pay some of their bills. My lack of satisfactory communication with the patient was frustratingly obvious because I did not speak Spanish, and I often had to look around to locate a translator. Moreover, many of her older relatives did not speak English either. The frequent exchange of smiles and gesticulation was not a sustainable substitute for real conversation.

There was only one remedy for my language handicap. I contacted Elmira College and enrolled in a two-semester Spanish evening course. Maintaining consistent attendance was difficult because of my unpredictable work schedule. Nevertheless, I bought every Spanish language CD I could find at Barnes & Noble; I listened and learned every day.

My patient's hospital stay was prolonged, and I admired her for her enormous strength and determination to recover from a very dangerous condition. Every once in a while, she would become understandably depressed. One day, while we were making our morning rounds, I noticed profound sadness in her face. She was completely withdrawn from her surroundings and was staring at her feet with a look of self-pity. She had lost all movement in them. I was determined to cheer her up—in Spanish, of course! I was barely three weeks into my Spanish class, and although I was not yet in a position to upstage Don Juan, I knew enough to declare, "*Eres una mujer hermosa.*"

Her instantaneous response deterred me from completing my Castilian prose. Her lips sprung apart to reveal a contagiously illuminating smile that inspired every team member in the room that morning.

Not long after this episode, she was discharged from the hospital before I had learned enough Spanish to mount a sustained conversation with her. Predictably, I went on to encounter many more Spanish-speaking patients, and my newly acquired language skills came in handy in facilitating a therapeutic bond between us. In taking care of her, I acquired much knowledge and appreciation for the remarkable resilience of the human mind and body, and I gained particular insights into patients' feelings and hopes regarding their outcomes after major surgery. Almost invariably, if a patient told me they would not make it home alive, they died during the hospital stay. Conversely, there were many who demonstrated an incredible determination to survive. There were times when we would reach a point of despair when a critically ill patient was no longer responding to massive, aggressive interventions, only to see that patient turn around spontaneously and ultimately be discharged home.

I remember a time when in our determination to resuscitate an elderly patient with a terrible cardiac problem, we shocked her about fifty times. Finally, I called an end to any further attempts at resuscitation and declared her dead. Then we removed her breathing tube. When I turned around to leave her bedside, the nurse called my attention to her cardiac monitor. The electrical pattern on display had suddenly changed from a flatline to a normal heart rhythm. Even more miraculous was the fact that she opened her eyes, sat up in bed, and was breathing on her own. I was flabbergasted. I walked over to her, held her hand, and asked her how she was feeling.

"I'm feeling fine. And you?" she asked.

I didn't know what else to say. So I stammered something like this: "You know, you had a cardiac arrest, and you were gone. We were working on you aggressively for quite some time."

"Oh! I don't know about you guys, but I'm fine," she responded.

At that moment, I was convinced I was dealing with a Higher Power than the medicine we knew, so I politely and humbly made my exit.

There was also a gregarious, zesty ninety-five-year-old man whose heart valve I had replaced. He was up and out of bed on the first postoperative day and asked to be discharged. When I questioned in all seriousness the secret for his longevity, his response was hardly cosmic. "Smile and be happy," he stated.

Three months later, he got married to a lovely lady who was much younger. She was seventy-five.

The lessons I have learned from my patients have been special and priceless. I often feel like I am the one benefiting more from treating them.

CHAPTER 74

Mission to Cambodia

I MADE SEVERAL MEDICAL mission trips during my tenure at the Guthrie Clinic. Most of those trips took me to Southeast Asia—specifically Cambodia, where many people were living in desperate social conditions. On my first trip to Cambodia, which was meant to be part vacation and part fact-finding mission, I traveled with two friends, Richard and Daniel, and we arrived in the capital city of Phnom Penh, where we remained a few days before venturing further north to Siem Reap.

During our stay in Phnom Penh, Richard arranged for the minister of health to give us a tour of the local general hospital. It was a hot, muggy day, and my suit was drenched with perspiration even before the hospital tour began. Nevertheless, I was full of enthusiasm about the possibility of learning about health-care challenges in that country. Our first stop was an operating room where a surgeon was involved in removing a patient's esophagus because of cancer. The patient himself was a surgeon. The room was spartan and had no ventilation system. I remember seeing several flies cruising freely in the air and occasionally making rest stops on the surgeon's mask and one of many other targets that would have made any Western surgeon squirm with concern. As we were walking in a particular ward, our tour guide, a physician, wanted to know my specialty.

"Cardiovascular and thoracic surgery," I said.

Slowly, he led us down a dark and gloomy hallway. In the first room was a thirteen-year-old boy with a severe heart problem involving his aortic valve. He was sitting straight up in bed and having difficulty with breathing, and his neck veins were severely distended because of his failing heart.

My own heart went out to that boy. On that day, we saw several more patients with a plethora of heart conditions. In one room, we encountered a cute little boy about two years old crawling naked on a filthy, pockmarked cement floor. He appeared to be oblivious to our presence. Barely visible in the dim light was a tiny mat in the corner of the room, supporting the fragile figure of an emaciated-looking female curled up in a fetal position and facing the wall. Our tour guide muttered something in Khmer (their language), and she slowly turned her head to face us. Then we were told she had a terrible heart condition from which she would face certain death. She had just recently been readmitted after several prior admissions for severe heart failure. She was only sixteen and married with a child. We learned that each time she was discharged, she would return to her family in the village, where she worked on her rice farm and supported many other poor villagers. I was moved by her story. We were all moved.

At that point, I reminded everyone that the patient's main problem was that she had been born on the wrong latitude and longitude. That reality was true for all the patients we had just seen. Had they been living in the United States, they would have all received lifesaving cardiac surgery. If I had my way, I would have taken all of them with me to the United States and performed the surgeries they so desperately needed. That little boy crawling on the floor faced an uncertain future without a mother. Through a translator, I asked the patient if she would like to travel to America to undergo surgery for her heart condition. She responded with a puzzled look. Well, as I thought further about my question, I realized how stupid it was. She was a poor girl who knew nothing about America's whereabouts in the universe. I asked our translator to tell her that I would do everything I could to bring her to America and address her health problem. Our next stop was the pediatric ward, where more medical destitution awaited us.

After our depressing tour, we returned to our hotel. I began to formulate a strategy for bringing Yea Luk, the young patient with a son, to the Guthrie Clinic and to personally perform her surgery free of charge. The next day, I solicited the help of the US consular officer in Phnom Penh to offer her a tourist visa. Realizing that she would have a difficult time making the journey by herself, I spoke with a local Cambodian cardiologist named Dr.

Hay, who agreed to travel with her to the United States, and I offered to take care of his travel expenses. That day, my friend Richard suggested a visit to the famous ancient temples in northern Cambodia, and we took a flight to hot, steamy Siem Reap, an important tourist destination in the north, where we were met by a couple of overly enthusiastic native tour guides who took us on a tour of the ancient temples at Angkor Wat.

A visit to Angkor Wat gave us a unique appreciation for the richness and vibrancy of Cambodian culture and history. Angkor Wat reminded me of the Egyptian pyramids, the Mayan temples, and the ruins of ancient Zimbabwe. It reminded me of the importance of appreciating and acknowledging the collective contributions to modern civilization from various corners of the globe. Our Cambodian experience was certainly rich and rewarding.

When I returned home from the trip, I began to make arrangements for Yea Luk's surgery. I presented her case to our CEO, and it didn't take much convincing to win his support. The hospital was prepared to offer the care she desperately needed free of charge. Next, I contacted Prince Rashid of the Jordanian royal family, who had just replaced me as president of the International Heart to Heart Foundation, a medical humanitarian organization I founded, which was based in London. He offered his support as well.

Back in Cambodia, things were moving feverishly but well after Yea Luk received a US entry visa. Not only was she shocked, stunned, and flabbergasted by the rapidity of events, but her entire village was also overjoyed.

Finally, a US Airways flight touched down at the Elmira Corning airport, and Yea Luk, accompanied by Dr. Hay, stepped out and alighted on foreign soil. She walked gingerly toward the passenger terminal, her thin, frail, delicate frame drooping from the fatigue of travel and the weight of her oversized garments. That morning, I had been overly anxious and full of hope that her journey would be smooth and uninterrupted. Knowing how delicate her clinical situation was, I did not want anything to go wrong; therefore, I drove to the airport about two hours before her scheduled arrival and waited impatiently. The airport authorities were gracious enough to permit me to meet her on the tarmac with a wheelchair. Yea Luk only spoke one language, Khmer.

Accompanied by one of Guthrie's outstanding nurses, I ran up to her with exuberant excitement to hug her, but she recoiled! Judging from the way she was looking at me, she did not know who I was. Instantly, it became obvious to me that on our first encounter, she was in terrible shape, and I was probably just another body among a dozen intruders in her hospital room that day. Then, as if on cue, Dr. Hay, who was standing behind her, whispered something to her. The only term I recognized was "Dr. Zama." She clasped her hands against her chest in a traditional Cambodian greeting and smiled.

Then we drove at once to the hospital, where the nurses had been anticipating her arrival and had prepared a very comfortable room for her on the telemetry floor. There, she underwent extensive testing in preparation for her anticipated surgery. Dr. Hay was extremely helpful with translation needs. Besides his native language, he spoke English and French fluently. I offered him a room in my house for the duration of his sojourn in the United States. The next day Yea Luk underwent a successful heart operation without complications. The new permanent heart valve I used to replace her damaged native valve had been donated by St. Jude, an American company. Afterward, well wishes came pouring in from the Sayre, Pennsylvania, community and beyond. Prince Rashid of Jordan made a special surprise visit from London to lend his support to our collective efforts in addressing her medical needs.

In a speech given at my house during a reception given in his honor by the hospital, he encouraged everyone to be concerned about the welfare of the less privileged in the developing world. On the second day after her surgery, Yea Luk was allowed to walk with a little assistance on the nursing floor. She did not like any of the food on the hospital menu, and after exhausting every menu option we could think of, we eventually solicited Dr. Hay's assistance. Yea Luk told him she wanted rice and nothing else.

"Plain rice?" her nurse asked with a look of incredulity.

Yes, that's all she wanted. Plain rice and a cup of water, while other patients on the floor were chomping away on "cardiac-unfriendly" menu items like Salisbury steaks, pork chops, bacon, and cheese.

During her hospital stay, she received visits from the Cambodian community in Ithaca, and eventually, she began to feel much better. She was energetic but was homesick and was missing her son. However, I insisted on keeping her in the United States for a few more weeks to be certain that nothing would go wrong with her recovery.

Her last day at the hospital was an emotional one. The entire staff of nurses, doctors, and housekeeping workers were fond of her and were pleased to see how much better she was feeling, but they were sad to see her go. On my part, I was touched by the generosity and kindness of many fellow Americans who, despite not knowing her, were moved by her story and sent cards, checks, shoes, and clothes for her and her son as a gesture of their support and love for her.

A Cambodian friend of mine in Lowell, Massachusetts, Nissay Liek, his family, and the rest of the Cambodian community offered to host her for the rest of her recovery in the United States. A short while after she arrived in Massachusetts, I received a clipping from a regional newspaper bearing a photo of her and a famous Vietnam veteran who was quite familiar with her part of the world. Senator John Kerry had met her to offer his support and best wishes. Yea Luk had become a celebrity!

I made several more humanitarian trips to Southeast Asia. On one of those trips, I donated boxes of hospital supplies and equipment, including multiple defibrillators, to a remote hospital in northern Cambodia. On that particular visit, I had no energy. I was tired and feeling physically and emotionally depleted because I had been operating nonstop for a few weeks preceding that trip.

I remember sitting on a park bench in Angkor Wat, enjoying a little respite from the heat, humidity, and a million chatty Western tourists, when I became aware of a persistent voice imploringly nudging me to buy something.

"Sir, would you like to buy a bracelet? Sir, kindly buy a bracelet. I can give you a good price."

I chose to ignore this unwanted intrusion, but then something hit me: the intruder was speaking with a perfect American English accent and proper grammar! I looked up. Standing in front of me was a little girl no more than ten years old carrying a small stack of bamboo bracelets. My curiosity was piqued at once. I fired off many questions at her in rapid succession.

"How old are you? Who made these bracelets? Where did you learn to speak English?"

Her responses not only stunned me but also impressed me immensely. Her name was Saren. She was ten years old and lived in a village nearby. Her family was poor (no surprise there), and she made and sold bamboo bracelets to pay for her education and to support her destitute family. She had learned to speak English by interacting daily with tourists. She had been hawking bracelets and other homemade trinkets for about five years. Listening to that kid reminded me of someone I was all too familiar with who had grown up in a not-so-different world in Africa. She had to sell a whole lot of bracelets to make a dollar! I asked her how many bracelets she would normally sell in a day.

"About five," she answered.

She added that she was hoping to sell me ten of them! *What an aggressive little entrepreneur*, I thought. Our conversation became livelier. I bombarded her with questions about her family, school, and community. Intermittently, she would bring the focus back to her bracelets and inject a reminder that I should buy a few of them. I thought to myself that here was a kid living in abject poverty but not feeling hopeless. I saw tremendous potential in her. Something told me I had to help that kid. I grabbed my camera and took a picture of her. Then I promised her I would be back to see her and meet her parents on a later visit.

When I stood up to look for my friends, she planted her feet firmly in front of me and reminded me that I had not bought any of her bracelets. I paused for a moment, smiled at her with great admiration for her importunity, and reached into my pocket for a twenty-dollar bill, which I exchanged for a few bamboo bracelets. I had a feeling that I had just made a fateful encounter with a future luminary. When I returned to the United States, I shared the story of my trip with some of my associates. In particular, I told them about my delightful encounter with that bright, ambitious village girl named Saren and how I intended to sponsor her education.

After several months of neckbreaking surgical procedures, I took off again to Cambodia. First, I wanted to spend a few days discovering a couple of other Asian countries. My friend Norm Shetler from Ohio decided to travel with me, and we made a whirlwind tour of Japan, China, South Korea, Vietnam, and Thailand. Finally, we arrived in Cambodia, our ultimate destination. I wanted to return to Siem Reap to fulfill a promise. Armed with a photo, I emerged in the Angkor Wat jungle in search of Saren. After showing it to a few locals, I was assured by one of them that she would be notified of my arrival. The next morning, I came back and waited at the same spot where we had met during my previous visit. I had barely sat down when I heard my name.

"Dr. Zama! Dr. Zama!"

Saren came running toward me. She collided with me, and I gave her a big hug. Then I observed an older woman walking softly toward us. Saren turned, looked at the lady, and announced, "My mother."

With her hands clasped vertically in the middle of her chest, her mom greeted me. We talked a while, with Saren translating for us. I told her I wanted Saren to continue making and selling bamboo bracelets and other items, as she had been doing. I wanted her to sell her merchandise fewer days a week so that she could concentrate on her schoolwork. I promised to provide sufficient funds to support her education and related expenses for as long as she remained in school and maintained good grades. I intended to channel my financial support through a friend who owned a popular souvenir shop nearby in that city. Her mother thanked me profusely. After that, I wished both of them well, and I left.

Saren went on to graduate and became an expert in computer technology in Cambodia, and I smile each time I see those bamboo bracelets adorning a wall in my living room.

CHAPTER 75

Economist Conference

ONE OF THE PARTICULARLY enriching experiences I had was participating in the Economist Conferences in Athens, Greece. The first time I attended one of these conferences, I learned about many regional European and global geopolitical issues impacting humanity. I met and interacted with several European leaders, as well as our former (now late) president George Bush and former secretary of defense William Cohen, who had been invited to address the attendees. On my first trip to the Economist Conference, I met Yevgeny Primakov, a former Russian prime minister and a vivacious conversationalist. It was interesting to see that despite our ideological differences, we had the same needs and desires in life.

At a lunchtime reception in the American Embassy that week, I found President Bush and his wife, former first lady Barbara Bush, to be warm and genuinely compassionate people. Barbara promised to fix me "a good meal" if I ever visited her family in Texas. During that first conference, I was invited to dinner at the home of Antonius, a Greek businessman, where I sat next to Dora Bokayannis, who was a parliamentarian at that time. Initially, I felt out of place among all those politicians and tycoons and pretty much stayed to myself.

Then a discussion emerged regarding the political controversies surrounding stem cell research and its usage in the United States. Suddenly, someone announced that there was a doctor in the room who might want to educate the dinner guests about stem cells. With all eyes on me, I proceeded to deliver a lecture on ongoing research efforts and potential clinical uses of stem cells. To my surprise, everyone appeared to be genuinely interested in what I had to say about that topic. Soon, other guests in attendance began to move closer to my table and to actively participate in subsequent discussions on the same topic. I remember listening as the night progressed to Dora's narrative about important events that had occurred in her life, especially the assassination of her husband by members of an infamous domestic gang. She talked about the lessons she had learned from her father, a former Greek prime minister, and her tireless efforts fighting for her people. Hearing this, I turned to her and gave her my prophecy that eventually, she would rise to a highly prominent position in her country. She chuckled and shrugged. About a year later, she became mayor of Athens and not long afterward, minister of foreign affairs.

Also sitting at my table that night was Despina, the daughter of a notable Greek industrialist. An attendee at the conference, she was a stunningly beautiful PhD student home on vacation from England. At the end of the dinner reception, she volunteered to give me a ride back to the Athens Hilton, where I was staying. I could not decline. When we got there, we remained sitting in her car for about three hours, talking about everything from protecting marine wildlife in Barbados to the Apollo space program while her chauffeur dozed off. The next day, she stopped by and took me to lunch, followed by a photographic and educational tour of the museums of Athens and other important historical sites in that remarkable city.

Afterward, we went on a casual walk on the beach and then back to her house, where I met her mother, who was just as friendly as she was. I was in the car alone with her chauffeur, heading back to my hotel, when he told me how much happier Despina was since meeting me. I only had about twenty-four more hours to be in Athens. That night, I hung out with her and her chauffeur until the wee hours of the morning of my departure. Then, when she went home to rest for a couple of hours before taking me to the airport, I returned to my hotel to prepare my luggage. On the way to the airport, it was obvious to both of us that we had developed an intense liking for each other.

The previous day, she had inquired with a travel agent in the hotel about flights to New York because she was interested in visiting me. She was also looking into the possibility of completing her graduate education, hopefully at Cornell University, which was located a short distance from my home. We were so involved in our conversation that I almost missed my flight to New York. After arriving at the Athens airport, I hugged her and promised to call within two days. It was a Thursday, and I had to go straight to work after arriving home because I had been scheduled to assume on-call duties at the hospital that night. We both agreed that she would visit within two weeks. As I was rushing through the security screening setup, I turned one last time to find her standing on the same spot I had just left her, tears rolling down her cheeks. I blew a kiss at her and disappeared behind a security curtain. Sadly, that would be the last image of her I would ever see.

When I got home, I received a visit from my friend Daniel Martin, an international attorney from London. He had come to discuss future humanitarian endeavors by our organization. On Saturday, as promised, I called Despina numerous times and left messages on her voice mail but received no response. I was surprised. All weekend, I called her intermittently, to no avail. On Sunday night, while having dinner with Daniel, I began to wonder why Despina had not responded to my messages. It seemed unusual in light of the very rich encounter we had enjoyed during my brief stay in Athens. Then something hit me.

"She is dead," I declared.

"No!" exclaimed Daniel. "Maybe she is not sure of your intentions. Maybe she needs reassurances. Send her flowers."

I called a local florist and sent her a large bouquet of roses. A day later, I received a fax message from her mother, written by Aspa, Despina's maiden-in-waiting. It informed me that Despina had fallen from a third-floor balcony and sustained serious injuries. She was on life support, and I would be receiving updates on her progress. It ended by acknowledging the arrival of flowers I had sent, which had been placed on her bedside table. I was shocked by the news, but I found no comfort in the fax message. A few days later, I received another fax from Aspa. It announced bad news. Despina had died. Furthermore, it stated that she would be buried at the First Cemetery of Athens because of her family's important social standing. I felt numb and heart-wrenched. She was so young, so bright, so caring and concerned about others. How could she be dead? She had spent time in the

Caribbean fighting to protect sea turtles and other marine wildlife. She had expressed an interest in joining me on future medical missions.

The following year, I received an invitation by the organizers of the annual Economist Conference in Athens to lecture European political and business leaders on the economic implications of challenging contemporary global health issues. I accepted the invitation and returned to Athens. In advance of my trip, I contacted Despina's mother, who agreed to meet and take me to visit her grave. I was lodged with other speakers, including some European leaders, in the Astir Palace Resort near Athens. Despina's mother came there to meet me, and we went to visit her final resting place. By the time we arrived at her mausoleum, we were both drenched in tears.

A beautiful photo of Despina that I had taken the first time we met was delicately and artfully laminated on the wall of her mausoleum. I reached out and touched it gently. It was one of the many pictures I had taken of her during our brief and blissful encounter. I had mailed copies of them to her home as soon as I returned from Athens. After she died, her mother requested the negatives. She considered them the happiest pictures she had ever seen of her daughter. It was hard to believe that Despina was gone, and it was even harder for a mother who had just lost her only daughter. Her father slipped into a deep depression.

During the conference, I met Javier Solana, the president of the European Union, who was an analytical strategist with a great sense of humor. The head of NATO, Mr. Robertson, was more laid-back, and my friend Richard and I had breakfast one morning with both of them. Among the many speakers at that conference was the former German chancellor Helmut Kohl, who gave a stirring, passionate speech stressing the value of designing political and economic policies that promoted peace among nations. He related in riveting and agonizing pathos his experiences as a child growing up during the Second World War and received a standing ovation at the end of his talk.

He was a tough act to follow by any measure. I spoke after him. Before heading to the podium, I was given a generous introduction by one of the conference organizers. The room was filled with powerful dignitaries, and I was feeling tense. I guess you could say I had a thousand knots in my stomach. I stood up after a brief round of applause and walked to the podium.

Then I delivered what I considered my best speech ever. I had spent months researching the topic of my talk and preparing for that occasion. I talked about epidemics, HIV, tuberculosis, malaria, famine and nutritional challenges, heart disease, and biological warfare.

I made a passionate plea to the leaders of developed nations to be more engaged with these problems that, by and large, afflicted the poor and especially those in developing countries. I emphasized that those challenges could and would wind up at our doorsteps in the West if they were not addressed rapidly and collectively by those who had the resources to do it. In the end, I was overwhelmed by the applause I received, and I was asked to remain at the podium for a panel discussion.

After I returned to my seat, an official came to me and informed me that Chancellor Helmut Kohl wanted to meet me. I was escorted to his table. He was a tall man with an impressive frame. He gave me a big bear hug and a crushing handshake, told me how much he had enjoyed my presentation, and asked to meet with me afterward. Later on, I was informed that he had been moved to tears by my speech and its impassionate delivery.

That night, I received a knock on my door as I was preparing to go to bed. I opened it and saw two gentlemen facing me. One of them stated, "Dr. Zama, Chancellor Kohl would like to have a few moments with you."

I hesitated. It was late, and I was in my pajamas. I requested to be allowed a few minutes so that I could get dressed and become presentable; after all, I did not consider it polite to meet the former chancellor of Germany in my pajamas. Instead, they interrupted me and told me there was no need for me to change my outfit.

"You may come as you are. He is in his pajamas as well," they stated.

So down the hall we went, and I was escorted to a private pajama party with the former chancellor of Germany! We had an extensive conversation, during which he disclosed to me that his wife was suffering from debilitating photophobia. He became quite emotional during that particular narrative. He talked about his own life and intermittent struggles with his weight. He was a brilliant conversationalist and highly knowledgeable about a broad range of issues. He asked many specific questions about my profession and was particularly fascinated with the conduct of heart surgery. He mentioned something about heart transplantation and his admiration for Dr. Christiaan Barnard. At the end of our conversation, he expressed a desire to keep in touch and shared his contact information with me. With a chuckle he declared, "You can be my heart doctor."

Upon hearing that, I assured him I would always be available to address whatever cardiovascular issues he might develop. We shook hands, exchanged good night wishes, and parted ways. When I returned to my room, I still couldn't believe what had just transpired. How did I get from being a scrawny, flea-infested little kid in a tiny village to the Astir Palace Hotel in Athens, Greece, sitting next to the German chancellor or hanging out with President George Bush? It was indeed an inexplicably humbling and incomprehensible experience.

Sometime during the conference, I met Mr. Chowdury, a kindhearted and elegant gentleman who was the CEO of Gorenje, a Slovenian appliance company in Athens, Greece. He invited me to join him and his beautiful daughter, Maya, for dinner. That would be the beginning of a rich and rewarding friendship between him, his lovely family, and me. Not long after we met, he invited me to visit Slovenia to meet the rest of his family. On that visit, I was honored to know his charming wife; his son, who held a doctorate in engineering; and his daughter, who was completing doctoral studies in the sciences. Her boyfriend, Iztok, took me on a whirlwind tour of Slovenia and its remarkably scenic countryside.

After we left Slovenia, Mr. Chowdhury drove across the border to a town known principally for its global movie superstar, Arnold Schwarzenegger. From there, I caught a flight to Vienna, Austria, for a brief visit with my cousin Charles and his family. A year later, I was honored with a reciprocal visit by my friend Mr. Chowdhury and his family. From then on, we enjoyed a special and endearing friendship until his untimely and devastating death about a decade later.

CHAPTER 76
Belgrade and Brazil

AFTER MY SPEECH AT the Economist Conference, I received a surprise call from Princess Katerina of the former Yugoslavia. She had heard about my presentation through one of her friends who had been at the conference in Athens and was interested in soliciting my involvement with her humanitarian projects in Serbia. Consequently, I flew to Belgrade to attend a major fundraising event at the White Palace. For me, it was an entirely fascinating experience because I had studied the history of Yugoslavia in secondary school. There I was, standing in a room where Emperor Tito used to sit and watch movies.

My hosts informed me that Tito's favorite movies were John Wayne Westerns. During that visit, I met Prince Alexander and many other global dignitaries, including the Prime Minister of Serbia, Zoran Dindic. This was our second encounter since we had crossed paths previously at one of the Economist Conferences in Athens, Greece, where he was a featured speaker. During the reception in Belgrade, I sat at a table with him and his gracious wife. They were a marvelous couple, full of zest and life. We talked about possibly meeting up again in the future to sail the Mediterranean. He spoke lovingly and passionately about his country. Sadly, a year later he was felled by a disgruntled assassin's bullet because of his Western leanings and his role in delivering Milosevic to the World Court.

While in Belgrade I accompanied Princess Katerina on a tour of several health-care facilities, all of which were rudimentary, deplorable, and very much in need of significant improvements. She had graciously donated a lot of equipment and supplies to assist most of them with their challenging efforts to provide decent health-care services to the people of that nation after the Bosnian war. Many ambulances were also donated by a few kind, generous philanthropists to support her humanitarian initiatives. It was devastating to witness the unintended destructive consequences of war on the only children's hospital and other health-care facilities in Belgrade.

At a final reception in the White Palace, I met a most dignified, erudite, sophisticated lady named Denise Hale from San Francisco. We enjoyed an open, unpretentious conversation about the events of that day and life in general. Afterward, she extended me an invitation to visit her in San Francisco. Indeed, she was special in many ways, as I would ultimately discover.

Of the many encounters that I had on that trip, the one that stands out the most in my mind was a Gypsy camp along the river in Belgrade. I had heard about Gypsies but had never quite met any of their members. I was told that they were living under sordid conditions; therefore, I asked someone to take me there to see how I could help them. Quite a few people cautioned me against making the trip because of the possible risk of harm to me, but I was stubborn. I explained to my driver that I had never been afraid of meeting new friends because I believed every human had some element of good in them.

When we arrived at the camp, one by one the Gypsies began to mill around me. They were curious about the motive of my visit. The scene appeared to be out of a post–World War I documentary. Their homes were precarious-looking sheds made of cardboard and sticks. I reached out and shook hands with each of them, and I was received with warm smiles, love, and laughter while we were communicating in a mixture of Spanish and French. Mostly they spoke Italian, and we got along just fine.

After I explained the purpose of my visit, one of them invited me into her cardboard house to meet her husband. I asked to know what kind of difficulties they were facing. They all seemed to be worried about how they were going to survive the coming winter. They had many other life challenges about which we talked, but none of them requested any assistance from me. Conversely, they offered me food, but I politely declined. I did promise to ship them blankets shortly to keep them warm during the upcoming winter. Therefore, as soon as I returned to the United States, I purchased a hundred blankets and shipped them to Belgrade. I have not been back to Serbia since that visit, but I'm hopeful those blankets reached my Gypsy friends and their families.

My host in Belgrade also had other guests from Greece, the Malamatinas, a young, personable couple, Katerina and her quiet husband, Kostas. I was told they were owners of one of the largest wine-producing companies in Europe and were very generous philanthropists. Katerina was a tall, smart, attractive, and dignified lady with an air of sophisticated simplicity who spoke softly and smiled readily. Kostas, on the other hand, was more reserved initially but opened up later, revealing his dynamic side. He was a very low-key person but had a poignant and hilarious sense of humor, which I enjoyed. From that encounter emerged a friendship that has flourished up till today.

When I returned home, I had a long list of surgical procedures to perform. As usual, I worked day and night for a few months until I was pretty much caught up before thinking about another missionary trip. One time, I was introduced to a cardiologist from Brazil who was working at an impoverished public hospital. He talked about so many patients who needed heart operations because of the high incidence of rheumatic heart disease in that country. Unfortunately, very few patients could afford lifesaving heart surgery. Hearing that, I contacted some of the heart-valve manufacturing companies in the United States, and after persistent solicitation, I was offered over $200,000 worth of artificial heart valves.

Armed with this huge bag of goodies, I arrived in a public hospital in Brazil, where I delivered them to a team of grateful surgeons. I remember helping the doctors in surgery and joining them afterward on their ward rounds. To witness the looks of gratitude in the eyes of patients who had received one of the valves I had donated was the most rewarding experience. My main problem was that I could not communicate with them in Portuguese. Nothing can be more frustrating than a language barrier between a doctor and a patient.

On the last day of my visit, I received an expression of gratitude from the chief medical officer of the hospital in an auditorium full of about two hundred doctors. On my part, I thanked them profusely for the warm hospitality they had extended me. Furthermore, I told them that everything had been wonderful except for my inability to communicate with patients in Portuguese. Then I made a promise that I would learn to speak fluent Portuguese before my next visit in three months. There was a lot of chuckling and laughter from the audience.

After I returned from Brazil, I went to my favorite Barnes & Noble in Elmira, New York, where I bought every Portuguese language CD I could find, as well as four dictionaries and two textbooks. Each day, I would spend at least two hours studying Portuguese. Applying immersion language learning strategies, I subscribed to TV Globo, a Brazilian TV network, and played Portuguese language lectures daily while sleeping or driving to and from work. About three months later, armed with boxes of medical equipment, I took off from JFK on a medical mission to Rio de Janeiro, with a six-hour layover in Miami.

I had been in touch with my college friend Ron Russo, the disco don from our college years, but I had not seen him in ages. Coincidentally, he was living in Miami, so I called him, and we agreed to meet at Miami International Airport. It was the most delightful encounter after so many years. Of all the people I knew, nobody understood my difficult college years, my struggles, and my sufferings like Ron did. He had not lost his sense of humor and wit after all those years. He took me home to meet his beautiful friend Becky, and we shared a hearty dinner and a lengthy conversation. Then Ron drove me back to the airport for my continuing flight to Brazil. We were at the Varig (Brazilian Airlines) check-in counter ready to drop off my luggage when the Brazilian attendant wondered why I was checking in so much luggage.

"Are you going on vacation to my country?" she asked.

"No. Heart surgery," I responded.

Without giving me a chance to clarify my response, she leaned far across the countertop, and with an honest look of deep compassion, she reassured me. "Don't you worry. We have the best heart surgeons in the world. Trust me. You will be just fine." Then she added enthusiastically, "I will put you in a better seat because you need to rest well before you get there."

With that, she completed the check-in process in a jiffy, and I thanked her. In the meantime, Ron kept nudging me, and when I leaned over, he said, "She thinks you are the patient, not the surgeon! Tell her you are the one who is going to do the heart surgeries."

I smiled but didn't respond. As we walked away from the ticket counter, I said, "Why ruin it for her? She is admirably proud of her country. This experience will probably be the highlight of her day. And I am OK with that."

When our plane landed in Rio de Janeiro, I greeted the customs official in Portuguese, and he welcomed me "back home," asking how my vacation to America was. Then, after seeing my passport, he looked confused. He had thought I was Brazilian. I smiled. When I arrived in Brazil and started my mission at the public hospital, no one believed I had just learned Portuguese in three months. My determination had paid off. The patients were happy and comfortable, and that's what I cared about the most.

CHAPTER 77

Denise Hale and
Kamala Harris

AFTER RETURNING FROM BRAZIL, I received a call from Denise Hale in San Francisco. She asked to know when I would be visiting. I picked a weekend, flew out to San Francisco, rented a car, and drove up to her ranch, where I spent the weekend enjoying the warm and beautiful mountainous geography of Northern California. She was the consummate host. Everything about her exuded elegance and charm.

That weekend, I met another guest of hers at the ranch who was an Egyptologist and a professor at the University of Richmond. We spent hours discussing philosophical issues in ethics and religion. During that weekend he became my teacher. Denise Hale was a celebrated socialite and an amazing human being with a strong philanthropic instinct. When we met for the first time in Belgrade, Serbia, I was told she had donated about fifteen furnished ambulances to serve the needs of the citizens of that country. She was highly prominent on all the powerful lists of celebrated socialites in San Francisco and gave generously to countless community causes, including the San Francisco Symphony orchestra. Most knew her as Liza Minnelli's stepmother.

On one of many visits to San Francisco, she talked about a single lady she wanted me to meet called Kamala Harris, who was a prosecutor in the district attorney's office. One evening, we stopped at a boisterous venue teeming with the newsmakers in San Francisco, where she chatted briefly with Nancy Pelosi's husband and a couple of other friends of hers, including the conductor of the San Francisco Symphony. In the middle of that social melee, she introduced me to Kamala, who was engaged in an animated conversation with a friend of hers from Sacramento. To escape the noise, she and I stepped outside, chatted for a while, and then exchanged contact information. She was talking excitedly about running for the district attorney position in San Francisco, and I encouraged her.

After I returned home, she and I talked often, and I gave her moral and financial support for her campaign and would often ship cartons of candy and snacks to her campaign headquarters to support her volunteers. Ultimately, she won the election, and I suggested a special celebration somewhere overseas. Initially, we agreed on Paris, and after I had made appropriate arrangements for the trip, we decided otherwise and settled on Rio de Janeiro, where we traveled at the end of that year and checked in at the Sofitel hotel on Copacabana Beach. While there, we would spend long hours each morning in conversation while exercising at the gym before setting out to explore Rio, go shopping, or take long walks on Copacabana Beach.

One time, we hired a driver who took us deep into Rocinha Favela, one of the largest crime-ridden shantytowns in South America, where hundreds of thousands of people reside, many of them living under the most inhumane and unsanitary conditions, just a stone's throw from enormously expensive, glistening, luxury high-rise condos hugging sun-drenched tropical beaches. It was considered a risky place to visit, but we did not encounter any problems during our tour.

Additionally, we visited the iconic Christ the Redeemer statue, which is almost a hundred feet high and perched at twenty-three hundred feet on Corcovado Mountain overlooking the picturesque city of Rio de Janeiro. To get there, we took a scary vertical train. I remember visiting Sugarloaf Mountain, which rises vertically from the Atlantic shores and is popular with rock climbers. To get to the summit, we had to take two glass-walled cable cars. The first car started at street level and ascended to a nearby mountain called Moro da Urca. At this point, we transferred to a second car, which whisked us up to the summit of Sugarloaf. Although nobody around me could appreciate it, at that time, I was in a heightened state of anxiety because of my morbid fear of heights. Therefore, I kept my eyes partially closed during the cable car trip. That night we topped it off with an experience at the Brazilian cultural show at a popular theater and a dinner dance afterward in the Lagoa district of Rio. Indeed, it was a delightful opportunity for us to experience the incomparable richness of Rio's hospitality and iconic landmarks.

CHAPTER 78

Surgical Moments

WHENEVER I WAS NOT on a medical mission overseas, I would have a packed surgical schedule, especially since I was operating at both the Guthrie Clinic in Sayre, Pennsylvania, and the Arnot Ogden Medical Center in Elmira, New York. Eventually, the operative load became lightened somewhat when the Arnot hospital signed an agreement with Columbia University to manage their heart institute and allowed Drs. Craig Smith and Mehmet Oz to assist with cardiac surgical cases. This arrangement freed me up so that I could work almost exclusively at the Guthrie with occasional cross-coverage at the Arnot.

I was also performing many surgeries on international patients. One time, my friend Katerina Malamatina, whom I had met in Belgrade, called me from Thessaloniki, Greece, telling me about her mother, a beloved eighty-year-old attorney and family matriarch, who had been exhibiting some mental status changes. After listening carefully to her narrative, I suspected her mother had coronary disease and had likely suffered a heart attack in the past. I had her flown to the United States for a diagnostic evaluation, which confirmed my suspicion, and subsequently, I performed a quadruple bypass operation on her. She survived into her nineties.

On the family front, my children were all doing well. Mankah was taking psychology in college with an interest in pursuing law. Robert was looking to graduate high school and begin college, while Ahleea was preparing to start her senior year in high school. I spoke frequently with them and provided guidance and support with their educational endeavors. I probably bored them often enough with my overly lengthy speeches about the importance of education and academic excellence. My lovely niece Yvonne, who was attending Mansfield University, spent most of her weekends with me during her college years, and eventually, she met a brilliant, humble, personable young man, Jacob, who was preparing to enter a PhD program in computer science at McGill University. After she graduated college, they decided to tie the knot, and I couldn't have been a happier and prouder uncle to be accorded the honor to give her hand away in marriage. That splendid wedding took place in Canada, where she had moved soon after graduation.

Increasingly, I was being asked to lecture overseas, and I would usually schedule missionary activities conjointly, even for just a few days. Within a few years of my joining the Guthrie Clinic, I remember receiving a surprising notice that I had been selected in Sayre to be Person of the Year. I was humbled to receive it, although I thought many great people in that region were more deserving of the honor than me.

I traveled to Argentina for a conference, and on my way back, I stopped in São Paulo, Brazil, for a visit when I received notice that my aunt Cecilia, who had taken me in after my mom died, had been diagnosed with large lung cancer, which was deemed inoperable. She was evaluated in Cleveland and Detroit and was left frustrated because she had been told she would die from surgery. And then she related to her son Augustin a dream she had had in which my father had encouraged her to seek my professional assistance in addressing her health problem. I remembered the love she gave me as a child, and it hurt me inside to think of the misery she was experiencing.

Therefore, I caught an earlier flight from Brazil that night and returned to New York. The next day, she arrived from Ohio to see me, and twenty-four hours later, she was in the operating room. Before the surgery, to remain emotionally disconnected from her and maintain my composure so that I could concentrate on the operation, I avoided eye contact with her and requested to be called to the operating room only after she had been prepared, draped, and was ready for incision.

It was a tedious and extensive operation that involved removing the tumor with her entire left lung. Everything went well, and she was alert and talking within an hour of the surgery. How ironic it was to have been allowed the opportunity to show her my appreciation for her love for me when she had come to my rescue decades earlier when I was mourning the loss of my mother. The morning after her surgery, when we walked into her hospital room to check on her, she began to cry. I asked her what could be wrong, and she said she had not been sleeping well during the preceding year because the enormous tumor in her chest had caused her to have severe breathing difficulty while lying down. However, the night after the operation, she did sleep like a baby. Then she told me she was feeling sad because most of her siblings had already died, thereby leaving her alone to enjoy the fruits of their collective labor. Her siblings never had the chance to experience the kind of modern, lifesaving marvels she had just received.

Not long after I operated on my aunt, I was approached by one of our cardiologists, who was concerned about a forty-five-year-old man with a large aneurysm in his chest and a bad heart valve associated with it. He needed a major operation that required disconnecting his main aorta from his heart, cutting out his heart valve below it, disconnecting his coronary arteries from his main aorta, and cutting out the aorta with the aneurysm. After doing all that extensive work, his anatomy had to be reconstituted to its natural form. To perform this operation, artificial materials were used to replace both the aorta and the valve. His coronary arteries also had to be accurately reattached to the new artificial aorta. That would be a monumental surgical undertaking.

The patient had very young children and a doting wife. On the day of surgery, a large crowd of family members and loved ones arrived to support him. I had just performed a similar operation the previous day and was assured that we had everything we would need for that operation.

After opening the patient's chest and cutting out the bad aorta completely, I turned to the nurse and asked for the new composite aorta. The circulating nurse left to fetch it in the adjourning supply room. Time was of the essence. I could tell she was back in the room even though she remained quiet. Again, I asked for the new aorta and the valve that comes attached as a composite. No response. Then I turned around, and our eyes met. Hers were telling me something no surgeon wants to hear. She looked ashen.

"Dr. Zama, we used the last one yesterday," she said with a tremulous voice.

I felt paralyzed. Someone had dropped the ball. I had already completely cut out the patient's natural aorta and valve and discarded the specimens. I took off my gown and gloves and stepped out in the hallway for a minute to recollect my thoughts. I had a young man on the operating table; I had stopped his heart and lungs, and he was being kept alive on a heart-lung machine. There were no options other than the scheduled procedure to address the situation at hand. His family, a million of them, were waiting downstairs in the lounge. The clock was indeed ticking fast.

Back in the room, I spoke to the nurse with emphatic calm: "Call the hospital helicopter now. Call every hospital in the region or the state, and find out who has what I need. Send a helicopter to pick it up right away. I will wait for it. We must complete this operation and give the patient the best outcome."

An artificial aorta and valve composite of appropriate dimensions was located, and a couple of hours later, the helicopter returned with it. The operation was successful, and afterward, I met with his family and gave them the good news. It had been a close call, and I could barely stay awake that night because I was extremely emotionally exhausted.

Cardiothoracic surgery is a very stressful profession. Critical decisions have to be made in split seconds. Any wrong decision or mishap can have immediate, fatal consequences. A cardiac surgeon adapts to always living in a heightened state of vigilance. It is a profession that invariably deals with issues of life and death every day. After that close call, I convened a meeting of my staff, and we formulated a stringent policy to avert any future possibilities of a similar event. Henceforth, a most effective and reliable inventory management protocol was implemented.

I remember being called urgently to see a teenager who presented with a stab wound to his chest. Allegedly it was a self-inflicted injury in response to his girlfriend's decision to end their relationship. (Incidentally, the first documented successful heart surgery in America was performed in 1893 by Daniel Hale Williams, an African American surgeon, to address a similar injury on a man in Chicago.) When I saw the young patient, I was surprised to discover that he was very calm and seemingly unconcerned about his injury despite having a knife sticking out of his chest. Immediately, we took him to the operating room, where I opened his chest, removed the knife, and repaired an injury in his heart. He had a very smooth postsurgery course and was discharged in a stable condition.

When I saw him about two weeks later in the clinic, I spent an enormous amount of time with him, giving fatherly advice. He expressed profound remorse for his previous actions after realizing how close he had come to dying. Several months later, I was pleasantly surprised to receive a card and a letter of thanks from him indicating that he had developed a new and more positive perspective on life in general. To this day, I often think of him with much hope in my heart that experience, age, and maturity have conspired to keep him in a better mental state.

At the Guthrie Clinic, we had a very strong team of perfusionists under the leadership of Dennis. At that time, there was a senior perfusionist who was excellent and highly skilled. One time, the hospital decided that a non-board-certified perfusionist could no longer be employed by the hospital. That decision was made following a state mandate on the issue. It was quite unfortunate because that particular perfusionist had maintained an outstanding track record for decades while providing extraordinary patient care. He also was at the end of his career and was profoundly upset with the decision. I couldn't understand why somebody with such technical talent and no performance issues had to be put in that position. Therefore, I called the appropriate administrator in Harrisburg at the state office and told him that if he was ever in my region and needed heart surgery electively or urgently, I would hope any of our perfusionists would be at the controls. They got the message, and our senior perfusionist was granted an extension and maintained a stellar job performance until his eventual retirement.

My operating room staff was made up of dynamic individuals. I could not have asked for a better team. During my tenure, one of my colleagues resigned and accepted an offer in a different state. He took one of our assistants with him, leaving only Rich Rockwell and me. Rich was outstanding, skilled, and committed. He practically walked on water. However, the many operations and emergencies we were addressing had begun to take a toll on him since he was working as a lone surgical assistant. His lovely family was making enormous sacrifices by not having him at home as often as he would have wanted. I approached the administration and requested an additional surgical assistant as soon as possible.

CHAPTER 79

Mrs. Alice Blair, Jennifer, and the Orphans

OVER DINNER IN WASHINGTON, DC, in the summer of 2006, my gentle friends Tom and Alice Blair and their daughter, Jennifer, had a long discussion about medical humanitarianism. During that conversation, everyone expressed an interest in participating in humanitarian endeavors in developing countries. They wanted very much to help the sick and unfortunate children in these countries. The Blair family had a long history of human service and philanthropy at both community and global levels.

After our discussion, Jennifer organized and formed Global Family, a not-for-profit organization through which people could channel their resources and talents to help others. Ultimately, we decided that Cameroon would be a good place to begin our international mission. At first, Mr. and Mrs. Blair were interested in sponsoring disadvantaged sick children from poor countries who needed advanced surgical care that could be given in the United States. However, in time, it was decided that a fact-finding mission to Africa would help illuminate and amplify their understanding and appreciation for the problems and needs of those children. A date was set for the trip to Africa.

On Friday, November 2, 2006, we took off from Dulles airport on the Blair family jet, which was filled with many gifts for children: shoes, school supplies, clothes, toys, games, over-the-counter medicines, and essential medical supplies like stethoscopes, blood-pressure-monitoring equipment, bandages, and countless other items that Mrs. Blair and her daughter Jennifer had meticulously packaged over several weeks in the Blair family home, which had essentially been converted into a mission staging center.

On that plane was the most interactive group anyone could assemble for such a trip. There were three superb pilots, James, Patrick, and Joe; a flight engineer; and Larry, a personal assistant to Mrs. Blair. Jennifer even brought two of her children—Emily, eleven, and Blair, ten—as well as their nanny, Michelle Carr. In advance of our departure, we notified Dr. Wali Muna in Yaoundé, Cameroon, to work out an itinerary for our visits to orphanages, elementary schools, and health-care facilities.

On the way to Africa, we made a refueling stop in Cape Verde. It was raining cats and dogs on Saturday evening when our plane touched down on the tarmac in Yaoundé, where we were greeted by the smiling face of Mary, an airport employee, and Mr. Bernard Muna, an attorney and brother to Dr. Wali Muna. Immediately, our plane was unloaded, and everything was transported to the Yaoundé Hilton, where we would be lodging.

That night, we were hosted at an exotic and delicious dinner at Dr. Muna's residence. His wife had spent several days cooking and preparing for our visit. We were informed that she had actually cut short her vacation in Europe in order to be there for us. Among the many invitees that night was the US ambassador to Cameroon, R. Niels Marquardt, and his lovely wife, Judith.

The very next day, we began our mission by driving to the poor parts of the city. The sight of so many children scavenging the streets for food and bare necessities was hard to swallow. We took along bags of lollipops and jump ropes, which were a hit with the children in the streets. It was such a delightful sight to witness so much joy in their eyes and the expressive faces of those lively children sucking on lollipops and hopping around with jump ropes. They responded to the gifts with words of "Thank you!" and *"Merci beaucoup!"* ringing all around us.

Our team was joined by a Spanish philanthropist named Nieves Castillo from Madrid. She had heard about our mission and wanted to join us. Her experience with poor children in other parts of West Africa was truly invaluable. The first hospital we visited touched a special chord in my soul. How could a trained physician from the West not be moved by the deplorable

376

conditions in a hospital devoid of basic medical equipment? There were mothers and their children sleeping in bunk beds. We saw a cute little girl with sickle cell disease roaming the halls with her pediatrician. She had her intravenous infusion bag strapped to her hip because there were no poles on which to hang it.

Family members had to care for their hospitalized loved ones. They cooked on makeshift stoves on the hospital grounds and did their laundry using plastic basins. It was particularly touching to see severely ill little children alone in hospital beds, having no family members with them. We were told that often a parent would have to return to the village to take care of important matters and therefore would leave their child all alone in the hospital. If you got sick and were hospitalized but had no one to help provide you food and assistance with basic needs, you would be in a very difficult situation.

I had witnessed such challenging conditions before in other parts of Africa, Southeast Asia, and South America, but one can never get accustomed to human deprivation and suffering. Mrs. Blair, Jennifer, Nieves, and the rest reached out to the children in the wards, offering support, hugs, and love. They donated basic medical supplies, medicine, and diapers to staff members at the facility. The response of the nurses, doctors, patients, and their families was heartwarming. Seeing the nurses and doctors in their heroic efforts under such stark circumstances reminded me that they were the real heroes in human service. We were told that the conditions in the hospitals had deteriorated not just where we were visiting but all over the country because so many good nurses had been lured to the West to fill their health-care needs. Hence, the nurse shortage was nearing a crisis state.

We visited a small orphanage deep in the rain forest that was run by three nuns who depended almost exclusively on charitable donations to support the facility. Their surroundings were inhospitable, but their home was filled with love. We gave them bags of medication and school supplies. Then we distributed shoes to all the children at the facility. Jennifer and Michelle took Polaroid snapshots of each kid and presented them with the photos. They were all laughing and beaming with excited smiles. The joy and happiness shared among us and the children reflected the deepest longings of the human spirit for love and compassion. Most of those children received their first-ever portraits.

At that particular orphanage, one of the boys, who must have been no more than ten years of age, came up and reminded us that he had no shoes. We were all feeling bad for him, and then someone ran back to one of our SUVs to see if we had any more left. Unfortunately, the only ones remaining were babies' sizes. Someone suggested giving the nuns money to buy a pair of shoes for the boy. He had a heart-wrenching look of sadness on his face. The children had all been barefoot before our arrival, and now everyone was wearing a pair of brand-new shoes except for that unfortunate kid. Then Blair, Jennifer's son, whispered something to his mother, and in a poignant gesture of love, he removed his shoes, a pair of handsome white sneakers, and offered them to his new friend, assisting him as he was putting them on. This was such a moving act of spontaneous generosity that spoke volumes of him, his background, and possibly his future. That experience shall certainly resonate in our hearts forever.

As I stood there beholding this gesture of kindness unfold in front of me, I was reminded of the many teachings of Martin Luther King Jr. and many other great men and women whose lives have impacted mine and others. I was reminded of the innate goodness in humans and the virtues of human service. On that day, we brought a little sunshine to the orphanage. At the time of our departure, emotions began to flow. With joyful tears drenching their eyes, the nuns were hugging everyone while the children huddling around them with their radiant faces were crying out in French, "*Merci! Merci!*" as we waved goodbye to each other. At that moment, I could see myself in a similar village a few decades earlier, shoeless and hopeful.

While lying in bed that night, I reviewed the previous days' activities and visits, and I thought about how easily Blair and Emily, two privileged American children from a loving family, had been interacting so well with their less fortunate peers in an African village. The foundation of their interaction was pure, untarnished love. Then I thought about how sad it was that so many adults were incapable of seeing the world through the eyes of children and how the innocent minds of so many children were poisoned with the hate and ignorance of adults who were painfully wedded to the status quo and whose visions were blinded by their prejudices, trapping them at the lowest rung of a universal moral social order.

Our next stop was an elementary school deep in the jungle, where we received the most surprising and vivacious reception ever. There were welcoming palm-leaf decorations planted at various locations on the dirt road leading to the school. When our three-vehicle motorcade arrived, the children were standing in line on the schoolyard in the searing tropical sun, where they had been patiently waiting for us. At once, the atmosphere was electrified by a dance troupe of village women who broke out in a vigorous song-and-dance number. Word of our visit had reached the principal government representative, and a regional medical leader, Dr. Obama, arrived at the elementary school and welcomed us to their community.

A handsome little boy presented Mrs. Blair with a welcome bouquet of tropical flowers. She was immensely touched by all the warmth and hospitality that we were receiving as she reached deep into the bottomless wells of her love and delivered a short and moving speech thanking everyone and especially the children for their generous welcome while reminding everyone that her experience as a teacher had made the occasion even more special to her. Then she stated that it was one of the most remarkable receptions she had ever received. Afterward, we met the teachers and discussed some of their needs and challenges. Then we donated a large collection of supplies to the school.

On the way back to the city, we made a quick stop at the village of one of our drivers so that he could greet his family. As we waited in the car, a young mother with a baby strapped on her back walked up to Jennifer and asked if she had a pair of shoes for her child. As it turned out, there was a pair of baby shoes left, and they were the right fit for the woman's baby. That made her day! She smiled broadly, curtsied, and with a kind and gentle look in her eyes, she thanked Jennifer and walked away.

As soon as she was gone, a child happened by with a large tray of ripe bananas on his head. I asked him how much all his bananas would sell for, and he looked perplexed. I imagined people generally didn't buy all of them at once. Several minutes elapsed before he blurted out that they were Fr. 1,000. I offered him Fr. 1,500 instead and took possession of a few. Then I asked him to sell the rest of them to someone else so that he could take home more money, but surprisingly, he refused. The look of confusion on his face spoke volumes. Meeting him brought back personal memories of my child-hood when I was a sweet hawker of oranges, bananas, and mangoes all day and sometimes to my mother's chagrin, I would sell very little. Therefore, I bought the rest of the bananas and shared them with our drivers.

Two days before leaving the country, we decided to visit another orphan-age, elementary school, and a hospital in Limbe at the foot of the Cameroon mountains. We flew to Douala, where we were received by Humphrey, another member of the Muna family. Additionally, Mr. Samuel Asongwed, the gentleman who had rescued me from the YMCA in Baltimore many years earlier, had made advanced arrangements for our visit to an orphanage in Limbe on the Atlantic coast.

The forty-minute drive from Douala to Limbe was uneventful. Our first stop was at an orphanage with about seventy children, where we met the director, a lady by the name of Rose, who appeared to be surprised by our visit. We were told that she and her orphans had just been evicted by their landlord without prior notification because he had wanted to sell his building. Having been suddenly rendered homeless, she decided to take the orphans on a long trek to the new home, where we met them. While trek-king, they had encountered an emaciated, dehydrated infant girl who had been abandoned on the wayside by someone. Rose and her children took the infant with them to their new home: a dilapidated motel with few beds, abominable sanitary conditions, and spartan surroundings.

Rose was so overwhelmed with emotion while sharing her experience with us that she broke down and sobbed uncontrollably. We were all moved by her plight with the children. Mrs. Blair took a brief tour of the facil-ity and was visibly shaken and horrified at the extent of the starkness and physical deprivation surrounding her. She was deeply moved by the sight of hungry, weak, listless, and malnourished children languishing on beds without mattresses in dark, desolate, musty rooms. The sound of her voice was choking with emotion as she declared, "These children need food! We must do something and do it now!"

With that rallying and passionate cry, we filed back into our SUVs and followed Samuel as he led us to a local market. At the market we bought enough produce and household supplies to fill four vehicles. We bought sacks of rice, beans, corn flour, green vegetables, vegetable oil, soap, and other supplies. When we returned to the orphanage, we discovered that the children had showered and were dressed in their Sunday best! They received the food and supplies with joy, laughter, and tears. They even entertained us with their beautiful songs. There was not a dry eye in that room.

Rose was transfixed by the chain of events that morning. We played games with the little ones, and we could see that a major burden of responsibility had been lifted from Rose's back due to the assistance Mrs. Blair had provided her. In addition to the food items, we donated several boxes of shoes, clothes, toys, books, diapers, among many other items. Rose told us about how she had been an orphan at eight years of age and had gone on after years of hard work to graduate from university. She stated that she had been motivated by God to open an orphanage.

About two months before our visit, two lovely infants had become the newest members of her family. They were found in the streets, dehydrated and near death, abandoned by their mother in her final days before succumbing to AIDS. Additionally, we learned that the monthly rent for the new home amounted to about $120. As we prepared to leave, Mrs. Blair hugged all of those children and thanked their mother, Rose, for the great work she was doing.

Our next stop was a local elementary school, which was no different than some of the other ones we had visited earlier—dirt floors, dilapidated buildings, and enthusiastic, disciplined, loving, and smiling children with their dignified, dedicated, and doting teachers. This stop was longer. Mrs. Blair, Jennifer, and Michelle became guest teachers for a while. They visited each and every classroom, singing songs with the children, playing games, and reading to them. It was electric and truly memorable. We donated many school supplies to the school headmaster, and after Mrs. Blair expressed a few words of thanks to the children and their teachers, we left their campus to travel to our final stop at a regional hospital.

It was a colonial hospital almost one hundred years old. After we pulled up, a cheerful, attractive staff nurse, exquisitely and elegantly dressed in a snow-white uniform complete with a nurse hat, came up and welcomed us, telling us she had been expecting our visit. As she spoke, I could not focus on her words because something about her demeanor and her looks was familiar to me. My curiosity was explosive. Calmly, I asked her where she was from, and she responded Bamenda—my original home. Upon further questioning, I discovered that she had graduated from the same elementary school I had attended over thirty-five years earlier. Then I asked her name, and it all came together in an amazing twist of fate. I was facing Beatrice, the girl I was crazy about in elementary school, whose father was our teacher.

I looked her straight in the eyes and said, "Beatrice, I had a terrible crush on you, but you refused to pay any attention to my romantic overtures. I tried everything—mangoes, oranges, more mangoes…still no interest or response from you. Just last week, I wrote something about it in my book."

She looked flabbergasted, but I did not stop there. I continued by describing exactly her family home, the bushes around her house where I would hide in the hopes of catching a glimpse of her. Then, excitedly, I reminded her of her best friend in those days, who was also called Beatrice and who was then living in Washington, DC. After I finished my spiel, she looked unflinchingly unimpressed, and with a calm demeanor, she blurted out, "I don't remember you."

I stood there frozen in the hot, humid hospital courtyard, not knowing what next to say. Suddenly, probably out of sympathy for my failed exuberance and persistent romantic overtures decades earlier, or maybe in a spirit of humanitarianism, especially given our visit to her hospital at that moment, her eyes shimmered, her lips parted to unveil a warming smile, and she reached out. We embraced warmly. Her gesture was met with peals of laughter and thundering handclaps from the entourage.

Beatrice and her colleagues had been expecting a group of American visitors, and I was sure that never in her wildest imagination did she think she would be accosted by one of them, a bona fide stalker from her past. We visited the pediatric unit and met the rest of her colleagues. Then, as an aside, I reminded Beatrice about how tired and frail she was in elementary school and about how much I wanted to help her and to be her friend. She didn't participate in any sports at that time, and neither did I. Years later, in medical school, while studying congenital diseases, I often wondered whether she had a congenital heart problem. She paused for a moment and then told me softly that she was born with sickle cell disease. She had done very well; she was happily married and had an eighteen-year-old daughter. Sadly, her father had died in 1996, the same year I lost mine.

It was time for us to leave. I promised her that I would keep in touch, and then I gave her additional boxes of stethoscopes and blood-pressure-monitoring devices, including a couple of medical appliances that I usually traveled with. Indeed, I had advanced from offering enticements of mangoes and oranges to more expensive and fancy stuff, but without expectations other than a motivation to support her noble purpose in the service of humanity.

As our vehicle was roaring off to the Douala, I couldn't stop thinking about life's amazing coincidences. That night in our hotel, we talked about Rose and the children. She was truly an angel, and her dedication was boundless in her love for those children. The next day, on the flight back to the United States, our discussions mostly centered on the plights of the people we had been blessed to meet, the joy and happiness in their faces, and their effusive gratitude. We talked about the universality of love and about how connected we are in the world.

Somewhere over the Atlantic, as we were individually preparing to get some shut-eye after a physically and emotionally grueling whirlwind trip, Mrs. Blair, in a deep, pensive moment, looked across at me and said, "I just can't get that lady [Rose] and those children off my mind." Then she reached into her purse and gave me $1,500. "Please send this money to Samuel so that he can pay her rent for the year."

CHAPTER 80

Pocono Medical Center

THE AFRICA TRIP TOOK a heavy toll on me. Jet lag didn't help things either. I slept for two days before I could resume my daily duties at the hospital. One night, I was called to operate urgently on an eighty-four-year-old man who had ruptured his heart muscle after a massive heart attack. He needed quadruple bypass surgery plus the replacement of a heart valve in addition to the insertion of a machine to support his failing heart. At 1:00 a.m., I was in the middle of that marathon operation all by myself with no assistant. Out of frustration, I contacted the CEO but only got his voice mail because he was on vacation, and I left a message about my urgent need for an assistant. Soon after that, I was promised one.

Weeks went by, and no updates came. And then one night, a hospital manager called me at home telling me that she had a secret that I couldn't divulge because she was afraid of losing her job. She said she felt bad about the long hours I was putting in and knew that the hospital had lied to me. She continued by telling me I would not be getting the assistant I requested because of a recent meeting in which a senior leader had expressed no interest in getting me the assistance I needed. I thanked her for the information and promised to keep it to myself. I had made significant sacrifices to rebuild the cardiothoracic program at that hospital, and I very much enjoyed serving the people in that region. I had served faithfully, and I felt betrayed.

The next day, I handed in my letter of resignation, and within a week, I began to receive calls with job offers. A good number of those calls were from Pocono Medical Center, where a brand-new heart and vascular institute had just been established and they were interviewing candidates for a director-ship position. Initially, I had no interest in that position.

The recruiter, Stephanie, was persistent in her efforts to bring me on board. A previous colleague, Dr. Gervais Charles, had recommended me to the search committee at that hospital. Then I received a phone call from the University of Pennsylvania encouraging me to consider it. They had been contracted to identify a top candidate to head up the new institute. In August 2006, to end the persistent calls from Pocono, I decided to go there for a visit and went through a daylong interview with all twenty members of the selection committee. All applicants for the position were required to present a business plan indicating how they planned to run the institute. At the end of the day, everyone assembled in a large conference room for my presentation. I did not have a business plan, but most importantly, in my opinion, they were going about the selection process the wrong way.

About 150 surgeons had submitted their résumés for that position. I told the committee that I did not have a business plan. Firstly, I assured them that my comments would be entirely objective as I was not in desperate need of a job. I told them that any candidate who came with a great business plan should not be considered for the position. I reminded them of all the great medical centers surrounding Pocono that were within its competitive landscape. Therefore, I added they should be looking for a surgeon with three major qualities:

90. **Affability.** A surgeon with an amiable personality who could interact well with patients, staff, and community members—someone whom the providers would embrace.

91. **Capability.** A highly competent, board-certified, technically strong surgeon with impeccable credentials who would shut up the com-petition. Anyone with weak credentials could lead to an eventual collapse of the program.

92. **Availability.** Whoever was hired would have to work alone around the clock. That could be both physically and mentally exhausting. I considered that criterion to be imperative.

Then I told them that if they chose to, they could hire a Harvard MBA to manage the business side of the practice. After I finished that part of my presentation, nobody said a word.

"Let me share with you what I did this week," I continued.

I presented a few complex cases I had performed that week, among which was a reconstruction of the heart in a patient with heart failure, a repair of a gigantic twelve-centimeter aneurysm in a patient from Ecuador, a triple heart-valve operation and a fourth-time-redo-coronary-bypass operation. In conclusion, I reminded them that any surgeon who could not perform these types of operations should not be given serious consideration for the job because there would be too many patients transferred out of the institute, and the competition would harp on this weakness to delegitimize and destroy the program. The room remained silent; therefore, I thanked them for a great visit and departed.

On my way home to Elmira, I admonished myself for having been somewhat hard on the search committee members. "You just screwed up. They're not going to look at you," I told myself. In essence, I decided my blunt and tactless comments had probably angered the committee members and that was the reason why they had remained silent throughout my presentation and afterward.

The next day, my phone began ringing off the hook. Dr. Ponnathpur, chairman of the search committee and distinguished cardiologist, called and told me that every committee member had ranked me their number-one candidate out of three finalists. I was shocked. I told him I would have to think about it. Indeed, I had been considering a move back to Boston. I thought for a moment about the Poconos. I thought about its mountains, rivers, waterfalls, ski resorts, and countless other outdoor opportunities. Then I called him back and accepted the offer.

The next phone call I received was from the CEO of Pocono Medical Center. He started by congratulating me in a peculiar manner. "As you know, they selected you to be the new director of the institute."

They? I wondered why he chose to insert that word in a congratulatory call. Strangely, he continued, "As you know, there are two other excellent candidates. Number two is a professor in Iowa who is just as outstanding, and so is number three, who is from New York."

I was thinking that these were not encouraging words from a CEO whose committee had just selected a cardiovascular and thoracic surgeon from a long list of contestants to lead a brand-new institute. It sounded like he didn't want me there. He continued rambling about a few other things without expressing any degree of interest in my candidacy, and then he requested a list of all the operations I had done since I was an intern. His voice was cold and detached. I complained to him that I had been practicing for about fifteen years and had done thousands of surgeries. I reminded him that I was the director of a prestigious surgical program at a teaching hospital. He was unfazed and insisted on seeing my list of cases starting from my internship years.

"That is preposterous," I said. "Nobody carries around a meaningless list of cases from internship years."

He ignored my comment. During my interview, I had told them I would expect to earn the same salary I was earning at my job at that time. The CEO continued, "Also, we cannot meet your salary demands."

Thus, he offered me only about 30 percent of the amount I was asking. Things were beginning to sound more comical than ridiculous, but I didn't want to miss an opportunity to educate him. So I gently reminded him accordingly: "Just so we both understand, I am being hired to perform thoracic operations, cardiac operations, esophageal operations, pacemaker devices, and therapeutic catheters. Furthermore, I will be completely and solely responsible for the cardiac ICU twenty-four-seven, running the institute, assuming on-call duties twenty-four- seven, and performing community outreach all by myself, while earning 75 percent less than what I'm earning now? In essence, I will be doing the job of three cardiothoracic surgeons all by myself for free!"

His response floored me.

"Well, take it or leave it. The other two candidates are just as skilled as you are, so if you don't like what we are offering you, we can shake hands and say, 'It's been nice knowing you.'" He rambled.

My brain kicked into supercharging mode. My parents often had reminded me of my best weapon whenever the bullies became overbearing. Therefore, I made a counterproposition. "How about this: you pay me whatever you choose. After one year, if my outcomes are not at the top percentile of the most stringent national measures, you can keep me at the same salary or fire me. If I am at the top percentile, then you can pay me the salary I am requesting [my then-current salary] if you choose."

He rejected my proposition. "Take it or leave it," he said.

His final response spoke volumes to me about him and his motivation and gave me an answer to the question I had been asking myself.

At that point, he requested a response to his initial offer as soon as possible because he intended to contact the alternate candidates. I promised to get back to him.

After we hung up, I smiled to myself. I was not desperate for work. I worked for a purpose, not a salary. However, I would never allow myself to be intimidated by anyone, including someone with nefarious intentions. I had purposely tricked him into revealing what he was thinking. Clearly, despite his committee's unanimous decision, he did not want me there at all. The offer I made him was the most ridiculous offer ever. In essence, I would have been working for free. If he wanted me, he would've jumped for it. During my interview, I had met a delightfully friendly and wonderful pulmonologist, Dr. Sedani, and we quickly became friends. I called him to let him know what position the CEO had taken, and he was furious.

A few days later, I received a concerned phone call about the CEO, who, while having dinner with a few staff members, allegedly posed the following question: "How do you think the people in this region will feel about a Black man touching their hearts?"

One of the doctors in attendance of Indian heritage rebuked him for what he perceived to be a racist question. When I talked to the pulmonologist about this, he was aghast. My suspicions about the CEO were confirmed.

The motivation for his actions was clear to me at that point. Everything smelled *racist*!

Later that day, I received several calls from the same CEO. I did not answer any of them. I was sitting at a dealership where my car was being serviced and decided to chat with Dr. Sedani. He recommended that I share my experience with the board chairman of Pocono Medical Center. I grabbed a computer, wrote an email to the CEO, and copied the chairman of the board, whom I had never met. In substance, I wrote the following: "You are sly. You are a crook. I do not trust you. I will not allow myself to be diminished by you or anyone. I am not an intern, and I'm not desperate for a job either. Therefore, I have withdrawn my candidacy."

Barely a couple of minutes after I hit the Send button, the CEO began to call me, but I refused to answer. Soon afterward, I received a call from a number I did not recognize. When I answered it, the voice on the other end announced, "This is Darrel Covington, and I'm the chairman of the board. I was not in town when you interviewed. I read your CV, and when I discovered that you had won the prestigious George C. Crile Award in surgery at the Cleveland Clinic, immediately, I realized you are the candidate we were looking for. Please do not pull out. I specifically gave the CEO a mandate to find the best surgeon to lead this program. I did not ask him to negotiate salary."

Then he pleaded with me to come back for another visit. He sounded like a quintessential leader, an intelligent person who was open-minded and with whom I could work. So I drove back to Pocono and met him and the CEO together, at which time I dictated the terms of my employment to the CEO, and we both signed the contract.

CHAPTER 81

ESSA Heart and Vascular Institute

ON JANUARY 1, 2007, I became the new medical director of the ESSA Heart and Vascular Institute at Pocono Medical Center. I must confess I was nervous that morning at breakfast, wondering if I had made the right decision in accepting the job. When I arrived at the hospital, there was no one to welcome me. I had no office and nowhere to sit. Within an hour of my arrival, I was called to see a patient with a bad lung infection who needed surgery right away. I took her to the operating room and addressed her problem expeditiously. Back in the locker room, I greeted every doctor I encountered, but none of them responded. Wow! I had been through that before. Then I met a marvelous person, the chairman of the anesthesia department, Dr. Anthony Nostro, who was also a cardiac anesthesiologist. He was extremely cordial, welcoming, and helpful.

The next day, I received a phone call from the doctor on whose patient I had performed surgery the previous day. Immediately, he began to yell at me and was vigorously admonishing me for not having notified him about operating on his patient. I apologized profusely, telling him that I had performed the operation on my first day at the hospital, I had neither office nor secretary, I was unfamiliar with the layout of the hospital, and I didn't even know where the restrooms were located. After we hung up, I contacted the telephone operator to know the location of his office, and I trudged in heavy snow to see him. Again, I apologized to him in person, promised to do better, and asked him to give me a chance to prove myself.

The CEO had made no onboarding arrangements for my anticipated arrival. Without an office, I roamed the hallways haphazardly to familiarize myself with the layout of the physical plant. A kind nursing leader became aware of my predicament and cleared an equipment storage room the size of a small closet in the ICU, where she placed a tiny desk for my use. This was my office for at least six months until a new office space was developed for me.

Within twenty-four hours of my arrival, I began to assemble a high-performance team for cardiothoracic surgery. Subsequently, I convened a meeting of operating room staff, anesthesia, surgical assistant, and ICU leaders to begin simulation procedures in anticipation of launching the open-heart-surgery program. There were multiple simulations and countless meetings with the operating room staff as well as ancillary staff and members of other service lines as well. Cardiology and cardiac catheterization laboratory representatives were also very involved in the planning process during this time. Within the space of a week, I designed patient-care protocols for the ICU.

Two months later, we scheduled the first heart surgery in the history of northeastern Pennsylvania in Monroe County. I had previously operated on that patient's husband at the Guthrie Clinic, and she wanted me to perform hers as well. Despite my many years of practicing cardiothoracic surgery, the hospital insisted on hiring an observer to proctor me on my first operation. The patient did undergo a successful quadruple bypass operation, and afterward, a call came in about a young lady in need of emergent heart surgery, and she became the second patient to undergo heart surgery at Pocono Medical Center on that day. Within four days, we had performed five major heart operations, including one on a delightful Pennsylvania senator.

Overnight, the new heart institute had become a mature facility. That year we performed about 250 heart procedures and over 180 thoracic cases. That first year, I worked with Traci, a spectacular nurse practitioner. She and I teamed up on certain afternoons and weekends to do house calls in the region. Many people thought it was unusual for a modern-day doctor—let alone a surgeon—to be doing patient home visits. However, our patients loved it, and that was good enough for me.

My surgical assistants, Jon and Robert, were highly competent, superbly trained, extremely reliable, and unquestionably respectable gentlemen. A few years later, we were joined by another rising star, Geno. The institute office was expertly managed by Stephanie, who was joined shortly afterward by Cathy. Both of them possessed caring personalities and were outstanding managers imbued with marvelous interpersonal skills. After about six months of my directing the new institute, the CEO came to me and acknowledged in many ways that he had been mistaken about my capabilities. I liked him as a person despite some of his initially misguided thought processes.

Our cardiology staff was a strong group with diverse skill sets and was highly responsive to our patients' needs. The ICU, a very important pillar in any cardiothoracic program, was staffed by an extremely distinguished, dedicated cohort of talented nurses under the esteemed leadership of Toni. Patient care was strictly protocol driven. I worked day and night, sometimes doing about thirty or more operations per month as a solo surgeon. My operating room staff of nurses and perfusionists was a dynamic and incomparably high-performance team.

Dr. Nostro, a phenomenal cardiovascular anesthesiologist, was one of the most skilled, dedicated, and sacrificial leaders I had worked with. We both toiled daily, and I barely slept continuously for more than two hours a night. One day, we did six operations, and we were done by 8:00 p.m. I was understandably exhausted the next day, and I needed a little respite from work. Therefore, I welcomed an offer to dinner by a kind, generous, illustrious local businessman and philanthropist, Rick Mutchler, at a quiet restaurant in a quaint historic town. It was wonderful to escape the hospital and engage in nonmedical conversation.

After I returned home that evening, I went straight to bed. I had not received any of the usual phone calls from the hospital during the time we were at dinner. I might have been asleep an hour when my phone started to ring. The call was from an operating room at the hospital. There was a nurse at the other end requesting my immediate presence to help with a trauma patient. I could hear an incredible amount of commotion in the background. I got in my car and rushed down to the hospital. As soon as I entered the operating room, I was given a brief report on the patient. He was a sixteen-year-old teenager who was at a party where an argument ensued, and he was shot by another teenager.

There were two trauma surgeons desperately trying to control massive bleeding in his pelvis. At the point of my arrival, the patient had lost several liters of blood. Practically everybody around the operating table was soaked in blood. I immediately joined my colleagues, and we worked concertedly on the patient. Every major structure in the patient's pelvis was shredded. The bullet had caused severe damage to several large arteries and veins. Despite the valiant efforts of three surgeons working frantically on the young man, it was practically impossible to control the bleeding. He suffered a cardiac arrest and died on the operating table. It was heart-wrenching to witness the pain and agony his poor parents were going through that night.

On the drive back home, I was consumed with anger and frustration at the senselessness of violence and murder in general, especially among youth. It was clear to me that until we addressed the social ills that created the conditions that made such violence possible, sad outcomes like that one would continue to devastate families and communities in perpetuity. Two weeks earlier, I had performed an urgent operation on a fifteen-year-old who had been shot in the chest. Fortunately for that victim, we were able to save his life. I remember giving him a long lecture about setting priorities in life and hoping that a long incisional scar on his chest would serve as a permanent reminder for him to pursue a more honorable and uplifting trajectory in life.

After about a year, I was nearing burnout, so I took a ten-day vacation to rest up. That year, my daughter Mankah entered law school in Madison. I could not contain my excitement. I took a couple of days off to visit her and attended one of her classes. While there, I met Everett Mitchell, a friend of hers with a great heart, who was not only highly intelligent but was also one of the most dynamic people I have known. He was a full-time student who was also a popular religious leader in Madison. A couple of years after we met, he flew out to the Poconos to spend some time with me. On that visit, he expressed a desire to marry my daughter, and I gave him my approval. I could think of no better man than him to be her husband. Therefore, I welcomed him to the family fold with open arms.

Eventually, they got married, and after graduating from law school, they decided to settle in Wisconsin. Robert also finished college and decided to enter the workforce at once. Within a couple of years, all my nieces and nephews, except one who was studying in Europe, graduated from college. I was extremely happy for all of them. My sacrifices had paid off, and I had fulfilled the promise I had made to my father before his death.

In the meantime, our new cardiac program was growing by leaps and bounds. Toward the end of my first year at the hospital, I was recognized with a Physician of the Year Award. Subsequently, I met with the CEO of the hospital as well as our recruiters and asked them to look for a second surgeon. In keeping with my strong beliefs in diversity, I specifically requested a female cardiothoracic surgeon. Serendipitously, I heard from a surgeon, Dr. Anne Cahill, in California. Eventually, she was hired and joined me a little over a year after the start of the program. She was a distinguished surgeon and educator, and she brought new surgical techniques to the program.

Later, we welcomed a highly trained and skilled cardiac anesthesiologist, Dr. Winston Thomas, who joined us after completing his training at the Cleveland Clinic. At that juncture, our surgical program was incomparably strong and dynamic. Consistently, every report on quality and outcomes in heart surgery ranked us among the best performers in the region and one of the top programs in the Commonwealth of Pennsylvania. Within a couple of years, we were ranked among the top in the nation, and all the naysayers disappeared. Our regional competitors could hardly keep up with us.

We espoused a patient-centered team philosophy in all our strategic decisions and the care we delivered. After the first year of our new institute, the University of Pennsylvania decided to affiliate with us, and Dr. Cahill and I received clinical associate professorships there. Our outcomes were outstanding among the University of Pennsylvania affiliate hospitals. Within three years we were featured in *Consumer Reports* among the top twenty-seven heart surgery centers in the United States, while our regional competitors didn't make the coveted list.

The CEO of a major regional hospital came to me and tried to lure me away from Pocono, but I refused. I started to publish a quarterly clinical newsletter to educate the community about cardiovascular diseases and heart-healthy living. To engage strong community support, I embarked on an aggressive outreach strategy, giving talks to local schools and colleges as well as community groups. The following year we were again featured in *Consumer Reports* among the exclusive list of top performers in cardiac surgery in the country. Additionally, our outcomes consistently received maximum star ratings by the Society of Thoracic Surgeons. These impressive awards were a tribute to the great men and women at the hospital, who were motivated by excellence in patient care at every station of the care continuum.

Once again, I was humbled to receive an Award for Patient Satisfaction on three separate occasions. I considered each of these awards a mandate for me to work even harder with my dedicated team and build a better practice to address the needs of the people we were privileged to serve. During this time, I received an award for preceptorship from the University of Pennsylvania in recognition of my involvement with teaching students on clinical rotation at our hospital.

At a meeting in New York City, our service line administrator met a prominent cardiologist, Dr. Tulloch-Reid from Jamaica, who expressed an interest in some kind of partnership with us. Following that meeting and conversation, I was invited to give a lecture at the Heart Institute of the Caribbean in Kingston, Jamaica. I accepted the invitation and traveled to Jamaica. After my talk, I had a long conversation with a marvelous couple who had done a remarkable job establishing and running the institute: Dr. Ernest Madu, a world-renowned cardiologist, and Dr. Dainia Baugh, a preeminent internist and holistic practitioner. I learned that Jamaican patients in need of heart operations were often referred to a center in Miami, which was prohibitively expensive despite having surgical outcomes that were unimpressive. On the spot, I offered to do all their heart surgeries with a comprehensive package at half the cost of those offered in Miami.

Soon afterward, we began to receive many patients from there and other countries. To meet their needs on a world-class level, we designed specific protocols for all international patients. The feedback from those patients and their providers was uniformly good. One of the Jamaican patients who underwent an extremely complex intervention at our facility was a former minister of health who expressed tremendous satisfaction with the care he had received. There were absolutely no complications or mortalities involving any of our international patients. On a couple of occasions, I flew to Kingston to perform surgical interventions, such as the implantation of heart-supporting devices in patients with weak hearts and problems related to the heart's electrical system.

In short, Pocono's heart program became vastly successful in a relatively short time following its inception because it epitomized the true meaning of a high-performance team consisting of strong, engaging, and committed individuals, from the housekeeping department down to physicians and surgeons. The chairman of the board, Dr. Darrel Covington, remained highly visible during those earlier years and kept his finger on the pulse of the program. He showed up frequently to see how things were going and was consistently supportive of the program by making sure every resource we needed to keep it a world-class program was at our disposal.

CHAPTER 82

Ahleea

IN THE FALL OF 2009, I drove to Cleveland to visit my daughter Ahleea, who was in her sophomore year of college. I arrived on a particularly cold, snowy night with poor visibility, and when I called her, she came outside her apartment building to meet me. I had not seen her in a while, and I wrapped my arms around her and gave her a big hug that lasted a while. While hugging her, I could feel her heart beating against my chest with a rhythm that was highly disconcerting to me. She had rushed out to see me wearing a T-shirt and pants in the cold weather. It was dinnertime, and I was hungry. I asked if we could share a meal and chat. So, she went back upstairs and grabbed a winter jacket, and we drove out to a nearby Asian restaurant.

While having dinner, we chatted about school, friends, and family. My thoughts kept drifting back to the specific heart rhythm I had felt earlier when hugging her. I had intentionally selected a table in a well-lit section of the restaurant where we were seated. While visually scanning her body, I noticed a few physical changes about her that were concerning, especially her skin and her eyes. I wanted to address my concerns without alarming her, so I set out to ask her questions that might help me with a diagnosis.

"How much sleep do you get each night?" I asked.

She responded that she did not need much sleep and that she did fine with a couple of hours of sleep each night. Then I inquired about her menstrual periods.

"Heavy, Daddy," she replied.

Furthermore, I asked her how she felt about the cold Cleveland winters.

"No problem, Daddy. Cold weather does not bother me. I don't always need a winter jacket."

After receiving her responses to my questions, which ranged from her moods to her bowel function, I had an idea about what could be going on with her. We enjoyed a delicious dinner, and I dropped her off and promised to meet her again the next day. Back in my hotel, I was convinced I had just diagnosed a condition in my daughter that she was unaware of. I found it disquieting that her pediatrician at a prominent medical center had failed to appreciate that condition, which, if left untreated, could lead to a lethal outcome. I began to map out a strategy to address her problem. I remembered her mother telling me about how her behavior had changed.

The following day, I took her to a restaurant for lunch. Afterward, I repositioned myself next to her at the table, held her hand, and asked her, "How often do you see your doctor?"

She replied, "Often enough."

"When was the last time you saw her?" I continued.

"Recently."

"What did you guys talk about?" I asked.

"Everything," she replied.

"Did she express any concerns about your health?" I asked.

"No. She always tells me I am fine," she replied.

In a very gentle and deliberate manner, I placed a hand on her shoulder and said, "My daughter, I don't want you to panic about what I'm going to tell you. I love you. After we parted last night, I was concerned about a health problem that you may have, which can be corrected permanently. Please don't be alarmed because I will stand by you and stay with you throughout the treatment process, and you will be fine."

She began to weep. I wrapped my arms around her. I have an enormous love for my children, and I will die for them. It was hard for me to be the harbinger of health-related news to her, but I could think of no better person to do it than her mother or me. I wiped away her tears and continued to reassure her.

"I am your father, and you are going to be OK eventually. Darling, you have a condition with your thyroid gland."

I pointed at the center of her neck, and I continue to explain what a normal thyroid gland does, why hers had become a problem, and what must be done to address that problem. She would need an operation, and I planned to be there with her, guiding and supporting her throughout the process. She was still teary-eyed when I hugged her and told her I was going to begin the process of addressing her health problem the next day. After dropping her off, I called her mother to inform her about my observations and conclusions. Then I got in my car on a long drive back to the Poconos.

On the way, I kept thinking about her. She was such a marvelous, beautiful young lady, and I had endless love for her and her siblings. I was upset about her doctor's failure to discern the findings that I just observed in her. Most of all, I was concerned about other children who might not be as fortunate to have doctor parents or loved ones with medical knowledge who could diagnose problems and have them addressed promptly. All in all, I decided to keep the focus on my daughter and her gland.

When I arrived at my office the next day, I spoke to her doctor, who denied having observed any unusual changes in Ahleea during her history and physical examination on her most recent visit. When I shared my diagnosis with the doctor, she was rattled by it and expressed contrition, but I didn't want her to feel bad. I just wanted her to draw up a plan of action to address the problem. Therefore, I assured her that even though I was upset, I didn't plan to focus on the past, and all I wanted was to take care of my daughter's health. As a surgeon who has expertise as well in the surgical treatment of specific thyroid problems, I was cognizant of what needed to be done. Therefore, I discussed and agreed to a plan of action for Ahleea.

Afterward, a team of doctors at that facility met and mapped out treatment options for her. Then I contacted a thyroid surgeon at that same institution, who evaluated her case and agreed that she would benefit from an operation. A surgery date was set, and I flew to Cleveland to be with her. In an operation that took five hours, her entire thyroid gland was removed. She came through it without turning a hair. The pathology report revealed abnormal cells within the gland.

If the operation had not been performed, her prognosis would have been terrible. Ahleea's mother and I were pleased with the outcome, but I was still concerned about her overall status, and my intuition propelled me to move her to Pennsylvania to live with me. She enrolled at East Stroudsburg University, where she demonstrated stellar academic performance and graduated with honors. After spending a year learning Spanish in Madrid, she completed a master's degree at Loyola Marymount in Los Angeles.

In 2014, I was delivering a lecture at a conference in Europe when someone casually asked what I considered the highlight of my career. I imagined they were expecting an answer along the lines of a dramatic event involving the performance of a highly complex operation to save a human life. My response triggered prolonged applause by the audience: "I have done thousands of operations; however, the highlight of my career was diagnosing a serious medical condition in my daughter while hugging her."

CHAPTER 83

Racial Prejudice and Stereotypes

THERE HAVE BEEN SOME racist experiences I have had within the confines of a hospital building that reminded me of the fact that the health-care environment is just a microcosm of society at large and many of the same attitudes in a larger community setting are just as prevalent within the health-care system. I have had my share of similar experiences in department stores and in other social settings that have probably bothered me less than they have the perpetrators.

I remember being called by my office one morning after a long night of surgeries because a lady had been diagnosed with a serious problem in her heart and was understandably nervous and upset and wanted to see me as soon as possible. Accordingly, I told my staff to make appropriate changes to my calendar so that I could see her before my scheduled clinic hours that morning. I skipped breakfast, darted out of my house, got in the car, and sped down to the clinic, hoping to address her needs first and then resume my breakfast afterward.

When the hospital elevator door opened, there was a lady already in there. I hopped in and the door shut. I greeted her, and she did not respond. At once, she avoided eye contact with me, lifted her purse, which had been hanging visibly at the level of her leg, and clutched it tightly against her chest wall with both hands. Then she swung her body around so that her face was almost touching the elevator wall panel. On my part, I pressed the button to the floor below my office because I intended to change into work scrubs. When I was making my exit, she relaxed her purse and allowed it to hang again by her leg in its previous position. She did not notice my grin.

Later on, when I arrived at my office, my manager apologized for having added another consult to an already packed schedule. I assured her that I was OK with it.

The add-on patient was already in the examination room and waiting. I knocked on the door and walked in. A purse sitting on the countertop looked familiar. So did its owner.

"Are you Dr. Zama?" she asked with a classic deer-in-the-headlight look on her face. She was sitting at the edge of her seat and appeared to be ready to take flight.

"Good morning. Yes, I am madam," I responded.

"I mean Dr. Zama, the heart surgeon?" she emphasized.

"Yes, ma'am, that's me. Welcome."

She dropped her chin on her chest. "I am so sorry. I did not know you were a doctor," she said with a look of profound remorse.

I chuckled. "That's OK. I did not know you were a patient, and I'm glad to meet you," I said.

After discussing the reason for her visit and reviewing her films, I gave her a thorough examination. At that point, I assured her that her heart problem was a treatable one and that I would take good care of her. We agreed on a date for surgery. When I turned around to leave the room, she resumed her apologies for what had happened earlier in the elevator, claiming that her behavior earlier was attributable to her life and experiences in New York City. I knew that as an adult, she understood the motives for her actions, and I was hopeful that her experience with me would teach her important, transformative life lessons. Her actions in that elevator were rooted in learned behavior. Therefore, I made light of the situation, defused the tension between us, and maintained my focus on her medical problem.

After she left, my manager had me laughing uncontrollably when she told me that while registering the patient before my arrival that morning, she talked about a frightening experience she had just had in the elevator and about how scared to death she was being alone with a "big colored man" who had suddenly walked into the elevator.

I have always held on to the fundamental belief that when one encounters an irrational and insensitive behavior, it is prudent to keep one's sensitivities in check before attaining an understanding of the root cause of such behavior. More often than not, if, during an encounter, you avoid jumping to stereotypes and conclusions about somebody's behavior and you engage them positively without resorting to animosity and losing your power, you may be able to discover the good in that person and possibly transform their attitudes and perceptions as well. Most negative social attitudes and actions are steeped in ignorance and learned behaviors.

I remember being called by an esteemed colleague, Dr. Fried, to see a patient who was having active chest pain. He had just undergone a major test revealing significant blockages in all his major coronary arteries and needed urgent heart surgery. Of note was the fact that his daughter was a nurse at our hospital. Without any hesitation, I walked over to the recovery room to see the patient. After I introduced myself, he responded, "Who are you?"

"I am Dr. Zama, a heart surgeon. I have been asked to see you because you need urgent surgery to fix the problem you have in your heart," I said.

Without flinching, he barked, "Another son of a bitch. I ain't gonna let you do it!"

His daughter, who was standing next to him, was embarrassed. She tried to convince me to allow my associate Dr. Cahill (a White female) to do the operation instead because her dad might be more receptive to her. I told him the choice was his to make. Then I thanked him and left.

When the cardiologist came back to see the patient, he asked bluntly, "Don't you have a better surgeon other than a nigger to do my operation?"

The cardiologist, obviously disgusted with such blatant racism, reprimanded the patient, telling him, "Dr. Zama trained at a tiny college in Boston called Harvard, and he would do my operation if I needed one."

He continued to tell the patient in no uncertain terms that he would have to choose Zama or the door. His chest pain must have disagreed with his attitude, so I was called again to see him. When I returned, he was unrelenting in his vitriolic verbiage and his overt animosity toward my skin color. This time I was enjoying the challenge. I did this by ignoring his words and his attitude. I have always believed that dwelling on hate can stunt a person's growth. I knew he would break down under the load of prejudice he was carrying, a load so chronic that even a threatening heart attack could not dissuade him otherwise! Then he went into a tirade about the president.

"Obama, son of a bitch, is gonna screw up the seniors like me, and I may not be able to pay for this fuckin' operation."

I assured him his insurance company would pay for the operation. When I told him that there were tens of millions of Americans without health insurance and that the Affordable Care Act was designed to address that problem, his hostility level surged.

"I'd like to get my hands on that Obama son of a bitch, take him out, and shoot him!"

I had to maintain complete control of the dialogue without allowing him to lose face.

"Let's respect our president, regardless of his color. President Obama has nothing to do with your heart problem. You need major, lifesaving heart surgery. We love you, and we are here to help you. I believe you are kinder than your hostile words."

At that point, he stopped talking abruptly and avoided any further eye contact with me. I continued to hold his hand, and I could feel the hesitation in it. I could tell the psychological pain he was harboring in his mind from a lifetime of hate exceeded the physical pain he was enduring from his threatening heart condition. Moments later, his hand relaxed under my grip.

Once again, I assured him about the competency of my team in the operating room and the ICU, and I concluded by thanking him for allowing us to take care of him before he willingly provided consent for the surgery. On that note, I left, feeling eternally hopeful for him, his beliefs, and his attitude.

In keeping with our protocol, the anesthesiologist was called to see him and prepare him for surgery. We had two of the best cardiac anesthesiologists: Anthony and Winston. Dr. Winston Thomas came to take the patient to the surgical suite. When he showed up, all hell broke loose again. The patient was hurling racial epithets so fast and furiously that you couldn't dodge them quickly enough. Dr. Thomas, an extraordinary gentleman who happens to be African American, ignored the patient's vile pronouncements and remained unperturbed in his professionalism. The patient was struggling to have greater control of a rapidly changing scenario. While maintaining a calm disposition in that stormy setting, Dr. Thomas wheeled the gurney to the operating room, where he gently injected the usual anesthetic into the patient's vein and knocked him out right away. Then he connected him to a ventilator, and we proceeded with the operation.

About an hour and a half later, we concluded a successful lifesaving triple bypass operation. The surgery had a remarkable effect on his personality! One of the nurses joked about the fact that surgery had released all the badness within him. He was much kinder to his caregivers during the rest of his hospital stay. Henceforth, we became the best of friends.

After many years of addressing the needs of patients under my care, I must say that it has always boggled my mind to understand why some patients would consciously express hate, disdain, and animosity toward me or my staff members, especially when we make personal sacrifices to serve them. Ultimately, I would rather maintain my focus on serving every patient with fairness and then moving forward without expecting any appreciation for my services, rather than allowing myself to become mired in endless analyses of patient personality idiosyncrasies. Invariably, true compassion never expects reciprocity.

CHAPTER 84

Back to Harvard

ON NEW YEAR'S EVE in 2009, I was on vacation in Miami, and during a late-evening stroll along the ocean, I thought about my career up to that point. I had been in leadership positions for many years, and I had been thinking about planning for the possibility of a future shift in my career path. Therefore, I decided to pursue a graduate degree in management while continuing my full-time duties as a cardiothoracic surgeon. After reviewing several prominent programs in the Northeast, I settled on Harvard.

Within a couple of weeks, I submitted my application to them, and a couple of months later, I received an acceptance letter. That summer, I enrolled in a management degree program that lasted two grueling years. I can say truthfully that it was the busiest period I had ever experienced in my life. After performing surgeries all day, I would drive five hours to Boston in the evening, check in at a hotel, study for a few hours, and participate in classroom lectures from 7:00 a.m. until about 6:00 p.m. Then I would immediately get back on the road to Pennsylvania to make rounds at midnight before heading home. The next morning I would wake up at 5:00 a.m. and resume my routine schedule of surgeries, followed by another long drive to the Northeast coast. Driving to and from Boston was often difficult and challenging. On several occasions, I had to pull over on the highway and take a long nap to avoid an accident. I had little time for sleep. Some months I performed about thirty-two major surgeries while pursuing one of the most rigorous educational programs at the same time.

At one point, in my desperation to stay awake for studies and driving, I resorted to caffeine. I had never taken it before that. Then I began to experience frequent palpitations and headaches. On one occasion, I asked one of the nurses to take my blood pressure, and I was shocked to discover it was 200/100. All along, I had been a strong advocate for fitness and rarely had blood pressure readings above 110/70. Immediately, I suspected caffeine as the culprit. After eliminating it from my liquid menu, a few days later, my blood pressure returned to normal levels.

I had not been back in Boston since the nineties. This time I was returning as a more mature student, and my academic experience was not as emotionally taxing as it had been during those earlier years. My cohort was diverse, and each person possessed unique skills, attributes, and talents. Participating in lectures with a group of brilliant yet unassuming and friendly individuals was nothing short of inspiring. The Harvard faculty members were expectedly extraordinary and exceptional; however, in many ways, I was learning more from my colleagues during intense classroom discussions and debates than from didactic lectures.

The experience at Harvard gave me a brand-new set of leadership tools and a new prism for better understanding organizational dynamics. It emphasized creative and innovative thinking and positive personal growth. It stimulated me to evaluate myself critically and appreciate my deficiencies better, and it enabled me to make appropriate, sustainable personal transformational changes.

In June of 2012, my friend Sebastiana and her mom, Reid (who was resilient and determined as ever despite being stricken with debilitating arthritis), stood by me as I joined many other graduates to receive my diploma at a Harvard Yard ceremony.

During my tenure at Pocono Medical, I was highly engaged in community affairs and events. I couldn't travel for medical missions like I used to because our program was new and vulnerable. I joined the board of directors of the American Red Cross and participated with other engaging board members to provide essential services to people in the region who needed acute interventions after destabilizing events in their lives. During that time, I was honored with an award for community service by the Red Cross, Kiwanis International, and three awards by the State of Pennsylvania for humanitarian work, community service, and promoting healthy living.

CHAPTER 85

The Diplomat's Wife

MY OLDER SISTER WAS visiting her daughter Yvonne, who was living in Ottawa with her husband, Jacob, and their energetic son, Daniel. It was wintertime, and despite my chronic fatigue and crazy work schedule, I decided to drive up there for the weekend. I asked my friend Alisa if she could travel with me and help me with the driving. The trip was uneventful, and I had a wonderful time with my nephew, who had grown remarkably since the last time I saw him.

While having lunch, Yvonne shared a sad story about a lady named Mercy, an ambassador's wife in the city who had undergone major heart surgery to address an aggressive infection in her heart. Following her heart surgery, it was discovered that the infection had spread throughout her body and had permanently destroyed her arms and legs. Consequently, all four extremities were amputated. She and her husband, Solomon, had two lovely children. While I was listening to Yvonne, my mind flashed back instantly to my mother. After lunch, I asked Yvonne if she could give me the ambassador's phone number. I called him at once, and we agreed to meet at the Ottawa Heart Institute. I had never heard of him, although he was aware of some of my humanitarian work in Africa.

After we exchanged greetings and shared a few connecting moments, we went up to see his lovely wife, Mercy, who had just come off the ventilator after weeks of multiple operations. In reviewing her medical history, I discovered she was a thirty-five-year-old geologist who had previously undergone a replacement of one of the heart valves in New York City and had gone on to give birth to the two adorable children. Years later, her husband was appointed high commissioner to Canada, and the family moved to Ottawa.

Not long after they had settled in their new home, she began to experience fevers, chills, and rigors. She was evaluated at a local emergency department, where she was thought to have the flu and was discharged home. She continued to feel worse and was reevaluated, but no obvious significant or concerning issues were detected. When she returned home the second time, she told her husband that she believed she was dying. In desperation, he took her back to the same emergency department, where further aggressive testing revealed a severe infection in her bloodstream, which also involved the artificial valve in her heart. This being a potentially lethal situation, she was taken to surgery, where the valve was removed and replaced with a similar one.

After the operation, she suffered severe bleeding and was rushed back to surgery to control it. However, after she was transferred to the ICU, she continued to bleed significantly. At one point, her doctors discussed the futility of further surgery with her husband, but due to his persistence and insistence, she was taken back to surgery a third time, and fortunately, the bleeding was controlled. As if the poor lady had not suffered enough, when she was examined after the last surgery, it was discovered that none of her limbs were viable because the infection in her bloodstream had destroyed them to a point where they could not be salvaged. Therefore, she was returned to the operating room, where she underwent the amputation of both her legs and arms.

On that fateful day, when I walked into the ICU with her husband and met her for the first time, she had just been disconnected from the ventilator and was still in a fog. I was stunned by the trauma she had been experiencing and mesmerized by her incomparable strength and tenacity. Understandably, as a surgeon, I had a more expansive view of her medical needs. I knew that she would be facing a long, nasty road in the weeks, months, and years ahead, a road littered with potentially troublesome complications and challenges such as stump infections, heart infections, wound infections, prolonged rehabilitation, and prosthesis management issues, to name a few. Not only that, because she was so young and her infected valve had been replaced with a tissue valve, which might last about ten years, she would be needing another operation to replace it! That would mean a fifth operation with all of the attendant risks! Neither she nor her husband were aware of these possibilities.

Within half an hour of my arrival, her mental fog lifted enough for her to appreciate my presence. I greeted her and expressed my best wishes to her for a smooth recovery and assured her that even though she did not know me, I was going to help and guide her through whatever milestones awaited her in the future. As I spoke, she teared up. I hugged her, and shortly afterward, I departed with her husband. Downstairs in the lobby, I shared my contact information with him, and again I assured him, "You will not walk alone. I will walk with you."

I encouraged him to reach out to me anytime. I must say that meeting his wife, Mercy, and learning about her journey had left an indelible mark on my heart. I got back in my car, unconcerned about the frigid temperatures, and sat for a minute facing a recurrent rhetorical question so many of us involved with direct patient care confront all too often: *Why her? When will all this human suffering end?*

When I returned home to Pennsylvania, I called the Kessler Institute for rehabilitation in New Jersey and shared my experience with the medical director of the facility. He agreed to see Mercy and address her rehabilitation needs. Three months later, she was admitted for inpatient rehabilitation. I drove out there to see her, and for some reason, I decided to take along my stethoscope.

When I got there, I was impressed with the degree of progress she was making at that facility in the use of her prostheses. At the end of my visit, I obtained her permission to listen to her heart. After I lifted the stethoscope from her chest, I made a concerted effort to maintain a surgeon's poker face because what my brief exam had just revealed was worrisome. I would have to engage in deep thinking afterward before I could muster enough courage to divulge my findings to her and Solomon.

Her husband was standing by attentively as usual. I hugged her and promised to see her again before she returned to Canada. Thoughts of her, Solomon, and their children filled my mind on the drive back to the Poconos.

Her husband's openly passionate and demonstrative love for her was a major reason for her resilience and strength. I was endeared by his doting attitude and his attentiveness to her every need and whim. I had witnessed him hoist her with his arms and place her gently on her wheelchair with an air of eternal commitment that could soften even the most hardened heart. These observations made what I had just heard in her heart more gut-wrenching. Unfortunately for her, one of her other heart valves had relayed a troublesome message through my stethoscope to my concerned mind. Her aortic valve was in bad shape! Her previous surgeries had involved her mitral valve.

Mercy completed her rehabilitation program and returned to Canada. Soon afterward, I called her husband and shared my findings with him, and I recommended an appointment with her cardiologist, who eventually performed a couple of tests that confirmed my previous findings. Subsequently, she went to see her surgeon. After that visit, I heard from her husband, who told me her surgeon was hesitant to operate on her again because her risk level was considered prohibitive and she might die from it. Moreover, the surgeon allegedly talked about the exorbitant cost of another operation. I suggested to both of them that I would come up to Canada to provide her support through the surgery experience. In the course of our conversation, I could sense their discomfort with consenting to undergo another operation at that same institution, especially since the next intervention would be astronomically difficult and could lead to her death. Solomon's voice conveyed a sad, somber, anxious tone indicative of his concern for his wife. Hence, I made a sudden remark: "I know it will be a high-risk surgery, and she may not survive it. If she is going to die, I want her to die in my hands so that I will know that I have done everything I know possible."

Their response was unanimous and instantaneous. "We want you to do the surgery."

To this day, I do not know what prompted me to volunteer to perform her surgery. I was not coerced, and I was just as concerned with the extraordinarily high likelihood of her dying in surgery. Once I committed myself, there was no turning back. Before hanging up the phone, I promised to get the wheels in motion so that she would be able to travel to Pennsylvania for the operation.

I was well aware of the fact that it would be one of the most difficult operations in cardiac surgery and would require careful planning and critical thinking. Whatever decisions I made about the conduct of that surgery would have to be final because there could be no second chance. Every decision had to be tailored specifically to her unique circumstances. Her chest would have to be entered for the fifth time. Scarring from her previous surgeries would be so extensive as to render any subsequent operation significantly more difficult, and with a greater likelihood of injury to the heart and other critical structures. Drugs and essential fluids that are usually infused in arm veins would present a challenge in her case because she had no limbs to be accessed. If we were successful in entering her chest, the recently diagnosed bad heart valve would have to be replaced with a permanent mechanical valve. Therefore, the previously replaced tissue valve in her heart would have to be replaced as well, with a similar permanent mechanical valve. To replace both valves with tissue valves that only last about ten years would not bode well for her in the long run.

Additionally, implanting two permanent mechanical valves in her heart would commit her to a lifetime of therapy with blood-thinning medication to prevent dangerous clots from forming on her artificial valves and possibly causing a stroke or killing her. Blood thinners can also cause serious bleeding in a small percentage of patients from blunt or penetrating injuries, for which she would be at risk because of her obvious gait challenges.

On the day before her operation, because of her special circumstances, she was admitted to the ICU overnight to prepare her for the procedure. I discussed with her and her husband in adequate detail my plans for the operation, the risks and benefits as well as alternatives. She was willing and ready to proceed with surgery the following day. That afternoon, I was feeling unsettled, so I decided to hike Tammany Mountain in the Poconos, where I sat on a large boulder on the summit alone, meditating, praying, and regaining composure with my inner self. Finally, I descended from the mountain in a much better-prepared mood. Driving home from that hike, I was visited by recurring images of the helpless little angels she had left at home, her two lovely children.

Early the next morning, she was taken to the operating room by Dr. Nostro. All of our outstanding superstar team members, Derek, nurses, circulators, and top perfusionists Anil and James, were present and ready. I stepped into the room and stayed long enough to fulfill our checklist requirements, all the while avoiding any eye contact with her. Suddenly, I began to feel nervous as the enemies of self-doubt gnawed away at me. I didn't know if I should be doing the operation. I was a wreck and desperately needed to slip away into "the zone" where I would always go before an extremely challenging operation, and I had to avoid any visual or emotional distractions to hinder my entry into that dimension. My performance was always at its best whenever I was in the quiet zone, and my staff understood and appreciated this fact. I walked out of the room to a connecting chamber, and after reconnecting with myself, I relaxed, said a quick prayer, and then started to scrub my hands. Words cannot adequately express the depth of technical difficulty that was involved in the conduct of the operation on that day. The entire room remained focused from the moment of incision to the final closure three hours later. The planned surgery was executed without a glitch. God was in that room!

Two hours after arriving in the ICU, she awakened completely, and her first question was "Is surgery over?"

"Yes. And you did fine! Everything was accomplished as planned," I said.

Her postsurgery recovery was uncharacteristically uneventful, despite her being a "fifth timer." Before the operation, given the tension surrounding her condition, emotions were high on both sides. On the first day after her surgery, when the nurses came to take her on a therapeutic walk in the ICU, I discovered a sharp wit and a sense of humor that were shrouded in her effervescent personality. Her leg prostheses were in position. Her male nurse was understandably confused about how to walk her since she had no arms. Without skipping a beat, Mercy declared, "Hold me like you are walking me down the aisle." The male nurse blushed, and down the hallway they went, strutting under the protective eyes of an eternally doting and ubiquitous husband, who was holding back tears of joy.

While I was standing there with my staff with cheerful delight and watching Mercy in action, a comforting thought crisscrossed my mind. Once again, I had just fulfilled a decades-long promise. I smiled! Then I relayed that promise in a mental message through my heart to the two precious angels in a distant city across our northern border.

"Don't worry. There is a doctor here. Mommy will be home soon!"

CHAPTER 86

Pocono Challenges

A COUPLE OF YEARS after I started at Pocono, I convened a team of experts from the various relevant departments—oncology, surgery, radiology, pathology, and social work—to establish a cancer forum, which met once a week to evaluate new patients and employ a team approach in deciding the appropriate care for our patients by following best practice guidelines and evidence-based medicine. Although this idea was well received and was subsequently successfully implemented, I encountered much animosity from the lead physician in the cancer department.

Initially, I was taken aback by his response and pushback. However, when I thought further about it, I realized I had truly made a mistake by not engaging him first. I was wrong in the way I went about designing the conceptual framework for addressing cancer patients' needs. I could have engaged him initially and allowed him to lead the charge as an oncologist, or I could have worked closely with him to make it a mutual, collaborative effort. I learned from that experience that friction between two high-profile leaders in an organizational setting can be detrimental even to the most constructive ideas and initiatives. When I realized my mistake, I apologized directly to him. We resolved our differences and worked harder and collaboratively with the administration to establish a bona fide cancer center with a transformative physical plant that has continued to provide state-of-the-art care to the community and beyond.

Every chance I had during this time, I encouraged community members to allow me to mentor their children. Many young men and women who participated in my mentoring program went on to attend college and medical and vocational schools. One of them in particular stands out. Yakira was only thirteen years old when her mother asked if I would mentor her. She would come in every morning on time and join the team for morning rounds in the ICU, and subsequently, I brought her in to observe surgery. She was shy and reserved but seemingly more mature than her chronological age, and we made every effort to give her a rich experience during her stint in our department. She was also a gifted artist. I received a painting from her through one of our state senators that still hangs proudly in my office. It was a painting of Dr. Daniel Hale Williams.

Years later, I was looking at the painting one day and curious to know how she was doing. When I searched the internet, I discovered to my delight that she was a student at Northwestern University in Chicago majoring in material sciences and engineering. During one of her student interviews, someone asked her what events in her life had been pivotal in determining her educational path. She responded by saying that when she was thirteen years old, a cardiothoracic surgeon took her under his wing, and that experience transformed her life. Reading that statement gave me enormous gratification, and I am sure she will be highly successful and will hopefully pay it forward and help many others so that the world can be a better place for everyone.

I believe adults have a noble responsibility to help the younger ones design a better future for themselves and, consequently, for humankind in general. Our children are truly the only message to a future we will never see.

Some of the challenges I encountered during my first five years in the Poconos were with top hospital administrators. When I came to the Poconos, my goal was not to lead an average program. I wanted to be part of a spectacular team and the best cardiothoracic surgery program, second to none! Additionally, it was my fervent desire to be a part of a program in medical tourism, the capabilities of which could address the surgical needs of patients from other nations. I wanted the reputation of our program to enable other service lines to be elevated to world-class status and attract patients not just from the region but also from other locations.

On my first meeting with the hospital board of directors when I arrived in 2007, I stated that my vision was to make Pocono a world-class cardiovascular program, among the top programs in the United States, within a few years. I remember looking across the room and witnessing a few smiles and wondered whether many of them were secretly saying, "You are full of s——."

I also remember many times during strategic discussions about our hospital that someone invariably would allude to some of our "prestigious" regional competitors in a subtle way designed to suggest that they were superior to us. Predictably, I would interject and openly attributed some of their responses to an inferiority complex, a concept that is foreign to my psychological bent. I often continued to remind them that we must embrace excellence in serving our patients, adding that we had the ability and the capacity to transform our thinking and consequently our institution because our competitors could learn a lot from us. We had a lot to offer the world! On one occasion, I had to admonish a doctor who kept harping on a certain neighboring medical big name during our discussions.

"Harvard is not better than us. Cleveland Clinic is not better than us. Our fears and insecurities are better than us!" I exploded.

I went on to say that we should be thinking instead about how to acquire the rest of our regional competitors! Ironically, eventually, it came out that one of the most powerful regional competitors had been losing sleep over several years because they had been unable to duplicate or attain the level of successful clinical outcomes we were experiencing at our new heart and vascular institute. We had taken our commitment to patient care to the highest level of challenge and excellence, operating on international patients and notable personalities and demonstrating distinguished and incomparable outcomes by all national measures. By taking on risky and high-profile cases, we were shining a critical spotlight on ourselves and our institution and also accentuating our vulnerabilities and capabilities. By positioning ourselves in this light, we challenged ourselves to rise to higher standards and to maintain consistently high degrees of excellence in patient care. This is the conceptual framework I espoused and promoted constantly.

There was significant buy-in from most individuals; however, with agonizing pathos, I must confess that some statements emanating from administrative leaders at that time, such as "I don't know about all this world-class stuff" and "We are a community hospital," were disabling. Sadly, my vision, values, and goals were in many ways not aligned with those of a few key leaders. I came to appreciate the fact that nebulous, whimsical support from the top can stifle growth, erode ambition, disable motivation, and sadly, squelch enthusiasm in any organizational setting where the values of progressive visionaries and provincial leaders are misaligned. I came to appreciate that in the competitive world where we live, provincial thinking can be a corrosive acid that imperceptibly eats away at the very core of an organizational structure and ultimately destroys its composite.

When I approached the board of directors with these concerns and my alternate vision for the institution, their response was not uniformly supportive. To add insult to injury, I had waited over a year to have my contract renewed, despite numerous reminders to this effect.

Not only that, but a clause in my initial employment contract also spelled out specifically that any future hiring of a cardiothoracic surgeon must be approved by me for quality reasons. Thus, I was flabbergasted one day when a gentleman walked into my office and declared, "Greetings, Dr. Zama. I am the new thoracic surgeon." And then he went on to tell me that he needed help getting his equipment ready for surgeries. This left me wondering whether such recruitment decisions were being made in a patient's best interest or to fulfill other personal motivations in contradistinction to my vision for the community we were charged to serve.

At that point, we only had one office manager, Cathy, who was toiling away all day by herself. The ultimate coup de grâce came when her position was furtively downgraded and her vacation time reduced. Consequently, her salary was reduced as well, to a pathetic level that was incongruent with her daily responsibilities managing a successful, high-profile service line. She was a struggling, hardworking single parent with a long-term commitment to the institution. She was serving nobly in an institute that was financially sound and solvent. I could not stand by and watch her suffer, so I marched up to the CEO's office and lodged a complaint about it. I was assured there had been a mistake because the CEO had not ordered her salary to be reduced. The blame for the reduction was placed on a different senior administrator.

I returned to my office and reassured my tearful office manager that the problem would be fixed.

Statements referring to me, such as "We do not need a rock star," that emanated from leadership at that time, were discouraging to me, especially given the enormous depth of my commitment to patients and the community. I chose to ignore these irritations for a while. During that time, I saw an opportunity to brand our hospital overseas—specifically the cardiac, oncology, plastics, orthopedic, and bariatric service lines. I had been operating on patients from Europe, the Caribbean, and South America, and I saw opportunities to attract more international patients to our enviable institution, the great Commonwealth of Pennsylvania, and specifically, the immensely and uniquely beautiful Poconos.

An opportunity did come by way of an invitation from one of the leaders of a Caribbean nation who was interested in discussing the possibility of a partnership in cardiovascular medicine and surgery with us. This gesture had the potential to become a huge win-win opportunity. Our CEO was invited to participate in those discussions. Unfortunately, I made the trip to the Caribbean nation with a lower-ranked administrator instead. Sensing a lack of interest and commitment on our part, our host retreated from the proposal, and subsequently, it fizzled. That did it for me. I saw no solution for this unfortunate collision in values. I saw no solution for the misalignment of ambition with the status quo. Therefore, I tendered my resignation, declined an offer amounting to a significant increase in my salary, and refused to make any compromise with decisions that were not patient centered, did not embrace growth, and were strictly provincial.

CHAPTER 87

Aria Jefferson Hospital

WITHIN TWO MONTHS, I joined a new team at a teaching hospital in Philadelphia, where I also continued my graduate teaching role with the University of Pennsylvania. I was particularly impressed with the engaging, honest, and sacrificial leadership of my new CEO, Kate Kinslow, who had a strong clinical background. She not only appreciated my drive, ambition, and motivation, but she also actively supported my initiatives for advanced quality patient care. She was highly communicative and predictably honest in her interactions and was driven principally by quality care and growth. She made a point of meeting all my international patients on their arrival and welcoming them to the hospital and the great city of Philadelphia. This impressive gesture had an immeasurable positive impact on those patients, their families, and loved ones, and it created new program disciples, thereby fostering exponential growth in our local and international programs.

One time, a prime minister from a faraway country came to us and received advanced care for his medical problem. He arrived with his family and an impressive entourage and was welcomed by the CEO, who met him at his hotel and had a productive conversation that left him with an immensely positive impression on the institution in particular and our state and country in general.

The cardiovascular ICU and operating rooms needed improvements in patient care protocols. Under the expert leadership of nursing staff, perfusionists, and cardiac anesthesiologists, we succeeded in establishing better protocols that were patient centered and grounded in evidence-based medical practice and best practice guidelines. The feedback from staff members was positive, and I was extremely happy with the nursing staff members who consistently performed superbly in providing the best care every day to all our patients. Things were a little rough initially, especially in the operating room, because I arrived with techniques that were different from what some of the team members had been used to.

One day, I was in the operating room and had just completed a double bypass operation on a seventy-three-year-old man. The operation took about thirty-five minutes. The heart resumed beating vigorously spontaneously. Then I asked the cardiac anesthesiologist to turn on the breathing machine so that I could wean the patient from the heart-lung machine. (This is a routine procedure in heart surgery.)

"No, it's not safe! The patient is not ready for weaning. We must wait twenty minutes," he protested in a loud voice.

Conversely, in a gentle voice, I told him it was OK. Then I instructed the perfusionist running the heart-lung machine to prepare for weaning the patient from his machine. This is also part of a routine protocol in heart surgery. To my surprise, the anesthesiologist resisted again.

"No! Don't wean!" he yelled.

"No! Don't wean!" he repeated.

He was a highly skilled, highly intelligent anesthesiologist but did not have much experience working with me.

"Trust me on this one," I said.

"No!" he yelled again.

"Please don't take this as an affront to your intelligence," I said.

"No!" he repeated.

It is the surgeon who makes the final decision about when to wean a patient from the heart-lung machine. This kind of pushback is highly unusual, especially when dealing with an experienced surgeon. "I have done thousands of these operations," I added gently.

"No!" he insisted.

"You have a TEE [special echocardiogram probe inserted through the mouth into the stomach before surgery to show live images of the heart]. You can see the heart is beating fine," I retorted.

"No!" he objected.

At that point, I asked his colleague standing next to him to go on and start the breathing machine.

"Not safe. No! You shouldn't!" his associate responded.

I had never encountered such a scenario in the operating room. I was flabbergasted, but I had to maintain my cool. Other staff members in the room were stunned by the recalcitrance of the anesthesiologists. This was a real-life mutiny in the operating room! And I thought I had seen it all! I guess not. I had to keep a calm and level head. One could feel the tension in the room. Besides, we were at a critical stage in the operation, and the patient's best interest was foremost. I am a fast surgeon, and it is just the way I've always worked. I had just completed the operation in thirty-five minutes, and the heart was beating strong. There was no clear reason to keep the patient hooked up to a machine for a prolonged interval. In the anesthesiologist's opinion, we needed to allow the heart to recover longer before weaning it. Conversely, the longer a patient stays on the heart-lung machine, the greater the risk of complications. I had a zero percent mortality that year doing that specific operation, which I had performed thousands of times during my career.

With a firm voice, I commanded the circulating nurse to summon the chairman of anesthesia to the room. He arrived, and after learning of what had transpired, he agreed to have the patient weaned. The rest of the protocol in the operating room went smoothly, and the patient was transferred to the ICU. He enjoyed an uneventful recovery and was discharged home.

The anesthesiologist resigned soon afterward and joined a major medical center in Pennsylvania. One day, I received a surprise call from him, and I was all ears. He started with an apology for his actions months earlier on that day in the operating room. He went on to tell me that he had developed a greater appreciation for my skill set since starting a new job with a team of cardiac surgeons at his new job. I still think he is a great anesthesiologist, and I recognize the fact that he was just not used to my preferences and the way I operated. However, I think he should have approached the situation by demonstrating greater reflection instead of disruptive confrontation. I strongly believe that change invites reflection.

Organizational conflicts are commonplace in every setting. We had our share of them at our institute. Despite our best intentions, there were a few cardiologists who openly declared hostilities toward Kate, our CEO, in ways that bordered on extreme sexism. I remember at one of our first meetings, the leader of that group and his primary disciple openly denounced every measure that she had proposed to produce positive changes in the hospital. She tried to engage them in every possible way, but to no avail. It came to a point at which they began referring to her as "the bitch" and reveling in what they perceived as the "better days" they had had under the previous CEO. I could not just sit there and take such nonsense any longer.

Accordingly, in no uncertain terms, I set out to educate them, and I expressed my disdain for the expletives they used in describing her and the implied sexism and discrimination in their pronouncements. In short, I told them that it was my firm belief that the CEO's heart was in the right place and that the health-care industry was changing rapidly; therefore, to remain competitive, our traditional strategic thinking had to be revised. I continued by emphasizing that ad hominem attacks would lead us nowhere and specifically what we needed to do was to become copilots in bringing about transformative change within the organization. Finally, in speaking about the fiercely competitive modern health-care arena, I alluded to the timeless African adage that "when you have no enemies within, you don't have to worry about enemies without."

That did not sit well with the rebels, whom I considered to be good doctors. Henceforth, I became the recipient of the vilest, uglies abuses anyone could imagine. They labeled me a terrible person, a horrible surgeon. Whatever misinformation they could fabricate to erode my position and disable my drive, they didn't hesitate to disseminate. All this was precipitated by my firm decision to stand up for justice, to stand up for fairness, to support our CEO, who was forward-thinking, creative, and innovative, and who had the best interest of the institution and patients at heart. Everyone knew that I had been hired to replace their friend, the former chief of cardiac surgery. Therefore, I could understand the root cause of their vociferous vilification of me, but I was unperturbed because of my conviction that genuine human service should never become a popularity contest.

CHAPTER 88

Education and Health Care

PEOPLE ALWAYS ASK ME why I speak so much about education and its importance in human life. It has a special place in my heart and has enabled me to realize my goals in life and to transform a few other lives. At a juncture in my career, I began to think about expanding my role in the service of humanity beyond the confines of surgical suites and physical hospital plants. For decades, my life has been steeped in two of the most important pillars in human life: education and health care.

Education is the greatest emancipator. As I look at my own life, I realize that education has engendered me with a deeper understanding of the world and has empowered me to do many things that I would have been unable to do without it. While living in Philadelphia, I spent a great deal of time visiting elementary and high schools to interact with students and learn about their hopes, dreams, and challenges. Additionally, I started a robust mentoring program to generate greater interest in health-care careers among students, especially those from poor backgrounds. This is something that I had been doing consistently for decades, and I began to appreciate how my perspective on matters relating to educational possibilities was evolving.

I have always been a subscriber to the powerful African perspective that it takes a village to raise a child, and indeed I am the quintessential beneficiary of that village effort. Some of the children I mentored were fundamentally brilliant but were from fractured homes and communities where education was not a "sexy" idea; hence, they became easily drawn to dishonorable endeavors, or they persisted in the educational arena with low-expectation clouds hovering ubiquitously over them.

I have always been cognizant of the power of education and health care in undergirding all the pillars of our lives: economy, security, housing, transportation, communication, and entertainment, and many others.

One day, I contracted a plumber to unclog a toilet in my house. It took him several minutes to extract a white sock from the depths of drainage pipes leading from my toilet unit. Embarrassed, I thanked him and paid for the cost of his visit, which amounted to about $175. He then rushed out to address multiple other appointments he had that day. I was not sure how the sock wound up where he found it, but instantly my mind drifted away from the sock drama to the plumber. I admired his professionalism, his expertise, the quality of his service, his experience, and his attitude. He was busy, appeared to be content with his job, and earned a very good living.

Then I realized something obvious. Often, we focus too much on classical education and related professions. America became the greatest nation in the world has ever known not because everyone was college educated. I think in developing countries, to a greater extent, there is justification for promoting classical education aggressively to create a critical mass of experts for nation building. However, when a nation has attained a high level of social, scientific, and technological maturity, professional diversification becomes a greater key driver in delivering significant value to the lives of its citizens.

Not everyone needs to go to college and earn a degree. Attending college is not the only educational option our young people have to make a good living. Vocational schools provide important options as well. In addition to learning about financial management in elementary school, I believe all our children should receive outstanding comprehensive education from kindergarten through high school. Additionally, it would likely serve them better to be introduced to a broad spectrum of professional and career options during this time to stimulate their interest in selecting avenues that they may consider attractive. For many of our young people, vocational and technical schools can be even better and more dignified options than college, and society must promote and support these earlier on. The skills they acquire from a technical education are lifelong and can provide them with financial independence, a meaningful life, and greater self-esteem. In short, the plumber and I have more in common than many people would think.

For those children who pursue an academic track, I discovered that many school systems do not prepare them for a competitive future. A good number of the students I have mentored were learning just enough to get by. It always amazes me how children in resource-poor village schools in Africa are more competitive than our students here in this great nation with enormous resources and impressive facilities. In Africa, a child's education is a collective concern because a successful child enables a secure village. When we look at our educational structures here, collectivity is an important missing element. As the world becomes increasingly one, America will rapidly and invariably lose its competitive edge unless we recognize the fierce urgency of now and institute a collective, concerted "Marshall Plan" for education across this nation. Therefore, I decided that I would become a prominent drum major not only for health care but also for education.

In November of 2012, my daughter Mankah; her wonderful husband, Everett; and beautiful daughter Sydney welcomed a new baby, Braylon, to their household. I immediately flew out to Wisconsin with my aunt to celebrate his birth. There can be nothing more heartwarming and energizing than earning the title of Granddad. In 2013, I took my younger daughter, Ahleea, to visit an orphanage I was supporting in Africa and also to visit my village and offer her a tantalizing glimpse of a vanishing way of life. The decades-long scourge of HIV, along with the economic downturn in the late 2000s, threatened to destroy the most cherished institutions in African life—the family and the village—and exacerbated the problem of orphans in many poor communities. We visited the Good Shepherd Orphanage in Cameroon, a place infused with love and the grace of God, which was started by Sister Jane, a consummate leader, mother, angel, and saint who was sacrificing her personal life in the service and salvation of orphans and abandoned children. After witnessing the great work she was doing for those little ones, I committed myself to join others in helping her with her mission for human service.

While we were in that region, I decided to visit a school in Musang, where I observed the first grade. I was surprised to discover that the campus had changed little since my elementary school years. I met a gracious missionary pastor from Vermont and the school headmistress, who was a delightful, energetic lady with an overflowing passion for education. She graciously gave us a tour of the classrooms and the tiny school campus. Afterward, I asked to know what challenges her students were facing.

In a somber tone, she related the following: almost one-third of the three hundred students dropped out each year because they could not afford tuition and fees. A significant number of the students were orphans, and others were being raised in single-parent homes due to the ravages of HIV on many families. In addition to these problems, most students could not afford the recommended books for their classes. Hearing these problems was particularly disturbing to me because, when I was at that stage, I suffered financial insecurities and my parents had difficulty paying my tuition. At one point, I had lived in a single-parent home due to my mother's untimely death, and finally, I resorted to stealing books because I could not afford them, and our educational resources were severely limited. What bothered me especially was that many decades later, children were still experiencing some of the same problems I had confronted in my earlier years. I knew I could make a difference, and I was prepared to commit myself to their futures.

I responded by telling the headmistress that I would offer yearly scholarships to every student who could not afford tuition, and I would buy enough books so that every child who needed one could borrow it for the semester. It was a moving experience. As soon as I returned to Philadelphia, I initiated a wire transfer to the school in fulfillment of my commitment to the students. About a year later, I received one of the most heartwarming messages on WhatsApp from that headmistress. In essence, it stated that because of my assistance, student enrollment was up 35 percent, there were no dropouts, and every child had the books they needed.

Such experiences remind me of the interconnectedness of humanity in this fabric we call life. That primitive elementary school prepared me for a future that has enabled me to provide beneficial services to thousands around the globe during my medical career. We are truly one!

When my daughter and I returned to the United States after our trip to Africa, I was invited to an event celebrating the value of the YMCA in the community. At that event, I was truly surprised when I received the third award for community service by the State of Pennsylvania and subsequently a Humanitarian of the Year Award from the chamber of commerce.

A chance encounter with a nun from New Jersey through a patient of mine led me to one of the most phenomenal people I have known, the Reverend Canon Elizabeth Rankin Geitz, a celebrated author and a brilliant, humble, God-fearing human being with the best in humanitarian instincts. She had met Sister Jane at the Good Shepherd Orphanage, where she learned about Sister Jane's eternal wish to build a school for her orphans. When she returned to the United States, she established the Good Shepherd Foundation as a framework for actualizing Sister Jane's dream.

I met with Elizabeth and a few others at my house after she solicited my participation on the board of directors of Good Shepherd. Together with Ms. Brenda Ruello (cofounder and vice-chair), Mr. Bertrand Delaney, Esq., and Mr. Sam Ruello, we mapped out a strategic vision for a meaningful and sustainable educational institution where students could acquire the skills to become creative and innovative thinkers, engaging leaders, and transformation agents in agriculture, science, technology, and the arts. Collectively, under Elizabeth's leadership, we engaged countless religious leaders and congregants, private individuals, community groups, and known philanthropists, and we embarked on an aggressive fundraising campaign that culminated in the realization of Sister Jane's dream.

In 2016, Good Shepherd Academy officially opened its doors to a group of eager, hope-infused youngsters, many of them orphans whom the world awaits patiently in the future. On my part, I was touched by my friends from Montgomery, Alabama, Joseph "Buddy" and Susie, who decided to honor my mother's legacy by building the Monica Neba Student Center at the school. Good Shepherd Academy's beautiful, expansive, state-of-the-art campus on a lush and scenic mountain range represents the best in human instincts and an understanding of our mutual destiny.

A couple of years after I left Pocono for Philadelphia, I received a barrage of telephone calls, texts, and emails one day from doctors, nurses, and board members as well as friends in the Pocono community notifying me of major leadership changes that had been effected at Pocono Medical Center. They were all persuading me to consider returning to the region. My home and heart were still in the Poconos. I suffered prolonged anguish with the decision, especially since I had begun to enjoy my practice in Philadelphia, and I shared my predicament with the CEO, who was sad to see me leave but was supportive of my decision. I had invested so much of my heart in Pocono's program that leaving had not been an easy decision. After I returned, my fabulous team rallied with me to reboot the cardiovascular program, and within a year and a half, we soared back to the top tier in both state and national rankings of quality outcomes.

CHAPTER 89
Bountiful Harvest

IN MANY WAYS, THINGS seemed to be going well on the family front as well. Within two years, my nephew Franklin in Belgium completed his master's degree, Robert began to occupy himself nobly by serving troubled youths, and my younger daughter Ahleea finished her master's at Loyola Marymount in Los Angeles and began to make plans for further studies. Mankah, my older daughter, completed her PhD studies, which she had begun during law school, and her husband, Everett, won an election and became a circuit court judge in Madison, Wisconsin, where he miraculously continued to maintain a full-time position as a pastor in addition to being a community organizer and a mentor for disadvantaged youths in that city.

For a while, it seemed as though I was spending most of my free time traveling to college graduation ceremonies. Nothing could be more gratifying than to witness the academic achievements of my children, nieces, nephews, and others for whom I had toiled relentlessly to provide financial support and psychosocial guidance in fulfillment of my moral obligation to the world and a promise to my late father. It was important for me to celebrate these milestones with my children and other family members, especially since I had not attended my college graduation because, at that time, I was alone and had no family members to share the experience with me.

When I left Madison on a flight to Philadelphia after celebrating Mankah's graduation, I found myself reminiscing about the events of that day. I remembered the collective joy in the eyes of every family member in attendance, including Denise and her mother, Ella-Ruth. The pride in Ahleea's eyes as she was witnessing her older sister being recognized for her outstanding performance in graduate school was touching. There had also been a sparkle in Everett's eyes as he watched his wife receive her diploma, and of course, I could not forget the alacrity in Mankah's step as she strutted to the podium to accept her PhD, the crowning glory for all her hard work in reaching a goal she had set for herself since graduating law school a few years earlier. My nieces and nephews from afar were also in attendance. I would have been amiss to forget the look of satisfaction in her professor's eyes. Afterward, I remember reminding her that she had been named after my grandmother, a name that meant "torchbearer." There was no doubt in my mind that she had proven herself to be a veritable torchbearer, not only for the family but also for the world.

Indeed, when I thought about all the events that unfolded that day, my mind took me back to the village in Africa, and it was clear to me that a seed that was planted in me decades earlier had begun to bear fruit. I was reminded of the celestial words of my father after he sold his house for three hundred dollars in a desperate bid to enable me to travel to America. At that time, I was so moved by his action that I promised to build him a house in the future. Although I may not have understood it then, his response was essentially a mandate for me to reciprocate instead by addressing the needs of others. He recognized I would be a trailblazer, a title that always comes with a mandate to provide assistance to succeeding generations so that their journeys will not be as arduous. In essence, the hardships my father experienced in his life motivated him to enable me to obtain the education he was denied and to enjoy a life he would have loved to live.

Epilogue

ONE DAY, I WAS sitting in my office and feeling extremely exhausted when I received a video call from my niece Bih. She was a highly ambitious young lady, the oldest child of my older sister, who graduated from nursing school and opened a clinic in Africa, where she took care of the health-care needs of her community. I can remember the broad smile on her radiant face when our video connection went through, and she screamed my name in joy when she saw my face. Our mutual greetings were laced with laughter and smiles.

I was feeling tired and practically half asleep because of the long working hours I had been keeping. Therefore, I asked her if it would be OK for me to call her back at a later time or date. Sadly, within forty-eight hours, she was dead from unknown causes. Again, I had to travel back to Africa to bury another family member. This time my daughter Ahleea and I joined other relatives from around the globe to mourn her death and celebrate her life.

While relishing a quiet personal moment in my hotel room after the funeral, I began to question whether the many years I had removed myself from my family had been worthwhile. This has been a recurring question for me. I was feeling nostalgic for having missed out on so many family activities over the years. I kept thinking about all the things I had done and began to wonder if they had brought much value to anyone. I thought about my bad habit of procrastinating or postponing social and family events in the interest of my work.

Even after I returned home to the United States, these thoughts kept bothering me. I was sitting in my home office one afternoon and rummaging through old files when I saw a letter from the family member of a previous patient. I read that letter several times. (I have appended it here.) In the final analysis, I became convinced to a greater extent that my journey has been worth the many personal sacrifices I have had to make over the years and it would be better for me to maintain a forward-looking perspective in my life than to worry about a past that I cannot change. It would be better to think about the countless lessons I have learned along the way than wallow in my past mistakes and failings.

First of all, I have learned not to save my proverbial "expensive china" for special occasions like my mother did because every day is a special occasion, and tomorrow is not guaranteed.

I have learned that the constraints to my dreams are intrinsic.

I have learned that I can never be considered successful when others around me are not.

I have learned that change demands reflection before acceptance or rejection.

I have learned that true compassion and commitment need no reciprocity.

I have learned that in the darkest of nights, there is a star out there.

I have learned that the enemies of self-doubt are universal and that to achieve any meaningful goals in life, I must appreciate them and overlook them.

I have learned that our common humanity must be the centerpiece of the decisions I make. Hence, I am because you are.

I have learned that all people have some good in them, and it is up to me to discover it.

I have learned that when you are well, you have many dreams, but when you are not, you only have one.

I have learned that until the lion can find its own historian, the story of the chase will always favor the hunter.

I have learned that to "conquer new lands," I must never be afraid to lose sight of the shore.

I have learned that when I am driving at a hundred miles an hour on life's expressway, I will crash if I keep my eyes on the rearview mirror.

I have learned that if I have long-term plans with sustainable benefits, I don't have to bother with short-term distractions.

I have learned that promises do not transform. Actions do!

I have learned that there will always be more for me to learn.

I started to think about many other children and succeeding generations right here in America who have been deserted by the wayside on life's highway and many others who have been marooned in a trailless social wilderness where they may never be able to realize their hopes and dreams. Then I wondered about the implications of the Ubuntu African philosophy "I am because you are" on current social realities and the future of America.

I bemoan the fact that we live in a world now where social disunity abounds. We live in a world where political expediency outweighs human necessity. We live in a world where the poor of all races, creeds, and colors are dominated and exploited to keep them down and so that they can be used as political pawns in arenas where their identities have been reduced to ballots, a world in which the poor are valued as tools to facilitate the political ascendancy of others to their aspired positions. We live in a world where the poor who have become impoverished aliens in an affluent society have been chronically psychologically anesthetized, marginalized, subjugated, and abandoned on the outskirts of hope, where their children are subliminally encouraged to strive for mediocrity and embrace life in protected statewide domestic colonies while the rest of society soars to the stratosphere.

We live in a world where our poor fellow Americans are forced to subsist on "perpetual promises" and are discouraged from working hard and mounting competitive emancipatory efforts to enable them to realize the true American dream. We live in a world where the good people, through passivity, comfort, and complacency, have allowed politicians and leaders with nefarious intentions to articulate sound bites and craft policies intended to divide humanity into racial groups, to promote classism, and to create bitter social dissensions and disruptive social upheavals.

The world now finds itself at the intersection of history with towering infectious, social, and economic challenges that may well determine the course of humanity. As I watched with shock and sadness the gut-wrenching video on George Floyd and the sad chain of events that unfolded at a street corner in Minneapolis, and I witnessed the images of the unprecedented scale of global protests for social justice and against racism, I prayed with unbridled hope in my heart that the world in general and America in particular might be witnessing the uterine contractions of a new world ready to be born.

I sat up that night and wrote two articles for Medium, one on what a cardiovascular and thoracic surgeon sees when he sees George Floyd and the other on racism and discrimination in the health-care industry, highlighting gender, racial, ethnic, and other discriminatory practices that are so prevalent in the largest industry in America.

A few weeks later, I found myself signing a legal document and agreeing to be a medical expert witness for the George Floyd case. I was charged with producing a professional opinion document detailing the mechanism of his death based on forensic data and supported by known biochemical, physiological, anatomical, and histopathological facts. Subsequently, I spent weeks meticulously sifting through a mountain of depositions, images, videos, forensic data, and all other pertinent information before generating a detailed report.

I continue to be concerned about the deep social divisions in this great nation that are being exposed and amplified by rapidly evolving global protests against the social ills of racism and sexism, and I wonder what kind of world we intend to pass on to future generations. I am concerned about the mounting cases of social and economic devastation triggered by COVID-19, the mismanagement of this scourge, and the surging numbers of deaths of despair among Americans of all races and ethnicities facing worsening social marginalization, discrimination, and economic hardships during these challenging times.

It is my fervent hope that from all these travails will emerge a new world without toxic, divisive social disharmony, a world where our overriding loyalty is to the common good and a recognition of the shared humanity in all of us. A world where the meaningless blight of racialism has no place in human lives. A world where individuals choose action over observation. A world where we can be united in our mission and goals for the welfare of humanity without being uniform in our principles. And, yes, a world where—because we are aware of our mortality—we can reflect objectively on our legacies and question our positions and actions on important issues affecting our communities.

To experience that world in all its greatness, we must not allow our minds to succumb to debilitating cynicism and social polarization. We must address our weaknesses, biases, and ignorance, which naturally stunt moral growth and relegate us to the miserable fringes of an enlightened global society. If we refuse to confront these social ills and to appreciate the existential reality of our mutuality, our offspring will invariably have to grapple with the burden of our collective negligence in the future.

As America has transitioned to a knowledge-based economy, it has become more apparent to many that those who were abandoned during that transition have found themselves in a much-disadvantaged position, especially during this COVID-19 scourge, when knowledge-requiring technologies and the jobs they engender have kept many skilled workers off unemployment ranks, allowing them to continue their participation in the labor market from the safe confines of their home offices.

Additionally, COVID-19 has lifted the veil on educational disparities. We see children of economically privileged classes weathering the challenging storms of a pandemic in the comfortable milieu of their resource-laden homes conducive to remote learning, whereas children of poor fellow Americans in remote communities and congested inner-city shanties are facing monumental challenges adapting to abruptly new educational paradigms as they lack not just home environments conducive to meaningful learning but additionally are woefully handicapped by the paucity of essential educational resources at their disposal to nourish their minds, amplify their experiences, and expand their future options.

These social asymmetries will continue to grow exponentially and widen the educational achievement gap between poor and rich children and expand the economic crevasse between rich and poor Americans. It is apparent that if the current situation is not addressed right away, poor children may never be able to catch up with their rich counterparts in this educational marathon, much to the future detriment of America in a competitive globalized economy. We must not forget that when education uplifts individuals, it uplifts nations!

The statistically greater mortality from COVID-19 among poorer Americans can be accounted for by centuries-old disparities in economic, health-care, and educational opportunities in this nation. These three important social pillars are interrelated and interdependent. Any community that faces educational and health-care challenges will have to confront economic hurdles as well. I have witnessed the hardships of countless White folks under my medical care for decades in the hills of Pennsylvania, as well as many Black and Brown people I have served in the sequestered enclaves of our sprawling cities. I have been appalled by the consequences of economic and social marginalization they have continued to endure, especially in a nation that can extinguish the leaping, searing flames of oblivion that threaten to consume them. We must come to see that the economic, educational, and health-care pillars in every community and their associated social determinants are inseparably interwoven. Hence:

Violence of any kind is a public health problem.
Discrimination is a public health problem.
Substandard housing is a public health problem.
Economic disparity is a public health problem.
Substandard education is a public health problem.

In every social determinant of health status—nutrition, housing, employment, education, genetics, clean water, safety, and security—the poor of every race, creed, and color come up short. Chronic diseases disproportionately affect poor Black, Brown, and White folks. When one looks at all these seemingly overwhelming challenges, the two mutually inclusive fundamental interventions that can address most of them directly or otherwise in our communities are educational and economic empowerment, which must begin at an early age.

Unfortunately, instead of providing constructive support so that individuals can acquire the skills and tools needed for personal uplift from childhood through adult life and realize the American dream by collecting a piece of the great American pie, so many actors have resorted instead through vitriolic propaganda to distracting the economically disadvantaged members of our great nation by shining the spotlight on meaningless social constructs like skin color and race, which does not elevate thought, drive competition, or deliver rewards. The timeless adage about teaching someone to fish so that they can feed themselves for a lifetime is still true. Poor Whites are manipulated, alienated, and marginalized by the power structures just as much as their Black and Brown brothers and sisters. The consequences of such overt and covert discriminatory practices may differ in substance but converge in their outcomes.

Long-term economic apartheid policies and practices have trapped large communities of Americans of all races in chronic despondency, leaving many people feeling hopeless and seeking magical solutions for their problems. Sadly, some have been driven by apathy to succumb to deaths of despair. This cancer in the body politic must be addressed. It needs a team approach and radical surgery. The focus of society should be the economic emancipation of its people from poverty by crafting actionable and sustainable educational and economic strategies within communities that uplift children from oblivion within those communities and steer them toward challenging, competitive paths, which will ultimately imbue them with a greater sense of self-worth and afford them more meaningful and productive lives.

This constitutes the very essence of the American Dream! Promises do not uplift; actions do.

With twenty dollars in my pocket, I landed on the shores of this great nation and discovered the true land of opportunity. While I have made countless mistakes along the way, I have learned an important lesson: that growing up disadvantaged does not have to be a permanent condition. Because of what America truly represents, I now have every advantage of having grown up disadvantaged. The transition from being disadvantaged to having advantages hinges on individual resolve and community abetment.

I believe that despite some of its failings, this nation offers the best and greatest opportunities for self-actualization, far beyond any other on this planet. Ours is a great nation, especially for those who are prepared and willing to compete and weather the storm along the way with the support of community institutions. Therefore, I deplore policies and strategies that do not focus on preparing individuals to uplift themselves and do not stimulate the competitive instincts within them.

We are at an alarmingly critical juncture in our erratic educational voyage, and we may be sailing in the wrong direction. Our children are abandoning the competitive American spirit and are performing miserably in the global educational arena, especially in science, mathematics, and technology, yet we choose to deny reality and instead look the other way. Consequently, policies and strategies that are not designed to critically evaluate and address this unfortunate trajectory are morally unfair and will only culminate in the marginalization in perpetuity of large segments of this great nation. The ultimate manifestation of this travesty would be the relegation of our nation to a position of subservience in the global community because any American who is left behind in a world that is rapidly becoming highly competitive and interconnected reduces our collective strength, power, and capabilities. Additionally, a nation that fails to encourage, stimulate, and support individual economic uplift in general runs the risk of fostering and amplifying unsustainable levels of dependency and entitlement, thereby generating domestic unrest, social acrimony, chronic social apathy, and a collective resentment toward leadership for failing to deliver on its promises.

Understandably, economic uplift for the poor can never be attained sustainability from mounting an assault on American capitalism, especially when such action is rooted in political expediency. By the same token, a commitment to social responsibility must be part of a global strategic policy and vision for American corporations and businesses because it creates community partnerships and generates and engages a broader, more skilled workforce that can enable and foster sustainable future national economic growth. Acting on that commitment would require strategic paradigms designed to unveil enormous talents and capabilities hibernating within our economically marginalized communities and tap into them.

It is precisely the availability of opportunities for economic growth and the pursuit of social freedoms that propelled America to a position of global prominence and continues to draw tens of thousands of immigrants to this nation each year.

Our children must be taught, encouraged, guided, and supported to be competitive and to strive to acquire *their* piece of the American pie and transform their communities and the world instead of being fooled into accepting intermittent palliative crumbs as an answer to their insatiable cravings for the real pie. Global commerce is evolving rapidly, and there is no stopping it. No affirmative action policy exists to govern participation in a globalized, knowledge-based economy. Only highly skilled and competitive candidates will succeed in that arena. Failure to empower our communities by mounting a positive thrust for education will invariably handicap our children domestically and globally, hence jeopardizing the future of this great nation.

Adults must understand that failure to address the chronic harm that economically challenged citizens endure in substandard education and poor health care will only place a greater burden on the future lives of our offspring, our nation, and our world. Without meaningful strategies, dumping dollars on these problems simply leaves us with solutions that don't solve and promises that don't deliver.

Nche Zama, MD, PhD

The realization of such harm must be collective. The appreciation of it is individual. The correction of it must be harmoniously collective.

In the end, ignoring the future does not eliminate it!

Acknowledgments

I THANK GOD FOR giving me the strength to scale this mountain called LIFE.

It has been said that wherever you are in this world, somebody helped you to get there.

I dedicate my life's journey to the village that raised me and to my loving, humble, God-fearing parents who enabled me to have the educational experiences that their circumstances did not afford them. They taught me to lead a purpose-driven life and to keep the focus on others.

I am particularly indebted to my grandmother Mankah for shaping my vision, coaching my heart, and teaching me resilience, patience, and unconditional love.

To uncles George, Daniel, Marcus, and Papa Manfred, who knew me before I knew myself, I will forever remain grateful to you for being the best male role models in the universe. I may never completely fill your shoes, but I will never stop trying.

To my sisters Kien, Siri, Mambo, Bih, and my brother Fru, who stood by patiently and did not desert me in frustration despite my complete, unending immersion in books, I assure you that I would never have made it without the bolstering tailwinds of your love.

To my rock Manwi Joanne, you have been a trusted bright ray of hope and an endless ocean of love and tranquility.

Thank you Everett and Jacob, for being exemplary dads. The torch has been passed, and I have no doubt you will continue to brighten the trails for others.

To the women who represent the valiant spirit of traditional mother-hood; Denise, Terry, Susan, Yvonne, Nemo Mankah, Delphine, Belinda, Corine, Nene, and Sylvia, I applaud you.

My dear Mankah, Robert, Ahleea, and Sofia I love you. Your lives give mine lasting fulfillment. You have been the most amazing children, always energizing and illuminating my life with your tireless love and robust compassion for humanity.

To my grandchildren, Sydney and Braylon, I pray you forgive me for preferring books over toys. I love you with all my heart and soul.

I am grateful to all my nieces and nephews the world over, for your strong sense of family and tradition.

I would like to thank all my teachers, including the missionaries and American Peace Corps volunteers, for their patience, sacrifices, determination, and dedication to excellence. Your collective value in my life is infinitesimal in its impact.

To my patients across this planet, I am indebted to you for making me a better servant.

To every classmate on my educational journey, I thank you for igniting a competitive spirit in me.

To all those angels stationed along my physically tasking and emotionally turbulent journey who were charged with strengthening my ethereal hopes, I owe you tremendous gratitude.

Finally and most importantly, to every child in the pursuit of knowledge, I love you. I encourage you to keep walking, keep dreaming, and never despair because you have what it takes to succeed. You do not walk alone! Therefore, always strive for excellence so that you can make the world better for everyone. You are because we are!

Made in the USA
Middletown, DE
03 May 2022

65178283R00254